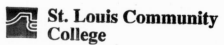

The 1904 Olympic Games

THE 1904 OLYMPIC GAMES

Results for All Competitors in All Events, with Commentary

by
Bill Mallon

RESULTS OF THE EARLY MODERN OLYMPICS, 3

McFarland & Company, Inc., Publishers
Jefferson, North Carolina, and London

British Library Cataloguing-in-Publication data are available

Library of Congress Cataloguing-in-Publication Data

Mallon, Bill.
    The 1904 Olympic Games : results for all competitors in all
events, with commentary / by Bill Mallon.
       p.   cm. — (Results of the early modern Olympics ; 3)
    Includes bibliographical references and index.
    ISBN 0-7864-0550-3 (library binding : 50# alkaline paper) ∞
    1. Olympic Games (3rd : 1904 : Saint Louis, Mo.)   2. Olympics —
Records.   I. Title.   II. Series: Mallon, Bill. Results of the
early modern Olympics ; 3.
GV721.8M35   1999
[GV722 1904]
796.48 — dc21   98-30989
                                            CIP

Manufactured in the United States of America

McFarland & Company, Inc., Publishers
  Box 611, Jefferson, North Carolina 28640

For Scruffy

Table of Contents

Introduction

At the end of contemporary Olympic Games it is customary for the committee that organized the Games to publish the Official Report of the Olympic Games. The Official Report describes every facet of the Olympics in great detail, including the results for every competitor in every event.

The 1904 Olympic Games were held in St. Louis, Missouri, but were quite different from what we know as the Olympics today. One difference, albeit minor, is that no true official report of the 1904 Olympic Games was ever published. Two books are often mentioned in lieu of a 1904 Official Report: *The Olympic Games 1904* by Charles J. P. Lucas, and *Spalding's Official Athletic Almanac for 1905 (Special Olympic Number)* by James E. Sullivan. However, Lucas' book mentions only the results of the track & field athletics competitions. Sullivan's book is more complete, as it should be, for he was the director of the 1904 Olympic Games. But while Sullivan's book reports all the events, it usually mentions only the first few finishers; in addition, it is fraught with errors.

This book is an attempt to reconstruct the complete records of the 1904 Games. While not trying to be a complete Official Report, it does attempt to substitute for that section of the Official Report which would contain the results.

The 1904 Games were highly unusual, in more ways than just the absence of an Official Report. They were originally scheduled to be held in Chicago. But St. Louis was planning to hold a World's Fair in 1904 — the Louisiana Purchase Exposition. It was planned that a large number of sporting events would take place at the Exposition, which would have been in direct competition with the Olympic Games. The International Olympic Committee (IOC), wishing to avoid this confrontation, decided to move the Games to St. Louis.

The Games were under the control of James Edward Sullivan, whose official title was Chief of Physical Culture for the Louisiana Purchase Exposition. Sullivan tried to hold a sporting event every day of the Exposition, which lasted over six months. In addition, Sullivan insisted on labeling every event as Olympic, thereby creating a plethora of so-called Olympic events.

Therefore, one problem facing anyone studying the 1904 Olympic Games is to decide which events are truly of Olympic caliber. The IOC was not present at St. Louis except for a very few members. Supposedly, after the Games had ended, the IOC convened and decided, rather arbitrarily, which events it would consider official. It is not, however, certain when this Committee meeting took place, or if, in fact, it actually did.

Though the IOC is the final arbiter of all things Olympic, its reasoning is not clear on the choosing of 1904 Olympic events. Subsequent Olympic historians have not entirely agreed with its selections. Therefore, one of the most difficult problems faced in this compilation was deciding which sports and events to include, thereby giving to them my imprimatur as "Olympic." I have included all events which could possibly be considered of Olympic caliber, but I have made my own decisions as to what should and should not be considered "Olympic" events.

"Olympic caliber" here means that the events were open to the best amateur athletes of all countries to compete on equal terms. This immediately eliminates handicap events (abundant in track & field athletics, swimming, and cycling), age-group events (held in track & field athletics throughout the summer), and events for limited groups (Irish nationals, Western AAU competitors, YMCA athletes). Events have not necessarily been eliminated because only Americans took part; this was a common occurrence in 1904. In many of these, as can be seen in Appendix II, there were foreign entrants who did not show up, which was not the fault of the people organizing the Olympic Games.

It seems like a long time since I began working on the 1904 Olympic Games. Studying the St. Louis Games was how I got started in the field of Olympic history, inspired by the doyen of Olympic historians, Erich Kamper of Austria. I self-published (photocopied) an 81-page pamphlet in 1981, entitled "A Statistical Summary of the 1904 Olympic Games," which is cited occasionally in the pages following using he abbreviation Mallon2.

A great deal has changed in the study of Olympic History since that beginning in 1981. Perhaps most importantly to me, Erich Kamper died on 9 November 1995. All Olympic historians will miss him. Secondly, a group devoted to the study of Olympic history, the International Society of Olympic Historians (ISOH), has been formed, which helps coordinate and stimulate research into the history of the Olympic Games.

My work on the history of the early Olympics has continued, however. With the help of McFarland & Company, Inc., Publishers, I am in the process of publishing a series of books on the history of the early Olympics. The works on 1896 and 1900 appeared in 1997, and this and the 1906 book are appearing in 1998. Volumes are planned for the Olympics of 1908, 1912, and 1920.

Many people have helped me with this project. Hoping not to omit anyone, I extend my thanks to the following: Harvey Abrams (USA), Bob Barnett (USA), June Becht (USA), Ian Buchanan (GBR), Bessie Carrington (USA), Wally Donovan (USA), Pim Huurman (NED), Wayne McFarland (USA), Robert Rhode (USA), Milton Roberts (USA), Jeffrey Tishman (USA), and C. Frank Zarnowski (USA).

My original work on the 1904 Olympics began only at the dawn of the computer age, and I did not have a computer. But I did have some help. So I'd like to thank Scruffy, our first dog, who mostly sat on my lap while I typed those notes on that old Smith-Corona, asking no greater privilege than to be close to me at all times. He probably knew more about the 1904 Olympics than any dog, but he is no longer with us to share that knowledge, nor his happy smile, with us. Karen and I miss him, and his smile.

Bill Mallon
Durham, North Carolina

Summer 1998

Abbreviations

General

A:	athletes competing	ko	knock-out (boxing)
AAU	Amateur Athletic Union	LAW	League of American Wheelmen
AC*	also competed (place not known)	LPE	Louisiana Purchase Exposition
bh	behind	NAA	National Archery Association
C:	countries competing	NAAO	National Association of Amateur Oarsmen
d.	defeated		
D:	date(s) of competition	NH	no-height
DNF*	did not finish	NM	no mark
DNS	did not start	NP	not placed
DQ	disqualified	or	Olympic Record
E	entered	qr	qualifying round
est	estimate(d)	scr	scratched
f	final	T:	time of competition starting
F:	format of competition	tko	technical knock-out (boxing)
GNYIAA	Greater New York Irish Athletic Association	USGA	United States Golf Association
		vs.	versus
IOC	International Olympic Committee	wo	walkover (won by forfeit)
jo	jump-off	WR	World Record

Sports

ARC	Archery	GOL	Golf
ATH	Athletics (Track & Field)	GYM	Gymnastics
BAS	Basketball	LAX	Lacrosse
BOX	Boxing	ROQ	Roque
CYC	Cycling	ROW	Rowing & Sculling
DIV	Diving	SWI	Swimming
FEN	Fencing	TEN	Tennis
FTB	Football (Soccer)	TOW	Tug-of-War

These abbreviations appear in lowercase in Appendix III.

| TUR | Turnverein Gymnastics | WLT | Weightlifting |
| WAP | Water Polo | WRE | Wrestling |

Nations

AUT	Austria	HUN	Hungary
CAN	Canada	IRL	Ireland
CUB	Cuba	SAF	South Africa
FRA	France	SUI	Switzerland
GER	Germany	USA	United States
GRE	Greece		

References

with Their Abbreviations as Cited in Text

Primary Sources

Abrams   Abrams, Harvey Lee. "The History of the United States Olympic Wrestling Team from 1896 to 1904." Diss., Southeast Missouri State University, 1979.

Barnett   Barnett, C. Robert. "St. Louis 1904: The Games of the IIIrd Olympiad," in *Historical Dictionary of the Modern Olympic Movement*. Westport, Conn.: Greenwood Press, 1996.

Barney   Barney, Robert K. "Born from Dilemma: America Awakens to the Modern Olympic Games, 1901–1903." *Olympika* 1 (1992): 92–135.

Bennitt   Bennitt, Mark, ed. *History of the Louisiana Purchase Exposition*. St. Louis: Universal Exposition Publishing Co., 1905.

Condon   Condon, Yvonne M. "St. Louis 1904: Louisiana Purchase Exposition," in *Historical Dictionary of World's Fairs and Expositions, 1851–1988*, edited by John E. Findling and Kimberly D. Pelle. Westport, Conn.: Greenwood Press, 1990.

Coubertin   Coubertin, Pierre de. *Une Campagne de vingt-et-un ans (1887–1908)*. Paris: Librairie de l'Education Physique, 1909.

CRB   Barnett, C. Robert. "1904 Olympic Swimming, Fancy Diving, and Water Polo Competition." *Swimming World and Junior Swimmer* 20, 12 (December 1979): 34–36.

DW   Wallechinsky, David. *The Complete Book of the Olympics*. Four editions. First edition, Middlesex, England: Penguin Books, 1983. Second edition, New York: Viking Penguin, 1988. Third edition, London: Aurum, 1991. Fourth edition, New York: Little Brown, 1996.

EK   Kamper, Erich. *Enzyklopädie der olympischen Spiele*. Dortmund: Harenberg, 1972. Parallel texts in German, French, and English. American edition issued as *Encyclopaedia of the Olympic Games* by McGraw-Hill (New York) in 1972.

EzM   zur Megede, Ekkehard. *Die olympische Leichtathletik*. Bands 1–3. Darmstadt: Justus von Liebig Verlag, 1984.

Find   Findling, John E. "World's Fairs and the Olympic Games." *World's Fair* 10 (December 1990): 13–15.

FJGVDM   Merwe, Floris J. G. Van der. "South Africa at the Olympic Games," forthcoming article in *Journal of Sports History.*

FM   Mező, Ferenc. *The Modern Olympic Games.* Budapest: Pannonia Press, 1956. English edition.

FW   Wasner, Fritz. *Olympia-Lexikon.* Bielefeld, Germany: Verlag E. Gunglach Aktiengesellschaft, 1939.

Gynn   Gynn, Roger. *The Guinness Book of the Marathon.* London: Guinness, 1984.

Henry   Henry, Bill. *An Approved History of the Olympic Games.* First edition. New York: G.P. Putnam, 1948.

Index   Gjerde, Arild and Teigen, Magne. *Index of Participants of Olympic Athletics 1896–1988: Part I: 1896–1812 Men.* n.p., 28 May 1992.

LucasCJP   Lucas, Charles J.P. *The Olympic Games 1904.* St. Louis: Woodward & Tiernan, 1905.

LucasJA   Lucas, John A. "Early Olympic Antagonists: Pierre de Coubertin versus James E. Sullivan." *Stadion* 3 (1977): 258–272.

Lyberg1   Lyberg, Wolf. *The History of the IOC Sessions. I. 1894–1939.* Lausanne: International Olympic Committee, October 1994.

Lyberg2   Lyberg, Wolf. *Fabulous 100 Years of the IOC: Facts-figures-and much, much more.* Lausanne: International Olympic Committee, 1997.

Mallon1   Mallon, Bill. *The Olympic Games 1896, 1900, 1904, and 1906: Part I — Track & Field Athletics.* Durham, N.C.: author, 1984.

Mallon2   Mallon, Bill. *A Statistical Summary of the 1904 Olympic Games.* Durham, N.C.: author, 1981.

Müller   Müller, Norbert. *One Hundred Years of Olympic Congresses: 1894–1994.* Lausanne: International Olympic Committee, 1994.

OlyTen   Gillmeister, Heiner. *Olympisches Tennis: Die Geschichte der olympischen Tennisturniere (1896–1992).* Sankt Augustin, Germany: Academia Verlag, 1993.

OR   1904 Official Report. The text that serves as 1904's Official Report is the following: Sullivan, James E. *Spalding's Official Athletic Almanac for 1905: Special Olympic Number, Containing the Official Report of the Olympic Games of 1904.* New York: American Sports Publishing, 1905.

OTAF   *Olympic Track and Field.* Editors of *Track & Field News.* Los Altos, Calif.: Tafnews Press, 1979.

Sayenga   Sayenga, Don. "The 1904 Basketball Championship ... or ... Were the 'Buffalo Germans' the Original Dream Team?" *Citius, Altius, Fortius* 4, 3 (1996): 7–8.

SG   Greenberg, Stan. *The Guinness Book of Olympics Facts and Feats.* First edition. Enfield, Middlesex, England: Guinness, 1983.

SpGolf   Spalding's Athletic Library. *Spalding's Official Golf Guide for 1905.* New York: American Sports Publishing, 1905.

SpHoop   Spalding's Athletic Library. *Spalding's Official Basketball Guide for 1905.* New York: American Sports Publishing, 1905.

SpTennis   Spalding's Athletic Library. *Spalding's Official Tennis Guide for 1905.* New York: American Sports Publishing, 1905.

TMF   Martin D.E., Gynn R.W.H. *The Marathon Footrace.* Champaign, Ill.: C.C. Thomas, 1979.

VK   Kluge, Volker. *Die olympischen Spiele von 1896 bis 1980.* Berlin: Sportverlag, 1981.

Who   Maritchev, Gennadi. *Who Is Who at the Summer Olympics 1896–1992.* 4 vols. Riga, Latvia: Demarko Sport Publishing, 1996.

Periodicals

American Golfer, New York.
Amerikanische Turnzeitung, Milwaukee.
The Archer's Register, London.
The Bicycling World, New York.
The Field, London.
Golf, New York.

The Golfers' Magazine, Chicago.
Illustrierte Athletik-Zeitung, Berlin.
Lawn Tennis Monthly, New York.
New York Athletic Club Journal, New York.
Outing, New York.

Newspapers

Atlanta Constitution, August–September 1904.
Boston Daily Globe, August–September 1904;
    April 1909; April 1910.
Chicago Daily News, July–October 1904.
Chicago Tribune, July–October 1904.
Cincinnati Enquirer, September 1904.
Cleveland Plain-Dealer, August–October 1904.
Indianapolis News, August 1904.
Los Angeles Times, July 1904.
Manitoba Free-Press, Winnipeg, June–July 1904.
Milwaukee Journal, August–September 1904.
Missouri Republican, August–September 1904.
New York Herald, July–October 1904.
New York Times, May–November 1904.
Newark Evening News, Newark, NJ, July–
    October 1904.

Philadelphia Inquirer, July–October 1904.
St. Louis Globe-Democrat, October 1903–
    January 1904; May–December 1904;
    October–December 1905.
St. Louis Palladium, August–September 1904.
St. Louis Post-Dispatch, June–November 1904.
St. Louis Register, August–September 1904.
St. Louis Republic, July–November 1904.
St. Louis Star-Times, August–October 1904.
St. Louis World, August–September 1904.
The Sporting News, June–November 1904.
Toledo News-Bee, September 1904.
Toronto Globe, July–November 1904.
Toronto Star, September 1904.
Washington Post, August–September 1904.
Weltliche Post, St. Louis, July–October 1904.

Miscellaneous Printed Material

Daily official programs: All-Around Event, Basketball, Cycling, International Turners contests,
    Golf, Marathon, Rowing, Swimming & Diving, Athletics (Track & Field), Water Polo.
Official rules and regulations: All-Around Event, Fencing, Golf, Gymnastics, Swimming &
    Diving, Athletics (Track & Field), International Turners contests, Wrestling, Water Polo.
Photographs of the 1904 Olympic Games at the Missouri Historical Society.
Scrapbooks of the Louisiana Purchase Exposition at the Missouri Historical Society, volumes
    31 and 32 concerning the Olympic Games.
Official results — Archery competitions, International Turners contests.

National Olympic Histories

Buchanan, Ian. *British Olympians: A Hundred Years of Gold Medallists*. London: Guinness, 1991.
Howell, Reet, and Howell, Max. *Aussie Gold: The Story of Australia at the Olympics*. South Melbourne: Brooks Waterloo, 1988.

Lennartz, Karl. *Geschichte des deutschen Reichsaußchußes für olympische Spiele. Heft 2 — Die Beteiligung Deutschlands an den olympischen Spielen 1900 in Paris und 1904 in St. Louis.* Bonn: Verlag Peter Wegener, 1983.

Lester, Gary. *Australians at the Olympics: A Definitive History.* Sydney: Lester-Townsend Publishing, 1984.

Mallon, Bill, and Buchanan, Ian. *Quest for Gold: The Encyclopaedia of American Olympians.* New York: Leisure, 1984.

Mező, Ferenc. *Golden Book of Hungarian Olympic Champions/Livre d'or des champions olympiques hongrois.* Budapest: Sport Lap. És Könyvkiadö, 1955. Parallel texts in English and French.

Roxborough, Henry. *Canada at the Olympics.* Third edition. Toronto: Ryerson Press, 1975.

Tarasouleas, At[hanassios]. *Helliniki simmetokhi stis sinkhrones olympiades* [transliterated title]. Athens: author, 1990.

1904 Olympic Games — Analysis and Summaries

Dates:	1 July–23 November 1904
Site:	St. Louis, Missouri, United States
Candidate Cities:	Buffalo, New York, USA; Chicago, Illinois, USA; New York, New York, USA; Philadelphia, Pennsylvania, USA
Official Opening By:	Mr. David Francis, President of the Louisiana Purchase International Exposition (the 1904 World's Fair)
Number of Countries Competing:	12 [12 Men—1 Women]
Number of Athletes Competing:	630 [624 Men—6 Women]
Number of Sports:	16 [16 Men—1 Women]
Number of Events:	91 [89 Men—2 Women]

Members of the International Olympic Committee in 1904 [31] (Years on IOC in brackets)

Argentina	José Benjamin Zubiaur [1894–1907]
Belgium	Count Henri de Baillet-Latour [1903–1942]
Bohemia	Dr. Jiří Guth-Jarkovský [1894–1943]
Denmark	Niels V. S. Holbeck [1899–1906]
France	Pierre Frédy, Baron Pierre de Coubertin [1894–1925]
	Ernst Callot [1894–1913]
	Henri Hébrard de Villeneuve [1900–1911]
	Count Albert Bertier de Sauvigny [1904–1920]
Germany	Karl August Willibald Gebhardt [1896–1909]
	Prince Eduard Max Salm-Horstmar [1901–1905]
	Count Julius Caesar Erdmann von Wartensleben [1903–1914]
Great Britain	Charles Herbert [1894–1906]
	The Rev. Robert Stuart de Courcy Laffan [1897–1927]
	Sir Howard Vincent [1901–1908]

1

Greece	Count Alexandros Merkati [1897–1925]
Hungary	Dr. Ferenc Kémény [1894–1907]
Italy	Count Eugenio Brunetta d'Usseaux [1897–1919]
Mexico	Miguel de Beistegui [1901–1931]
The Netherlands	Baron Frederik Willem Christiaan Hendrik van Tuyll van Serooskerken [1898–1924]
New Zealand	Leonard Albert Cuff [1894–1905]
Peru	Carlos de Candamo [1903–1922]
Russia	Prince Sergey Beloselsky-Belotsersky [1900–1908]
	Count Nikolao Ribeaupierre [1900–1916]
Spain	Count Gonzalo Mejorada del Campo, Marquis de Villamejor [1902–1921]
Sweden	General Viktor Gustaf Balck [1894–1921]
	Count Carl Clarence von Rosen [1900–1948]
Switzerland	Baron Godefroy de Blonay [1899–1937]
United States	Professor William Milligan Sloane [1894–1924]
	Theodore Stanton [1900–1904]
	Caspar Whitney [1900–1904]
	James Hazen Hyde [1903–1908]

1904 Organizing Committee

Honorary President of the Olympic Games of 1904: President Theodore Roosevelt
President of the Olympic Games of 1904: David Rowland Francis
Chief, Department of Physical Culture, Louisiana Purchase Exposition: James Edward Sullivan
Director of Exhibits, Louisiana Purchase Exposition: Frederick James Volney Skiff
President of the Amateur Athletic Union (AAU): Walter H. Liginger
President of the Western Division of the AAU: John J. O'Connor
Past-President of the Amateur Athletic Union: Harry McMillan
Past-President of the Western Division of the AAU: Henry Garneau

Purchase of the Louisiana Territory

The award of the 1904 Olympic Games to St. Louis really must be traced back to the 18th century and political struggles which involved the British, French, Spanish, and the United States. It is an award with historical links to Napoleon Bonaparte, James Monroe, and Thomas Jefferson.

A large central portion of the American subcontinent was called Louisiana, which belonged to France at the dawn of the 18th century. At the end of the Seven Years' War with Spain, France ceded control of this huge territory to the victorious Spanish in 1763. The land was bordered on the east by the Mississippi River and included the present-day states of Arkansas, Missouri, Iowa, Minnesota, North Dakota, South Dakota, Nebraska, Oklahoma, Kansas, and portions of Louisiana, Montana, Wyoming, and Colorado. The territory covered an expanse of 828,000 square miles (2,144,520 square kilometers).

In a secret treaty between France and Spain, promulgated on 1 October 1800, Spain returned Louisiana to France in exchange for the rights to certain portions of Tuscany, which Napoleon had threatened to conquer. But Napoleon soon abandoned his attack on the Tuscan region and Spain continued to administer Louisiana. In October 1802, Spain revoked American traders' rights of deposit, which essentially closed the Mississippi River to American trade. Almost concurrently, France sent troops to Santo Domingo, Hispaniola (now the Dominican Republic) to quell a rebellion there.

President Thomas Jefferson greatly feared France's re-taking the Louisiana Territory. France was at the time a nominal ally of the United States, but Jefferson feared a war between England and France for control of Louisiana, and especially feared England's controlling over one-third of the American sub-continent.

With these thoughts in mind, Jefferson sent James Monroe, then U.S. minister to England, to Paris to assist the American minister in France, Robert Livingston, to negotiate the possible purchase of at least parts of Louisiana by the United States. Monroe was instructed to attempt one of four possible scenarios favorable to the United States: (1) purchase all of Florida and New Orleans; (2) purchase New Orleans alone; (3) purchase land on the eastern bank of the Mississippi River for an American port; or (4) acquire perpetual rights of navigation and deposit on the Mississippi River.

On 11 April 1803, before Monroe actually arrived in France, Napoleon's Prime Minister, Duke Charles Maurice de Talleyrand-Périgord, asked Livingston how much Jefferson would offer to purchase the entire Louisiana territory. Napoleon's new attitude was spurred by events in America, in which his armies suffered terrible losses in Hispaniola and retreated. The army had been destroyed both by the enemy and by encroaching yellow fever, and Napoleon greatly feared war with the English at this time.

After Monroe's arrival, he and Livingston continued negotiations on Jefferson's behalf, and on 2 May 1803, France sold the Louisiana Territory to the United States for 60 million francs, then about $15 million. Of this, 45 million francs were paid outright to France and 15 million francs were to be paid to U.S. citizens to satisfy their claims against France. The United States territory had more than doubled overnight at a cost of approximately three cents per acre.

President Jefferson was concerned about the constitutionality of the acquisition and even considered whether an amendment to the United States Constitution was necessary. The Constitution, however, gave the United States President the power to make treaties, and the United States Senate ratified the purchase as a treaty on 20 October 1803.

Besides doubling the land area of the new country, and protecting the new nation against foreign invasion, the purchase helped Jefferson solve one major "problem." The American "West," then defined as the area between the Appalachian Mountains and the Mississippi River, was quickly filling up with settlers escaping the crowded Eastern seaboard. But Native American Indians occupied much of these lands and skirmishes between the settlers and the Indians were becoming frequent. Expansion further west gave more room for the settlers to seek land, and the United States Government also helped "solve" the problem by forcing the Indians to seek land further west as well.

The Selection of St. Louis

The Games of the Ist Olympiad of the Modern Era were celebrated in 1896 in Athens, Greece, and the Games of the IInd Olympiad were held in 1900 in Paris, France. The Olympic Games had basically been resurrected through the efforts of a Frenchman, Baron Pierre de Coubertin, although as has been recently elucidated, he had significant historical precedent in the works of an Englishman, Dr. William Penny Brookes, and a Greek, Panagiotis Soutsos.[1]*

*See Notes on pages 25–26.

Shortly after the 1900 Olympic Games, Coubertin and the other members of the IOC realized that it was now necessary for them to choose a city to host the 1904 Olympic Games. There is some historical evidence that Coubertin had always intended the Olympics to be held first in Athens, next in his home city of Paris, and then in an American city.

Recently, a superb summary of the selection of the host city for the Games of the IIIrd Olympiad has been published by Professor Robert Barney of the University of Western Ontario (London, Ontario, Canada). Entitled "Born from Dilemma: America Awakens to the Modern Olympic Games, 1901–1903," it was published in *Olympika*, in the first volume of that journal in 1992. Much of what follows is based primarily on Barney's article and his research.[2]

Barney states that Coubertin, in his last published book, *Mémoires Olympiques*, noted "that the 1900 Games planned for Paris would be followed four years later by an Olympic festival in America, completing, as he phrased it '...the original trinity chosen to emphasize the world character of the institution and establish it on a firm footing.'"[3] But the historical evidence from the early years of the Olympic Movement does not completely support this statement. In an article in *The Century Magazine* published in 1896, Coubertin himself stated, "Where will those [Games] of 1904 take place? Perhaps at New York, perhaps at Berlin or at Stockholm. The question is too soon to be decided."[4] Thus there is documentation that other cities, and other nations, were being considered to host the 1904 Olympic Games.

But no serious challenger to the American cities ever emerged for 1904. And eventually, five American cities would be considered as possible hosts for the 1904 Olympic Games: Buffalo, Chicago, New York, Philadelphia, and St. Louis.

Philadelphia was the first U.S. city to consider making a bid for the 1904 Olympics. In late July 1900, *The New York Times* and the *Chicago Tribune* both ran stories discussing the "probability" that the 1904 Olympics would come to the City of Brotherly Love.[5] But it never came to pass, and the Philadelphia bid was truly an ephemeral one. It always seemed to be based mainly on the Pennsylvania city's interest in track & field athletics, not on holding a true multi-sport festival.[6]

The two cities from New York State which broached the possibility of bidding for the 1904 Olympic Games also did so only transiently. The possibility of New York as 1904 Olympic host can be traced to the thinking of William Milligan Sloane, a Princeton history professor and the senior American member of the IOC. Coubertin often consulted with Sloane, who was one of the very early supporters of the Olympic Movement, and Coubertin's major ally in the United States. After consultation with Sloane, Coubertin actually announced on 11 November 1900 that either New York or Chicago would be the site of the 1904 Olympic Games, and this was published in *The New York Sun*.[7]

The bid by Buffalo for the 1904 Olympic Games is even more mysterious. At the 1901 IOC Session in which the host city was decided, the minutes document that the three American candidates were Buffalo, Chicago, and St. Louis. But Buffalo did not even have a representative at the session (nor did St. Louis), and the bid appeared to be a misrepresentation. In actuality, it appears Buffalo had no intention of bidding for the 1904 Olympic Games, but rather for a sports festival in 1901. In 1901, Buffalo hosted a major international fair, the Pan-American Exposition, and wished to host the Olympic Games as part of that Exposition,[8] not fully aware that the Olympics were only to be held every four years and were not scheduled for their next celebration until 1904. In addition, the IOC decision in May 1901 would have left them no time to host a major international athletic event. Buffalo's bid was never considered seriously by the IOC.[9]

After Coubertin's pronouncement concerning an American host city was published in *The New York Sun*, it was noticed by James E. Sullivan, who was at the time the president of the Amateur Athletic Union (AAU), and probably the most powerful sports administrator in America in 1901. Barney notes, "There is little doubt that Sullivan viewed his AAU as the sole certifying agent for staging Olympic Games in America, based solely, of course, on his perception that when amateur athletics occurred in the United States they were subject to the rules of domestic sports governing bodies."[10] The relationship between Coubertin and Sullivan was complex and decidedly confrontational, and is described in detail in the article by Lucas, "Early Olympic Antagonists: Pierre de Coubertin versus James E. Sullivan."[11]

In response to Coubertin's support of New York and Chicago, Sullivan immediately fired off a response to *The New York Sun* on 13 November 1900. Sullivan stated that Coubertin had no right to make any such announcement concerning Olympic Games in the United States as he had "been stripped of his athletic powers by the French governement"[12] and was "thus no longer in control of international meetings."[13] Referring to the President of the University of Chicago, William Rainey Harper (1856–1906), Sullivan noted:

> … provided the other delegates of the International Union agree to hold the games in the U.S. in that year, but President Harper will have to apply to the new union, as it will be impossible to hold a successful meeting without the consent of that body. Baron de Coubertin has no right to allot dates for such a meeting.[14]

Sloane and Coubertin then began a correspondence debating the merits of New York and Chicago as Olympic host cities. This eventually prompted Coubertin to publish the following statement in the *Revue Olympique*, "It seems now very probable that the next Olympian games will take place in America, and people agree generally that, at the meeting which will be held shortly, the members of the International Olympic Committee will have to decide in favor of the New World. A rivalry was thought to arise between New York and Chicago; but Chicago seems to have already taken the lead."[15]

The precise origins of Chicago's Olympic bid are mired in obscurity, but Barney has shed some light on communications which transpired from the end of 1900 through February 1901 between President Harper, Henri Merou, chief delegate of the French Consulate in Chicago, and Henri Bréal, secretary of the Franco-American Committee in Paris. But Barney also notes that the most important person in the Chicago bid was probably Henry Jewett Furber, Jr. (né 1866), a Chicago corporate lawyer with multiple real estate and insurance interests around 1900. A letter of late 1900 from Furber documents his involvement and the early interest of Chicago:

> Now my dear Dr. Harper, inasmuch as Consul Merou of Chicago, at present in Paris, and Mr. Bréal, as well as myself, have undertaken to create a movement in favor of Chicago, we must ask that, in justice to all concerned, a committee, such as we already have considered, be appointed in order that we may formulate some definite plan of action and be able to follow up our general declaration of intention.[16]

Chicago's formal Olympic bid began when President Harper presided over a banquet on 13 February 1901 at the Chicago Athletic Association, at which a committee organized by Furber publicly announced Chicago's interest in obtaining the bid as host city of the 1904 Olympic Games.[17]

But Coubertin had not yet heard from the Chicago Bid Committee, as it were, and knew only that which he read in the papers. The Chicago announcement was published in both the *Chicago Tribune* and *The New York Times*. The IOC Session for 1901 was only three months away, scheduled for May 1901.

Correspondence took place during those three months between Coubertin and the three

American IOC Members: Sloane, Caspar Whitney, and Theodore Stanton. The American IOC Members were strongly in favor of Chicago, and they eventually were able to convince James Sullivan that Chicago was an appropriate choice for the 1904 Olympics.

The Chicago Olympian Games Committee sent an official request to host the 1904 Olympic Games to Coubertin on 1 May 1901.[18] The document was signed by 13 prominent Chicago citizens, who constituted the bid committee.

The 1901 IOC Session took place in Paris from 21 to 23 May at Le Club Automobile de France. Until just before the session, it appeared that Chicago was the only candidate city. But events in St. Louis transpired to yield a second possible host city.

With 1903 marking the 100th Anniversary of the Louisiana Purchase, St. Louis planned a large World's Fair, the Louisiana Purchase International Exposition. But even by 1901 it had become obvious that the plans could not be completed in time to celebrate the anniversary in 1903. It was expected that the Exposition would be postponed to 1904. Anticipating this, on 30 April 1901, Caspar Whitney wrote to Harper, conveying the news of the probable postponement and the expected St. Louis challenge to host the 1904 Olympic Games.[19]

Almost concurrent with Whitney's letter, Coubertin received a St. Louis resident at his home in Paris, Count de Penaloza, who gave the Baron an informal confirmation of the St. Louis bid. He noted that a formal invitation would arrive momentarily. In a few days, the expected invitation did not materialize, and Penaloza sent Coubertin a note to the effect that St. Louis could not formally bid "at this time" and asked the IOC to postpone their decision until 1902.[20]

This was untenable to the IOC, who decided to procede with choosing a 1904 host city during their 1901 Session. Of the American IOC Members, only Theodore Stanton was present in Paris.[21] With Henri Bréal assisting, Stanton presented the formal Chicago bid to the IOC. No representative of St. Louis was present, only the vague request from Penaloza to delay the selection. On 22 May 1901, Chicago was elected unanimously by the IOC as the host city for the 1904 Olympic Games.[22]

Shortly thereafter, Coubertin wrote to the United States President, William McKinley, asking him to accept the Honorary Presidency of the 1904 Olympic Games. But no response from McKinley ever occurred.[23] And if it had, events of September 1901 would have rendered it moot. While visiting the Buffalo Pan-American Exposition, McKinley was mortally wounded on 6 September by an anarchist, Leon Czolgosz, and died on 14 September 1901, the victim of the assassin's bullet. His replacement as President would be a man known for his love of the outdoors and his support of sports, Theodore "Teddy" Roosevelt.

Coubertin quickly turned his attention to Roosevelt and wrote him with a similar request.[24] He was rebuffed: "My dear Sir ... It is a matter of real regret to me that I do not feel at liberty to accept your very kind request that I become honorary president of the Chicago Olympic Games. Unfortunately, after consultation with members of the cabinet, I feel it would not do for me to give the unavoidable impression of governmental connection with the Games."[25]

Barney documents that Roosevelt never acquiesced to Coubertin's request, although future Olympic historians have not always recorded it in that manner. Specifically, he notes that Bill Henry, in his book *An Approved History of the Olympic Games*, erroneously stated that Roosevelt accepted the Honorary Presidency on 28 May 1902.[26]

And like President Roosevelt's rebuffs, Chicago's Olympic bid would soon come crashing down around it, the victim of the delay in St. Louis' hosting of the Louisiana Purchase Exposition. St. Louis, although it had failed to win the 1904 Olympic Games, apparently planned an ambitious series of athletic events to be contested in conjunction with the 1904 World's Fair.

Henry Furber learned of St. Louis's ambitions just before he left on a cruise in August 1902, and he understood well the significance of this announcement. He cabled President Harper in Chicago, "I have just been informed that the St. Louis Exposition is trying to secure the AAU championship contests in 1904. As the AAU virtually controls athletics in the United States, this would seriously injure the Olympian Games."[27]

Shortly after his cruise ended, Furber learned of further possible problems. The officials of the Louisiana Purchase Exposition were requesting a meeting with him in New York, in which they wished to explore avenues by which the nation's best athletes could compete in both the 1904 Olympic Games in Chicago, and the 1904 AAU Championships, by then scheduled for the same time period in St. Louis. Furber met in New York with Frederick Skiff, Director of Exhibits at the Louisiana Purchase Exposition, and Alfred Shapleigh, a member of the Exposition's Executive Committee. Exact records of that meeting do not exist, but Barney has unearthed a letter from Furber to Coubertin which discussed the St. Louisan's hardball tactics: "They informed me politely but clearly, that the Olympian Games of 1904 threatened the success of their World's Fair, and that if we insisted in carrying out our program they would develop their athletic department so as to eclipse our games...."[28]

Shortly after Furber's return to Chicago, more bad news awaited him. This was in the form of a message from David R. Francis, former Governor of Missouri, and then the President of the Louisiana Purchase Exposition, requesting an audience with the Chicago Organizing Committee's entire board of directors. A dinner meeting was arranged for 10 November 1902, at the Chicago Athletic Association. Francis' committee also expressed their hopes that Chicago would transfer the 1904 Olympics to St. Louis. The Chicago committee voted narrowly to place the decision in the hands of Coubertin and the IOC.[29]

Within two weeks, Furber sent two letters to Coubertin. In them he gave details of the Chicago proposal. Barney quotes from the letters in his article:

> St. Louis has an organized and paid corp of officials that could outstrip us in promptness and efficiency of work; the official recognition of the national government which would embarrass us in our missions abroad; a huge (over $6,000,000) appropriation from the government, plus sums from states involved, thus blocking our own efforts; and St. Louis might place Chicago in the light of mischievously competing in an enterprise in whose success the honor of the nation is involved....
>
> If we try to carry out our program in 1904, St. Louis will jeopardize our enterprise. She will ... injure us in a thousand different ways ... it would be better to accept the invitation of St. Louis and transfer the Games to that city, than to attempt to conduct them at Chicago in the face of difficulties with which St. Louis would oppose us. Still, my dear friend, I do not believe that this would be the wisest course. In my official letter I have suggested a postponement to 1905. If this plan should meet with your approval, I see the greatest possible success for us.[30]

Coubertin later wrote that he would allow a transfer but never a postponement. In December 1902, he sent off letters to the IOC Members discussing the situation and the problem, and asking for their opinion. Seven responses from IOC members have survived, all of them opposed to transferring the Olympics to St. Louis.[31]

It was obvious to Coubertin that he had to make a decision, and after pondering it in January 1903, he did so early in February. On 10 February 1903, he cabled Furber, "Transfer accepted."[32] On February 12th, Coubertin received a cable from Furber. The message approached the Baron's in brevity and succinctness: "Instruction just received. Will transfer accordingly."[33]

The 1904 Olympic Games would be held in St. Louis in conjunction with the Louisiana Purchase Exposition. Baron Pierre de Coubertin would forever rue that decision.

A Brief History of St. Louis

The earliest known inhabitants of what is now St. Louis were the Hopewell Indians who settled there between 500 B.C. and A.D. 400. Also known as the mound builders, they built round, earthen structures to be used as temples, forts, and burial sites on the banks of the Mississippi. Some of these mounds survive today in the St. Louis area, particularly in Cahokia Mounds State Park across the river in Illinois. These mounds are responsible for St. Louis's original nickname of the "Mound City."

In approximately 1700, French Jesuit priests founded a mission at the mouth of the Rivière des Peres, near the current site of St. Louis. Kaskaskia and Tamaroa Indians came from Illinois to live with the priests for three years, but after they left, the mission failed.

St. Louis, Missouri, was originally settled in December 1763 by the French fur trader Pierre Laclède Liguest of New Orleans, who started a fur trading post on the site. He named the post in honor of Louis IX, the Crusader King of France, who ruled from 1214 to 1270 and was canonized in 1297. He was beloved by the French people for his benevolence, economic successes, his efforts to form a lasting peace, and his initiative to allow direct appeal to the Crown in all cases.

Following the Louisiana Purchase in 1803, St. Louis became a part of the United States. It was immediately made the seat of government of the District of Louisiana (1805), and later served as the capital of the Louisiana Territory (1805) and the Territory of Missouri (1812). It relinquished the seat of Missouri government when Missouri was made a state of the United States of American in 1820. The Missouri Compromise of 1820 resulted in Missouri being admitted to the United States as a slave state in exchange for Maine being admitted as a free state. Slavery was then forbidden in all states north and west of Missouri.

However, St. Louis was always the major city in Missouri and served as the entry point for settlers to the American West. Beginning with the steamboat era of the mid–19th century, and helped by its location on the banks of the Mississippi, St. Louis served as a major transportation hub, and was the United States' busiest inland river port well into the 20th century. St. Louis quickly prospered because of a booming fur trade and the influx of immigrants to the area. By the 1840s, St. Louis was surpassed only by New Orleans as a port on the Mississippi. After the Civil War, St. Louis enjoyed great prosperity. Many of the city's landmarks which still exist today were built in this era, including Forest Park (where the 1904 Louisiana Purchase Exposition would take place), Tower Grove Park, and the Missouri Botanical Gardens. The world's first skyscraper, the ten-story Wainwright Building, was built in 1890 by Louis B. Sullivan.

St. Louis was incorporated as a town in 1821 and as a city in 1823. By 1900 it was the fourth largest American city, trailing only New York, Chicago, and Philadelphia, with a population of 575,000. Almost 20 percent of the St. Louis population was foreign-born in 1904, with about 10 percent of the population of German descent.[34] As late as 1950, St. Louis was the eighth most populous U.S. city, then with 855,000 citizens, but by 1994, it ranked 43rd with a population of 368,000. The city is now dominated by a huge (630 foot [190 meter]) stainless-steel Gateway Arch, begun in 1963 and finished in 1966, a monument symbolizing St. Louis' status as "Gateway to the West."

The Louisiana Purchase International Exposition: The 1904 St. Louis World's Fair[35]

The 1904 St. Louis World's Fair was officially known as the Louisiana Purchase International Exposition, but was usually called the Louisiana Purchase Exposition. It was held in commemoration of the centennial of the 1803 Louisiana Purchase. As noted above, the fair was originally planned for 1903, but was delayed in order to accommodate the foreign exhibitors, who were unable to plan their exhibits by the 1903 deadline.

A commemoration of the Louisiana Purchase had been discussed in St. Louis as early as 1889. Then Governor David R. Francis led a delegation from Missouri to Washington in 1890 to secure the Columbian Exposition for St. Louis, but they lost out to Chicago. Francis was upset, but he determined that St. Louis should hold a bigger and better celebration in 1903 for the Louisiana Purchase centennial. Is it possible that Francis' defeat by Chicago in the efforts to host the 1893 World's Fair led to his intransigence in dealing with Chicago on the subject of the Olympic Games in 1902–1903?

On 3 March 1901, the U.S. Congress passed the Louisiana Purchase Exposition Bill, which authorized funding for the St. Louis Fair.[36] By May 1901 Francis was elected President of the Louisiana Purchase Exposition Company. A board of directors was appointed, made up of 93 business and civic leaders. Francis and his board planned a fair with several themes. They wished to repair St. Louis' tarnished image resulting from a violent turn-of-the-century transit workers' strike. The benefits of American Imperialism were one theme of the Louisiana Purchase Exposition. As a result of the Spanish-American War, the United States had recently acquired possessions and established protectorates in the Caribbean and the Pacific. The 1904 World's Fair purported to show the benefits reaped by recently conquered countries because of American civilization. Francis further noted that the fair promoted universal peace by bringing together diverse people of many nationalities in peaceful co-existence. The St. Louis World's Fair also emphasized the latest technological developments in all exhibits.

The site of the Louisiana Purchase Exposition was chosen as the western half of Forest Park, and the fairgrounds covered 1,272 acres—1.75 by 1.05 miles. St. Louis determined to put on its best face for the international visitors it expected. The city joined with private corporations to improve the appearance and services of St. Louis. The transit company added 450 new cars; trains ran to the fair every 15 minutes; and an intramural railroad was built to transport people in and around the fairgrounds. Water filters were installed to improve the notoriously bad St. Louis water. Mayor Rolla Wells directed the rebuilding of over 70 miles of streets and the construction of 30 miles of new streets.

The center of the Louisiana Purchase Exposition was the Pike, an amusement and concession area, which extended 1½ miles from the main fair entrance. St. Louis architect Isaac Taylor was appointed as director of works, and he chose Emmanuel L. Masqueray as his chief design assistant. Masqueray developed the fan-shaped plan for the exhibit palaces, and also designed the colonnades and pavilion restaurants, as well as structures on the Pike.

Director of Exhibits Frederick J. V. Skiff planned the exhibits to demonstrate man and his works, emphasizing education. There were twelve major classifications of "man and his works": (1) education, (2) art, (3) liberal arts and applied sciences, (4) agriculture, (5) horticulture, (6) mining and forestry, (7) manufacturing, (8) transportation, (9) electricity, (10) anthropology, (11) social economy, and (12) physical culture. The exhibits concluded with physical culture, stressing a strong body as essential to a keen intellect. The 1904 Olympic Games were conducted as a section of the Physical Culture Exhibit, which was led by the Director, James Edward Sullivan.

The exhibits at the 1904 fair were designed to demonstrate the progress of humanity from barbarism to the pinnacle of Anglo-Saxon civilization, and this was exemplified by a series of historical and anthropological exhibits contrasting various races and peoples. Emphasizing this, there were American Indian exhibits, and exhibits of Philippine natives, both of which contrasted modern civilization against the relative barbaric cultures of those two groups at that time.

The opening day of the Louisiana Purchase Exposition was Saturday, 30 April 1904, and it drew an estimated crowd of 200,000. The fair was opened by President Theodore Roosevelt from Washington, who pressed the key of a telegraphic instrument to signal the start. At Roosevelt's signal, an artillery battery fired a national salute in the direction of Washington, while David R. Francis lifted his hands and issued an invitation to "enter herein, ye sons of men." Concurrently, 10,000 flags unfurled, fountains sprayed into the air, water tumbled down the Cascades, and bands played to signal the start of the fair. Francis then gave a rather lengthy speech.

Visitors could choose among some 540 amusements and concessions. The Pike stayed open in the evening when exhibit palaces had closed, and it also featured the Cliff Dwellers, Zuni, and Moki Indians who had "never been shown before"; it had burros conveying visitors along steep inclines, Mysterious Asia with camel rides along its winding streets, and the Geisha Girls entertaining visitors to Fair Japan. But with a separate admission price for each concession, the Pike proved to be too expensive for many families.

The Louisiana Purchase Exposition can claim the distinction of staging the first successful demonstration of wireless telegraphy between the ground and the air in the United States, and the St. Louis World's Fair is credited with mounting the first meteorological balloon experiments in the United States. However, there is no truth to the oft-quoted rumors that iced tea, hot dogs, and ice cream cones originated at the St. Louis World's Fair.

The Louisiana Purchase International Exposition drew to a close on 1 December 1904. President Francis gave the closing remarks: "Farewell, a long farewell, to all thy splendor." A band struck up "Auld Lang Syne," great geysers of fireworks blazed forth, ending with the fiery words "Farewell — Goodnight." According to official attendance figures, 19,694,855 people passed through the turnstiles during the seven months of the fair.

The 1904 World's Fair was a financial success. Profits from it were used to build the Jefferson Memorial in Forest Park, which was the first national monument to Thomas Jefferson and cost nearly $500,000 to build. On a negative note, the fair reinforced unfortunate racial stereotypes in the ordering of exhibits contrasting "civilized" peoples with their "barbaric, hardly human" counterparts, and in the Old Plantation exhibit, which cast the antebellum South in a golden glow. On the local level, the 1904 fair paved the way for reforms instituted by Dwight Davis (who was elected park commissioner in 1911). Forest Park had lost most of its wilderness character as a result of clearing the land and its landscaping for the fair, but Davis established public recreational facilities in these new open spaces.

The 1904 Louisiana Purchase Exposition was not soon forgotten. In 1944, a popular movie, *Meet Me in St. Louis* (MGM), was centered around life at the 1904 World's Fair. Starring Judy Garland and directed by her future husband, Vincente Minnelli, the movie introduced the popular song, "Meet Me in St. Louis, Louis." The movie also starred Margaret O'Brien, Mary Astor, Lucille Bremer, Tom Drake, June Lockhart, and Harry Davenport. It won a National Board of Review Award as one of the 10 best films of 1944. The song was written by Andrew B. Sterling (lyrics) and Kerry Mills (music) and was also sung by Leo Ames in the movie *By the Light of the Silvery Moon* (Warner Bros., 1953). In addition a group devoted to studying the 1904 World's Fair was formed in 1986, "The 1904 World's Fair Society," which has a web page devoted to its activities (www.inlink.com/%7Eterryl/), a newsletter, and over 400 members as of 1998.

Games of the 3rd Olympiad

The Olympic Games were held in St. Louis from 1 July through 23 November 1904. Sporting events as part of the Physical Culture Section of the Louisiana Purchase Exposition actually began on 14 May 1904, with an Interscholastic Meet, which was actually the Missouri State High

School Championships for 1904. But James Sullivan, whose official title was "Chief of the Department of Physical Culture Section of the Louisiana Purchase Exposition" and who was thus the Director of the Olympic Games, termed almost every event which occurred in conjunction with the Louisiana Purchase Exposition an Olympic event. The State High School Meet's "official" title was the Olympic Interscholastic Meet. The sporting events conducted at the Fair ended a few days after the Olympic Games events, with a football game played between the two Indian schools, Carlisle and Haskell, on 26 November 1904. Carlisle defeated Haskell, 34–4.

There was something approximating a modern day Opening Ceremony at the 1904 Olympic Games, but it took place on 14 May 1904, at the Olympic Interscholastic Meet. It was scheduled to start at 2:30 P.M. (1430), but the functionaries had begun by touring the Louisiana Purchase Exposition and were late. At about 2:50 P.M. (1450), President Francis arrived at Francis Field accompanied by the United States Secretary of State John Milton Hay (1838–1905). They led in a double line of silk-hatted officials and commissioners and proceeded to their boxes in the grandstand. After they were seated, the band struck up "The Star Spangled Banner." Francis, Hay, and Sullivan then walked down to the starting line. Sullivan called the athletes to the line for the first heat of the 100 yards, and the "Olympic Games" were opened when Francis fired the starting pistol at 3:00 P.M. (1500).

Most of the events of the 1904 Olympic Games took place on the campus of Washington University. Francis Field, the Washington University athletic stadium which was named after David Francis, Director of the Louisiana Purchase Exposition, had a new, then-modern, stadium built for it, called the Olympic Stadium. Adjacent to the stadium was the Physical Culture Gymnasium which housed many of the physical culture exhibits and in which several of the indoor sports were conducted. Francis Field and the Olympic Stadium still exist in their original forms, although the 1904 cinder track was replaced, but not until the 1980s. The Physical Culture Gymnasium also still exists, almost as it did in 1904, and is still the main gymnasium for Washington University physical education classes.

After the debacle of 1900, Coubertin was hoping for better from the United States and St. Louis in 1904, but did not see his hopes realized. The Games were very similar to those in 1900 — they lasted almost five full months; many of the events were not truly Olympic, but only championships of the Fair; it is difficult to know which sports and events were definitely on the Olympic program; a number of unusual sports and events saw their way to the program; and the Games were mostly an afterthought to the Fair. Attendance at many of the events was minimal. The local newspapers followed Sullivan's lead and termed almost everything an "Olympic event," but nationally, the newspapers seemed concerned only with the track & field athletic events, which occurred at the end of August and first of September. Little nation-wide publicity was given to other sports. Again, the number of competing nations and athletes cannot be determined with absolute accuracy, although we can do better than we can with 1900.

The athletics (track & field) events were virtually an American club championship, and, in fact, a trophy was donated by Albert Spalding for the American club scoring the most points in the sport. The trophy was hotly contested between the Chicago Athletic Association and the New York Athletic Club, and the New York AC's victory was disputed by the Chicago club when they claimed a "ringer" had been used in the tug-of-war event (which was considered part of track & field athletics). Though surpassed by athletes in other sports, the American foursome of Archie Hahn, Harry Hillman, James Lightbody, and Ray Ewry won three gold medals each in track & field and received the bulk of the media attention.

In other sports, American dominance was almost as complete, owing to the fact that only a few other countries attended the Games, and very few foreign athletes competed. Only 12 nations can be considered to have competed in 1904, and the participation of several nations consisted of only a few athletes. Only track & field athletics had a true international flavor, with

10 nations competing. Swimming had competitors from four nations. Gymnastics also had four nations participating, but with only one athlete each from Austria and Switzerland.

It should be noted that in those years, athletes often competed virtually as individuals, with no real national teams. Thus the case of Felix Carbajal of Cuba, who travelled to St. Louis using money raised in staging various exhibitions in Havana. He stopped in New Orleans and lost his money in a crap game. So he hitchhiked to St. Louis to run in the marathon. He showed up on the starting line wearing heavy shoes, long trousers, and a long-sleeved shirt, but legend relates that American weight thrower Martin Sheridan helped him by using scissors to trim off his trousers and the sleeves on his shirt. Carbajal finished fourth. Two black Tswana tribesmen, Len Tau and Jan Mashiani, who were part of the Boer War exhibition at the fair, also competed in the marathon. Ironically, they are considered to be the first Olympic competitors from South Africa.

In other events, the first black men earned Olympic medals in track & field athletics, both Americans. These two athletes were George Poage, who won two bronze medals in the 200 and 400 meter hurdles; and Joseph Stadler, who won a silver medal in the standing high jump and a bronze medal in the standing triple jump.

The great hoax of the athletic events at the 1904 Olympics occurred in the marathon race. The winner was English-born American Tom Hicks, but the first runner to come into the stadium was Fred Lorz, also of the United States. He had his picture taken with Alice Roosevelt, daughter of Teddy Roosevelt, before it was revealed that he had stopped running and taken a car ride to just outside the stadium. He was disqualified by the AAU "for life," although that ruling was rescinded in time for Lorz to win the 1905 Boston Marathon.

Pierre de Coubertin was appalled when he heard of the happenings in St. Louis, but never more so than when he heard about the "Anthropological Days." The Fair organizers included several days of "Olympic" competitions among several so-called primitive tribes which were being exhibited at the Exposition. Among these were Pygmies, Patagonians, Filipinos, Native American Indian tribes, Japanese Ainus, and certain Asian tribes. Events included throwing bolos, mud fighting, and climbing a greased pole.

The Baron de Coubertin was informed of these events by Ferenc Kémény, who stated, "I was not only present at a sporting contest but also at a fair where there were sports, where there was cheating, where monsters were exhibited for a joke." Of this last reference to "Anthropological Days," Coubertin presciently noted, "As for that outrageous charade, it will of course lose its appeal when black men, red men, and yellow men learn to run, jump and throw, and leave the white men behind them."[37]

Coubertin would vow after 1904 to never again hold the Olympics as a sideshow to a major international fair, although 1908 would have a loose connection with one. Notably, he did not even attend the Olympics in 1904, sending two IOC delegates from Hungary (Kémény) and Germany (Willibald Gebhardt) in his place. In addition, the 1904 Olympic Games are also the only Olympics in history at which a formal session of the International Olympic Committee (IOC) was not conducted. With the events of 1900 and 1904, the nascent Olympic Movement was reeling. It would be revived by an "Olympic Games" held outside of the cycle, in 1906 in Athens, which now receives little recognition for its import, but definitely resuscitated Coubertin's flagging Olympic Movement.

Which Events and Sports Were the Olympic Games?

In my recent work on the 1900 Olympic Games, I devoted a large section to this problem as related to the Paris Olympics of 1900. A similar difficulty exists in 1904, because of Sullivan's inane insistence on labelling every sporting event that occurred in St. Louis in the summer and fall of 1904 as "Olympic." Fortunately, the problem is not quite so difficult for 1904 as it is for 1900, although it is by no means simple.

First of all, to my knowledge, the IOC has never *officially* made any determination of what should be considered Olympic sports and events for 1904, nor did they for 1900. In my 1900 report, I discussed this in more detail, but suffice to say that multiple rumors exist that such a determination has been made, but no documentation to support that fact can be found. The same is true for 1904.

In the introduction to the statistical summary on the 1904 Games that I wrote in 1981, I stated that I would not attempt such a determination, and simply included most of the usually listed events and sports, allowing the readers and historians to make their own judgments. But that was a cop-out on my part, and herein I will attempt to determine which events should be considered part of the official Olympic program for 1904. As with my work on 1900, I propose to make the attempt, with the justification being, if not in this book, where else would it be done? Nobody else has looked at as many sources. Much of what follows will be similar to my arguments concerning the determination of the Olympic program in 1900.

In making this determination, I am using the principles of what constitutes an Olympic event in the 1990s, what was discussed officially by the IOC from 1894 to 1903, and will also extrapolate a bit to consider Coubertin's philosophy of Olympism. I think this last point is important, for Coubertin certainly had nothing in mind like what took place in 1900 and 1904, and he never would have considered all the events of 1900 or 1904 to be Olympic in nature.

Four criteria currently must be met for any event or sport to be considered an Olympic event in current nomenclature. One, the event should be international in scope, allowing entries from all nations.[38] Two, no handicap events should be allowed. Three, the entries must be open to all competitors (which means mainly that limitations based on age, religion, national origin, or competency, such as junior, intermediate, or novice events, should not be allowed). And four, the events should be restricted to amateurs only. While amateur status is no longer a criterion for inclusion on the Olympic program, it certainly was in 1904.

Applying current criteria to 1904, a completely different era, is hardly good history. But if we look at the above criteria in the context of 1904, little should actually change.

First, that the events should be international was true in 1904 as well as today. Coubertin strongly desired the Olympics to be an international event, and did not wish to restrict entry on national origin in any manner. Thus, events in 1904 which were open to Americans only, such as American collegiate championships, or regional athletic sports, should not be included on the 1904 Olympic program.

Second, that handicap events should not be allowed was also definitely true in 1904. Even by 1904, the IOC had adopted the motto of "Citius, Altius, Fortius," and definitely desired the Olympic events to be contests among the world's best athletes competing on an even basis. This would eliminate all handicap events from Olympic consideration in 1904.

Third, any restriction of the events to certain classes of competitors was antithetical to Coubertin's principles even in 1904. Coubertin did not wish to restrict the Olympics in any way,[39] with the exception of amateurism. He wanted them open to all amateur athletes in all parts of the world. To consider events for juniors, intermediates, novices, or Irish athletes only, would certainly violate his philosophy, in 1904 as well as today. I know of only a few exceptions to this principle. In 1896 a swimming event for sailors only was on the program. And until 1952, equestrian events were open only to military personnel, specifically officers.

Fourth, amateurism was certainly a requirement for an event to be considered Olympic in 1904, with one exception. At the 1894 Sorbonne Congress which re-established the Olympic Games, one of the conclusions of the Congress was, "Except in fencing only amateurs [will be] allowed to start."[40] Fencing professionals were allowed, and professional fencing was included in 1896 and 1900. Fencing teachers, or masters, were considered professionals but were also considered "gentlemen" in this era, and it was apparently considered acceptable for them to compete in the Olympic Games initially. There were no professional fencing events conducted as part of the 1904 Louisiana Purchase Exposition, probably because fencing was never that popular in the United States. Professional events in any other sport, however, should not be considered Olympic events.

Now given all this, here is a list of all the sports and events which were conducted during the 1904 Louisana Purchase Exposition. Included in this list are the above criteria, and I have designated which events I think should be included as Olympic and which should not. Within each separate sport section, I have usually discussed the criteria for inclusion as an Olympic sport, and whether or not the sport met these criteria.

	Amateurs/Pros	Int'l	Hdcp	Open	Olympic
Anthropology Days	Amateurs	Yes	No	No	
Archery					
Double York Round, Men	Amateurs	No	No	Yes	✓
Double American Round, Men	Amateurs	No	No	Yes	✓
Team Round, Men	Amateurs	No	No	Yes	✓
Double Columbia Round, Women	Amateurs	No	No	Yes	✓
Double National Round, Women	Amateurs	No	No	Yes	✓
Flight Shooting, Men	Amateurs	No	No	No	
Flight Shooting, Women	Amateurs	No	No	No	
Athletics (Track & Field)					
Olympic Track & Field Athletics	Amateurs	Yes	No	Yes	✓
Olympic Handicap Meet	Amateurs	Yes	Yes	Yes	
Missouri Interscholastic Meet	Amateurs	No	No	No	
Open Handicap Meeting	Amateurs	No	Yes	No	
School Meet for LPE Territory	Amateurs	No	No	No	
St. Louis Elementary School Meet	Amateurs	No	No	No	
AAU Handicap Meet	Amateurs	No	Yes	No	
AAU Junior Championships	Amateurs	No	No	No	
Collegiate Championships	Amateurs	No	No	No	
Interscholastic Handicap Meet	Amateurs	No	Yes	No	
Interscholastic Championships	Amateurs	No	No	No	
Special Athletic Events	Amateurs	No	No	No	
Public Schools Athletic League Meet	Amateurs	No	No	No	
Irish Sports	Amateurs	No	No	No	
Western AAU Handicap Meet	Amateurs	No	Yes	No	
Western AAU Championship Meet	Amateurs	No	No	No	
YMCA Team Pentathlon Championships	Amateurs	No	No	No	
YMCA Handicap Track and Field Meet	Amateurs	No	Yes	No	
YMCA Track and Field Championship	Amateurs	No	No	No	
Military Athletic Carnival	Amateurs	No	No	No	
Basketball					
Olympic Basketball Championship	Amateurs	No	No	Yes	
Olympic College Basketball Championship	Amateurs	No	No	No	
Public School Ath. League Basketball	Amateurs	No	No	No	
YMCA Basketball Championships	Amateurs	No	No	No	
Boxing	Amateurs	No	No	Yes	✓

	Amateurs/Pros	Int'l	Hdcp	Open	Olympic
Cycling					
Olympic Amateur Events	Amateurs	No	No	Yes	✓
Olympic Amateur Events, Handicap	Amateurs	No	Yes	Yes	
Olympic Professional Events	Pros	No	No	Yes	
Olympic Professional Events, Handicap	Pros	No	Yes	Yes	
Diving	Amateurs	No	No	Yes	✓
Fencing					
Foil	Amateurs	Yes	No	Yes	✓
Dueling Swords (Épée)	Amateurs	Yes	No	Yes	✓
Saber	Amateurs	Yes	No	Yes	✓
Single Sticks	Amateurs	Yes	No	Yes	✓
Team Foil	Amateurs	Yes	No	Yes	✓
Junior Foil	Amateurs	No	No	Yes	
Football					
Olympic Association Football	Amateurs	Yes	No	Yes	✓
Olympic College Football	Amateurs	No	No	No	
Gaelic Football Championships	Amateurs	No	No	No	
Golf					
Men's Individual	Amateurs	Yes	No	Yes	✓
Men's Team Championship	Amateurs	No	No	Yes	✓
President's Match	Amateurs	Yes	No	No	
Consolation Flights	Amateurs	Yes	No	Yes	
Team Nassau Match	Amateurs	No	No	Yes	
Driving Contest	Amateurs	Unk.	No	Yes	
Putting Contest	Amateurs	Unk.	No	Yes	
Gymnastics					
AAU Events	Amateurs	No	No	Yes	✓
Turnverein Gymnastics	Amateurs	Yes	No	Yes	✓
YMCA Individual Gymnastics	Amateurs	No	No	No	
YMCA Team Athletic-Gymnastics	Amateurs	No	No	No	
Lacrosse					
Olympic Lacrosse Championships	Amateurs	Yes	No	Yes	✓
Irish Hurling Championships	Amateurs	No	No	No	
Roque	Amateurs	No	No	No	
Rowing & Sculling					
Single Sculls	Amateurs	No	No	Yes	✓
Double Sculls	Amateurs	No	No	Yes	✓
Coxless Pairs	Amateurs	No	No	Yes	✓
Coxless Fours	Amateurs	No	No	Yes	✓
Coxed Eights	Amateurs	Yes	No	Yes	✓
Intermediate Single Sculls	Amateurs	Yes	No	No	
Association Single Sculls	Amateurs	Yes	No	No	
Intermediate Double Sculls	Amateurs	No	No	No	
Intermediate Coxless Pairs	Amateurs	No	No	No	
Intermediate Coxless Fours	Amateurs	No	No	No	
Intermediate Coxed Eights	Amateurs	No	No	No	
Swimming					
Olympic Swimming Championships	Amateurs	Yes	No	Yes	✓
Olympic Handicap Meet	Amateurs	Yes	Yes	Yes	

	Amateurs/Pros	Int'l	Hdcp	Open	Olympic
Tennis (Lawn)					
Olympic Men's Singles	Amateurs	Yes	No	Yes	✓
Olympic Men's Doubles	Amateurs	Yes	No	Yes	✓
World's Fair Men's Singles	Amateurs	Yes	No	Yes	
World's Fair Men's Doubles	Amateurs	Yes	No	Yes	
Louisiana Purchase Open Singles	Amateurs	No	No	Yes	
Interscholastic Men's Singles	Amateurs	No	No	No	
Tug-of-War	Amateurs	Yes	No	No	✓
Water Polo	Amateurs	No	No	No	
Weightlifting					
Two-Hand Lift	Amateurs	Yes	No	Yes	✓
All-Around Dumbbell Contest	Amateurs	No	No	Yes	✓
Wrestling	Amateurs	No	No	Yes	✓

SUMMARY STATISTICS

1904 Olympic Games — Medals Won by Countries

The following medal lists (nations and individuals) includes *my* determination of which sports and events should be considered of Olympic caliber in 1904. Notably, *not* included are the following, which are often listed in Olympic reference books: Basketball, Roque (Croquet), Water Polo, and the Swimming 4 × 50-yard relay.

	Gold	Silver	Bronze	Medals
United States	74	79	80	233
Germany	4	4	4	12
Canada	4	1	1	6
Hungary	2	1	1	4
Cuba	3	–	–	3
Austria	1	1	1	3
Ireland (Great Britain)[41]	1	1	–	2
Greece	1	–	1	2
Austria/United States	1	–	–	1
Cuba/United States	1	–	–	1
Switzerland	1	–	1	2
France	–	1	–	1
France/United States	–	1	–	1
Totals (91 events)	93	89	89	271

Note: *No third in 4-mile team race (athletics — men); no third in flyweight, bantamweight, and middleweight classes (boxing); two thirds in welterweight class (boxing); no third in team foil fencing; two firsts/no second in horizontal bar (gymnastics — men); two firsts/no second in horse vault (gymnastics — men); no third in eights (rowing); two thirds in men's individual event (golf); two thirds awarded in all events [two] in 1904 tennis.*

Ladies' team round (archery) in 1904 was not contested, although several records books continue to list it as an event, with the United States winning and no second or third.

Basketball, roque (croquet), and water polo are not included in the above list as Olympic sports in 1904. American football and the anthropology days events, which are never included as Olympic sports in Olympic reference books, are likewise not included in the above list. In addition, I have eliminated the swimming 4 × 50-yard relay as an Olympic sport — for details see the swimming section.

Most Medals (2 or more) [73: 70 Men, 3 Women]

Men

	Gold	Silver	Bronze	Medals
Anton Heida (USA-GYM)	5	1	–	6
George Eyser (USA-GYM)	3	2	1	6
Burton C. Downing (USA-CYC)	2	3	1	6 [3]
Marcus L. Hurley (USA-CYC)	4	–	1	5
Albertson Van Zo Post (USA-FEN)	2	1	2	5
William A. Merz (USA-GYM)	–	1	4	5 [6]
James D. Lightbody (USA-ATH)	3	1	–	4
Charles M. Daniels (USA-SWI)	2	1	1	4
Francis Gailey (USA-SWI)	–	3	1	4
Edwin "Teddy" Billington (USA-CYC)	–	1	3	4 [10]
Frank Kungler (USA-TOW/WLT/WRE)	–	1	3	4 [11]
Raymond C. Ewry (USA-ATH)	3	–	–	3
Ramón Fonst Segundo (CUB-FEN)	3	–	–	3
C. Archibald "Archie" Hahn (USA-ATH)	3	–	–	3
Harry L. Hillman, Jr. (USA-ATH)	3	–	–	3
Julius Lenhart (AUT-GYM)	2	1	–	3
G. Phillip Bryant (USA-ARC)	2	–	1	3
Emil A. Rausch (GER-SWI)	2	–	1	3
Robert W. Williams, Jr. (USA-ARC)	1	2	–	3
Ralph W. Rose (USA-ATH)	1	1	1	3 [20]
Arthur L. Newton (USA-ATH)	1	–	2	3
William H. Thompson (USA-ARC)	1	–	2	3
Charles T. Tatham (USA-FEN)	–	2	1	3
William P. Hogensen (USA-ATH)	–	1	2	3
Emil Voigt (USA-GYM)	–	1	2	3 [25]
Manuel D. Diaz Martinez (CUB-FEN)	2	–	–	2
Zoltán von Halmay (HUN-SWI)	2	–	–	2
Edward A. Hennig (USA-GYM)	2	–	–	2
Oliver L. Kirk (USA-BOX)	2	–	–	2
Meyer Prinstein (USA-ATH)	2	–	–	2 [30]
Beals C. Wright (USA-TEN)	2	–	–	2 [31]
Walter Brack (GER-SWI)	1	1	–	2
H. Chandler Egan (USA-GOL)	1	1	–	2
George V. Finnegan (USA-BOX)	1	1	–	2
John J. Flanagan (USA-ATH)	1	1	–	2
John Grieb (USA-GYM)	1	1	–	2

(Men)	Gold	Silver	Bronze	Medals
Charles Mayer (USA-BOX)	1	1	–	2
John J. F. Mulcahy (USA-ROW)	1	1	–	2
Oscar P. Osthoff (USA-WLT)	1	1	–	2
Harry J. Spanger (USA-BOX)	1	1	–	2 [40]
Howard V. Valentine (USA-ATH)	1	1	–	2
William P. Varley (USA-ROW)	1	1	–	2 [42]
Edgar W. Leonard (USA-TEN)	1	–	1	2
Adolf Spinnler (SUI-GYM)	1	–	1	2
Georg Zacharias (GER-SWI)	1	–	1	2 [45]
Nathaniel J. Cartmell (USA-ATH)	–	2	–	2
Albert Coray (FRA-ATH)	–	2	–	2
Georg Hoffmann (GER-SWI/DIV)	–	2	–	2
Charles M. King (USA-ATH)	–	2	–	2
Robert LeRoy (USA-TEN)	–	2	–	2 [50]
W. Frank Verner (USA-ATH)	–	2	–	2
Frank L. Waller (USA-ATH)	–	2	–	2 [52]
A. F. Andrews (USA-CYC)	–	1	1	2
Alphonzo E. Bell (USA-TEN)	–	1	1	2
Jack Eagan (USA-BOX)	–	1	1	2
William Grebe (USA-FEN)	–	1	1	2
Lacey E. Hearn (USA-ATH)	–	1	1	2
Géza Kiss (HUN-SWI)	–	1	1	2
Charles Krause (USA-GYM)	–	1	1	2
J. Scott Leary (USA-SWI)	–	1	1	2 [60]
Joseph P. Lydon (USA-BOX/FTB)	–	1	1	2
Burt P. McKinnie (USA-GOL)	–	1	1	2
Francis C. Newton (USA-GOL)	–	1	1	2
Joseph F. Stadler (USA-ATH)	–	1	1	2
Wilhelm Weber (GER-GYM)	–	1	1	2
George E. Wiley (USA-CYC)	–	1	1	2 [66]
John Duha (USA-GYM)	–	–	2	2
Frank Kungler (USA-WLT)	–	–	2	2
George C. Poage (USA-ATH)	–	–	2	2
Robert S. Stangland (USA-ATH)	–	–	2	2 [70]

Women	Gold	Silver	Bronze	Medals
Lida Scott Howell (USA-ARC)	2	–	–	2
Emma C. Cooke (USA-ARC)	–	2	–	2
Jessie Pollock (USA-ARC)	–	–	2	2 [3]

Most Gold Medals (2 or more) [21: 20 Men, 1 Woman]

Men	Gold	Silver	Bronze	Medals
Anton Heida (USA-GYM)	5	1	–	6 [1]
Marcus L. Hurley (USA-CYC)	4	–	1	5 [2]
George Eyser (USA-GYM)	3	2	1	6

James D. Lightbody (USA-ATH)	3	1	–	4
Raymond C. Ewry (USA-ATH)	3	–	–	3
Ramón Fonst Segundo (CUB-FEN)	3	–	–	3
C. Archibald "Archie" Hahn (USA-ATH)	3	–	–	3
Harry L. Hillman, Jr. (USA-ATH)	3	–	–	3 [8]
Burton C. Downing (USA-CYC)	2	3	1	6
Albertson Van Zo Post (USA-FEN)	2	1	2	5 [10]
Charles M. Daniels (USA-SWI)	2	1	1	4
Julius Lenhart (AUT-GYM)	2	1	–	3
G. Phillip Bryant (USA-ARC)	2	–	1	3
Emil A. Rausch (GER-SWI)	2	–	1	3
Manuel D. Diaz Martinez (CUB-FEN)	2	–	–	2
Zoltán von Halmay (HUN-SWI)	2	–	–	2
Edward A. Hennig (USA-GYM)	2	–	–	2
Oliver L. Kirk (USA-BOX)	2	–	–	2
Meyer Prinstein (USA-ATH)	2	–	–	2
Beals C. Wright (USA-TEN)	2	–	–	2 [20]

Women

Lida Scott Howell (USA-ARC)	2	–	–	2 [1]

Youngest Medalists[42] (10 athletes/11 performances)

Yrs-days
15-124 Henry B. Richardson (USA-ARC, Team Round)
16-007 John Duha (USA-GYM, Combined exercises, team)
16-023 Louis J. Menges (USA-FTB)
16-125 Duha (USA-GYM, Parallel bars)
16-295 Charles J. January, Jr. (USA-FTB)
16-326 Alexander Cudmore (USA-FTB)
17-168 Frank R. Castleman (USA-ATH, 200 hurdles)
17-301 Robert E. Hunter (USA-GOL, Team)
17-326 Peter J. Ratican (USA-FTB)
18-082 Warren G. Brittingham (USA-FTB)
18-166 George Passmore (USA-LAX)

Youngest Medalists, Individual (10 athletes/20 performances)

Yrs-days
16-125 John Duha (USA-GYM, Parallel bars)
17-168 Frank R. Castleman (USA-ATH, 200 hurdles)
18-185 H. Jamison Handy (USA-SWI, 440 breaststroke)
18-240 Frank L. Waller (USA-ATH, 400 meters)
18-242 Waller (USA-ATH, 400 hurdles)
18-261 John C. Hein (USA-WRE, Light-flyweight)
18-357 Albert Zirkel (USA-WRE, Lightweight)
19-164 Charles M. Daniels (USA-SWI, 100 yd. freestyle)

19-164	Ralph W. Rose (USA-ATH, Hammer throw)
19-165	Charles M. Daniels (USA-SWI, 220 yd. freestyle)
19-165	Daniels (USA-SWI, 50 yd. freestyle)
19-166	Daniels (USA-SWI, 440 yd. freestyle)
19-166	Rose (USA-ATH, Shot put)
19-169	Rose (USA-ATH, Discus throw)
19-177	Burton C. Downing (USA-CYC, ½ mi)
19-178	Downing (USA-CYC, ¼ mile)
19-178	Downing (USA-CYC, 2 mile)
19-180	Downing (USA-CYC, 25 mile)
19-180	Downing (USA-CYC, 1 mile)
19-180	Downing (USA-CYC, ⅓ mile)

Youngest Gold Medalists (10 athletes/12 performances)

Yrs-days

17-301	Robert E. Hunter (USA-GOL, Team)
18-192	Kenneth P. Edwards (USA-GOL, Team)
18-284	Mason E. Phelps (USA-GOL, Team)
19-165	Charles M. Daniels (USA-SWI, 220 yd. freestyle)
19-166	Daniels (USA-SWI, 440 yd. freestyle)
19-166	Ralph W. Rose (USA-ATH, Shot put)
19-178	Burton C. Downing (USA-CYC, 2 miles)
19-180	Downing (USA-CYC, 25 miles)
19-270	Samuel Berger (USA-BOX, Unlimited class)
20-009	Louis Abell (USA-ROW, Coxed eights)
20-026	H. Chandler Egan (USA-GOL, Team)
20-084	Georg Zacharias (GER-SWI, 440 breaststroke)

Youngest Gold Medalists, Individual (10 athletes/17 performances)

Yrs-days

19-165	Charles M. Daniels (USA-SWI, 220 yd. freestyle)
19-166	Daniels (USA-SWI, 440 yd. freestyle)
19-166	Ralph W. Rose (USA-ATH, Shot put)
19-178	Burton C. Downing (USA-CYC, 2 miles)
19-180	Downing (USA-CYC, 25 miles)
19-270	Samuel Berger (USA-BOX, Unlimited class)
20-084	Georg Zacharias (GER-SWI, 440 breaststroke)
20-154	Oliver L. Kirk (USA-BOX, Featherweight)
20-154	Kirk (USA-BOX, Bantamweight)
20-223	Marcus L. Hurley (USA-CYC, ½ mile)
20-224	Hurley (USA-CYC, ¼ mile)
20-226	Hurley (USA-CYC, ⅓ mile)
20-226	Hurley (USA-CYC, 1 mile)
20-327	William P. Dickey (USA-SWI, Plunge)
21-007	Ramón Fonst Segundo (CUB-FEN, Foil)

21-007   Fonst Segundo (CUB-FEN, Épée)
21-164   Oscar P. Osthoff (USA-WLT, Dumbbell contest)

Oldest Medalists (10 athletes/17 performances)

Yrs-days

68-193   Samuel H. Duvall (USA-ARC, Team Round)
64-001   Galen C. Spencer (USA-ARC, Team Round)
63-239   Robert W. Williams, Jr. (USA-ARC, Team Round)
63-238   Williams, Jr. (USA-ARC, Double York Round)
63-237   Williams, Jr. (USA-ARC, Double American Round)
56-194   William H. Thompson (USA-ARC, Team Round)
56-193   Thompson (USA-ARC, Double York Round)
56-192   Thompson (USA-ARC, Double American Round)
53-264   Lewis W. Maxson (USA-ARC, Team Round)
50-251   Charles T. Tatham (USA-FEN, Team Foil)
50-250   Tatham (USA-FEN, Épée)
50-250   Tatham (USA-FEN, Foil)
46-028   George S. Lyon (CAN-GOL, Individual)
45-023   Lida S. Howell (USA-ARC, Double National Round)
45-022   Howell (USA-ARC, Double Columbia Round)
42-303   Cyrus E. Dallin (USA-ARC, Team Round)
42-028   Jesse L. Carleton (USA-GOL, Team)

Oldest Medalists, Individual (10 athletes/23 performances)

Yrs-days

63-238   Robert W. Williams, Jr. (USA-ARC, Double York Round)
63-237   Williams, Jr. (USA-ARC, Double American Round)
56-193   William H. Thompson (USA-ARC, Double York Round)
56-192   Thompson (USA-ARC, Double American Round)
50-250   Charles T. Tatham (USA-FEN, Épée)
50-250   Tatham (USA-FEN, Foil)
46-028   George S. Lyon (CAN-GOL, Individual)
45-023   Lida S. Howell (USA-ARC, Double National Round)
45-022   Howell (USA-ARC, Double Columbia Round)
40-214   James S. Mitchel (USA-ATH, 56 lb. weight throw)
37-251   Albertson Van Zo Post (USA-FEN, Saber)
37-251   Van Zo Post (USA-FEN, Single sticks)
37-250   Van Zo Post (USA-FEN, Épée)
37-250   Van Zo Post (USA-FEN, Foil)
34-313   Thomas F. Kiely (IRL-ATH, All-Around)
32-301   George Eyser (USA-GYM, Rope climbing)
32-301   Eyser (USA-GYM, Pommelled horse)
32-301   Eyser (USA-GYM, Horizontal bar)
32-301   Eyser (USA-GYM, Horse vault)
32-301   Eyser (USA-GYM, Parallel bars)

32-301	Eyser (USA-GYM, Combined exercises)
31-234	John J. Flanagan (USA-ATH, 56 lb. weight throw)
31-231	Flanagan (USA-ATH, Hammer throw)

Oldest Gold Medalists (10 athletes/14 performances)

Yrs-days

64-001	Galen C. Spencer (USA-ARC, Team Round)
63-239	Robert W. Williams, Jr. (USA-ARC, Team Round)
56-194	William H. Thompson (USA-ARC, Team Round)
53-264	Lewis W. Maxson (USA-ARC, Team Round)
46-028	George S. Lyon (CAN-GOL, Individual)
45-023	Lida S. Howell (USA-ARC, Double National Round)
45-022	Howell (USA-ARC, Double Columbia Round)
37-251	Albertson Van Zo Post (USA-FEN, Single sticks)
37-251	Van Zo Post (USA-FEN, Team Foil)
37-068	John O. Exley, Jr. (USA-ROW, Coxed eights)
34-313	Thomas F. Kiely (IRL-ATH, All-Around)
32-301	George Eyser (USA-GYM, Rope climbing)
32-301	Eyser (USA-GYM, Horse vault)
32-301	Eyser (USA-GYM, Parallel bars)

Oldest Gold Medalists, Individual (10 athletes/15 performances)

Yrs-days

46-028	George S. Lyon (CAN-GOL, Individual)
45-023	Lida S. Howell (USA-ARC, Double National Round)
45-022	Howell (USA-ARC, Double Columbia Round)
37-251	Albertson Van Zo Post (USA-FEN, Single sticks)
34-313	Thomas F. Kiely (IRL-ATH, All-Around)
32-301	George Eyser (USA-GYM, Rope climbing)
32-301	Eyser (USA-GYM, Horse vault)
32-301	Eyser (USA-GYM, Parallel bars)
31-231	John J. Flanagan (USA-ATH, Hammer throw)
31-208	Étienne Desmarteau (CAN-ATH, 56 lb. weight throw)
30-324	Raymond C. Ewry (USA-ATH, LJs)
30-324	Ewry (USA-ATH, TJs)
30-321	Ewry (USA-ATH, HJs)
30-153	Manuel D. Diaz Martinez (CUB-FEN, Saber)
30-113	George H. Sheldon (USA-DIV, PF)

Female Medalists, Ages (2 athletes/4 performances)

Yrs-days

45-023	Lida S. Howell (USA-ARC, Double National Round)
45-022	Howell (USA-ARC, Double Columbia Round)

20-190   Emma C. Cooke (USA-ARC, Double National Round)
20-189   Cooke (USA-ARC, Double Columbia Round)[43]

Total Known Competitors (Men and Women)

	Arc	Ath	Box	Cyc	Div	Fen	Ftb	Gol	Gym	Lax	Row	Swi	Ten	Tow	Wlt	Wre	Subtotal/Totals	
AUS	-	2	-	-	-	-	-	-	-	-	-	-	-	-	-	-	2	2
AUT	-	-	-	-	-	-	-	-	1	-	-	1	-	-	-	-	2	2
CAN	-	5	-	-	-	-	11	3	-	24	9	-	-	-	-	-	52	52
CUB	-	1	-	-	-	2	-	-	-	-	-	-	-	-	-	-	3	3
FRA	-	1	-	-	-	-	-	-	-	-	-	-	-	-	-	-	1	1
GER	-	2	-	-	3	1	-	-	7	-	-	4	1	-	-	-	18	17
GRE	-	10	-	-	-	-	-	-	-	-	-	-	-	5	1	-	16	14
HUN	-	2	-	-	-	-	-	-	-	-	-	2	-	-	-	-	4	4
IRL/GBR	-	3	-	-	-	-	-	-	-	-	-	-	-	-	-	-	3	3
SAF	-	3	-	-	-	-	-	-	-	-	-	-	-	5	-	-	8	8
SUI	-	-	-	-	-	-	-	-	1	-	-	-	-	-	-	-	1	1
USA	29	88	18	18	2	8	23	74	112	12	35	16	35	20	4	41	535	523
Total	29	117	18	18	5	11	34	77	121	36	44	23	36	30	5	41	645	630
Nations	1	10	1	1	2	3	2	2	4	2	2	4	2	3	2	1		12

Women

	Arc	Totals
USA	6	6
Totals	6	6
Nations	1	1

Known Competitors by Nation

	Subtotal Men	Total Women	Sub-Total	Men 2-sport	Men 3-sport	Men Total	Total
Australia	2	–	2	–	–	2	2
Austria	2	–	2	–	–	2	2
Canada	52	–	52	–	–	52	52
Cuba	3	–	3	–	–	3	3
France	1	–	1	–	–	1	1
Germany	18	–	18	1	–	17	17
Greece	16	–	16	2	–	14	14
Hungary	4	–	4	–	–	4	4
Ireland (GBR)	3	–	3	–	–	3	3
South Africa	8	–	8	–	–	8	8

	Subtotal Men	Total Women	Sub-Total	Men 2-sport	Men 3-sport	Men Total	Total
Switzerland	1	–	1	–	–	1	1
United States	529	6	535	10	1	517	523
Totals	639	6	645	13	1	624	630
Nations	12	1	12	3	1	12	12

Known Competitors, Nations, and Events by Sports

	Total Comp.	Men Comp.	Women Comp	Nations	All Events	Women Events
Archery	29	23	6	1	5	2
Athletics (Track & Field)	117	117	–	10	24	–
Boxing	18	18	–	1	7	–
Cycling	18	18	–	1	7	–
Diving	5	5	–	2	1	–
Fencing	11	11	–	3	5	–
Football (Association) [Soccer]	34	34	–	2	1	–
Golf	77	77	–	2	2	–
Gymnastics	121	121	–	4	12	–
Lacrosse	36	36	–	2	1	–
Rowing & Sculling	44	44	–	2	5	–
Swimming	23	23	–	4	9	–
Tennis (Lawn)	36	36	–	2	2	–
Tug-of-War	30	30	–	3	1	–
Weightlifting	5	5	–	2	2	–
Wrestling	41	41	–	1	7	–
Subtotals	645	639	6	12	91	2
Multi-Sport Athletes	14	14	–	3	–	–
Totals	**630**	**624**	**6**	**12**		**2**

Athletes Competing in Two or More Sports in 1904 [14]

Three Sports [1] — *United States* [1]: Kungler, Frank. Tug-of-War/Weightlifting/Wrestling.
Two Sports [13] — *Germany* [1]: Hoffmann, Georg. Diving/Swimming. *Greece* [2]: Georgantas, Nikolaos. Athletics/Tug-of-War. Kakousis, Perikles. Tug-of-War/Weightlifting. *United States* [10]: Chadwick, Charles. Athletics/Tug-of-War. Emmerich, Max. Athletics/Gymnastics. Feuerbach, Lawrence Edward Joseph. Athletics/Tug-of-War. Haberkorn, Charles. Tug-of-War/Wrestling. Jones, Samuel Symington. Athletics/Tug-of-War. Lydon, Joseph Patrick. Boxing/Football (Soccer). McKittrick, Ralph. Golf/Tennis. Mitchel, James Sarsfield. Athletics/Tug-of-War. Olson, Oscar G. Tug-of-War/Weightlifting. Semple, Frederick Humphrey. Golf/Tennis.

NOTES

1. The contributions of Brookes have been known by Olympic historians for many years. Soutsos' involvement in the formative years of the Olympic Movement in the 19th century was only recently unearthed through the pioneering efforts of Prof. David Young, who published a landmark description of the origins of the modern Olympics in his recent book, *The Modern Olympics: A Struggle for Revival* (Baltimore: Johns Hopkins University Press, 1996). Young's work describes well the influence of Brookes and Soutsos on Coubertin's eventual efforts.

2. Bob Barney has reviewed this material, and kindly allowed me to use much of his original work, although his work is far more comprehensive than this short introduction.

3. Pierre de Coubertin, *Mémoires olympiques* (Lausanne: Bureau International de Pédagogie Sportive, 1931), p. 60; quoted in Barney, p. 93.

4. Pierre de Coubertin, "The Olympic Games of 1896," *Century Magazine*, November 1896, p. 50; quoted in Barney, p. 93.

5. *The New York Times*, 28 July 1900; and *Chicago Tribune*, 27 July 1900.

6. Lucas JA, "Early Olympic Antagonists: Pierre de Coubertin versus James E. Sullivan," *Stadion* 3 (1977): 258–272. See especially p. 261 for discussion of this fact.

7. Barney, p. 95; and "Olympian Games for America," *The New York Sun*, 12 November 1900, p. 8.

8. "The Olympic Games at Buffalo," *Public Opinion* 29 (1 November 1900): 567.

9. Barney does not even mention the Buffalo bid. The above comes basically from notes by Wolf Lyberg in his summary of the IOC Sessions, *The History of the IOC Sessions: I. 1894–1939*, by Wolf Lyberg (Lausanne: IOC, 1994), pp. 24–25; and in Bill Henry, *An Approved History of the Olympic Games* (New York: G. P. Putnam's Sons, 1948), p. 69.

10. Barney, p. 95.

11. Lucas JA, *op. cit.*

12. Here Sullivan was referring to Coubertin being replaced by the French organizers of the 1900 Exposition Universelle as the administrator of the sporting events conducted as part of that World's Fair, which are considered the 1900 Olympic Games. In addition, he was alluding to a Union Internationale which had been formed in Paris in 1900 by him, de Saint Clair (FRA), Pierre Roy (FRA), and Lieutenant Bergh (SWE). Bergh, however, hearing of Sullivan's proclamation, noted that he himself had not been at the meeting at which the group was supposedly formed.

13. Lucas JA, p. 262.

14. "The Next Olympian Games," *The New York Sun*, 13 November 1900, p. 5; quoted in Lucas, p. 262, and Barney, p. 95.

15. *Revue Olympique*, January 1901, p. 11.

16. Barney, p. 98. His source is listed as Furber to Harper, 30 October 1900, Harper Papers, Box 50, Folder 13, held at the University of Chicago.

17. Barney, p. 99; Lucas, p. 264.

18. Barney, p. 101.

19. *Ibid.*, p. 102.

20. *Ibid.*

21. *Ibid.*, and Lyberg1, p. 24.

22. Lyberg1, p. 25.

23. Coubertin to President William McKinley, 28 May 1901, IOC Archives, Coubertin Personal Correspondence; quoted in Barney, p. 104.

24. Coubertin to Theodore Roosevelt, 15 November 1901, IOC Archives, Coubertin Personal Correspondence; quoted in Barney, p. 105.

25. Roosevelt to Coubertin, 7 December 1901, Presidential Papers Microfilm Series 1, Reel 327, Lamont Library, Harvard; quoted in Barney, p. 105.

26. Henry, p. 70; quoted in Barney, p. 105.

27. Furber to Harper, 30 August 1902, Harper Papers, Box 50, Folder 13, University of Chicago; quoted in Barney, pp. 106–107.

28. Furber to Coubertin, 26 November 1902, IOC Archives, Coubertin Personal Correspondence; quoted in Barney, p. 108.

29. Barney, pp. 108–109.

30. *Ibid.*, pp. 110–111.

31. *Ibid.*, pp. 112–114.

32. Coubertin to Furber, 10 February 1903, IOC Archives, Coubertin Personal Correspondence; quoted in Barney, p. 115.

33. Furber to Coubertin, 12 February 1903, IOC Archives, Coubertin Personal Correspondence; quoted in Barney, p. 115.

34. Barnett, p. 19–20.

35. Much of my background material on the Louisiana Purchase Exposition comes from Yvonne M. Condon, "St. Louis 1904: Louisiana Purchase International Exposition," in *Historical Dictionary of World's Fairs and Expositions, 1851–1988*, edited by JE Findling and KD Pelle (Westport, Conn.: Greenwood Press, 1990). Further material comes from the Internet Web Page for the 1904 World's Fair Society: www.inlink.com/%7Eterryl/

36. Barnett, p. 19.

37. Killanin/Rodda, p. 67.

38. "Allowing" is important here. In most cases, I have copies of the original rules. The fact that no foreign athletes competed should not necessarily exclude the sport or event, especially for 1904, when the long travel time to the United States and St. Louis discouraged many foreign athletes from attempting to compete.

39. The only possible exception to this concerns women. Coubertin never liked the idea of women competing at the Olympics and resisted it to the end.

40. Lybergl, p. 12.

41. All three "British" competitors were from Ireland, which in 1904 was still a dependent nation of Great Britain.

42. No "Youngest Competitors" or "Oldest Competitors" lists are included, as in my other books on the early Olympic Games. So few dates of birth are known for non-medalists at the 1904 Olympic Games that there is currently no difference between those lists and the lists of Youngest and Oldest Medalists.

43. There were three female medalists in the 1904 Olympics, all in archery. The other was Jessie Pollock, but her birthdate is not known.

The 1904 "Official Reports"

The current *Olympic Charter* states, under Rule 60.4, "A full and complete official report on the celebration of the Olympic Games shall be printed by the OCOG for the IOC, at least in French and English, within two years of the closing of the Olympic Games."[1]* No such rule existed in 1904 and, in fact, there was no Olympic Charter in 1904. Not only that, but no true "rules" governing the Olympic Games existed in 1904, as Baron de Coubertin only formulated an embryonic list in 1908, that being a handwritten set of basic rules. The Olympic "rules" in 1904 existed essentially only in the mind of Coubertin.

Since Coubertin did not attend the 1904 Olympics and had little interest and no governing role in them, the Olympic "rules" for 1904 basically fell to James Sullivan, who was in charge of the Olympics as the Director of the Department of Physical Culture at the Louisiana Purchase Exposition.

Nothing resembling a modern Official Report was ever produced concerning the 1904 Olympic Games. Two books were written which are usually given the imprimatur as the Official Report(s) of the 1904 Olympic Games. One was *Spalding's Official Athletic Almanac for 1905: Special Olympic Number, Containing the Official Report of the Olympic Games of 1904: Official Report of Anthropological Days at the World's Fair, containing a Review of the First Series of Athletic Contests ever held, in which Savage Tribes were the Exclusive Contestants,* published in 1905 in New York by the American Sports Publishing Company. This book was compiled by Sullivan and is the only work with a legitimate claim to being an Official Report. It should be noted that Sullivan not only ran the Olympics, and compiled this report, but he owned the American Sports Publishing Company which published this and multiple other publications in the series termed "Spalding's Athletic Library." Sullivan's book contains the results of most of the sports events contested at the Louisiana Purchase Exposition, although the results are not complete, and are replete with errors.

The other book was written by Charles J. P. Lucas. Entitled simply *The Olympic Games 1904,* it was published in 1905 by Woodward & Tiernan of St. Louis. It contains much more detail than Sullivan's book on the track & field athletic events, but that is all it contains. No other sports are mentioned.

Because of the importance of these two books, and their rarity, I have reproduced the introductions to both of them herein. They are reproduced exactly as written, except in a few rare cases where I have abbreviated some names of sporting clubs, including all their errors of statistics and name spellings.

OLYMPIC GAMES
James E. Sullivan

The Olympic games of 1904, held in the stadium of the Louisiana Purchase Exposition, at St. Louis, were without question the greatest athletic games ever held in the world. This was the third Olympic gathering under the auspices of the International Olympic Committee, of which Baron Pierre DeCoubertin of Paris is the President. To Baron DeCoubertin is entirely due the idea of the revival of the Olympic games as well as the organization of the International Olympic Committee.

The first Olympic games approved by the International Committee were held in Athens in 1896, the second at Paris in 1900, and it was decided by the International Committee to hold the third Olympic meeting in the city of Chicago during 1904. When it became apparent that the World's Fair was to have a well established Department of Physical Culture, with athletic games of all descriptions, it suggested itself to those interested that it would not do to have in America during the year 1904 two large athletic gatherings, as one must necessarily [*sic*] suffer. Chicago had organized an association for the conduct of this meeting and had also appointed committees, and it looked at one time as though there was a possibility of a conflict. This, however, was averted mainly through the instrumentality of Mr. A. G. Spalding and Mr. Frederick J. V. Skiff, both Chicago men, Mr. Skiff being the Director of Exhibits at the World's Fair. The result was that Chicago gave way and recommended to the International Olympic Committee the giving of the games to St. Louis, which was agreed to. There is no necessity here of dwelling at any great length upon the Olympic games contests or upon the success of future Olympic games. It is fair to say, however, that to America must be given the absolute credit of carrying to a success the Olympic games, the like of which will never again be equaled until the Olympic games are brought back to America, as America has set a standard that certainly will be hard for the other countries to follow.

Early in the season the Department of Physical Culture was notified that it was the desire of the International Committee that all sports that were to be given under the auspices of the Louisiana Purchase Exposition must bear the name "Olympic," and as a result Olympic championships in different sports were announced.

The different governing bodies of America appreciated thoroughly the great good that the Olympic games would do to all organized amateur sport in America and co-operated cheerfully with the Department of Physical Culture toward making the year's sports a gigantic success.

Owing to the conditions in America, particularly the athletic conditions, and the advanced stage we are now in, the Olympic games were held for many classes. The sports in the stadium commenced early in May with an interscholastic meeting, open to schoolboys of the State of Missouri. An open handicap meeting followed, for residents of Missouri, and intercollegiate meetings for the colleges of the Western territory. Interscholastic championships were also held, as were sectional college championships and National college championships, the idea being to select the particular Olympic champions in each class, because it would be manifestly unfair to ask an elementary schoolboy to compete with the preparatory schoolboy and the scholastic champion to compete with the college champion, for changes and conditions make it impossible for all to compete in one class with any degree of success.

We have had in St. Louis under the Olympic banner, handicap athletic meets, interscholastic meets, Turners' mass exercises, base ball, public schoolboys, lacrosse championships, swimming championships, basket ball championships, one of the best rowing regattas ever contested, bicycle championships, roque tournaments, fencing tournament, a special week for the Olympic Young Men's Christian Association championships, tennis tournament, golf tournament, archery tournament, wrestling, boxing and gymnastic championships tournaments, as well as the Olympic games, that decided the world's championships at track and field sports.

The Department received over 4,000 entries for the games decided in the Olympic series and when we include the team competitions and mass exercises the number of athletes that participated in the stadium during the year will come close to 9,000. This is certainly a showing from a numerical standpoint of which those who have been connected with this year's work can justly feel proud.

After the Louisiana Purchase Exposition Company secured the right to hold the Olympic games under the auspices of the Department of Physical Culture, the programme for this meeting was given a great deal of consideration. The Department had been created, the Chief had been appointed, and the International Committee, through its President, Baron Pierre DeCoubertin, delegated its powers to arrange the programme to the special committee of the Amateur Athletic Union of the United States. This committee met and as far as it could consistently arranged the athletic programme in conjunction with the Department. The powers of the American members of the International Olympic Committee, who are Caspar Whitney, of New York, editor of *Outing*; Prof. Wm. Sloane and James H. Hyde, were sought by the Department, and Mr. Whitney gladly at all times co-operated toward making the meeting a success; in fact, he aided materially in the organization of the Physical Culture Department of the Louisiana Purchase Exposition.

After preliminary work with the Amateur Athletic Union's committee, it was necessary for the Department to enlist the sympathies of the other governing bodies throughout America, for it was felt imperative that in order to make the Olympic games of 1904 a pronounced success the official endorsement and co-operation of all American governing bodies was essential, and as a result the National Lawn Tennis Association, the National Golf Association, the National Roque Association, National Archery Association, National Association of Amateur Oarsmen, and the American Amateur Fencers' League gladly co-operated with the Department, took unto themselves the active management of the different Olympic championships for their associations and made the same a pronounced success.

The Amateur Athletic Union of the United States, under whose rules the athletic features were held, deserves the highest kind of praise for the co-operation it gave to the Department, and so do the individual active associations that make up that body, together with all its allied members.

After the preliminary arrangements were perfected and programmes of the games published and distributed, the question of the Presidency of the Olympic games received the attention of the Department. The result was that through the efforts of Mr. Caspar Whitney, the Hon. Theodore Roosevelt, President of the United States, accepted the Honorary Presidency of the Olympic games of 1904 and David H. Francis accepted the Presidency of the Olympic games of 1904.

The acceptance of the Honorary Presidency of the Olympic games by President Roosevelt was a tribute to all concerned in the creation of the Olympic games for 1904. His acceptance proved conclusively that he approved of the organization, had given the subject a great deal of thought and believed that the successful carrying out of the programme meant much to the future success of this country as an athletic nation. He can certainly feel proud, as Honorary President, of the way the Louisiana Purchase Exposition conducted the games. There was not the slightest hitch; everything was carried on in a high class manner, and purely in an amateur way, and more has been accomplished for the future of athletics in this country than could ever be accomplished by any other method.

The Olympic games, held from August 29 to September 3, brought together in the stadium the greatest athletes of the world. Never before in America or any other country were such contests witnessed. World's records were made, Olympic records were equaled and surpassed and the competitions were keen and interesting. When one looks over the list of Olympic winners and then over the list of eligible men in the world, there are perhaps two men living today who were not in the stadium who could have won Olympic honors.

These particular games were made more interesting from the fact that handsome special Olympic souvenir cups were donated to the winners in the different events. The following is a list of the donors:

Marathon race — Hon. David R. Francis
100-meter run — Frederick J. V. Skiff
400-meter run — A. L. Shapleigh
Running broad jump — J. S. Huyler
1,500-meter run — Norris B. Gregg
800-meter run — Abram G. Mills
Throwing the discus — Isaac S. Taylor
Throwing the 56-lb. weight for distance — Charles J. Dieges
Pole vault for height — H. H. Baxter
Throwing the 16-lb. hammer — R. Wells, Jr.
For the club scoring the greatest number of points — A. G. Spalding
200-meter hurdle — J. J. Lawrence
400-meter hurdle — George B. Parker
200-meter run — William G. Thompson
Running the high jump — J. A. Holmes
Putting the 16-lb. shot — Goodman King
Running hop, step and jump — W. J. Kinsella
Three standing jumps — Lemp Boys
Lifting bar bell — Corwin H. Spencer

The Entry List

The entry that was received for the Olympic games shows conclusively what interest was taken in different athletic fixtures, and it is confidently stated by those who ought to know, that this is the largest entry that has ever been received by any one organization or corporation that ever held an athletic meeting or a series of athletic meetings. The following is a complete list of entries received, making a grand total of ...

List of Events and Numbers of Entries

May 14	Interscholastic meet for State of Missouri	136
May 21	Open handicap athletic meeting	90
May 28	Interscholastic meet, schools of Louisiana Purchase Territory	122
May 30	Elementary school championships	68
June 2	AAU handicap meeting	195
June 3	AAU junior championships	187
June 4	AAU senior championships	183

June	Amateur base ball tournament	99
June 11	Western college championships	124
June 23	Turners' mass exhibition	3,500
June 25	Olympic college championships	110
June 29–30	Interscholastic championships	258
July 1–2	Turners' international and individual team contest	789
July 1	Athletic games in honor of Cardinal Satolli	68
July 4	AAU all-around championships	7
July 4–6	Public school championships, elementary and high	415
July 5–7	Lacrosse	33
July 11–12	Olympic basket ball championships	44
July 13–14	College basket ball	15
July 20–23	Irish sports	140
July 29–30	Olympic world's regatta	131
July 29	Handicap meeting of the Western Association	90
July 30	Championships of the Western Association	100
Aug. 1–6	Bicycling	124
Aug. 1–12	Roque	3
Aug. 11	Bohemian Gymnastics	800
Aug. 15–20	YMCA athletics	393
Aug. 29–Sept. 3	Tennis	92
Aug. 29–Sept. 3	Olympic games	545
Sept. 5–7	Swimming and water polo championships	308
Sept. 68	World's fencing championships	42
Sept. 19–24	Golf tournament	74
Sept. 21–23	World's boxing championships	28
Sept. 19–21	Archery	35
Oct. 14–15	AAU wrestling championships	62
Oct. 28–29	AAU gymnastic championships	38
Nov. 12	College foot ball	340
Nov. 16–18	Association football	50

To President D. R. Francis, Director F. J. V. Skiff and the directors of the Louisiana Purchase Exposition, the American athletes and the American governing bodies owe a great deal. The object of the Department of Physical Culture was not to make money. It was believed that the subject of physical training and athletics had advanced to such a stage that a department could be created that would, in the broadest educational way, show to what an advanced state of affairs athletics had reached. A large sum of money was voted to give games, to encourage amateur sport, and to show in an educational way what steps forward had been made. And it is fair to state that the officials of the Exposition, from the very first meeting, knew that the whole work of the department would have to be classified as educational.

The final results of the Olympic games prove conclusively what has often been claimed, that the colleges of America will furnish the champion athletes of the future.

During the Olympic games, which extended from May to November, the prominent colleges of America (with the exception of a few of the Eastern ones) were represented by teams or individuals who wore the colors of their colleges or club.

Olympic Lecture Course

The scientific aspects of physical training and athletics were given prominence equal to that of the athletic competitions themselves by the presentation of courses of lectures by many of the world's authorities on the various subjects. These lectures embraced in most instances the results of original work not heretofore available to the public. The whole body of lectures, which are being published by the Exposition, constitute by far the most extended exposition of the science of physical training that has ever been made. The most cursory survey of the titles to these lectures will indicate the vast range of topics discussed. The plane upon which the work was carried out is indicated by persons who delivered these lectures, as well as by the distinguished positions they hold in the physical training, educational and medical world.

The number of lectures given by each person varied from one to ten. The names of the lecturers and their subjects are as follows:

E. H. Arnold, M.D., New Haven Normal School of Gymnastics, New Haven, Conn.—"The Organization and Conduct of School Games."

C. Ward Crampton, M.D., High School of Commerce, New York City—"The Correlation of Hygiene and Physical Training"; "Some Recent Advances in the Science of Physical Training."

George T. Hepbron, New York City—"The Equipment and Construction of Gymnasium and Athletic Fields."

H. S. Curtis, Ph.D., DeWitt Clinton High School, New York City—"The Playground Movement."

Cassius H. Watson, B.S., Pratt Institute, Brooklyn, N.Y.—"Muscular Movement and Human Evolution."

C. Stanley Hall, Ph.D., LL.D., President, Clark University, Worcester, Mass.—"Health as Related to Civilization."

Paul C. Phillips, M.D., Amherst College, Amherst, Mass.—"Anthropometric Methods."

R. Tait McKenzie, M.D., McGill University, Montreal, Canada—"Artistic Anatomy in Relation to Physical Training."

G. W. Ehler, B.S., YMCA, Chicago, Ill.—"The Adaptation of Physical Exercises to the Modern Conditions of Life."

F. A. Schmidt, M.D., Bonn, Germany—"The Physiology of Exercise."

William G. Anderson, M.D., Yale University, New Haven, Conn.—"Gymnastic Dancing and its Place in Secondary and Collegiate Schools."

Jakob Bolin, New York City—"Developmental Gymnastics."

David F. Lincoln, M.D., Boston, Mass.—"The Treatment of Feeble Minded, with Special Reference to Their Education in a Public School System."

G. E. Johnson, A.B., Superintendent of Schools, Lowell, Mass.—"Play in Relation to Education."

Joseph E. Raycroft, M.D., University of Chicago, Chicago, Ill.—"The Organization and Administration of Physical Training."

Frederick J. V. Skiff—"The General Advantages of Athletic Exercises to the Individual."

W. J. McGee, Chief, Department of Anthropology, Louisiana Purchase Exposition.—"The Influence of Play in Racial Development with Special Reference to Muscular Movement."

Luther Halsey Gulick, M.D., Brooklyn, N.Y., Chairman Physical Training Committee.—"Athletics and Social Evolution"; "The Place of the Social and Aesthetic Elements in Physical Training as Exemplified by German Gymnastics."

James E. Sullivan, Chief, Department of Physical Culture — "Sketch of the Development of Athletic Implements."

Aside from that, the Department had a fully equipped gymnasium with hundreds of exhibits from schools, colleges, and athletic clubs, showing the advancement made in athletics and physical training in this and other countries.

Previous Olympic Games

For purposes of comparison we herewith publish the winners and performances at the Olympic games at Athens in 1896 and at Paris in 1900, and on the following pages will be found a summary of the events at St. Louis.[2] In nearly all the St. Louis events new Olympic records were made, equaled or surpassed, and in many, world's records were established.[3]

Athens, 1896

100 meters — 12s., T. E. Burke, Boston AA

400 meters — 54 1-5s., T. E. Burke, Boston AA

800 meters — 2m. 11s., E. H. Flack, London AC

1,500 meters — 4m. 33 1-5s., E. H. Flack, London AC

110 meters hurdles race — 17 3-5s., T. P. Curtis, Boston AA

High jump — 5 ft. 11¼ in., E. H. Clark, Boston AA

Long jump — 20 ft. 9¾ in., E. H. Clark, Boston AA

Running triple jump — 45 ft., J. Connolly, Suffolk AC. The winner took two hops and a jump, there being no restrictions as to style.

Pole jump — 10 ft. 9¾ in., W. W. Hoyt, Boston AA

Putting 16 lb. weight (from 6 ft. 3¾ in. square without follow) — 36 ft. 2in., R. Garrett, Jr., Princeton U. AA

Throwing the discus — 95 ft. 7½ in., R. Garrett, Jr., Princeton U. AA. The discus was lens shaped, of hard wood, surrounded by iron, with brass center, and weighed 2 kilos (4½ pounds). It was thrown from an 8' 4½" square.

Weight lifting (two hands) — 245 pounds 12 ounces, V. Jenson, Copenhagen A. C.

Weight lifting (one hand) — 156 pounds 8 ounces, L. Elliott, London A. W. L. C. The contestants are required to lift a bar-bell (two hands) and a dumbbell (one hand), repeating to the shoulder, and thence vertically above the head.

Marathon race (24 miles 1,500 yards) — 2h. 55m. 20s., S. Loues, Greece, Greece. [*sic*]

Paris, 1900

60 meter run (65.62 yards) — 7s., A. D. Kraenzlein.

100 meter run (109.36 yards) — 10 4-5s., F. W. Jarvis, Princeton University and J. W. B. Tewksbury, University of Pennsylvania.

200 meter run (218.72 yards) — 22 1-5s., J. W. B. Tewksbury, University of Pennsylvania.

400 meter run (437.44 yards) — 49 2-5s., M. W. Long, New York AC

800 meter run (874.89 yards) — 2m. 1 2-5s., A. E. Tysoe, Salford Harriers, England.

1,500 meter run (1,640.41 yards) — 4m. 6s., C. Bennett, England.

2,500 meter steeplechase (1½ miles, 94.03 yards) — 7m. 34s., G. W. Orton, University of Pennsylvania.

Marathon race, 40 kilometers (24.85 miles)—2h. 59m., Teato, France.
4,000 meter steeplechase (2 miles 850.44 yards)—12m. 58 2-5s., C. Reinmer, England.
110 meter hurdle race (120.30 yards)—15 2-5s., A. C. Kraenzlein, University of Pennsylvania.
200 meter hurdle race (218.72 yards)—25 2-5s., A. C. Kraenzlein, University of Pennsylvania.
400 meter hurdle race (437.44 yards)—57 3-5s., J. W. B. Tewksbury, University of Pennsylvania.
Running high jump—6 ft. 2⅘ in., I. K. Baxter, University of Pennsylvania.
Running broad jump—23 ft. 6⅞ in., A. C. Kraenzlein, University of Pennsylvania.
Standing high jump—5 ft. 5 in., Ray C. Ewry, New York AC
Standing broad jump—10 ft. 6⅔ in., Ray C. Ewry, New York AC
Standing triple jump—34 ft. 8½ in., Ray C. Ewry, New York AC
Pole vault—10 ft. 9%0 in., I. K. Baxter, University of Pennvylania.
Running hop, skip and jump—47 ft. 4¼ in., M. Prinstein, Syracuse, N. Y.
Putting 16-lb. shot—46 ft., 3⅛ in., R. Sheldon, New York AC
Throwing 16-lb. hammer—167 ft. 4in., J. Flanagan, New York AC
Throwing the discus—118 ft., 2%0 in., Bauer, Hungary.

Testimonial to Director F. J. V. Skiff

After the Department of Physical Culture became thoroughly established and it was readily seen what good benefits were resulting therefrom, many gentlemen interested in the advancement of athletics in the United States decided that it would be only proper to recognize the man that created the Department, and at a dinner given within the exposition grounds early in June the following testimonial was presented to Director Skiff, the presentation speech being made by the Hon. Joseph B. Maccabe, the present President of the Amateur Athletic Union of the United States.

Testimonial

Presented to Mr. Frederick J. V. Skiff, Director of Exhibits, Louisiana Purchase Exposition, St. Louis, 1904.

Mr. Frederick J. V. Skiff.

Dear Sir: The undersigned, believing that a sound mind in a healthy body is conducive to good citizenship, and that the systematic training of the young in athletic exercises tends to promote all the manly virtues and to better our race in all the relations of life, desire to express our hearty appreciation of your broad-minded, far-sighted and patriotic action in establishing, for the first time in the history of international expositions, a conspicuous, thoroughly equipped department, devoted wholly to physical culture, in connection with the universal exposition in St. Louis.

The far-reaching, beneficial results of this new department are already recognized by our foremost statesmen, notably by the acceptance of the honorary president of the Olympic games by the President of the United States. We do not hesitate to predict that, whatever other benefits may accrue from this great exposition, those resulting from the Department of Physical Culture will be most widespread, most beneficent, and permanent in real value to our people.

Walter H. Liginger, President Amateur Athletic Union
J. E. Sullivan, Secretary-Treasurer Amateur Athletic Union
Harry McMillan, Ex-President Amateur Athletic Union

Bartow S. Weeks, Ex-President Amateur Athletic Union; Member AAU Championship Committee

Edward E. Babb, Ex-President Amateur Athletic Union

A. G. Mills, Chairman Legislation Committee Amateur Athletic Union

J. B. Maccabe, Delegate-at-Large of the Amateur Athletic Union

Gustavus T. Kirby, Delegate-at-Large of the Amateur Athletic Union; Chairman Advisory Board ICAAAA

C. C. Hughes, Delegate-at-Large of the Amateur Athletic Union

J. F. Harder, Delegate-at-Large of the Amateur Athletic Union

Luther Halsey Gulick, Chairman Physical Training Committee; President American Physical Education Association; Director Physical Training Public Schools of Greater New York

W. Scott O'Connor, Secretary Amateur Fencers' League of America

Thomas F. Riley, New England Association Amateur Athletic Union

A. A. Stagg, Director Athletics Chicago University

E. H. Arnold, Physical Training Committee

George T. Hepbron Secretary Athletic League YMCA of North America

James Pilkington, President National Association Amateur Oarsmen

C. H. Sherrill, Chairman Yale Graduate Advisory Committee Track Athletics, Captain, New York Athletic Club

James W. Greig, Secretary, New Jersey Bowling Green Club

H. Laussat Geyelin, President Athletic Association University of Pennsylvania

P. Gorman, Canadian Amateur Athletic Association

John McLachlan, Central Association Amateur Athletic Union

Dr. George K. Herman, Secretary and Treasurer Central Association AAU

T. J. Nevin, Metropolitan Association Amateur Athletic Union

Fred R. Fortmeyer, Secretary National Association of Amateur Oarsmen

H. W. Garfield, Chairman Regatta Committee National Association Amateur Oarsmen

Jakob Bolin, Member Physical Training Committee

Walter Camp, Yale College

Kriegh Collins, Member Lawn Tennis Committee

Clark W. Hetherington, University of Missouri

George A. Huff, University of Illinois

Darwin R. James, Jr., Princeton University

A. E. Kindervater, Supervisor Physical Culture Public Schools, St. Louis, Mo

George S. McGrew, Glen Echo Country Club, St. Louis

Frederick B. Pratt, Pratt Institute, Brooklyn

Joseph E. Raycroft, University of Chicago

Gustavus Brown, President South Atlantic Association AAU

M. F. Winston, President New England Association AAU

W. B. Hinchman, President Pacific Association Amateur Athletic Union

Frank Fisher, President Atlantic Association Amateur Athletic Union

John J. O'Connor, President Western Association Amateur Athletic Union

J. Frank Facey, Secretary and Treasurer New England Association of the Amateur Athletic Union

Herbert Hauser, Secretary and Treasurer Pacific Association Amateur Athletic Union

C. H. Pyrah, Secretary Atlantic Association Amateur Athletic Union

J. C. O'Brien, Chairman Registration Western Association Amateur Athletic Union

C. H. Mapes, Representative Intercollegiate Amateur Athletic Association

Theo. S. Gamble, South Atlantic Association of the Amateur Athletic Union

Alfred J. Lill, Jr., New England Association Amateur Athletic Union
Julian W. Curtiss, President Yale Club, Chairman Yale Advisory Athletic Committee
Henry G. Penniman, South Atlantic Association Amateur Athletic Union
J. C. McCaughern, Pacific Association Amateur Athletic Union
Theodore E. Strauss, South Atlantic Association Amateur Athletic Union
Harry E. Kelsey, South Atlantic Association Amateur Athletic Union
George W. Ehler, Physical Director Central YMCA, Chicago
John J. Dixon, Military Athletic League
Clifford E. Dunn, National Skating Association
James H. Sterrett, National Swimming Association
G. H. Walker, Chairman Equestrian Polo Committee
F. W. Gerould, Chairman Olympic Golf Committee
Charles Jacobus, Chairman Roque Committee
L. T. Doyle, Chairman Lacrosse Committee; Crescent Athletic Club, Brooklyn
A. G. Batchelder, President National Cycling Association
John T. Dooling, Metropolitan Association Amateur Athletic Union
W. A. E. Woods, Columbia College
B. P. Sullivan, Secretary and Treasurer Southern Association AAU
J. S. Fleming, Western Association Amateur Athletic Union
John Steil, North American Gymnastic Union
Watson L. Savage, President New York Normal School of Physical Education
Theo. Strempfel, Secretary National Executive Committee, N. A. Gymnastic Union
Herman Lieber, President National Executive Committee, N. A. Gymnastic Union
Edward B. Weston, Chairman Archery Committee
Beals C. Wright, Member Olympic Lawn Tennis Committee
Solon Jacobs, President Birmingham Athletic Club, Birmingham, Ala
C. H. Miles, Secretary Birmingham Athletic Club, Birmingham, Ala
Graeme M. Hammond, New York City
P. J. Conway, Greater New York Irish Athletic Association

TRIBUTE TO DIRECTOR F. J. V. SKIFF.

At the annual meeting of the Amateur Athletic Union, held at the Grand Union Hotel, New York City, Nov. 21, 1904, the following resolutions were adopted:

Resolved, That the Amateur Athletic Union of the United States in Annual Convention assembled do extend to Mr. F. J. V. Skiff the sincere thanks of the athletes and lovers of sport of the country for his earnest and successful effort in behalf of Amateur Athletics and Physical Training, both personally and by virtue of his honorable office as Director of Exhibits of the Louisiana Purchase Exposition. And be it further

Resolved, That this body set forth upon its minutes its appreciation of the substantial gain to the cause of Physical Training, both as a scientific investigation and study, and in the practical application and effect, resulting from the work of the Physical Training Department of the Universal Exposition at St. Louis.

Resolved, That this testimonial be engrossed and suitably presented to Mr. Skiff.

TRIBUTE TO CHIEF J. E. SULLIVAN.

At the annual meeting of the Amateur Athletic Union, held at the Grand Union Hotel, New York, Nov. 21, 1904, the following resolutions were adopted:

Resolved, That the Amateur Athletic Union desires to be recognized by a vote of thanks and congratulation the distinguished services of its Secretary-Treasurer, James E. Sullivan, Chief of the Department of Physical Culture of the Louisiana Purchase Exposition.

The great difficulties of the situation have been met with extraordinary skill and enthusiasm. The great success of the meeting, the high character of the competitions, the excellence of the arrangements, the superior character of the trophies, all testify to his great services.

While the Amateur Athletic Union feels that great honor has been given to it by the selection of its Secretary-Treasurer, as Chief of this new and important department of a Universal Exposition, it recognizes the fact that his superior equipment, both in natural qualifications and experience of such work.

Resolved, That this testimonial be suitably engrossed and presented to Mr. Sullivan.

CHIEF SULLIVAN TO BE AWARDED COMMEMORATIVE MEDAL.

Chief J. E. Sullivan, of the Department of Physical Culture of the Louisiana Purchase Exposition, has received the following letter from Baron Pierre DeCoubertin, President of the International Olympic Committee:

COMITE INTERNATIONAL OLYMPIQUE

PARIS, Oct. 19, 1904

Dear Mr. Sullivan:

On behalf of the International Olympic Committee, I beg to send you our warmest congratulations and thanks for the wonderful work you have succeeded in carrying out the organization of the third Olympiad.

As a token of our gratitude, I have the pleasure to state that the medal commemorating the revival of the Olympic games will be awarded to you on the occasion of the International Congress to be held in Brussels in June, 1905, under the presidency of his Majesty the King of the Belgians.

The value of the souvenir comes from the fact that only a very few copies have been given away since ten years, their Majesties the Emperor of Germany and the King of Spain and their Royal Highnesses the Crown Prince of Greece, the Crown Prince of Sweden and Norway and the Prince of Wales being among those who said were glad to receive it. President McKinley also received it after the vote making the third Olympiad an American one.

We expect you to present a short but substantial report on the St. Louis games to the Brussels Congress.

Thanking you for the numerous documents and the medals you sent us and congratulating you once more.

I am, dear Mr. Sullivan,

Very truly yours,
BARON PIERRE DeCOUBERTIN
President of the International Olympic Committee

NOTES

1. International Olympic Committee. *Olympic Charter*, in force as from 18 July 1996, Rule 60.4, p. 76.
2. I have omitted Sullivan's extensive listing of the top four places in the track & field athletics events, which he termed the "Olympic games."
3. I have not corrected any of Sullivan's errors here in terms of marks and name spellings.

THE OLYMPIC GAMES 1904
Charles J. P. Lucas

PREFACE

In presenting "The Olympic Games, 1904," the author has made no attempt to consider the sports held before them, as the Olympic Games were those events which opened August 29, continuing up to, and including, the games contested September 3. The Olympic Games Committee, consisting of James E. Sullivan, Chief of the Department of Physical Culture at the Exposition; Walter H. Liginger, President of the Amateur Athletic Union; John J. O'Connor, President of the Western Division of the Amateur Athletic Union; Harry McMillan, ex-President of the Amateur Athletic Union, and Henry Garneau, ex-President of the Western Division of the Amateur Athletic Union, performed its duties well. William Nash and John J. Conlon, secretaries of the committee; the officials of the Western Division of the Amateur Athletic Union, and the officers and members of the Missouri Athletic Club, are to be commended for the many pleasant entertainments which were prepared for foreign and domestic athletes, making the Olympic Games a pleasant occasion. The athletes of America are grateful to the following gentlemen, who donated valuable trophies to the winners of the different events: Marathon race, Hon. David R. Francis; 400-meter run, A. L. Shapleigh; 100-meter dash, F. J. V. Skiff; 1500-meter run, Norris R. Gregg; 800-meter run, Abram G. Mills; 200-meter hurdle, J. J. Lawrence; 400-meter hurdle, George B. Parker; 200-meter run, William G. Thompson; running broad jump, J. S. Huyler; throwing the discus, Isaac B. Taylor; throwing the 56-pound weight, Charles J. Dieges; pole vault, H. H. Baxter; throwing the 16-pound hammer, R. Wells, Jr.; running high jump, J. A, Holmes; putting 16-pound shot, Goodman King; running hop, step and jump, W. J. Kinsella; three standing jumps, Lemp boys; lifting the bar bell, Corwin H. Spencer; team championship trophy, A. G. Spalding.

CHARLES J. P. LUCAS
St. Louis, Mo., February 14, 1905

INTRODUCTION

During the second week of March, 1896, a little band of athletes, led by John Graham, athletic instructor of the Boston (Mass.) Athletic Association, sailed from the United States, bound for Europe, to compete in the first revival of the Olympic Games, which were contested at Athens the first week of April, in 1896. Several months previous to this time a group of men, each a lover of amateur athletics and interested in international sport, had assembled at Paris for the purpose of considering the advisability of renewing the Olympic Games, so far as might be feasible. Among those who took especial interest in this plan were Baron de Coubertin, of

France, and Comte Alex Mercati, of Athens, Greece. After due consideration, in 1895, it was decided by the International Committee to hold the first revival of the games at Athens, and this announcement was spread broadcast throughout the world.

At this time athletics both in New England and in the Metropolitan Divisions of the A.A.U., were in a very flourishing condition, and only a year previous, on Manhattan Field, America had defeated England in an international meeting. The great Wefers had tied a world's record; Kilpatrick and Sweeney had performed almost incredible feats, and many other American athletes, including Thomas E. Burke, of the Boston A.A., had won honors for America. Therefore, when the announcement was received in America that these games were to be contested, the board of directors of the Boston A.A. decided to send a team abroad, and this visit of American athletes marked the beginning of a series of hitherto unheard-of athletic victories, the most important of which was won in St. Louis, in 1904, at the third revival of the Olympic Games.

In the summer of 1900, the second revival of the games was held at Paris in connection with the Paris Exposition, and America was again victorious, almost sweeping the board. Every record made at Athens was broken at the Paris meeting. One-third of the competing athletes at Paris were Americans: this shows the intense interest displayed by Americans in these games.

It is really deemed unnecessary to go into the ancient history of the Olympic Games, for almost every schoolboy in the country knows the history of these games: how the ancients came from almost every part of Greece, at stated intervals, to display their prowess, and how each winner was awarded a wreath of laurel, which was the only prize he received for his victory. Circumstances were different, however, at the three modern revivals of the games; for, besides the laurel wreaths of victory, every winning athlete was awarded a gold medal, and to the athletes who won second and third places in every event, silver and bronze medals were awarded in addition.

But the Olympic Games of 1904 afforded a few changes in this respect, whereby, in connection with medals and wreaths, the winning athletes received silver trophies of considerable value.

During the progress of the Olympic Games at Paris, the International Committee held a meeting and decided, in view of the two victories of American athletes and the lively interest America had shown in the games, that it would be eminently just and proper to award to America the third revival of games, and, as Chicago was considered the most central point in the country, that city was selected for the games. An association known as the Olympic Games Company was organized for the purpose of arranging for the contests.

In the meantime an organization composed of business men and others was formed in the city of St. Louis, Missouri, for the purpose of holding an Exposition commemorating the purchase of the Louisiana Territory, and the American committee in charge of the Olympic Games was approached with a view to securing for the St. Louis Exposition authorities permission to hold the games during the progress of the Fair. This permission was granted, and James E. Sullivan, of New York, Secretary-Treasurer of the Amateur Athletic Union of the United States, the controlling body of amateur athletics, was chosen as Chief of the Department of Physical Culture, which was selected to handle these sports, Mr. Sullivan had been assistant chief of this department at the Paris revival of the Olympic Games.

The Olympic Games of 1904 had a long introduction, so to speak, and entries were promised from every athletic nation on the globe. While some of these nations responded, those countries which were most expected to enter did not do so. England and France did not send a single competitor to America, and the French people showed their ingratitude by an entire absence of representation. America made the Paris games a success, and without American entries the second revival of the games would have been a farce. Neither France nor England were missed from the games of 1904, however, and it is doubtful, indeed, if a single Frenchman could have finished even fourth in any of the events. In fact, only one Englishman would have stood a chance of winning any event whatever, and that man was Shrubb, who holds several world's records in the distance events.

But England and France were not alone in furnishing cause for censure in this connection. Harvard University showed the spirit which prompts its every move when it decided it would be inadvisable to send representatives to St. Louis to compete, as there were many athletes whose amateur standing was questionable. A few months later this same institution adopted the most ludicrous rule ever found in sporting annals, by deciding that any athlete, no matter how professionally he competed up to his twentieth year, if he remained at Harvard for two years thereafter he could compete on a Harvard team. Yale, Pennsylvania, Columbia, Dartmouth, Georgetown and Amherst, together with Michigan, Wisconsin, Minnesota, and the Western minor colleges, were conspicuous by reason of non-participation. In fact, the American colleges displayed very poor sportsmanship in this respect, and, with the exception of Princeton, Chicago, Washington, Leland Stanford, University of Oklahoma, St. Louis University, Missouri University, and University of Colorado, the American colleges are not to be thanked in the least for the clean-cut victory of America in the Olympic Games of 1904.

True it is, American collegians competed in several events, but their care, training and expenses were undertaken by members of the Amateur Athletic Union of the United States, and not by colleges.

There are several foreign nations to whom American athletes owe their thanks for sending teams thousands of miles to compete in the Olympic Games of 1904. Germany, Greece, Hungary, Canada, Australia, Zululand, the Transvaal and Cuba were represented in the games. To the athletes of these nations the American athlete tenders thanks for their co-operation. To the Athletic Clubs of America the St. Louis Exposition management is also deeply grateful for sending so many athletes to the games; for making them so successful in an athletic way.

One great objection has arisen regarding the Olympic Games, *i.e.*, the celebration of these great revivals in connection with Expositions. The attendance at the revival of 1904, while greater than that at Paris, was far below the daily attendance at Athens, and Baron de Coubertin, the honorary President of the International Committee, has gone on record by saying the games will never again be held in connection with an Exposition. The fourth Olympiad will be held at Rome in 1908.

Before closing the introduction to The Story of the Olympic Games, the author desires to pay tribute to the spirit of sportsmanship displayed by Comte Alex Mercati, of Athens, Greece, for the manner in which he sent Grecian athletes to the Olympic Games. Greece was represented directly by two great athletes, Nicholas Georgantos and Perikles Kakousis, both men having been victors in the games. Then twelve athletes, representing Greece competed in the Marathon race and performed credibly. It is not the performance of Greek athletes which prompts this tribute, but rather the words of Count Mercati, in a letter addressed to Mr. James E. Sullivan, in which the nobleman said: "The Grecian athletes do not go to America with the expectation of winning all the trophies, but that they may meet their American colleagues, and those of other nations, and become better acquainted; that they may carry back to Athens and to Greece the good fruits of this meeting, and in this manner benefit their native land."

In considering and writing of the Olympic Games of 1904, the fact must be thoroughly understood, when records are compared, that conditions governing competitions in Paris and St. Louis were widely different. The Olympic Games at Paris were contested on grass-plots, part of the course lying in a clump of trees; the course of the sprints was wet and soggy, and the hammer-throwing was impeded by trees. On the other hand, conditions for good performances, for records, at St. Louis, were ideal. Mr. James E. Sullivan exploited his ideas in a manner that called forth commendation.

The running track was oval in shape, one-third of a mile in circumference, and constructed in the most modern manner; the course for the 100- and 200-meter dashes being straightaway and well rolled. Each sprinter had his own lane through which to travel and could in no way interfere with his opponent. The track was 20 feet wide, thereby enabling the 800- and 400-meter races to be run in one heat.

The apparatus used by the competing athletes was of the most modern manufacture. The infield was laid off so that the weight events could, and were, contested at one time, insuring rapidity in running off the games. Each circle out of which the weights were thrown was marked so that the spectators could thoroughly understand what event was being contested on the field and easily note the winner. The time or performance of the winning athletes was announced by Mr. Charles J. Harvey, of New York. In a word, the field arrangements and acoustics at the Olympic Games of 1904 were a revelation to Americans themselves.

The gentlemen invited to fill the various offices in connection with the Olympic Games were as follows:

REFEREES — Walter H. Liginger, Milwaukee AC, Milwaukee, Wis., Monday; David R. Francis, St. Louis, Mo., Tuesday; Gustavus V. Kirby, New York City, Wednesday; Caspar Whitney, New York City, Thursday; Bartow S. Weeks, New York City, Saturday.

HONORARY REFEREES — A. L. Shapleigh, St. Louis, Monday; Dr. Luther H. Gulick, New York, Tuesday; John R. Van Wormer, New York AC, New York, Wednesday; President Seig, Milwaukee AC, Milwaukee, Wis., Thursday; Frederick J. V. Skiff, St. Louis, Mo., Saturday.

REFEREE ALL-AROUND DUMB BELL COMPETITION — Harry E. Buermeyer, New York.

JUDGES — Dr. A. J. Kennedy, St. Louis, Mo.; Otto Boettger, St. Louis, Mo.; C. W. Bassett, Missouri AC, St. Louis.

JUDGES TUG OF WAR — Clark W. Hetherington, M.D., Missouri University; John C. Meyers, St. Louis; Myles McDonough, St. Louis.

JUDGES AT FINISH — Harry McMillan, Philadelphia, Pa.; E. E. Babb, Boston AA, Boston, Mass.; Thomas F. Riley, Cambridgeport Gym, Cambridgeport, Mass.; John J. O'Connor, President Western AAU, St. Louis, Mo.; John McLachlan, Pullman AC, Pullman, Ill.

TIMERS — Charles J. Dieges, Pastime AC, New York; C. J. Hughes, New York; J. C. O'Brien, St. Louis; George W. Ehler, Chicago, Ill.; Mortimer Bishop, New York; Herbert Brown, Montreal, Canada; Everett C. Brown, Chicago, Ill.

FIELD JUDGES — Herbert Hauser, San Francisco; Ben Fell, St. Louis; F. W. Hulme, St. Louis; Steve Kane, St. Louis; Hugh Baxter, New York; Jerome Karst, St. Louis; Charles Pyrah, Philadelphia; M.J. Flynn, New York; John J. Dooling, New York; C. S. Middleton, San Francisco.

CHIEF INSPECTOR — Hon. Joseph B. Maccabe, East Boston, Mass.

INSPECTORS — Frank E. Boyd, Charles Sherrill, P. J. Conway, Harry G. Penniman, H. Garneau, B. P. Sullivan, J. W. Curtiss, F. W. Gerauld, Robert Kammerer, David R. Francis, Jr., F. B. Ellis, M. H. Butler, P. Gorman.

MARSHAL — Charles P. Senter, St. Louis, Mo.

CLERK OF COURSE — Fred Stone, Chicago AA.

ASSISTANT CLERKS OF COURSE — R. G. Campbell, Edward E. Lee, Joseph S. Fleming, J. J. O'Brien, M. Ferriss.

OFFICIAL REPORTER — John J. Conlen, New York.

ANNOUNCER — Charles J. Harvey, New York.

STARTERS — W. H. Robertson, New York, Monday; David R. Francis, St. Louis, Marathon Race, Tuesday; Thomas Aitken, St. Louis, Wednesday; Hugh McGrath, Boston, Mass., Thursday; Martin Delaney, St. Louis, Saturday.

Some of the above gentlemen were not present at the games, and there were representatives of foreign amateur athletic associations present who did officiate. Among the latter were Franz Kemeny, Hungary; S. Stanovitz, Hungary; Dr. H. H. Hardy, Germany; Dr. Willibald Gebhardt, Germany; P. J. Mueller, Germany; Gyula de Muzsa, Hungary; Hector M. E. Pasmezoglu, Greece; Demetrius Jannapoulo, Greece; Dr. Ralph Hager, Philippine Islands.

Archery

The archery events of the 1904 Olympics were contested at the World's Fairgrounds on 19–21 September 1904. These events were actually the United States National Championship, whose formal name was the 26th Grand Annual Target Meeting of the National Archery Association (NAA) of the USA. Fortunately, due to the efforts of Mr. Robert Rhode, historian of the National Archery Association, there are available to us absolutely complete results of the archery events of the 1904 Olympics in four different forms. One is a printout from the National Archery Association. A second is the actual handwritten scores from the Secretary of the National Archery Association in that year, Lewis Maxson. The third is the results which were published in the British archery magazine, *The Archer's Register*, while the fourth is the results as published in *Spalding's Official Athletic Almanac*.

However, I consider the archery events of 1904 to be of marginal Olympic caliber. These were essentially United States National Championships. No professionals competed, and unfortunately, no foreign archers competed either. There were some foreign entrants from the Philippine islands and Lanao Moro tribe. However, the Filipino archers did not show or compete.

The rules of the archery events were listed in the program as stating that "Medals of the NAA open only to competitions of members. Competitions for medals offered by universal exposition open to all archers." Thus it would appear that the events were open to all archers. Still, with no foreign athletes competing, it is really difficult to call these events much more than the United States National Championships.

There are also some problems with several of the events that were contested. Men competed in the Double York round and Double American round. The women competed in the Double National round and Double Columbia round. There was also a gentlemen's team round which was contested. A ladies' team round was scheduled but not held as only one team appeared, that from Cincinnati. Several Olympic reference books often list that a women's team round did occur and that medals were given out, but this is not listed in any of the final results from 1904.

The Archer's Register also listed medals given for the "Olympic range medals" for each of the individual events and also for flight shooting for men and women. The Olympic range medals basically were for the highest score at each separate distance of the various individual rounds. Although a medal was given out for these, they are certainly of marginal Olympic significance and, in effect, similar to giving out medals in the modern pentathlon for the best score in each of the events. Flight shooting is more difficult to dismiss. The men's flight shooting was won by Lewis Maxson with a distance of 259 yards, while the women's flight shooting was won by Mabel Taylor with a distance of 219 yards. No other results are given. Possibly these two events carried as much importance as the individual rounds that were contested, but it is also possible that they were considered only a championship of the NAA, which is more likely. Given that, I have omitted them as Olympic events.

The archery events were dominated by G. Phillip Bryant of Boston who won both of the men's individual rounds and helped his Boston team to a bronze medal in the team round. The men's team round saw Reverend Galen Carter Spencer win a gold medal with the Potomac Archers of Washington. Spencer turned 64 years of age on the day prior to winning his gold medal, which makes him the oldest American Olympic gold medalist ever. Finishing second in that event was a team of Cincinnati archers who included even an older marksman, Samuel Duvall, who was 68 years of age at the 1904 Olympics and is the oldest American Olympic medalist.

The archery events for women were dominated by Lida Scott Howell who was 17 times American ladies' archery champion, had no peer at all in that era, and is considered one of the greatest women archers of all time in the United States.

Placings in the individual events were determined as follows: one point was awarded for the high score at each distance, one point for the high number of hits at each distance, two points were for the high total score, and two points for the high total number of hits; making ten points possible in all. Ties were broken by total score. Any remaining ties were broken by total number of hits.

Site:	Francis Field				
Dates/Times:	19–21 September				
Events:	5 [3 Men — 2 Women]				
Competitors:	29[1]* [23 Men — 6 Women]				
Nations:	1 [1 Men —1 Women]				

Totals	*Competitors*	*1st*	*2nd*	*3rd*	*Totals*
United States	29	5	5	5	15
Totals	29	5	5	5	15
Nations	1	1	1	1	1
Men	*Competitors*	*1st*	*2nd*	*3rd*	*Totals*
United States	23	3	3	3	9
Totals	23	3	3	3	9
Nations	1	1	1	1	1
Women	*Competitors*	*1st*	*2nd*	*3rd*	*Totals*
United States	6	2	2	2	6
Totals	6	2	2	2	6
Nations	1	1	1	1	1

2,3

*See Notes on pages 47–48.

Men

Double York Round

A: 16; C: 1; D: 20 September; F: The Double York round consisted of two Single York rounds, one shot in the morning, one in the afternoon. A Single York round consisted of 72 arrows at 100 yards (91.44 meters), 48 arrows at 80 yards (73.15 meters), and 24 arrows at 60 yards (54.86 meters).

			100y[4]	80y	60y	Pts.	Hits	Score
1.	George Bryant	USA	79/281	67/293	46/246	7	192	820
2.	Robert Williams	USA	78/274	73/345	40/200	2	191	819
3.	William Thompson	USA	70/264	72/314	48/238	1	190	816
4.	Wallace Bryant	USA	55/235	54/224	35/159	–	144	618
5.	Benjamin Keys	USA	45/151	50/210	37/171	–	132	532
6.	Edward Frentz	USA	46/144	47/187	37/197	–	130	528
7.	Homer Taylor	USA	39/127	50/198	41/181	–	130	506
8.	C. S. Woodruff	USA	33/95	47/201	43/191	–	123	487
9.	Henry Richardson	USA	26/88	47/205	36/146	–	119	439
10.[5]	Cyrus Dallin[6]	USA	38/142	44/150	37/113	–	119	405
11.	D. F. McGowan	USA	33/111	40/172	22/100	–	99	383
12.	Lewis Maxson[7]	USA	33/133	35/115	34/134	–	102	382
13.	Thomas Scott	USA	33/101	37/137	29/137	–	99	375
14.	Ralph Taylor	USA	16/56	45/145	33/127	–	94	328
15.	Edward Weston	USA	22/66	23/81	31/121	–	76	268
16.	Edward Bruce	USA	11/45	33/127	18/66	–	62	238

Double American Round

A: 22; C: 1; D: 19 September; F: The Double American round consisted of two Single American rounds, one shot in the morning, one in the afternoon. A Single American round consisted of 30 arrows at 60 yards (54.86 meters), 30 arrows at 50 yards (45.72 meters), and 30 arrows at 40 yards (36.58 meters).

			60y	50y	40y	Pts.	Hits	Score
1.	George Bryant[8]	USA	56/270	60/366	60/412	8.2	176	1,048
2.	Robert Williams	USA	52/276	59/311	60/404	1.2	171	991
3.	William Thompson	USA	51/261	56/290	60/398	0.2	167	949
4.	C. S. Woodruff	USA	50/218	56/285	60/404	0.2	167	907
5.	Wallace Bryant[9]	USA	46/212	54/272	60/334	0.2	160	818
6.	William Clark	USA	50/242	55/273	59/265	–	164	880
7.	Benjamin Keys	USA	49/233	51/263	58/344	–	158	840
8.	Cyrus Dallin	USA	43/203	55/289	58/324	–	156	816
9.	Henry Richardson	USA	46/246	59/285	58/282	–	163	813
10.	Homer Taylor	USA	49/185	52/264	58/362	–	159	811
11.	Charles Hubbard	USA	46/186	48/242	57/351	–	151	779
12.	Lewis Maxson	USA	42/188	56/272	59/317	–	157	777
13.	Galen Spencer	USA	47/221	53/241	53/239	–	153	701

14.	Samuel Duvall	USA	40/158	43/219	58/322	–	141	699
15.	Edward Frentz	USA	31/117	50/240	54/308	–	135	665
16.	Amos Casselman	USA	36/132	45/227	55/269	–	136	628
17.	Thomas Scott	USA	36/126	44/192	50/244	–	135	562
18.	Ralph Taylor	USA	33/129	43/207	45/197	–	121	533
19.	Edward Bruce	USA	22/100	35/159	55/257	–	112	516
20.	E. H. Weston	USA	30/146	36/144	46/218	–	112	508
21.	Edward Weston	USA	26/108	34/132	46/210	–	106	450
22.	W. G. Valentine	USA	9/27	27/117	47/201	–	83	345

Team Round

A: 16; C: 1; D: 21 September; F: The team round consisted of four men per team each shooting 96 arrows from 60 yards (54.86 meters).

			Hits	Score
1.	Potomac Archers	USA	300	1,344
	William Thompson	83/413		
	Robert Williams	82/386		
	Lewis Maxson	71/283		
	Galen Spencer[10]	64/262		
2.	Cincinnati Archers	USA	303	1,341
	C. S. Woodruff	85/429		
	William Clark	79/317		
	Charles Hubbard	71/315		
	Samuel Duvall	68/280		
3.	Boston Archers	USA	282	1,268
	George Bryant	85/443		
	Wallace Bryant	68/296		
	Cyrus Dallin	65/267		
	Henry Richardson[11]	64/262		
4.	Chicago Archers	USA	224	942
	Benjamin Keys	71/345		
	Homer Taylor	71/321		
	Edward Weston	45/139		
	Edward Bruce	37/137		

Women

Double National Round

A: 6; C: 1; D: 20 September; F: The Double National round consisted of two Single National rounds, one shot in the morning, one in the afternoon. A Single National round consisted of 48 arrows at 60 yards (54.86 meters), and 24 arrows at 50 yards (45.72 meters).

			60y	50y	Pts.	Hits	Score
1.	Lida Howell	USA	87/417	43/203	7½	130	620
2.	Emma Cooke[12]	USA	60/230	43/189	½	103	419
3.	Jessie Pollock	USA	68/272	35/147	–	103	419
4.	Laura Woodruff	USA	29/101	37/133	–	66	234
5.	Mabel Taylor	USA	24/94	22/66	–	46	160
6.	Louise Taylor	USA	21/85	18/74	–	39	159

Double Columbia Round

A: 6; C: 1; D: 19 September; F: The Double Columbia round consisted of two Single Columbia rounds, one shot in the morning, one in the afternoon. A Single Columbia round consisted of 24 arrows at 50 yards (45.72 meters), 24 arrows at 40 yards (36.58 meters), and 24 arrows at 30 yards (27.43 meters).

			50y	40y	30y	Pts.	Hits	Score
1.	Lida Howell	USA	45/245	48/274	48/348	9½	141	867
2.	Emma Cooke	USA	34/150	44/202	48/278	½	126	630
3.	Jessie Pollock	USA	37/141	44/204	47/285	–	124	630
4.	Laura Woodruff	USA	27/101	39/165	47/281	–	113	547
5.	Mabel Taylor[13]	USA	14/50	15/57	30/136	–	59	243
6.	Louise Taylor	USA	5/19	17/73	31/137	–	53	229

NON-OLYMPIC EVENTS

Flight Shooting, Men

A: ?; C: 1; D: Unknown.

    1.   Lewis W. Maxson   USA   259 yards

Flight Shooting, Women

A: ?; C: 1; D: Unknown.

    1.   Mabel Taylor   USA   219 yards
[14]

NOTES

1. EK and VK did not list the number of competitors by event but listed 31 competitors overall in archery. This is incorrect as the evidence for the results here is very strong.

2. The very complete archery results came from the files of Robert Rhode, historian of the National Archery Association. Rhode provided the original results of the events in the handwriting of the Secretary of the National Archery Association of 1904, Lewis W. Maxson.

3. EK and FM both list a ladies' team event. This event was scheduled but, according to Rhode, never took place because only one ladies' team was present, the Cincinnati Archers. Both EK and FM list the Potomac Archers as finishing second, but their only female representative was Emma

Cooke. Kamper and other authors writing on the women's movement in the Olympics state that eight women competed at St. Louis. This must be an assumption that there were two archery teams of four women each. There were, in fact, only six women — those listed herein.

4. Scores at each distance show the number of the hits and the archer's score at that distance.

5. Places 10–13 are listed differently than in Maxson's original results. He made several clerical errors which I have corrected here. These were the only places in the 1904 archery events for which he had any errors.

6. EK and FM list this athlete as Claude Allen. Rhode confirmed his name as Cyrus Edwin Dallin, a famous sculptor.

7. EK lists this athlete as Louis Maxon, but in his own handwriting he spelled it Lewis Maxson.

8. FM is not even close here, listing the medalists as: (1) H[omer] Taylor, (2) C. R. Hubbard, (3) L[ewis] W. Max[s]on. I have no idea where this came from as they finished, respectively, 10-11-12.

9. Most sources list Clark 5th and Keys 6th (DW, EK, VK), but this is based only on score and not on the point system used for placements, as described above.

10. The Reverend Galen Carter Spencer was 64 years, 1 day old on the day of the team round. This would make him the oldest American to win a gold medal at the Olympics.

11. Often seen as Harry Richardson. The spelling of Henry Barber Richardson was confirmed via his *New York Times* obituary and listings in *American Medical Association Directories*. Richardson was only 15 years old when he competed in the archery events at the 1904 Olympics.

12. Several sources list the runners-up in these two events as two different women — Emma C. Cooke, and Emma C. Coolen. They were the same person, Emma C. Cooke.

13. EK has Mabel and Louise Taylor reversed although, oddly, he lists their scores correctly.

14. EK, FM, and VK list the women's team round, which was not contested. See above in the introduction.

Athletics (Track & Field)

The track & field athletics events held from 29 August through 3 September 1904 at Francis Field in St. Louis were considered to be the main event of the Olympic Games by all the media which covered them in that year. To some media, they were the only events worthy of being considered "true" Olympic events.

There were many other track & field meets held during the summer of 1904 in St. Louis, and James Sullivan, Director of the Department of Physical Culture at the Louisiana Purchase Exposition, insisted on calling all of them "Olympic" events. There were also handicap events conducted during the same days as the Olympic meet. I've included the results of everything below, although the "true" Olympic events are listed first and with the most detail.

There were a few foreign competitors, but the meet was essentially a U.S. championship, although the Olympic meet was *not* the 1904 AAU Championship. That had been held in St. Louis, but earlier in the summer, on 4 June (results given below).

The track was specially built for the Olympic Games and was very modern — for 1904. It was ⅓ of a mile in length (586 yards, 2 feet = 536.44 meters), with one very long straightaway, four turns, and three shorter straights. It was built on the campus of Washington University in St. Louis and was composed of cinders. (Through the mid–1980s, the track existed in its original form, but Washington University has now replaced it with a synthetic surface track. Amazingly, however, the stadium still exists in its original form.) The weather was excellent. It was sunny every day of the Games, with temperatures in the high-70s to mid-80s (F.) (25–30° C.).

Site:	Francis Field, Washington University
Dates/Times:	4 July, 29 August–3 September
Events:	24
Competitors:	117
Nations:	10

	Competitors	1st	2nd	3rd	Totals
Australia	2	-	-	-	-
Canada	5	1	-	-	1
Cuba	1	-	-	-	-
France	1	-	1	-	1
France/United States	-	-	1	-	1

Germany	2	-	-	1	1
Greece	10	-	-	1	1
Hungary	2	-	-	-	-
Ireland	3	1	1	-	2
South Africa	3	-	-	-	-
United States	88	22	21	21	64
Totals	117	24	24	23	71
Nations	10	3	3	3	6

60 Meters

A: 15[1]*; C: 3; D: 29 August; F: Winners of each heat advance to the final. Runners-up in the heats advance to the semi-finals. Top two in the semi-finals advance to the final.

This was the first event of the Games, and it was also the first time that many of the eastern sprinters had seen Archie Hahn, although he had won the 1903 AAU title at 100 yards. With Hahn, the favorites were Lawson Robertson, who earlier in the summer had won the AAU 100; Nate Cartmell, second in the 1904 IC4A 100; and Fay Moulton, winner of the 1903 IC4A title at 100 yards. All of the favorites advanced to the final where Hahn got the jump on them at the gun. He was ahead by two yards at the halfway mark and held this to the finish.

Competing in a heat but not qualifying, was George Poage of the University of Wisconsin and the Milwaukee AC. Poage was a black man and his appearance in this heat was the first time a black American competed in the Olympic Games.

Final A: 6; C: 1; D: 29 August

1.	Archie Hahn	USA	7.0
2.	William Hogensen	USA	7.2
3.	Fay Moulton	USA	7.2
4.	Clyde Blair	USA	7.2
5.	Meyer Prinstein[2]	USA	
6.	Frank Castleman	USA	

Semi-finals A: 4; D: 29 August

=1.	Frank Castleman[3]	USA	7.2
	Meyer Prinstein	USA	7.2
AC.	Nate Cartmell	USA	
	Robert Kerr	CAN	

Heats A: 15; D: 29 August

Heat 1 A: 4; D: 29 August

1.	Clyde Blair	USA	7.0
2.	Meyer Prinstein	USA	
AC.	William B. Hunter	USA	
	George Poage	USA	

*See Notes on pages 106–108.

Heat 2 A: 4; D: 29 August

1.	William Hogensen	USA	7.0
2.	Frank Castleman	USA	

Heat 3 A: 4; D: 29 August

1.	Archie Hahn	USA	7.2
2.	Robert Kerr	CAN	
3.	Lawson Robertson	USA	
4.	Béla de Mező	HUN	

Heat 4 A: 3; D: 29 August

1.	Fay Moulton	USA
2.	Nate Cartmell	USA

100 Meters

A: 13[4]; C: 3; D: 3 September; F: Winners and runners-up in the heats advance to the final.

By now, Archie Hahn was a heavy favorite, as he had already won the 60 and 200 meter events. Hahn was again off ahead at the start, and opened a lead of three yards in the first 20 meters. Cartmell got off to his usual poor start and was last at 40 meters, but closed rapidly again to finish second, 1½ yards behind Hahn.

Hahn had won the sprint double at the 1903 U.S. and Canadian championships, and he again won the AAU 220 in 1905. Though he was only 5'6", in 1906 he would become the first person to win the Olympic 100 twice, a feat not duplicated until 1984–88 by Carl Lewis. He later became a track coach, first at Princeton and then at the University of Virginia, and his book, *How to Sprint*, is considered a classic.

Final A: 6; C: 1; D: 3 September

1.	Archie Hahn	USA	11.0
2.	Nate Cartmell	USA	11.2
3.	William Hogensen	USA	11.2
4.	Fay Moulton	USA	
5.	Fred Heckwolf	USA	
6.	Lawson Robertson	USA	

Heats A: 13; D: 3 September

Heat 1 A: 4; D: 3 September

1.	Archie Hahn	USA	11.4
2.	Lawson Robertson	USA	
3.	Béla de Mező	HUN	

Heat 2 A: 4; D: 3 September

1.	William Hogensen	USA	11.6
2.	Fred Heckwolf	USA	
3.	Robert Kerr	CAN	
4.	Meyer Prinstein	USA	

Heat 3 A: 5; D: 3 September

1.	Nate Cartmell	USA	11.4
2.	Fay Moulton	USA	
3.	Clyde Blair	USA	
4.	Frank Castleman	USA	

200 Meters

A: 7; C: 2; D: 31 August; F: Winners and runners-up in the heats advance to the final. The event was run on a straight course.

After his victory in the 60, Hahn was the favorite. The other top finishers from the 60, Robertson, Moulton, Hogensen, and Cartmell, were also given a chance.

Hahn was helped when the three other finalists were all penalized a yard for false starts. Hahn opened an immediate lead, with Nate Cartmell getting a horrible start, falling behind by seven yards at the 20-yard mark. At 75 yards, Cartmell gathered himself and began to gain on the leaders. He picked off Hogensen and Moulton, but Hahn's early lead was too much for him, and he finished two yards behind at the tape.

Final A: 4; C: 1; D: 31 August

1.	Archie Hahn	USA	21.6
2.	Nate Cartmell[5]	USA	21.9
3.	William Hogensen	USA	
4.	Fay Moulton	USA	

Heats A: 7; D: 31 August

Heat 1 A: 4; D: 31 August

1.	Archie Hahn	USA	22.2
2.	Nate Cartmell	USA	

Heat 2 A: 3; D: 31 August

1.	William Hogensen	USA	22.8
2.	Fay Moulton	USA	
3.	Robert Kerr	CAN	

400 Meters

A: 13[6]; C: 3; D: 29 August; F: Final only — no heats.

Harry Hillman was probably the favorite, although Canada's Percival Molson would also be closely watched, based on his victory over Hillman at the 1904 Canadian championships. There were no heats, as the thirteen runners started together, with twelve men on the line, and one unknown soul forced to start behind the front line. Herman Groman went into the lead at 70 meters, and quickly opened a gap. The field immediately sorted itself out into two groups. At 200 meters Hillman, who had been running third, took the lead, while Joseph Fleming left the second pack and joined the main group. Into the last turn, George Poage tried to pass but was cut off by Fleming and Frank Waller. The final sprint involved Hillman, Waller, Groman, Fleming, and Prinstein, as Poage fell back. Hillman powered ahead to win by about three yards over Waller, with Groman on Waller's heels and Fleming and Prinstein finishing almost together, another two yards back.

Though Percival Molson failed to place, he would achieve his fame later, but it would cost him his life. Molson, the great-grandson of John Molson, founder of Molson Breweries of Canada, attended McGill, from which he graduated in 1900 after serving as president of his senior class and gaining every athletic honor the university could offer. When World War I broke out, he joined the Princess Patricia's Canadian Light Infantry, and fought with them at the Battle of Mount Sorrel in 1916. He was wounded during the battle and returned home, receiving the Military Cross for his efforts. He insisted he be allowed to rejoin the company, and on 5 July 1917, while fighting on the outskirts of Avignon, France, he was hit by mortar fire while attempting to rescue a fallen friend. Both were killed. In his honor, the main athletic stadium at McGill University is known as the Percival Molson Memorial Stadium.

1.	Harry Hillman	USA	49.2
2.	Frank Waller	USA	49.9
3.	Herman Groman	USA	50.0
4.	Joseph Fleming	USA	
5.	Meyer Prinstein[7]	USA	
6.	George Poage	USA	
AC.	Clyde Blair	USA	
	Percival Molson	CAN	
	Paul Pilgrim	USA	
	Johannes Runge	GER	
	George Underwood	USA	
	Howard Valentine	USA	

800 Meters

A: 13[8]; C: 3; D: 1 September; F: Final only — no heats.

Most of America's top middle-distance men were present, save for Eli Parsons of Yale, the 1904 IC4A champion. There were several theories as to the favorites, but James Lightbody, a young Chicago runner, was not one of the prominent names mentioned. At the start, Harvey Cohn took the lead, followed by Emil Breitkreutz and Germany's Johannes Runge, with Lightbody running last in the early going. At the 400-meter mark, Runge took over the lead, as Cohn flagged badly, and Lightbody began a sustained drive, passing the entire field on the outside. Coming into the final stretch, Breitkreutz and George Underwood led, but Lightbody was gaining fast. He eventually pulled away to win by two yards, with Breitkreutz holding onto second until the last yards. He was then passed by Howard Valentine, who closed quickly. This was probably the top race of the 1904 Olympics, as several runners were so badly spent they were carried from the track in exhaustion. Runge was hampered because three days earlier he had competed in the 800 meter handicap event, and not understanding the English instructions, thought it was the Olympic final.

1.	James Lightbody	USA	1:56.0
2.	Howard Valentine	USA	1:56.3

3.	Emil Breitkreutz	USA	1:56.4	
4.	George Underwood	USA		
5.	Johannes Runge	GER	4 meters bh 4th[9]	
6.	William Verner	USA		
AC.	George Bonhag	USA		
	Harvey Cohn	USA		
	Peter Deer	CAN		
	Lacey Hearn	USA		
	John Joyce	USA		
	John Peck	CAN		
	Paul Pilgrim	USA		

1,500 Meters

A: 9; C: 3; D: 3 September; F: Final only — no heats.

This race was mostly noteworthy for the athletes not in attendance, primarily Alfred Shrubb of Britain, the 1903 and 1904 AAA champion, and four-time AAU mile champion Alex Grant from Penn. Off past records, the favorite among those present had to be David Munson, the 1904 champion in both the IC4A and the AAU meet, but he would prove to be a disappointment.

The race began with Harvey Cohn and Peter Deer taking the lead, with Frank Verner third for most of the first lap. Deer dropped back on the second circuit, and at the bell, it was Cohn, Verner, and Lightbody, in that order, with Munson struggling in fourth place. On the backstretch, Lightbody made easy work of the field and coasted in a victor by six yards, Verner held onto second and was followed by Lacey Hearn who closed fast to take third. Lightbody's time was 4:05.4, which was a "world record," but was equivalent only to a 4:25.7 mile, far inferior to the amateur world record of 4:15.6 held by Tom Conneff.

1.	James Lightbody	USA	4:05.4	WR[10]
2.	William Verner	USA	4:06.8	
3.	Lacey Hearn[11]	USA		
4.	David Munson	USA		
5.	Johannes Runge	GER		
6.	Peter Deer	CAN		
7.	Howard Valentine	USA		
8.	Harvey Cohn	USA		
9.	Charles Bacon	USA		

110 Meter Hurdles

A: 8; C: 2; D: 3 September; F: Winners and runners-up in the heats advance to the final.

America's top hurdler was Edwin Clapp, IC4A champion in both 1903 and 1904, who entered but did not appear. This left the favorite role to Tad Shideler who in June had equaled Alvin Kraenzlein's world record of 15.0, only to see it not stand up because only two watches registered a time. Fred Schule won the first heat, and Frank Castleman nipped Shideler in the second heat. This gave the final to the last two AAU champions (Schule—1903, and Castleman—1904) in addition to Shideler. In the final, Castleman was never a factor, as Schule and Shideler fought it out, the former winning by about two yards.

1.	Frederick Schule	USA	16.0
2.	Thaddeus Shideler	USA	16.3
3.	Lesley Ashburner	USA	16.4
4.	Frank Castleman	USA	

12

Heats A: 8; D: 3 September

Heat 1 A: 4; D: 3 September

1.	Frederick Schule	USA	16.2
2.	Lesley Ashburner	USA	
3.	Ward McLanahan	USA	
4.	Corrie Gardner	AUS	

Heat 2 A: 4; D: 3 September

1.	Frank Castleman	USA	16.2
2.	Thaddeus Shideler	USA	
AC.	Leslie McPherson	AUS	

200 Meter Hurdles

A: 5[13]; C: 1; D: 1 September; F: Final only—no heats.

Yale's Edwin Clapp, the 1901, 1903, and 1904 IC4A champion, was again not present, which left the title basically up for grabs. Harry Hillman had won the AAU title in this event in 1902 and been the runner-up in 1904, and was probably a weak favorite off that record. Hillman and George Poage fought it out as they had in the 400 meter hurdles, with Hillman winning by about two yards, most of it gained on the final run-in.

For Harry Hillman it was his third individual gold medal of the Olympics. He would later compete at both the 1906 and 1908 Olympics, winning a silver medal in the 1908 400 meter hurdles. In 1910, Hillman began a coaching career at Dartmouth which lasted until his death in 1945. With fellow 1904 Olympian Lawson Robertson, Hillman is still listed as the co-holder of the fastest time for the three-legged 100 yard race—11.0 seconds.

1.	Harry Hillman	USA	24.6
2.	Frank Castleman	USA	24.9
3.	George Poage	USA	
4.	George Varnell	USA	
5.	Frederick Schule[14]	USA	

400 Meter Hurdles

A: 4; C: 1; D: 31 August; F: Final only—no heats.

Hillman led from start to finish and had the race well in hand until the eighth hurdle. He hit that hurdle very hard, almost falling, and Waller caught him at the ninth hurdle. Somehow, Hillman regained his momentum and took the run-in by two yards. In third place, George Poage won what is usually described as the first Olympic medal ever won by a black man, but on the same afternoon Joseph Stadler was winning a silver medal in the standing high jump, and in 1900, a black man had competed in the tug-of-war for France, winning a silver medal.

Hillman's time could not qualify as a world record for two reasons: 1) he knocked over a hurdle, which in those days invalidated hurdle marks for record purposes, and 2) the hurdles used were only 2'6" high, as opposed to the event standard of three feet.

1.	Harry Hillman	USA	53.0[15]
2.	Frank Waller	USA	53.2
3.	George Poage	USA	30 yards bh 2nd
4.	George Varnell[16]	USA	

2,590[17] Meter Steeplechase

A: 7[18]; C: 2; D: 29 August; F: Final only — no heats. The event was five laps to complete the distance. On each lap there was a water jump and several other jumps.[19]

The runners had to clear several hurdles and a 14-foot water jump on each lap. The favorite was the Irishman, John Daly, while the top American runner, James Lightbody, was contesting his first steeplechase. After one lap, Daly led by 10 yards over Cohn, with Lightbody in second, another 10 yards back. After two laps, Daly had opened up a 40-yard lead, and he still led going to the last lap, though the margin is given variously as either 15 or 60 yards. At this point, Daly must have virtually collapsed, for not only was he caught by Lightbody on the last lap, but Lightbody pulled away to win by about 10 yards. Arthur Newton, who had never contended, finished third, another 30 yards behind Daly.

Jim Lightbody attended the University of Chicago and represented the Chicago AA. Although he won three gold medals at the 1904 Olympics, he was relatively unknown prior to that time. After winning the 880 yard/mile double at the 1905 AAU championships, he repeated his 1500 meter victory at the 1906 Athens Games, but failed by a narrow margin to defend the 800 meter crown.

1.	James Lightbody	USA	7:39.6
2.	John Daly	IRL	7:40.6
3.	Arthur Newton	USA	30 yards bh 2nd
4.	William Verner	USA	
AC.	Harvey Cohn	USA	
	David Munson	USA	
	Richard Sandford	USA	

20

Marathon

A: 32[21]; C: 5; D: 30 August; F: 40,000 meters[22] (24.85 miles). The runners ran five laps clockwise around the track before exiting via the east gate. They ran up an incline, made a right turn onto Olympian Way (now known as [nka] Forsyth) passing eventually into downtown Clayton. They turned left onto South Meramec, then onto Sappington Drive (nka Shaw Park Drive), and then went down a hill to North and South Road (nka South Brentwood). The route continued on North and South up a very steep hill before going onto Manchester Road. After a bit the runners turned right onto Ballas Road, followed by a right turn onto Clayton Road, then a left onto Denny Road (nka Lindbergh). At about 19 miles, the route turned onto Olive Street, shortly becoming Olive Street Road. After a short stretch there, a right turn was made on North and South Road, which led into North Meramec. The road led again onto Forsyth, turning left, which led back to Francis Field via the east gate. The race finished on the track in front of the press box on the south side.[23]

The race was 40 km. and was held on a 90° F. (32° C.) day. In addition it was run over dusty country roads, and the lead automobiles kicked up so much dust that the runners practically choked on it throughout the race. There was also only one water stop on the course, that being a well at 12 miles.

Among the Americans there were several top distance runners. Sam Mellor, winner of the 1902 Boston Marathon; John Lordon, winner of Boston in 1903, Michael Spring, winner of Boston in 1904, and Arthur Newton, who had finished fifth at Paris in the 1900 Olympic marathon. The top foreign distance runners were not present, but a 5-foot tall Cuban named Felix Carbajal had come to St. Louis.

Carbajal had raised money for the trip by staging exhibitions and running the entire length of Cuba. Arriving in New Orleans, he lost all his money in a crap game, which forced him to hitch-hike to St. Louis. He showed up on race day wearing heavy street shoes, long trousers, a beret, and a long-sleeved shirt. Martin Sheridan helped him out by trimming the pants and the shirt. During the race, Carbajal would stop to eat some green apples which caused stomach cramps and didn't help his cause any. Still, he finished fourth.

The first two South African Olympians were ironically, black men named Len Tau and Jan Mashiani, who ran the marathon. Both Tsuana Tribesmen, they were present at the South African exhibit of the Louisiana Purchase Exposition. They had been dispatch runners during the recent Boer War and were noted to be "the fleetest in the service." They finished the marathon in 9th and 12th place, respectively.

The race started at 3 P.M. and the runners ran five laps of the stadium before heading out into the country. Fred Lorz had the early lead, but dropped out at nine miles. At that point, the lead was held by Arthur Newton, veteran of the 1900 Olympic marathon, and Sam Mellor. Shortly thereafter, Mellor slowed to a walk (he eventually withdrew), and Tom Hicks moved up on the leaders. Through 16 miles, Mellor had regained the lead, with Newton second, Hicks third, and Albert Coray and William Garcia together in fourth. Garcia would eventually drop out, and suffered so badly from the heat, dust, and lack of water that he spent several days in the hospital, his life in the balance, before recovering.

At this point, Hicks began to flag badly. His handlers helped him, administering strychnine sulfate in an egg white, giving him water, and sponging him down. The early sports medicine seemed to work as he had the lead at 19 miles. At 20 miles he was again ready to collapse when he was given the same treatments, along with sips of brandy. He was then passed by Fred Lorz, who was refreshed after having ridden in an automobile most of the race.

Lorz entered the stadium first and received the crowd's plaudits, as they were oblivious to his scheme. Hicks came shortly after, almost dead on his feet. He had finished the race by slow jogging interspersed with periods of walking. Lorz was soon found out and was banned from amateur competition for life, only to see the ban rescinded in time for him to win the 1905 Boston Marathon.

				5m	10m	15m	20m
1.	Thomas Hicks	USA	3-28:53	5	3	2	1
2.	Albert Coray[24]	FRA	3-34:52	6	5	3	2
3.	Arthur Newton	USA	3-47:33	1	1	1	3
4.	Felix Carbajal de Soto	CUB		9	6	5	4
5.	Dimitrios Veloulis	GRE		7	9	8	=7
6.	David Kneeland[25]	USA		10	12	=9	=7
7.	Henry Brawley	USA		8	13	10	8
8.	Sidney Hatch	USA		11	14	=9	10
9.	Len Tau[26]	SAF		12	16	14	13
10.	Christos Zekhouritis	GRE		13	20	19	11
11.	F. P. Devlin	USA		2	4	6	12
12.	Jan Mashiani[27]	SAF		14	23	15	=14
13.	John Furla[28]	USA		15	11	13	15
14.	Andrew Oikonomou	GRE		18	17	16	=14

AC. Frank Pierce [USA], Samuel Mellor [USA], Edward Carr [USA], Michael Spring [USA], Fred Lorz[29] [USA], John Lordon [USA], William Garcia [USA], Robert Fowler [USA], Thomas Kennedy [USA], Guy Porter [USA], John Foy [USA], Robert W., "Bertie" Harris [SAF], Georgios Vamkaitis [GRE], Charilaos Giannakas [GRE], Georgios Drosos [GRE], Georgios Louridas [GRE], Ioannis Loungitsas [GRE], Petros Pipiles [GRE]

Four-Mile Team Race (6437.4 Meters)[30]

A: 10; C: 2; D: 3 September; F: Point-for-place scoring.

There were only two teams entered, the New York Athletic Club and the Chicago Athletic Association. This was the last event of the Games, and the team trophy for high scoring American club also hinged on its outcome. Arthur Newton jumped into the lead immediately and opened space on the pack quickly. After one mile he led by about thirty yards, with Lightbody leading the pack in second place. In the next two miles Newton lapped both Sidney Hatch and Albert Corey, and held a lead of 200 yards over Lightbody. In the last mile, Newton did nothing but stretch out his lead to win by "hundreds of yards." Though Chicago finished 2nd, 3rd, and 4th, the 9th and 10th place finishes of Coray and Hatch cost them the race, 27–28, and the overall team trophy.

1.	New York Athletic Club			USA	27 pts.[31]
	Arthur Newton	1	21:17.8		
	George Underwood	5			
	Paul Pilgrim	6			
	Howard Valentine	7			
	David Munson	8			
2.	Chicago Athletic Association			USA/FRA[32]	28 pts.
	James Lightbody	2			
	William Verner	3			
	Lacey Hearn	4			

Albert Coray (FRA)	9
Sidney Hatch	10

High Jump

A: 6; C: 3; D: 29 August.

The *Globe-Democrat* predicted an easy victory for Sam Jones, who had won the 1901 and 1902 IC4A title, the 1902 AAA crown, and the AAU championship in 1901, 1903, and 1904. They were right. After winning with 5'11", Jones tried, but failed, to clear 6'2½". Second place was won by Garrett Serviss, but only after a jump-off of a tie with Paul Weinstein. Apparently, Weinstein competed in this event concurrently with the standing broad jump, and was running back and forth between the two.

The styles of the leading jumpers were different. The two Americans both used the scissors, while descriptions of Weinstein's form make it apparent that he was actually using the Eastern roll, years before it was ever called this. Gönczy probably had the best vertical jump of the contenders as his method is described as simply curling his legs up under him as he cleared the bar!

1.	Samuel Jones	USA	5-11	(1.80)
2.	Garrett Serviss[33]	USA	5-9¾	(1.77)
3.	Paul Weinstein	GER	5-9¾	(1.77)
4.	Lajos Gönczy	HUN	5-9	(1.75)
5.	Emil Freymark	USA		
6.	Ervin Barker	USA	5-7	(1.70)

Standing High Jump

A: 5[34]; C: 1; D: 31 August.

As he had in 1900, Ray Ewry dominated the three standing jumping events. In the standing high jump, Lawson Robertson and Joseph Stadler tied and settled second place on a jump-off. This went to Stadler, a black man from Cleveland, who became one of the first of his race to win an Olympic medal.

1.	Ray Ewry	USA	5-3[35]	(1.60)
2.	Joseph Stadler[36]	USA	4-9[37]	(1.44)[38]
3.	Lawson Robertson	USA	4-9	(1.44)
4.	John Biller	USA	4-8	(1.42)
5.	Lajos Gönczy	HUN	4-5	(1.35)

Pole Vault

A: 7; C: 2; D: 3 September.

Of the top American vaulters, only H. Louis Gardner, 1903 IC4A and 1904 AAU champion, and Stanford's Norman Dole, a former world record holder though never the winner of a major title, were missing. Also missing was France's Fernand Gonder, who in June had broken Dole's world record.

The bar was apparently raised 3" for each new height. At 11'3", five vaulters remained: Charles Dvorak, Leroy Samse, Louis Wilkins, Ward McLanahan, and Claude Allen. Only Dvorak was able to clear 11'3", clinching the victory, and he also made 11'6" before missing three attempts at a new world record of 12'2". The other four began a jump-off at 10'9", which all made. Allen and McLanahan then missed 11', while Wilkins and Samse made that, and also 11'3". In a second series of jump-offs, McLanahan defeated Allen and Samse defeated Wilkins.

1.	Charles Dvorak	USA	11-6	(3.50)[39]
2.	LeRoy Samse	USA	11	(3.35)
3.	Louis Wilkins	USA	11	(3.35)
4.	Ward McLanahan	USA	11	(3.35)
5.	Claude Allen	USA	11	(3.35)
6.	Walter Dray	USA		
7.	Paul Weinstein	GER		

Broad Jump (now known as Long Jump)

A: 10[40]; C: 3; D: 1 September; F: Each athlete received three jumps. The three leaders received an additional three jumps.

With world record holder and multiple AAA champion Peter O'Connor absent, Meyer Prinstein was the favorite, but he had recently been beaten by Daniel Frank at the Metropolitan AAU meet. An expected battle between the two never really materialized, however, as Prinstein led throughout and stretched his lead by posting his winning mark in the final round. This gave him the long jump gold medal which he thought he had deserved four years earlier in Paris.

1.	Meyer Prinstein	USA	24-1	(7.34)
2.	Daniel Frank	USA	22-7¼	(6.89)
3.	Robert Stangland	USA	22-7	(6.88)
4.	Fred Englehardt	USA	21-9	(6.63)
5.	George Van Cleaf	USA		
6.	John Hagerman	USA		
AC.	John Oxley	USA		
	Béla de Mező	HUN		
	Corrie Gardner	AUS		
	Leslie McPherson	AUS		

Standing Broad Jump

A: 4; C: 1; D: 29 August; F: Each athlete received three jumps. The three leaders received an additional three jumps.

1.	Ray Ewry	USA	11-4⅞	(3.47)[41]
2.	Charles King	USA	10-9	(3.27)
3.	John Biller	USA	10-8¼	(3.25)
4.	Henry Field	USA	10-5½	(3.18)

Hop, Step, and Jump (now known as Triple Jump)

A: 7; C: 1; D: 1 September; F: Each athlete received three jumps. The three leaders received an additional three jumps.

It was virtually impossible to predict a favorite as the event was rarely held. Meyer Prinstein defended the title he had won four years earlier, but failed to break his own Olympic record, missing it by four inches. Prinstein never led until his last jump, when he came through for the victory.

1.	Meyer Prinstein	USA	47-1	(14.35)[42]
2.	Fred Englehardt	USA	45-7¼	(13.90)
3.	Robert Stangland	USA	43-10	(13.36)
4.	John Fuhler	USA	42-4½	(12.91)
5.	George Van Cleaf	USA		
6.	John Hagerman	USA		
7.	Samuel Jones[43]	USA		

Standing Hop, Step, and Jump

A: 4; C: 1; D: 3 September; F: Each athlete received three jumps. The three leaders received an additional three jumps.

1.	Ray Ewry	USA	34-7¼	(10.54)
2.	Charles King	USA	33-4	(10.16)
3.	Joseph Stadler	USA	31-6	(9.60)[44]
4.	Garrett Serviss	USA	31-3¼	(9.53)[45]

Shot Put

A: 8; C: 2; D: 31 August; F: Each athlete received three attempts. The three leaders received an additional three attempts.

The first event on 31 August was the shot put, and the betting choice was Ralph Rose, who held the world's record but had yet to win a major championship. With Ireland's Denis Horgan, the top non–American, not in attendance, Rose's main competition was expected to be several times AAA champion, Wesley Coe. The two made a Mutt-and-Jeff pair as Rose stood 6'6", weighing 265 lbs., while Coe was only 5'10" and weighed 210 lbs.

Rose opened the competition and threw 47', while Coe opened with a mark described only as less than 46'. On the first throw of the finals, Rose put the shot 47'1", to extend his lead slightly, only to see Coe take the lead with 47'3". On his fifth attempt, Rose unleashed a new world's record, throwing 48'7", which held up to win.

1.	Ralph Rose	USA	48-7[46]	(14.81)	WR
2.	Wesley Coe	USA	47-3[47]	(14.40)	
3.	Lawrence Feuerbach[48]	USA	43-10½	(13.37)	
4.	Martin Sheridan	USA	40-8	(12.39)	
5.	Charles Chadwick	USA			
6.	Albert Johnson	USA			
7.	John Guiney[49]	USA			
AC.	Nikolaos Georgantas	GRE	DQ[50]		

Discus Throw

A: 6; C: 2; D: 3 September; F: Each athlete received three attempts. The three leaders received an additional three attempts.

The 1904 AAU champion, Martin Sheridan, was a slight favorite, but Ralph Rose was given a good chance, as was Greece's Nikolas Georgantas. After six throws, Rose and Sheridan were tied, and had a throw-off of the tie, in which each was accorded another three throws. This was won by Sheridan by 7'3½", with 127' 10¼" to Rose's 120' 6¾".

Martin Sheridan was an Irish immigrant who was inspired to take up athletics by his brother Richard, who won the discus throw at the 1902 AAU championships. Sheridan eventually became one of the great athletes of his time, setting several world discus records, winning nine Olympic medals (five gold), and three times winning the AAU title in the all-around championship.

1.	Martin Sheridan	USA	128-10½	(39.28)[51]
2.	Ralph Rose	USA	128-10½	(39.28)
3.	Nikolaos Georgantas	GRE	123-7½	(37.68)
4.	John Flanagan	USA	118-7	(36.14)
5.	John Biller	USA		
6.	James Mitchel[52]	USA		

Hammer Throw

A: 6[53]; C: 1; D: 29 August; F: Each athlete received three attempts. The three leaders received an additional three attempts.

John Flanagan had won over ten national titles in all, counting America, Britain, and Ireland. He was also the defending Olympic champion and the heavy favorite. His chief rivals were expected to be John DeWitt, IC4A champion from 1901 through 1904, and Ralph Rose. There were reports that Rose had recently thrown 190 feet in practice in California. The most notable absences were Alfred Plaw, who had delivered a rare defeat to Flanagan at the 1904 AAU meet; and Tom Nicolson, Britain's AAA champion in 1903-04.

Throwing from a seven-foot circle, and using two turns, Flanagan opened with 168'1", which eventually proved to be the winning mark. Rose and DeWitt also made their best efforts on their first throw, Rose using but a single turn.

1.	John Flanagan	USA	168-1	(51.23)[54]
2.	John DeWitt	USA	164-11	(50.26)[55]
3.	Ralph Rose	USA	150-0½	(45.73)[56]
4.	Charles Chadwick	USA	140-4½	(42.78)
5.	James Mitchel	USA		
6.	Albert Johnson[57]	USA		

56-lb. (25.4 kg.) Weight Throw

A: 6; C: 2; D: 1 September; F: Each athlete received three attempts. The three leaders received an additional three attempts.

This was expected to be one of the few international battles, as John Flanagan and Canada's Étienne Desmarteau were co-favorites. They had met once, at the 1902 AAU meet, and Desmarteau had beaten Flanagan at that time. In July of 1904, Flanagan had broken the world record with 40'2", but this was with an unlimited run-and-follow, while at St. Louis the weight was thrown from a seven-foot circle.

Ralph Rose opened the proceedings with a foul, and Desmarteau followed with 34'4". This eventually proved to be the winning mark, as Flanagan also followed with his best throw, 33'4". It was a warm day, and Flanagan was reported to be suffering from the flu, which may have hurt him a bit. An infection treated Étienne Desmarteau, however, much more severely. Within a year, he was dead of typhoid fever.

1.	Étienne Desmarteau	CAN	34-4	(10.46)
2.	John Flanagan	USA	33-4	(10.16)[58]
3.	James Mitchel	USA	33-3	(10.13)
4.	Charles Hennemann	USA	30-1½	(9.18)
5.	Charles Chadwick	USA		
6.	Ralph Rose	USA[59]	(ca28-0)	(8.53est)

All-Around Championship

A: 7[60]; C: 2; D: 4 July; F: Ten events all held in one day. Scoring by specialized point tables.

The all-around was the early forerunner of the decathlon and consisted of ten events held in one day as follows: 100 yards, shot put, high jump, 880 yards, hammer throw, pole vault, 120 yard hurdles, 56 lb. weight throw, long jump, and one mile run. Scoring was by point tables, but since in the sprints, times were only taken for the winner, the points for the others in the 100 and high hurdles were derived by estimating the distance they were behind the winner. For each foot behind the winner, seven points were deducted from the winner's score in the 100, and five points in the hurdles. The event was held in July, as part of the gymnastics championships, rather than with the other track & field events.

This was expected to be a battle between the Irish champion, Tom Kiely, and the two-time U.S. champions, Ellery Clark and Adam Gunn. But Clark was ill his entire stay in St. Louis and he fell behind early before dropping out. Kiely was fifth after four events, but then his great strength in the weight throws pulled him into the lead after the eighth event and he held on to win.

1.	Thomas Kiely	IRL	6,036
2.	Adam Gunn	USA	5,907
3.	Truxtun Hare	USA	5,813
4.	John Holloway	IRL[61]	5,273
5.	Ellery Clark	USA	2,778[62]
6.	John Grieb	USA	2,199
AC.	Max Emmerich	USA	DNF

EVENT SUMMARIES

100 Yards (91.44 meters)[63]

Heat 1

Truxtun Hare	10.8	790
John Holloway	@ 3 feet	769
Thomas Kiely	@ 11 feet	713

Heat 2

Ellery Clark	11.0	748
Adam Gunn	@ 4 feet	720
John Grieb	@ 4 feet	720
Max Emmerich	DNF	WD

Shot Put

Adam Gunn	40-1	(12.21)	668	1,388	[2]
Truxtun Hare	39-8	(12.09)	648	1,438	[1]
Thomas Kiely	35-6	(10.82)	448	1,161	[3]
John Grieb	34-7	(10.54)	404	1,124	[4]
Ellery Clark	33-8	(10.26)	360	1,108	[5]
John Holloway	32-10	(10.01)	320	1,089	[6]

High Jump

John Holloway	5-6	(1.68)	672	1,761	[3]
Adam Gunn	5-5	(1.65)	640	2,028	[1]
John Grieb	5-4	(1.62)	608	1,732	[4]
Ellery Clark	5-4	(1.62)	608	1,716	[5]
Thomas Kiely	5-0	(1.52)	480	1,641	[6]
Truxtun Hare	5-0	(1.52)	480	1,918	[2]

880 Yard (804.67 Meters) Walk

Thomas Kiely	3:59.0		717	2,358	[5]
John Holloway	3:59.0		717	2,478	[3]
Ellery Clark	4:11.0		657	2,373	[4]
Adam Gunn	4:13.0		647	2,675	[1]
Truxtun Hare	4:20.0		612	2,530	[2]
John Grieb	4:49.0		467	2,199	[6]

Hammer Throw

Thomas Kiely	120-7	(36.76)	706	3,064	[3]
Truxtun Hare	119-0	(36.28)	687	3,217	[1]
Adam Gunn	103-0	(31.40)	495	3,170	[2]
Ellery Clark	95-6	(29.11)	405	2,778	[5]
John Holloway	90-3	(27.51)	342	2,820	[4]
John Grieb	No mark		0	2,199	[6]

Pole Vault

Adam Gunn	9-9	(2.97)	616	3,786	[1]
John Holloway	9-6	(2.89)	568	3,388	[4]
Thomas Kiely	9-0	(2.74)	472	3,536	[2]
Truxtun Hare	8-0	(2.44)	280	3,497	[3]
Ellery Clark	No mark — withdrew		0	2,778	[5]
John Grieb	No mark — withdrew		0	2,199	[6]

120 Yard (109.73 Meters) High Hurdles

Thomas Kiely	17.8	670	4,206	[2]
Adam Gunn	@ 3 feet	655	4,441	[1]
Truxtun Hare	@ 14 feet	600	4,097	[3]
John Holloway	@ 16 feet	590	3,978	[4]

56-lb. Weight Throw

Thomas Kiely	29-3	(8.91)	684	4,890	[1]
Truxtun Hare	24-10¾	(7.59)	475	4,572	[3]
Adam Gunn	23-8½	(7.22)	418	4,859	[2]
John Holloway	19-7½	(5.98)	222	4,200	[4]

Broad Jump

Truxtun Hare	19-11	(6.07)	652	5,224	[3]
Thomas Kiely	19-6	(5.94)	612	5,502	[1]

Adam Gunn	18-2	(5.53)	484	5,343	[2]
John Holloway	18-2	(5.53)	484	4,684	[4]

One Mile (1,609.34 Meters)

Truxtun Hare	5:40.0	589	5,813	[3]
John Holloway	5:40.0	589	5,273	[4]
Adam Gunn	5:45.0	564	5,907	[2]
Thomas Kiely	5:51.0	534	6,036	[1]

NON-OLYMPIC EVENTS

60 Yards, Handicap

A: ?; C: ?; D: 3 September.

Final A: ?; C: ?; D: 3 September.

1.	Culver L. Halstedt	USA	6.2	(off 4 ft.)
2.	E. F. Annis	USA		(off 4 ft.)
3.	Fred Englehardt	USA		(off 7 ft.)

Heats A: ?; C: ?; D: 3 September.

Heat 1 A: ?; C: ?.

1.	Fred Englehardt	USA	6.6	(off 7 ft.)
2.	Fred Heckwolf	USA		(off 3 ft.)

Heat 2 A: ?; C: ?.

1.	Will C. Blome	USA	6.8	(off 5 ft.)
2.	Culver L. Halstedt	USA		(off 4 ft.)

Heat 3 A: ?; C: ?.

1.	E. F. Annis	USA	6.6	(off 4 ft.)
2.	Ollie F. Snedigar	USA		(off 3 ft.)

100 Yards, Handicap

A: ?; C: 4; D: 31 August.

Final A: 5; C: 2; D: 31 August.

1.	Culver L. Halstedt	USA	10.4	(off 4 yds.)
2.	Charles H. Turner	USA		(off 2 yds.)
3.	James D. McGann	USA		(off 4 yds.)
4.	Béla de Mező	HUN		()
5.	Will C. Blome	USA		(off 2 yds.)

Semi-Final A: ?; C: ?; D: 31 August; F: Runners-up in heats competed in the semi-final, with the winner advancing to the final.

Heat 1 A: 4; C: 3.

1.	Béla de Mező	HUN	10.6	
AC.	Corrie H. Gardner	AUS		
	Robert G. Kerr	CAN		
	J. T. Nehman	CAN		

Heats A: ?; C: ?; D: 31 August.

Heat 1 A: ?; C: ?.

1.	Culver L. Halstedt	USA	10.6	(off 4 yds.)
2.	Béla de Mező	HUN		

Heat 2 A: ?; C: ?.

1.	Will C. Blome	USA	10.6	(off 2 yds.)
2.	Corrie H. Gardner	AUS		(off 6 yds.)

Heat 3 A: ?; C: ?.

1.	James D. McGann	USA	10.6	(off 4 yds.)
2.	Robert G. Kerr	CAN		(scratch)

Heat 4 A: ?; C: ?.

1.	Charles H. Turner	USA	10.6	(off 2 yds.)
2.	J. T. Nehman	CAN		(off 4 yds.)

220 Yards, Handicap

A: ?; C: ?; D: 1 September.

1.	James D. McGann	USA	22.8	(off 10 yds.)
2.	J. T. Lukeman	CAN		(off 10 yds.)
3.	Charles H. Turner	USA		(off 2 yds.)

440 Yards, Handicap

A: ?; C: ?; D: 3 September.

1.	Frank O. Darcy	USA	50.8	(off 12 yds.)
2.	George Underwood	USA		(scratch)
3.	John B. Peck	CAN		(off 6 yds.)

880 Yards, Handicap

A: 10; C: ?; D: 29 August.

1.	John Runge	GER	1:58.6	(off 10 yds.)
2.	John B. Peck	CAN	at 5 yds.	(scratch)
3.	F. C. Roth	USA		(off 15 yds.)
4.	A. J. Betchestobill	USA		(off 50 yds.)

One Mile, Handicap

A: ?; C: ?; D: 31 August.

1.	John J. Daly	GBR/IRL	4:27.4	(off 20 yds.)
2.	David C. Munson	USA		(off 15 yds.)
3.	Peter Deer	CAN		(off 20 yds.)

One Mile Team Race, Handicap

A: ?; C: ?; D: 3 September.

1.	Missouri AC	USA	3:52.2	(scratch)
	(Paul H. Behrens, Joseph S. Fleming, Harry J. Kiener)			
2.	St. Louis Turnverein	USA		(off 80 yds.)
	(A. W. Solomon, Culver L. Halstedt, F. G. Quinn)			

120 Yard Hurdles, Handicap

A: ?; C: ?; D: 29 August.

Final A: 4; C: 2; D: 29 August.

1.	Lesley Ashburner	USA	15.8	(off 4 yds.)
2.	Frederick W. Schule	USA		(scratch)
3.	Thaddeus R. Shideler	USA		(scratch)
4.	Corrie H. Gardner	AUS		(off 4 yds.)

Semi-Finals A: ?; C: ?; D: 29 August.

Heat 1 A: ?; C: ?.

1.	Thaddeus R. Shideler	USA	16.4	(scratch)
2.	Corrie H. Gardner	AUS		(off 4 yds.)

Heat 2 A: ?; C: ?.

1.	Lesley Ashburner	USA	15.8	(off 4 yds.)
2.	Frederick W. Schule	USA		(scratch)

220 Yard Hurdles, Handicap

A: 3; C: 1; D: 1 September.

1.	L. G. Sykes	USA	27.2	(off 10 yds.)
2.	William H. McGann	USA		(off 6 yds.)
3.	E. J. Saddington	USA		(scratch)

High Jump, Handicap

A: ?; C: ?; D: 31 August.

1.	Ervin J. Barker	USA	6-2½	(off 0-4½)
2.	Lajos Gönczy	HUN	6-2	(off 0-3)
3.	Emil Freymark	USA	6-2	(off 0-4)
AC.	Paul Weinstein	GER		(off 0-2½)
	Samuel S. Jones	USA	6-0	(scratch)

Pole Vault, Handicap

A: 6; C: 3; D: 31 August.

1.	Leroy Samse	USA	11-10	(off 0-1)
2.	Walter R. Dray	USA	11-10	(off 0-10)
3.	Claude Allen	USA	11-9	(off 0-7)
4.	Paul Weinstein	GER		(off 0-8)
AC.	William Hapenny	CAN		(off 0-4)
	Ward McLanahan	USA	11-0	(scratch)

Broad Jump, Handicap

A: ?; C: ?; D: 29 August.

1.	Fred Englehardt	USA	22-5½
2.	George Van Cleaf	USA	21-6½
3.	J. Percival Hagerman	USA	21-6½
4.	Ervin J. Barker	USA	20-5½

Shot Put, Handicap

A: ?; C: ?; D: 29 August.

1.	W. Wesley Coe	USA	45-4	(scratch)
2.	Lawrence Feuerbach	USA	44-8½	(off 2-0)
3.	Martin Sheridan	USA	44-8½	(off 3-0)
4.	John J. Guiney	USA	43-8½	(off 4-0)

Discus Throw, Handicap

A: ?; C: ?; D: 1 September.

1.	Martin Sheridan	USA	132-0	(scratch)
2.	John J. Flanagan	USA	129-11	(off 6-0)
3.	John A. Biller	USA	128-3	(off 24-0)
4.	James S. Mitchel	USA	119-2	(off 10-0)

Hammer Throw, Handicap

A: 3; C: 1; D: 3 September.

1.	John J. Flanagan	USA	153-4	(scratch)
2.	Albert A. Johnson	USA	151-7	(off 30-0)
3.	James S. Mitchel	USA	151-6½	(off 23-0)

56-lb. Weight Throw, Handicap

A: ?; C: ?; D: 1 September.

1.	Albert A. Johnson	USA	36-8	(off 11-0)
2.	Charles Chadwick	USA	36-0	(off 8-0)
3.	L. E. Heyden	USA	35-11¾	(off 10-0)
4.	Étienne Desmarteau	CAN	34-10¾	(scratch)

NON-OLYMPIC MEETS

Olympic Interscholastic Meet
(State of Missouri) D: 14 May 1904

100 Yards

1.	Frank M. Mason	Central High School	10.8
2.	Keenan Shock	Central High School	
3.	B. R. Orr	Central High School	
4.	Grable Weber	Central High School	

Heat 1

1.	B. R. Orr	Central High School	11.0
2.	Grable Weber	Central High School	
3.	Earl Fraser	Christian Brothers College	

Heat 2

1.	Frank M. Mason	Central High School	11.0

2.	Richard Murray	St. Louis University	
3.	H. Smith	Smith Academy	

Heat 3

1.	Keenan Shock	Central High School	10.8
2.	F. Martinez	Christian Brothers College	

220 Yards

1.	Keenan Shock	Smith Academy	24.6
2.	B. R. Orr	St. Joseph High School	
3.	Earl Fraser	Christian Brothers College	
4.	A. Porselius	St. Joseph High School	

440 Yards

1.	Eugene Tittman	Central High School	55.4
2.	Peter J. Ratican	Christian Brothers College	
3.	Oliver G. Heimbucher	Manual Training School	
4.	R. P. Waters	St. Joseph High School	

880 Yards

1.	Oscar O'Connell	Central High School	2:08.0
2.	Milton A. Hellman	Smith Academy	
3.	R. Culbertson	Central High School	
4.	H. Bohn	St. Louis University	

One Mile

1.	Oscar O'Connell	Central High School	4:58.4
2.	Robert Potts	St. Joseph High School	
3.	James Duncan	Central High School	
4.	R. Robinson	Central High School	

120 Yard Hurdles

1.	Hugh Fullerton	Central High School	20.6
2.	Frank O'Brien	St. Joseph High School	
3.	Irving Labeaume	Smith Academy	
4.	Walter Sigmund	Smith Academy	

220 Yards Hurdles

1.	H. Smith	Smith Academy	29.2
2.	Earle Smith	Central High School	
3.	David White	Smith Academy	
4.	Frank M. Mason	Central High School	

4 × 440 Yard Relay

1. Central High School   3:54.6
   (Eugene Salisbury, Eugene Tittman, Harry Castlen, Frank M. Mason)
2. Smith Academy
   (Gerald Lambert, Milton A. Hellman, Skinner, R. Rutter)
3. St. Joseph High School
   (R. P. Waters, J. Brednus, A. Porselius, Breckinridge)

High Jump

1.	Frank Bader	Central High School	5-4
2.	Hugh Fullerton	Central High School	5-2
3.	Gerald Lambert	Smith Academy	5-2
4.	E. C. Rogers	St. Joseph High School	5-0

Broad Jump

1.	Frank Bader	Central High School	20-7
2.	Gerald Lambert	Smith Academy	19-9½
3.	Frank M. Mason	Central High School	19-6
4.	Earle Smith	Central High School	19-0

Pole Vault

1.	Gerald Lambert	Smith Academy	10-8
2.	E. C. Rogers	St. Joseph High School	10-6
3.	Paul J. Wall	Central High School	10-4
4.	Eugene Salisbury	Central High School	10-4

Shot Put (12-lb.)

1.	David Lamb	Central High School	36-5
2.	William Silliard	Central High School	36-3½
3.	Edward A. Stanard	Smith Academy	35-9
4.	William H. Burg	Smith Academy	32-8

Discus Throw

1.	David Lamb	Central High School	83-6
2.	Frank Bader	Central High School	83-4½
3.	William H. Burg	Smith Academy	81-1
4.	B. R. Orr	St. Joseph High School	77-5

Hammer Throw (12-lb.)

1.	Edward A. Stanard	Smith Academy	140-5½
2.	David Lamb	Central High School	129-4¼

3.	Fred Bock	Central High School	106-9½
4.	A. C. Priebe	St. Joseph High School	106-7

Team Championship

1.	Central High School	65½
2.	Smith Academy	44½
3.	St. Joseph High School	33
4.	Christian Brothers College	5
5.	Manual Training School	2
=6.	St. Louis University	1
	McKinley High School	1

Olympic Open Handicap Meeting

D: 21 May 1904

100 Yards

1.	Culver L. Halstedt (2½ yd)	Christian Brothers College	10.2
2.	Fred Heckwolf (scr)	Missouri Athletic Club	
3.	H. K. Tootle (scr)	Washington University	
4.	Charles H. Turner (1 yd)	St. Louis AAA	

Heat 1

1.	Charles H. Turner (1 yd)	St. Louis AAA	10.2
2.	H. K. Tootle (scr)	Washington University	

Heat 2

1.	Gwynne Evans (1 yd)	Missouri Athletic Club	10.4
2.	C. Glassner (scr)	St. Louis AAA	

Heat 3

1.	Fred Heckwolf (scr)	Missouri Athletic Club	10.0
2.	Paul Behrens (2½ yd)	Christian Brothers College	

Heat 4

1.	Culver L. Halstedt (2½ yd)	Christian Brothers College	10.6
2.	A. E. Garcia (6 yd)	St. Louis YMCA	

220 Yards

1.	H. K. Tootle (scr)	Washington University	23.2
2.	Charles H. Turner (scr)	St. Louis AAA	
3.	Culver L. Halstedt (4 yd)	Christian Brothers College	

Heat 1

1.	Culver L. Halstedt (4 yd)	Christian Brothers College	
2.	H. K. Tootle (scr)	Washington University	

Heat 2

1.   Charles H. Turner (scr)   St. Louis AAA
2.   Fred Heckwolf (scr)   Missouri Athletic Club

440 Yards

1.   L. E. Cornelius (6 yd)   Central YMCA   51.0
2.   Paul H. Behrens (scr)   Christian Brothers College
3.   A. W. Solomon (18 yd)   Missouri Athletic Club

880 Yards

1.   Harry J. Kiener (scr)   Missouri Athletic Club   2:05.0
2.   F. B. Fauntleroy (40 yd)   Missouri Athletic Club
3.   G. H. Boyer (1 yd)   Central YMCA

2-Mile Run

1.   Joseph A. Forshaw (80 yd)   Missouri Athletic Club   10:24.6
2.   W. Cavanaugh (120 yd)   Central YMCA
3.   Dan J. Weir (scr)   1st Regiment
      –– Grancer (20 yd)   West St. Louis Turnverein   DNF

120 Yard Hurdles

1.   L. G. Blackmere (scr)   Missouri Athletic Club   16.8
2.   Walter Sigmund (8 yd)   Smith Academy
3.   M. S. Shaw (4 yd)   Missouri Athletic Club

220 Yard Hurdles

1.   Dan Dillon (2 yd)   St. Louis University   26.8
2.   H. Smith (4 yd)   Smith Academy
3.   Walter Sigmund (15 yd)   Smith Academy

High Jump

1.   Gwynne Evans (1")   Missouri Athletic Club   5-9½
2.   G. D. Mattis (4½")   Missouri Athletic Club   5-7
3.   L. G. Blackmere (scr)   Missouri Athletic Club   5-5½

Pole Vault

1.   Paul H. Behrens (3")   Christian Brothers College   10-6½
2.   Dan Dillon (2")   St. Louis University   10-5½
3.   M. S. Shaw (scr)   Missouri Athletic Club   9-9

Broad Jump

1.	George H. Stadel (16")	Missouri Athletic Club	21-5½
2.	Culver L. Halstedt (7")	Christian Brothers College	21-4½
3.	Roy Gray (14")	St. Louis YMCA	20-6

Shot Put (16-lb.)

1.	Fred C. Warmboldt (scr)	Missouri Athletic Club	38-7½
2.	F. T. Bokern (36")	St. Louis Turnverein	36-10½
3.	W. Newman (24")	St. Louis University	35-10½

Discus Throw

1.	W. Newman (scr)	Missouri Athletic Club	95-8
2.	Edward A. Stanard (scr)	Smith Academy	93-9½
3.	A. B. Birge (scr)	Missouri Athletic Club	91-10¼

Hammer Throw (16-lb.)

1.	A. B. Birge (6 ft)	Missouri Athletic Club	125-7
2.	J. J. Sweeney (9 ft)	Christian Brothers College	118-6
3.	Edward A. Stanard (scr)	Smith Academy	106-5

Team Championship

1.	Missouri Athletic Club	52
2.	Christian Brothers College	20
3.	Washington University	10
4.	Central YMCA, St. Louis	10
5.	Smith Academy	9
6.	North St. Louis Turnverein	5
7.	St. Louis AAA	4
8.	St. Louis Turnverein	3
9.	St. Louis University	3
10.	1st Regiment	1

Olympic Athletic Meet for Schools in Louisiana Purchase Exposition Territory

D: 28 May 1904

100 Yards

1.	Frank M. Mason	Central High School	10.8
2.	Richard Murray	St. Louis University	
3.	Keenan Shock	Smith Academy	

Heat 1

1.	Keenan Shock	Smith Academy	11.0
2.	Richard Murray	St. Louis University	

Heat 2

1.	Frank M. Mason	Central High School	11.0
2.	R. Rutter	Smith Academy	

Heat 3

1.	Milton A. Hellman	Smith Academy	11.4
2.	F. Baylor		

220 Yards

1.	Grable Weber	Central High School	23.8
2.	Richard Murray	St. Louis University	
3.	R. Rutter	Smith Academy	

440 Yards

1.	Eugene Tittman	Central High School	54.0
2.	Keenan Shock	Smith Academy	
3.	Oliver G. Heimbucher	Manual Training School	

880 Yards

1.	Oscar O'Connell	Central High School	2:06.8
2.	Milton A. Hellman	Smith Academy	
3.	John E. Weinal	Manual Training School	

One Mile

1.	Oscar O'Connell	Central High School	4:58.6
2.	Edward Robinson	Central High School	
3.	James Duncan	Central High School	

120 Yard Hurdles

1.	Eugene Salisbury	Central High School	17.0
2.	Hugh Fullerton	Central High School	
3.	Walter Sigmund	Smith Academy	

220 Yard Hurdles

1.	Frank M. Mason	Central High School	27.0
2.	David White	Smith Academy	
3.	William Prosser	Smith Academy	

4 × 440 Yard Relay

1.	Manual Training School		3:53.4
2.	Central High School		
3.	Smith Academy		

High Jump

1.	Edward Mitchell	Central High School	5-2¼
2.	Hugh Fullerton	Central High School	5-1¼
3.	Robert Lamkin	Manual Training School	5-0¼

Pole Vault

1.	Gerald Lambert	Smith Academy	9-0
2.	Paul J. Wall	Central High School	8-10½
3.	Omar Langenberg	Central High School	8-0

Broad Jump

1.	Gerald Lambert	Smith Academy	19-4
2.	Grable Weber	Central High School	19-0½
3.	William Prosser	Smith Academy	17-3¾

Shot Put (12-lb.)

1.	William Lillard	Central High School	39-1
2.	David Lamb	Central High School	36-7¼
3.	William H. Burg	Smith Academy	34-7

Discus Throw

1.	Ludwig C. Collins	Lincoln High School	90-4½
2.	Edward A. Stanard	Smith Academy	88+
3.	David Lamb	Central High School	78+

Team Championship

1.	Central High School	67
2.	Smith Academy	31
3.	Lincoln High School	10
4.	Manual Training School	8
5.	St. Louis University	6

Olympic Elementary School Championship (St. Louis)

D: 30 May 1904.
For Boys Over 13 Years.

100 Yards

1.	A. Eilers	Garfield School	12.0
2.	E. Franquemont	Stoddard School	
3.	Roy Gray	Washington School	

220 Yards

1.	E. Franquemont	Stoddard School	27.6
2.	W. Haydock	Arlington School	
3.	W. Drack	Garfield School	

440 Yards

1.	E. Franquemont	Stoddard School	1:07.0
2.	W. Haydock	Arlington School	
3.	E. Hunter	Wyman School	

Relay Race

1.	Garfield School	1:59.8
2.	Clinton	

High Jump

1.	A. Eilers	Garfield School	4-4
2.	E. Wintermann	Sherman School	
3.	R. Newman	Charles School	

Broad Jump

1.	A. Eilers	Garfield School	13-10¼
2.	E. Wintermann	Sherman School	
3.	T. Duby	Marshall School	

Shot Put (12-lb.)

1.	A. Eilers	Garfield School	29-6½
2.	E. Mack	Stoddard School	
3.	E. Wintermann	Sherman School	

Boys Under 13 Years.

50 Yards

1.	R. Sauerbrunn	Emerson School	7.0
2.	E. Krutzsch	Sherman School	
3.	E. Kindervater	Clinton School	

100 Yards

1.	E. Illisen	Hodgen School	13.2
2.	R. Sauerbrunn	Emerson School	
3.	F. Mulrooney	Divoll School	

220 Yards

1.	H. Hunter	Crow School	31.8
2.	J. Turner	Marquette School	
3.	B. Wagoner	Eugene Field School	

High Jump

1.	R. Van Dach	Charles School	3-10
2.	N. Coleman	Hodgen School	

Team Championship

1.	Garfield School	26
2.	Stoddard School	16
3.	Sherman School	10
=4.	Emerson School	8
	Hodgens School	8
=6.	Charles School	6
	Arlington School	6
8.	Crow School	5
9.	Clinton School	4
10.	Marquette School	3
=11.	Marshall School	1
	Wyman School	1
	Washington School	1
	Divoll School	1
	Eugene Field School	1

AAU Handicap Meet

D: 2 June 1904.

100 Yards

1.	Joseph McGowan	Bethlehem Prep School	10.2
2.	J. J. Danaher	Xavier Athletic Association	
3.	Chester E. Peabody	New West Side Athletic Club	

220 Yards

1.	Joseph McGowan	Bethlehem Prep. School	22.2
2.	W. D. Randall	Maryland Athletic Club	
3.	Paul H. Behrens	Christian Brothers College	

880 Yards

1.	F. A. Rodgers	Mott Haven Athletic Club	1:57.0
2.	H. Lamble	Westminster, Pa.	
3.	Frank Hanlon	Mohawk Athletic Club	

One Mile

1.	W. Hall	Washington University	4:34.8
2.	L. H. Burkhardt	Young People's Association	
3.	Edward P. Carr	Xavier Athletic Association	

Two Miles

1.	Robert Todd	New West Side Athletic Club	10:04.2
2.	J. M. Lonergan	National Athletic Club	
3.	Joseph A. Forshaw	Missouri Athletic Club	

120 Yard Hurdles

1.	Seth P. Smith	Washington University	
2.	J. E. Gerity	Pastime Athletic Club	
3.	L. G. Blackmere	Missouri Athletic Club	

220 Yard Hurdles

1.	J. S. Hill	Maryland Athletic Club	25.2
2.	Seth P. Smith	Washington University	
3.	Dan Dillon	St. Louis University	

High Jump

1.	J. J. Ryan	St. Bartholomew Athletic Club	5-8
2.	Frank Olmstead	Temple Prep. School	
3.	J. W. Price	St. George Athletic Club	

Pole Vault

1.	Dan Dillon	St. Louis University	8-6
2.	Gwynne Evans	Missouri Athletic Club	
3.	R. C. Williams	Washington University	

Broad Jump

1.	J. S. Hill	Maryland Athletic Club	22-0
2.	R. L. Williams	Washington University	
3.	Seth P. Smith	Washington University	

Shot Put (16-lb.)

1.	Fred C. Warmboldt	North St. Louis Turnverein	39-8½
2.	Hans Wulff	Missouri University	
3.	F. T. Bokern	St. Louis Turnverein	

Discus Throw

1.	John Hines	Star Athletic Club	98-4¾
2.	J. E. Landon	Missouri University	
3.	J. J. Ryan	St. Bartholomew Athletic Club	

Hammer Throw

1.	Alfred D. Plaw	Pacific Athletic Club	158-6½
2.	W. H. Williams	Iowa State University	
3.	Jack E. Cannon	Missouri University	

56-lb. Weight Throw

1.	W. H. Williams	Iowa State University	26-11
2.	John Hines	Star Athletic Club	
3.	L. L. Hayden	Maryland Athletic Club	

Team Championship

1.	Washington University	18
2.	Maryland Athletic Club	14
3.	Bethlehem Prep. School	10
=4.	Iowa State University	8
	Star Athletic Club	8
6.	Missouri University	7
=7.	New West Side Athletic Club	6
	St. Louis University	6
	St. Bartholomew Athletic Club	6
=10.	Mott Haven Athletic Club	5
	Missouri Athletic Club	5
	North St. Louis Turnverein	5
	Pacific Athletic Association	5
14.	Xavier Athletic Association	4
=15.	Westminister, Pa.	3
	Pastime Athletic Club	3
	Young People's Association	3
	National Athletic Club	3
	Temple Prep. School	3
=20.	Mohawk Athletic Club	1
	Christian Brothers College	1
	St. George's Athletic Club	1
	St. Louis Turnverein	1

AAU Junior Championships

D: 3 June 1904

100 Yards

1.	William Hogenson	Chicago Athletic Association	10.2
2.	Ollie F. Snedigar	Pacific Athletic Club	
3.	William Eaton	Cambridgeport Gymnasium	

220 Yards

1.	William Knakel	GNYIAA	22.8
2.	J. Walz	GNYIAA	
3.	E. F. Larson	Chicago Central YMCA	

440 Yards

1.	D. H. Meyer	Buffalo 74th Regt	51.0
2.	J. McGucken	Bethlehem (Pa.) Prep. School	
3.	L. E. Cornelius	St. Louis YMCA	

880 Yards

1.	George Shipley	Chicago Athletic Association	2:06.2
2.	Henry Christoffers	St. George Athletic Club	
3.	J. A. Taylor	GNYIAA	

One Mile

1.	H. J. Buehler	Chicago Central YMCA	4:39.4
2.	Harvey Cohn	GNYIAA	
3.	A. Rose	Chicago Athletic Association	

Two Miles

1.	C. C. Naismith	GNYIAA	10:17.8
2.	Robert Todd	New Westside Athletic Club	
3.	A. H. Haigh	Chicago Central YMCA	

Five Miles

1.	Edward P. Carr	Xavier Athletic Association	29:58.8
2.	J. M. Lonergan	National Athletic Club	
3.	F. P. Devlin	Mott Haven Athletic Club	

120 Yard Hurdles

1.	Frank R. Castleman	GNYIAA	17.2
2.	J. E. Gerity	Pastime Athletic Club	
3.	Seth P. Smith	Washington University	

220 Yard Hurdles

1.	J. S. Hill	Missouri Athletic Club	27.4
2.	Seth P. Smith	Washington University	
3.	Dan Dillon	St. Louis University	

High Jump

1.	Channing Hall	Pacific AA	5-6½
2.	Frank Olmstead	TPS	
3.	J. W. Price	St. Georges AC	

Pole Vault

1.	Charles S. Jacobs	Chicago Central YMCA	10-1
2.	R. G. Rennacker	Chicago Central YMCA	10-1

Broad Jump

1.	Seth P. Smith	Washington University	20-1¼
2.	E. L. Greene	GNYIAA	19-7¼
3.	E. Clark	Kansas City YMCA	18-8½

Shot Put

1.	John J. Ray	St. Bartholmew AC	38-2
2.	Carl Van Duyne	GNYIAA	37-3
3.	John J. Schommer	Central YMCA	37-1

Discus Throw

1.	C. S. Rodman	Illinois	122-10½
2.	Hans Wulff	Missouri	104-5
3.	W. H. Banks	Indiana	

Hammer Throw

1.	H. L. Thomas	Purdue	144-9
2.	W. H. Banks	Illinois	
3.	O. S. Fowler	Colorado	

56-lb. Weight Throw

1.	Patrick J. Walsh	Washington	19-11½
2.	J. E. Landon	Missouri	
3.	J. J. Sweeney	Christian Brothers College	

Team Championship

1.	Indiana	32
2.	Stanford	27

3.	Purdue	24
4.	Colorado	16
5.	Missouri	15
6.	Washington	14
7.	Illinois	6
8.	Christian Brothers College	1

AAU Championships

D: 4 June 1904

100 Yards

1.	William P. Hogensen	10.5[64]
2.	Ollie F. Snedigar	at 4 inches
3.	William D. Eaton	
4.	Lawson N. Robertson	
5.	Patrick Walsh	
6.	E. F. Annis	

Heat 1

1.	Lawson Robertson	10.4
2.	Patrick Walsh	
3.	William Hogensen	

Heat 2

1.	William Eaton	10.2
2.	Ollie F. Snedigar	
3.	E. F. Annis	

220 Yards Straightaway

1.	William Hogensen	22.8
2.	Lawson Robertson	at 4 yds
3.	William Knakel	at 1 ft

440 Yards

1.	D. H. Meyer	51.2
2.	Harry Hillman	
3.	Henry Christoffers	

880 Yards

1.	Howard Valentine	2:00.8
2.	Charles Bacon	
3.	Paul Pilgrim	

One Mile

1. David C. Munson   4:41.2
2. Harvey Cohn
3. Edward P. Carr

Two Miles

1. Alexander Grant   10:06.2
2. C. C. Naismith
3. George Bonhag

Five Miles

1. John Joyce   28:25.2
2. Daniel Frank
3. David C. Munson

120 Yard Hurdles

1. Frank R. Castleman   16.2
2. Lawrence Ketchum
3. Seth P. Smith

220 Yard Hurdles (Straightaway)

1. J. S. Hill   27.4
2. Seth P. Smith
3. Dan Dillon

High Jump

1. Samuel S. Jones   5-9
2. W. C. Lowe
3. Channing Hall

Pole Vault

1. H. Louis Gardner   10-5¼
2. Louis Wilkins   10-5¼
3. J. H. Williams   9-11¼

Broad Jump

1. Meyer Prinstein   22-4¾
2. Robert Stangland   21-3¼
3. Ollie F. Snedigar   21-1½

Shot Put

1.	Martin Sheridan	40-9½
2.	Alfred D. Plaw	39-4½
3.	Carl Van Duyne	38-1¼

Discus Throw

1.	Martin Sheridan	119-1½
2.	James S. Mitchel	
3.	Carl Van Duyne	

Hammer Throw

1.	Alfred D. Plaw	162-0
2.	John J. Flanagan	153-4
3.	Carl Van Duyne	152-6¼

56-lb. Weight Throw

1.	John J. Flanagan	35-9
2.	James S. Mitchel	34-0
3.	J. J. Hines	25-5

Team Championship

1.	GNYIAA	61
2.	New York AC	45
3.	Pastime AC (SF)	13
4.	Chicago AA	8
=5.	74th Regt (Buffalo)	5
=5.	Maryland AC	5

Olympic Collegiate Championships

D: 25 June 1904

100 Yards

1.	Victor S. Rice	Chicago	10.0
2.	H. E. Moon	Michigan Agricultural College	
3.	Frank R. Castleman	Colgate	
4.	Clyde A. Blair	Chicago	

220 Yards

1.	Victor S. Rice	Chicago	22.6
2.	H. E. Moon	Michigan Agricultural College	
3.	T. B. Taylor	Chicago	
4.	W. H. Heckersall	Chicago	

440 Yards

1.	John C. Atlee	Princeton	52.4
2.	T. B. Taylor	Chicago	
3.	G. E. Cochrane	Princeton	

880 Yards

1.	L. M. Adsit	Princeton	2:00.6
2.	R. E. Williams	Princeton	
3.	G. E. Cochrane	Princeton	
4.	S. B. Parkinson	Chicago	

One Mile

1.	R. E. Williams	Princeton	4:41.2
2.	G. M. Chaplin	Princeton	
3.	R. L. Henry	Chicago	
4.	S. A. Lyon	Chicago	

Two Miles

1.	John L. Eisel	Princeton	10:01.4
2.	W. G. Mathews	Chicago	
3.	G. M. Chaplin	Princeton	
4.	S. A. Lyon	Chicago	

120 Yard Hurdles

1.	M. S. Catlin	Chicago	15.6
2.	Frank R. Castleman	Colgate	
3.	Hugo M. Friend	Chicago	
4.	J. M. Carter	Princeton	

220 Yard Hurdles

1.	M. S. Catlin	Chicago	26.0
2.	J. M. Carter	Princeton	
3.	E. R. Ferris	Chicago	

High Jump

1.	M. B. Tooker	Princeton	5-6
2.	E. R. Ferris	Chicago	5-4

Pole Vault

1.	H. L. Moore	Princeton	11-9
2.	Norman E. Dole	Stanford	11-9

Broad Jump

1.	Hugo M. Friend	Chicago	22-6
2.	G. Fox	Princeton	21-4½
3.	C. F. Kennedy	Chicago	20-11⅜
4.	E. R. Ferris	Chicago	20-9¼

Shot Put

1.	John R. DeWitt	Princeton	43-4¼
2.	R. M. Maxwell	Chicago	42-2½
3.	G. C. Gale	Chicago	41-6
4.	F. A. --	Chicago	40-1

Discus Throw

1.	C. S. Rodman	Illinois	120-8
2.	M. S. Catlin	Chicago	117-3
3.	E. E. Parry	Chicago	116-4¾
4.	John R. DeWitt	Princeton	114-0

Hammer Throw

1.	John R. DeWitt	Princeton	161-0
2.	J. F. Tobin	Chicago	140-1
3.	R. M. Maxwell	Chicago	133-1
4.	E. E. Parry	Chicago	132-2

Team Championship

1.	University of Chicago	69
2.	Princeton University	60
3.	University of Illinois	6
4.	Michigan Agricultural College	6
5.	Colgate University	5

Olympic Interscholastic Handicap Meet

D: 29 June 1904

100 Yards

1.	Grable Weber	Central High School	10/8
2.	William M. Crysler	McKinley High School	
3.	Keenan Shock	Smith Academy	

220 Yards

1.	Grable Weber	Central High School	23.8
2.	William M. Crysler	McKinley High School	
3.	William P. Warmer	Blees Military Academy	

440 Yards

1.	Keenan Shock	Smith Academy	54.6
2.	C. Lewis	Manual Training School	
3.	Harry Castlen	Central High School	

880 Yards

1.	Mel Sheppard	Brown Prep. School	2:06.8
2.	Milton A. Hellman	Smith Academy	
3.	Alec Hay	Christian Brothers College	

One Mile

1.	Mel Sheppard	Brown Prep. School	4:43.4
2.	Oscar O'Connell	Central High School	
3.	Edward Robinson	Central High School	

120 Yard Hurdles

1.	Eugene Salisbury	Central High School	17.6
2.	Walter Sigmund	Smith Academy	
3.	W. Flunk	Central High School	

220 Yard Hurdles

1.	Frank M. Mason	Central High School	27.4
2.	David White	Smith Academy	
3.	Milton A. Hellman	Smith Academy	

High Jump

1.	Edward Mitchell	Central High School	5-3
2.	Milton A. Hellman	Smith Academy	
3.	Omar Langenberg	Central High School	

Pole Vault

1.	T. W. Crouch	Lawrenceville School (N.J.)	10-2
2.	Gerald Lambert	Smith Academy	
3.	Justin Kendrick	Smith Academy	

Broad Jump

1.	Earle Smith	Central High School	21-7
2.	Frank M. Mason	Central High School	
3.	Milton A. Hellman	Smith Academy	

Shot Put (12 lb.)

1.	R. Higgins	Christian Brothers College	42-1
2.	W. B. Williams	Central High School	
3.	Edward A. Stanard	Smith Academy	

Hammer Throw

1.	Edward A. Stanard	Smith Academy	127-3
2.	David Lamb	Central High School	
3.	Fred Bock	Central High School	

Interscholastic Championships

D: 30 June 1904

100 Yards

1.	Grable Weber	Central High School	11.2
2.	William P. Warmer	Blees Military Academy	
3.	Keenan Shock	Smith Academy	

220 Yards

1.	Grable Weber	Central High School	24.2
2.	William P. Warmer	Blees Military Academy	
3.	William M. Crysler	McKinley High School	

440 Yards

1.	Keenan Shock	Smith Academy	58.6
2.	C. Lewis	Manual Training School	
3.	Harry Castlen	Central High School	

880 Yards

1.	Mel Sheppard	Brown Prep.	2:10.0
2.	Oscar O'Connell	Central High School	
3.	R. Culbertson	Central High School	

One Mile

1.	Mel Sheppard	Brown Prep. School	4:47.2
2.	D. M. Warren	D. U. High School	
3.	Oscar O'Connell	Central High School	

120 Yard Hurdles

1.	Eugene Salisbury	Central High School	17.8
2.	Hugh Fullerton	Central High School	
3.	Walter Sigmund	Smith Academy	

220 Yard Hurdles

1.	Frank M. Mason	Central High School	28.0
2.	Earle Smith	Central High School	
3.	David White	Smith Academy	

Pole Vault

1.	A. Van Schrader	Georgetown Prep.	9-8
2.	T. W. Crouch	Lawrenceville (N.J.) School	
3.	J. Brednus	S. B. High School	

High Jump

1.	Edward Mitchell	Central High School	5-3
2.	Hugh Fullerton	Central High School	
3.	A. Van Schrader	Georgetown Prep. School	

Broad Jump

1.	William P. Warmer	Blees Military Academy	21-1
2.	Edward Robinson	Central High School	
3.	Frank M. Mason	Central High School	

Shot Put (12 lb.)

1.	R. Higgins	Central High School	38-8½
2.	J. Brednus	S. B. High School	
3.	Edward A. Stanard	Smith Academy	

Hammer Throw (12-lb.)

1.	Edward A. Stanard	Smith Academy	129-3½
2.	David Lamb	Central High School	
3.	J. Brednus	S. B. High School	

Team Championship

1.	St. Louis Central High School	47
2.	Smith Academy, St. Louis	14
3.	Blees Military Academy	11
4.	Brown Prep. School, Philad.	10
5.	Georgetown Prep.	6
=6.	Christian Brothers College	5
	S. B. High School	5
=8.	Manual Training School	3
	D. U. High School	3
	Lawrenceville (N.J.) School	3
11.	McKinley High School	1

Special Athletic Events

D: 2 July 1904

100 Yards

1.	Rufus Seay	Central YMCA	10.2
2.	Charles H. Turner	St. Louis AAA	
3.	Joseph P. Lydon	Central YMCA	

440 Yards

1.	Rufus Seay	Central YMCA	48.8
2.	Daniel A. Frank	St. Louis AAA	
3.	Joseph P. Lydon	Central YMCA	

880 Yards

1.	Mel Sheppard	Brown Prep. School	2:01.4
2.	Harry J. Kiener	Missouri Athletic Club	
3.	W. W. Minges	St. Louis AAA	

One Mile

1.	Joseph A. Forshaw	Missouri Athletic Club	4:41.6
2.	Walter Kavanaugh	Central YMCA	
3.	D. M. Warren		

120 Yard Hurdles

1.	L. G. Blackmere	Missouri Athletic Club	16.8
2.	John H. January	Christian Brothers College	
3.	Oscar B. Brockmeyer	Christian Brothers College	

Olympic Championships of the Public Schools Athletic League

D: 4–6 July 1904

Open to High School and Elementary School Boys under 19 and 15 years of age, respectively.

High School Events

50 Yards

1.	–– Jessup	New York	5.6
2.	–– Sherman	Boston	
3.	–– Wiley	San Francisco	
4.	–– Donnell	Los Angeles	

100 Yards

1.	–– Jessup	New York	10.8
2.	–– Donnell	Los Angeles	
3.	–– Hayes	Boston	
4.	–– Anderson	Boston	

220 Yards

1.	–– Jessup	New York	24.6
2.	Grable Weber	St. Louis	
3.	–– McAlpin	New York	
4.	–– Pfletschinger	New York	

440 Yards

1.	–– Quigley	Rushville (Ill.)	53.6
2.	–– Krischeldorf	New York	
3.	–– Dierrsen	Chicago	
4.	–– Severy	Pasadena (Cal.)	

880 Yards

1.	–– Comstock	Chicago	2:13.2
2.	–– Severy	Pasadena (Cal.)	
3.	–– Harder	New York	
4.	–– Herrmann	New York	

One Mile

1.	–– Farrell	Boston	4:57.6
2.	–– Stiles	Ventura (Cal.)	
3.	D. M. Warren	Chicago	
4.	–– Bonner	San Francisco	

High Jump

1.	-- Bronjes	Chicago	5-6
2.	-- Hotaling	Pasadena (Cal.)	
3.	-- Nelson	Chicago	

Broad Jump

1.	-- Bonner	San Francisco	20-9½
2.	-- Norton	Boston	
3.	-- Bronjes	Chicago	
4.	-- Smith	St. Louis	

Shot Put (12-lb.)

1.	-- Strom	New York	42-8¼
2.	-- Graham	Chicago	
3.	-- Fuller	Pomona (Cal.)	
4.	-- Norton	Boston	

4 × 440 Yard Relay

1.	New York (Krischeldorf, Fackner, Geis, McNulty)	3:36.0
2.	Chicago	
3.	Los Angeles	
4.	Boston team	

Elementary School Events

50 Yards

1.	-- Gluckman	New York	6.4
2.	W. Sholes	Los Angeles	
3.	-- Thomas	New York	
4.	E. Franquemont	St. Louis	

100 Yards

1.	-- Sholes	Los Angeles	11.6
2.	-- Crawford	New York	
3.	-- Held	New York	
4.	-- Witham	New York	

220 Yards

1.	-- Crawford	New York	25.4
2.	-- Perry	Chicago	
3.	-- Kaestner	New York	
4.	-- Bailey	Los Angeles	

4 × 220 Yard Relay

1.	Chicago	1:45.2
2.	New York	
3.	Los Angeles	
4.	Boston	

High Jump

1.	-- Johnson	Chicago	4-7
2.	-- Bressi	San Francisco	
3.	W. Sholes	Los Angeles	
4.	-- Williams	Chicago	

Broad Jump

1.	-- Kilbourne	Chicago	19-10
2.	-- Hansler	Pomona (Cal.)	
3.	-- Kaestner	New York	
4.	-- Gluckman	New York	

Shot Put (12-lb.)

1.	-- Gluckman	New York	36-7¼
2.	-- Lamorsaine	San Francisco	
3.	-- Heintz	New York	
4.	-- Wilson	Chicago	

Team Championship

1.	New York	95 (46 elementary/49 high school)
2.	Chicago	65
3.	Los Angeles	23
4.	San Francisco	21
5.	Boston	19
=6.	St. Louis	7
	Pasadena	7
=8.	Rushville	5
	Pomona	5
10.	Ventura	3

Olympic Irish Sports

D: 20 July 1904

100 Yards

1.	Charles H. Turner	St. Louis AAA	10/4
2.	Fred Heckwolf	Missouri Athletic Club	
3.	A. J. Huff	Central YMCA	

220 Yards

1.	Charles H. Turner	St. Louis AAA	23.0
2.	Fred Heckwolf	Missouri Athletic Club	
3.	Paul Behrens	Missouri Athletic Club	

880 Yards

1.	W. W. Minges	St. Louis AAA	2:12.0
2.	John E. Weinal	unattached	
3.	E. A. Grimley	Columbia	

One Mile

1.	Joseph A. Forshaw	Missouri Athletic Club	5:10.8
2.	S. W. Root	Princeton	
3.	W. W. Minges	St. Louis AAA	

120 Yard Hurdles

1.	Thomas F. Kiely	GNYIAA	17.2
2.	W. R. McCullough	Worcester Academy	
3.	John J. Holloway	GNYIAA	

High Jump

1.	Emil Freymark	North St. Louis Turnverein	5-8
2.	John J. Holloway	GNYIAA	5-7
3.	Z. R. Pettit	First Regiment AC	5-3

Broad Jump

1.	John J. Holloway	GNYIAA	20-10¾
2.	Thomas F. Kiely	GNYIAA	20-9¾
3.	Z. R. Pettit	unattached	20-3½

Two Hops and a Jump

1.	Thomas F. Kiely	GNYIAA	43-9
2.	John J. Holloway	GNYIAA	43-3
3.	Paul Behrens	Missouri Athletic Club	43-2½

Standing Triple Jump

1.	John J. Holloway	GNYIAA	29-9
2.	Paul H. Behrens	Missouri Athletic Club	29-8
3.	W. Fleming	Fenian AC (Chicago)	24-4

Shot Put (16-lb.)

1.	John J. Guiney	Missouri Athletic Club	38-6½
2.	Albert A. Johnson	Missouri Athletic Club	33-10½
3.	T. K. Barrett	St. Leo's Gymnasium (Baltimore)	33-7

Hammer Throw (16-lb.)

1.	Thomas F. Kiely	GNYIAA	139-0½
2.	Albert A. Johnson	Missouri Athletic Club	124-6
3.	W. P. Hurley	unattached	118-1

56-lb. Weight Throw

1.	Thomas F. Kiely	GNYIAA	29-6½
2.	T. K. Barrett	unattached	28-9
3.	Albert A. Johnson	Missouri Athletic Club	17-6

42-lb. Stone Throw

1.	Thomas F. Kiely	GNYIAA	23-8½
2.	John J. Holloway	GNYIAA	21-8
3.	T. K. Barrett	GNYIAA	21-6

Western AAU Handicap Meeting

D: 29 July 1904

100 Yards

1.	Joseph P. Lydon (7 yd)	Central YMCA	10.2
2.	Charles H. Turner (2 yd)	St. Louis AAA	
3.	Fred Heckwolf (2½ yd)	Missouri Athletic Club	
4.	–– Loveland (5 yd)	Denver Athletic Club	

Heat 1

1.	Fred Heckwolf (2½ yd)	Missouri Athletic Club	10.6
2.	–– Loveland (5 yd)	Denver Athletic Club	

Heat 2

1.	Charles H. Turner (2 yd)	St. Louis AAA	10.0
2.	Joseph P. Lydon (7 yd)		

220 Yards

1.	Charles H. Turner (2 yd)	St. Louis AAA	22.6
2.	Joseph P. Lydon (12 yd)	Central YMCA	
3.	A. J. Huff (12 yd)	Central YMCA	
4.	Culver L. Halstedt (6 yd)	Missouri Athletic Club	

Heat 1

1.	A. J. Huff (12 yd)	Central YMCA	23.2
2.	Charles H. Turner (2 yd)	St. Louis AAA	

Heat 2

1.	Joseph P. Lydon (12 yd)	Central YMCA	22.4
2.	Culver L. Halstedt (6 yd)	Missouri Athletic Club	

440 Yards

1.	Roy Gray (30 yd)	Central YMCA	51.2
2.	Joseph P. Lydon (36 yd)	1st Regiment	
3.	A. W. Solomon (34 yd)	Missouri Athletic Club	

880 Yards

1.	Milton A. Hellman (20 yd)	Missouri Athletic Club	2:07.0
2.	W. W. Minges (15 yd)	St. Louis AAA	
3.	F. B. Fauntleroy (35 yd)	Missouri Athletic Club	

One Mile

1.	J. J. Reuter (150 yd)	1st Regiment	4:38.8
2.	C. L. Dodd (60 yd)	Central YMCA	
3.	W. Hall (40 yd)	St. Louis AAA	

Two Miles

1.	Joseph A. Forshaw (100 yd)	Missouri Athletic Club	10:59.0
2.	Dan J. Weir (150 yd)	1st Regiment	
3.	Milton A. Hellman (100 yd)	Missouri Athletic Club	

High Jump

1.	Emil Freymark (scr)	Missouri Athletic Club	5-9½
2.	Gwynne Evans (2½")	Missouri Athletic Club	
3.	G. D. Mattis (4½")	Missouri Athletic Club	

Pole Vault

1.	Paul Behrens (7")	Missouri Athletic Club	10-1
2.	Gwynne Evans (9")	Missouri Athletic Club	
3.	R. Mills (2")	R. S. Turnverein	

Broad Jump

1.	Culver L. Halstedt (7")	Missouri Athletic Club	20-10
2.	G. D. Mattis (9")	Missouri Athletic Club	
3.	George H. Stadel (5")	St. Louis AAA	

Shot Put (16-lb.)

1.	John J. Guiney (scr)	Missouri Athletic Club	40-2
2.	F. T. Bokern (5-4)	St. Louis Turnverein	
3.	Hans Wulff (2-4)	Missouri Athletic Club	

Discus Throw

1.	Seth P. Smith (21 ft)	Missouri Athletic Club	117-0
2.	H. A. Weinecke (??)	unattached	
3.	Hans Wulff (??)	Missouri Athletic Club	

Hammer Throw (16-lb.)

1.	Hans Wulff (scr)	Missouri Athletic Club	124-10
2.	H. A. Weinecke (8 ft)	unattached	
3.	John J. Guiney (scr)	Missouri Athletic Club	

56-lb. Weight Throw

1.	H. A. Weinecke (scr)	unattached	24-10
2.	Hans Wulff (3 ft)	Missouri Athletic Club	
3.	F. T. Bokern (5-4)	St. Louis Turnverein	

Team Championship

1.	Missouri Athletic Club	60
2.	Central YMCA	17
3.	St. Louis AAA	13
4.	First Regt. Ath. Assoc.	11
5.	St. Louis Turnverein	2
6.	R. S. Turnverein	1

Western AAU Championship Meeting

D: 30 July 1904

100 Yards

1.	Fay R. Moulton	Kansas City Athletic Club	10.0
2.	Fred Heckwolf	Missouri Athletic Club	
3.	Charles H. Turner	St.Louis AAA	

220 Yards

1.	Fay R. Moulton	Kansas City Athletic Club	21.8
2.	Charles H. Turner	St. Louis AAA	
3.	Fred Heckwolf	Missouri Athletic Club	

440 Yards

1.	Paul H. Behrens	Missouri Athletic Club	51.8
2.	Joseph S. Fleming	Missouri Athletic Club	
3.	J. C. Darling	Univ. of Oklahoma	

880 Yards

1.	Harry J. Kiener	Missouri Athletic Club	2:03.4
2.	H. F. Cotton	Kansas City Athletic Club	
3.	W. W. Minges	St. Louis AAA	

One Mile

1.	B. Gallagher	Kansas City Athletic Club	4:40.4
2.	Jack E. Cannon	Kansas City Athletic Club	
3.	Joseph A. Forshaw	Missouri Athletic Club	

Two Miles

1.	B. Gallagher	Kansas City Athletic Club	10:35.0
2.	C. L. Dodd	Central YMCA	
3.	Jack E. Cannon	Kansas City Athletic Club	

120 Yard Hurdles

1.	Seth P. Smith	Missouri Athletic Club	16.8
2.	J. C. Masker	Kansas City Athletic Club	

220 Yard Hurdles

1.	Frank M. Mason	Missouri Athletic Club	26.8
2.	Seth P. Smith	Missouri Athletic Club	
3.	J. C. Darling	Univ. of Oklahoma	

High Jump

1.	Emil Freymark	Missouri Athletic Club	5-10
2.	W. A. McElroy	Kansas City Athletic Club	
3.	Gwynne Evans	Missouri Athletic Club	

Pole Vault

1.	W. A. McElroy	Kansas City Athletic Club	10-4
2.	Gwynne Evans	Missouri Athletic Club	
3.	Paul Behrens	Missouri Athletic Club	

Broad Jump

1.	Seth P. Smith	Missouri Athletic Club	20-8½
2.	George H. Stadel	St. Louis AAA	
3.	Roy Gray	Central YMCA	

Shot Put (16 lb.)

1.	John J. Guiney	Missouri Athletic Club	40-9½
2.	Hans Wulff	Missouri Athletic Club	
3.	E. B. Alexander	Kansas City Athletic Club	

Discus Throw

1.	Hans Wulff	Missouri Athletic Club	103-10
2.	Seth P. Smith	Missouri Athletic Club	
3.	E. B. Alexander	Kansas City Athletic Club	

Hammer Throw (16-lb.)

1.	Albert A. Johnson	Central YMCA	131-3½
2.	Hans Wulff	Missouri Athletic Club	
3.	E. B. Alexander	Kansas City Athletic Club	

56-lb. Weight Throw

1.	H. A. Weinecke	Central YMCA	24-4
2.	Albert A. Johnson	Central YMCA	
3.	Hans Wulff	Missouri Athletic Club	

Team Championship

1.	Missouri Athletic Club	65
2.	Kansas City Athletic Club	41½
3.	Central YMCA	12
4.	St. Louis AAA	8
5.	Univ. of Oklahoma	2

YMCA Team Pentathlon Championships

D: 17 August 1904; F: 100 yards; Hammer Throw; High Jump; Pole Vault; One Mile.

1.	Chicago Central YMCA	1,286.40
2.	Kenosha YMCA	824.20
3.	St. Louis Central YMCA	273.31

YMCA Handicap Track and Field Meet

D: 20 August

100 Yards

1.	William B. Hunter (2½ yd)	Louisville	10.4
2.	Joseph P. Lydon (7 yd)	Central Branch, St. Louis	
3.	E. Russell (7 yd)	Cincinnati	

220 Yards

1.	William B. Hunter (?)	Louisville	22.6
2.	Joseph P. Lydon (?)	Central Branch, St. Louis	
3.	George H. Queyrouze (?)	New Orleans	

440 Yards

1.	E. Russell (24 yd)	Cincinnati	52.2
2.	J. Hargrave (20 yd)	Cincinnati	
3.	A. L. Brown (16 yd)	Cincinnati	

880 Yards

1.	W. H. Brown (25 yd)	Cincinnati	2:03.2
2.	L. L. Bayley (35 yd)	New Orleans	
3.	H. L. Lamb (25 yd)	Central Branch, St. Louis	

One Mile

1.	J. Barclay (40 yd)	Cincinnati	4:48.0
2.	C. L. Dodd (90 yd)	Louisville	
3.	G. H. Boyer (90 yd)	Central Branch, St. Louis	

Two Miles

1.	J. Barclay (scr)	Cincinnati	15:25.0
2.	C. L. Dodd (scr)	Louisville	
3.	W. L. Martin (scr)	Lynchburg, Va.	

120 Yard Hurdles

1.	L. C. Bailey (scr)	Central Department, Chicago	16.4
2.	A. Sandow (3 yd)	Cincinnati	
3.	W. R. McCullough (scr)	Central Branch, St. Louis	

220 Yard Hurdles

1.	A. Sandow (4 yd)	Cincinnati	28.2
2.	W. R. McCullough (2 yd)	Central Branch, St. Louis	
3.	L. C. Bailey (scr)	Central Department, Chicago	

High Jump

1.	J. C. Talcot (2½")	Central Department, Buffalo	5-4½
2.	E. E. Utz (1½")	Central Department, Chicago	5-3½
3.	W. G. Wood (2")	Cincinnati	5-2

Pole Vault

1.	H. R. Gilbert (9")	Central Branch, St. Louis	8-3
2.	J. S. Brown (7")	Cincinnati	8-1
3.	A. Sandow (scr)	Cincinnati	8-0

Broad Jump

1.	William B. Hunter (scr)	Cincinnati	20-3
2.	H. E. Wallace (12")	Omaha	19-7
3.	J. G. B. McLaughlin (10")	Cincinnati	19-4½

Shot Put (16-lb.)

1.	Albert A. Johnson (scr)	Central Branch, St. Louis	33-9½
2.	W. G. Wood (6")	Cincinnati	33-4
3.	J. J. Greene (scr)	Central Department, Chicago	32-2½

Discus Throw

1.	Albert A. Johnson (scr)	Central Branch, St. Louis	96-3
2.	William B. Hunter (6 ft)	Louisville	93-0½
3.	H. G. Frantz (10 ft)	Cincinnati	91-8

Hammer Throw (16-lb.)

1.	H. G. Frantz (?)	Cincinnati	130-9½
2.	Albert A. Johnson (?)	Central Branch, St. Louis	127-10½
3.	W. G. Wood (?)	Cincinnati	105-3

YMCA Track and Field Championship

D: 20 August

100 Yards

1.	C. L. Parsons	Los Angeles	10.0
2.	Nathaniel Cartmell	Louisville	
3.	William B. Hunter	Louisville	

Heat 1

1.	Nathaniel Cartmell	Louisville	10.2
2.	C. L. Parsons	Los Angeles	
3.	E. F. Larson	Chicago	

Heat 2

1.	William B. Hunter	Louisville	10.2
2.	G. Waite	Buffalo	
3.	R. H. Albertson	Chicago	

220 Yards

1.	Nathaniel Cartmell	Louisville	22.0
2.	C. L. Parsons	Los Angeles	
3.	William B. Hunter	Louisville	

440 Yards

1.	Harry C. Dane	St. Louis Central	52.8
2.	L. H. Powell	Chicago Central	
3.	L. E. Cornelius	St. Louis Central	

880 Yards

1.	W. A. Brown	Cincinnati	2:04.2
2.	L. H. Powell	Chicago Central	at 15 yds
3.	Richard L. Sandford	Brooklyn Central	
4.	F. Milhouse	St. Louis	

One Mile

1.	H. J. Buehler	Chicago Central	4:38.8
2.	E. Raum	Cincinnati	
3.	H. Monroe	New Orleans	

Two Miles

1.	A. H. Haigh	Chicago Central	10:19.6
2.	A. E. Small	Buffalo Central	
3.	C. L. Dodd	Louisville	
4.	H. Albert	St. Louis Central	

120 Yard Hurdles

1.	L. C. Bailey	St. Louis Central	16.6
2.	J. Percival Hagerman	Los Angeles	
3.	W. R. McCullough	St. Louis Central	
4.	O. E. Granberg	St. Louis Central	

Heat 1

1.	J. Percival Hagerman	Los Angeles	16.8
2.	W. R. McCullough	St. Louis Central	

Heat 2

1.	L. C. Bailey	St. Louis Central	16.8
2.	O. E. Granberg	St. Louis Central	

220 Yard Hurdles

1.	A. Sandow	Cincinnati	27.4
2.	L. C. Bailey	St. Louis Central	
3.	Charles S. Jacobs	Chicago Central	

4 × 440 Hard Relay

1.	Los Angeles	3:36.21
2.	Chicago Central	
3.	Cincinnati Central	

High Jump

1.	John J. Schommer	Chicago Central	5-8
2.	D. B. Crommell	Los Angeles	5-6
3.	J. G. B. McLaughlin	Cincinnati	5-4
4.	Adam B. Gunn	Buffalo Central	5-4

Pole Vault

1.	R. V. Norris	Chicago Central	10-8
2.	Charles S. Jacobs	Chicago Central	10-4
3.	R. H. Albertson	Chicago Central	10-4

Broad Jump

1.	William B. Hunter	Louisville	21-7
2.	J. Percival Hagerman	Los Angeles	19-9½
3.	Roy Gray	St. Louis Central	19-7½

Shot Put

1.	Adam B. Gunn	Buffalo Central	40-7
2.	D. B. Crommell	Los Angeles	38-6½
3.	W. H. Stevenson	Cincinnati	37-5

Discus Throw

1.	Adam B. Gunn	Buffalo Central	106-3½
2.	John J. Schommer	Chicago Central	97-7⅗
3.	Albert A. Johnson	St. Louis Central	96-11½

Hammer Throw

1.	Albert A. Johnson	St. Louis Central	128-7
2.	D. B. Crommell	Los Angeles	116-8½
3.	Adam B. Gunn	Buffalo Central	109-9

Military Athletic Carnival

D: 26 September — 1 October

NOTES

1. EK, FW, and VK have 12 competitors.
2. Prinstein's first name is often seen spelled as Myer. An alumni information form from Syracuse University has Prinstein signing his own name and spelling it Meyer.
3. Castleman was originally announced as the winner but the result was later changed to a dead heat.
4. EK, FW, and VK have 15.
5. Cartmell, Hogensen, and Moulton were to be penalized two yards for a false start in accordance with the rules of the era. However, the clerk of the course could set them back only one yard because there was no more room.
6. FW has 11.
7. Several sources mention Percival Molson as finishing fifth, but Prinstein's finish was confirmed by a photograph of the race.
8. FW has 14.
9. VK gives the times for Underwood and Runge as 1:56.5 and 1:57.1 respectively.
10. While technically a world record, Lightbody's time was only equivalent to a 4:25.0 mile, vastly inferior to the world mile record (amateur) of 4:15.6 held by Thomas Conneff.
11. In an obvious typo, FW has this athlete listed as "L. Verner."
12. FW has Gardner fifth, who did not qualify for the final.
13. EK, FW, and VK list four.
14. Most sources do not list Schule. He is listed in the *Chicago Tribune* which had a correspondent at the Olympic Games.
15. Except for two important problems, Hillman's time would have been a world record. However, he knocked over a hurdle which invalidated the mark as a record by the rules of 1904. In addition, and more importantly, the hurdles were only two feet, six inches in height, rather than three feet tall.
16. Varnell fell at the seventh hurdle. It is not known if he finished the race.
17. In older sources, the distance is usually listed as 2,500 meters, although FW has it correct. The St. Louis papers of 1904 and Lucas are unanimous in their description of the race as being 2,590 meters.
18. EK and VK list 10.
19. The number of jumps per lap is listed differently in the various St. Louis papers.
20. FW and OTAF list George Bonhag as finishing fifth. The *St. Louis Globe-Democrat* lists the complete starting field, as given here, omitting Bonhag. The paper listed only the top four finishers.
21. Various sources list between 29 and 37 starters. The number listed above, 32, was determined from many sources. All runners mentioned here have been confirmed as actually having run the race by photos or newspaper accounts of the race. EK and VK both have 31.
22. The course is always listed as 40,000 meters (24.85 miles) but June Becht and Wayne McFarland of St. Louis have studied this event in great detail and estimate its true length as closer to 42 km.
23. The course was determined by June Becht and Wayne McFarland. The above account is from their description.
24. Coray is always listed as from the United States. Several newspapers have confirmed that he was a Frenchman who came to Chicago and the United States only in 1903. Most sources also spell the name Corey, but French track & field historians insist that the correct spelling is Coray.
25. The *St. Louis Globe-Democrat* mentions Kneeland as having dropped out of the race but then lists him as finishing sixth. All sources list him as finishing.

26. Listed in all previous sources as Lentauw, Prof. Floris J. G. van der Merwe (University of Stellenbosch, South Africa) notes in a forthcoming article on South Africa at the Olympics (to be published in the *Journal of Sports History*) that the name is most likely "Len Tau."

27. Listed in all previous sources as Yamasini, Prof. Floris J.G. van der Merwe (University of Stellenbosch, South Africa) notes in a forthcoming article on South Africa at the Olympics (to be published in the *Journal of Sports History*) that the name is most likely "Jan Mashiani."

28. Furla, often misspelled as Thula, is usually listed as a Greek. His American citizenship was discovered in 1980 by June Becht and Wayne McFarland. Most of the other Greeks in the marathon were probably also Greek-Americans.

29. Lorz was actually the first runner across the line. He was disqualified when it was discovered that he had ridden in a car for several miles near the end of the race.

30. Most sources (including EK and SG) list this as a cross-country race, but the St. Louis newspapers of 1904 describe it as being held on the track. In particular, Newton is described as having lapped all the other runners.

31. EK does not list points for the teams but lists 21:17.8 for the New York Athletic Club. This was the winning time of Arthur Newton.

32. Usually listed solely as a United States' team. See above footnote in marathon concerning Coray's French nationality.

33. Serviss won second in a jump-off.

34. I was able to find five competitors in the St. Louis newspapers. The number of competitors in the standing long and triple jumps is taken from EK. No confirmations or contradictions could be found but I suspect there were other starters. There were several other entrants who were definitely present in St. Louis which makes one suspicious that the above are not the full fields. The other entries who were in St. Louis are as follows: Standing High Jump: Frederick Schule, John Fuhler; Standing Broad Jump: Joseph Stadler, Lawson Robertson, Frederick Schule; Standing Hop, Step, and Jump: Henry Field, John Biller, Paul Weinstein, Frederick Schule, John Fuhler, Lawson Robertson.

35. EK, FM, and VK have 1.50 and 1.498 meters, respectively (4–11). All St. Louis papers mention that Ewry won at that height but went on to clear 5–3.

36. Stadler was a black man. He and George Poage are the first American blacks to win medals in the Olympics. Who was first is impossible to tell as it depended on the order of the events on 31 August 1904.

37. Stadler won second in a jump-off by again clearing 4–9 (1.44 meters).

38. VK has 1.447 for Stadler and Robertson.

39. EK, FW, VK, and OTAF have Dray fifth and Allen sixth. The event went as follows. Samse, Wilkins, Allen, and McLanahan tied at 11–0. In a jump-off all four cleared 10–9. Samse and Wilkins also cleared 11–0 and 11–3, while Allen and McLanahan failed at 11–0. In a second jump-off Samse defeated Wilkins and McLanahan defeated Allen. Thus, listed marks for Samse and Wilkins of 11–3, included in my earlier report, are not correct, as they were only done in the jump-off.

40. EK, FW, and VK have only seven competitors.

41. Ewry also jumped 11–2 (3.40), 11–2¼ (3.41), and 11–4¼ (3.46).

42. Prinstein won the triple jump on his last attempt having, until that time, trailed Englehardt.

43. OTAF does not list Jones as a competitor. This was discovered from a photo in the Missouri Historical Society.

44. EK lists 9.53 (31–3¼). The distance 31–6 was given in St. Louis papers.

45. EK lists 7.95 meters (26–1). The distance 31–3¼ was found in the St. Louis papers.

46. Rose had other throws of 47–1 (14.35) and 47–10 (14.58).

47. Coe had other throws of 44–0 (13.41) and 47–1 (14.35).

48. Lawrence Edward Joseph Feuerbach's name is commonly given incorrectly as Leon E. J. Feuerbach.

49. Guiney is listed in only one source, the *St. Louis Republic*.

50. Georgantas' first two throws were disallowed for throwing the shot. He declined his third throw. His first two throws were approximately 43–0 (13.10).

51. In a throw-off of the tie, Sheridan defeated Rose. The marks in the throw-off were Sheridan: 127–10¼ (38.97); and Rose: 120–6¾ (36.74). This was listed only in the *Louisville Courier-Journal*.

52. Incorrectly spelled "Mitchell" in almost all sources.

53. EK and FW have five.

54. Flanagan had another throw of 167–0 (50.90).

55. DeWitt had another throw of 152–8 (46.53).

56. Rose had another throw of 145–6 (44.35).

57. Johnson was listed only in the *St. Louis Republic*.

58. This was Flanagan's only fair throw. He had five fouls.

59. Rose's best throw is described in the *St. Louis Globe-Democrat* as a trifle over 28–0 (8.53).

60. Most sources list seven, including EK and VK, which is reasonable, since Emmerich's participation was very brief and only listed in St. Louis newspapers.

61. Holloway is usually listed as from the United States. He was from Tipperary, Ireland and was several times Irish pole vault champion.

62. Clark is listed in OR, VK, and EK as sixth with 2,078 points. This is because of a clerical error in Spalding/OR. They correctly listed Clark's event-by-event totals but added them incorrectly.

63. In the 100 yard dash and the 120 yard high hurdles, times were taken only for the winners. The other runners' points were determined by how much they trailed the winner at the end of the race. In the 100 yard dash, seven points were deducted from the winner's score for each foot by which they trailed him. In the high hurdles, five points were deducted from the winner's score for each foot by which they trailed him.

64. Hogensen finished first with Robertson fourth. A finish judge gave the victory to his clubmate, Robertson, as he had done in a junior event earlier. The referee and all observers agreed Hogensen had won, but there was apparently no appeal from the decision of the judges.

Boxing

Boxing was held in the Physical Culture Gymnasium adjacent to the Olympic Stadium at Washington University, 21–22 September 1904. It was a very boring competition. In seven classes, only 17 boxers competed. Only the 135 pound and 145 pound classes had more than three competitors and three classes had only two competitors, who fought a single bout for the Olympic championship.

The Olympic boxing matches in 1904 were not the U.S. National Championships or the AAU Championships. They were a separate event contested solely as the Olympic contest. In addition, they were open to amateurs only and to entrants from all nations. Thus, they probably should be considered as an Olympic event. The only negative for consideration as an Olympic sport is that there were no foreign competitors and no foreign entrants that I can find. This does not mean, however, that the boxing events were not open to them, and in fact, they were, according to the rules. It means simply that no foreigners entered. Possibly this is due to the fact that the boxing tournament took place late in September, and many of the foreign athletes may have returned to Europe.

The most memorable feat at the 1904 boxing championships was performed by Oliver Kirk who won both the 115 pound and 125 pound classes, the only boxer in Olympic history to have won two gold medals at the same Olympics.

Site:	Physical Culture Gymnasium	
Dates/Times:	21–22 September	
Events:	7	
Competitors:	18	
Nations:	1	

	Competitors	1st	2nd	3rd	Totals
United States	18	7	7	5	19
Totals	18	7	7	5	19
Nations	1	1	1	1	3

Flyweight Class (≦ 105 lbs. [47.6 kg.])

A: 2[1]*; C: 1; D: 22 September.

1.	George Finnegan	USA
2.	Miles Burke	USA[2]

Tournament Draw

22 Sep

Finnegan
　　　　　Finnegan
Burke　　　TKO1

Bantamweight Class (≦ 115 lbs. [52.2 kg.])

A: 2[3]; C: 1; D: 22 September.

1.	Oliver Kirk	USA[4]
2.	George Finnegan	USA[5]

Tournament Draw

22 Sep

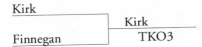

Kirk
　　　　　Kirk
Finnegan　TKO3

Featherweight Class (≦ 125 lbs. [56.7 kg.])

A: 3[6]; C: 1; D: 21–22 September.

1.	Oliver Kirk	USA[7]
2.	Frank Haller	USA[8]
3.	Fred Gilmore[9]	USA

Tournament Draw

21 Sep　　　　**22 Sep**

See Notes on page 113.

Lightweight Class (≦ 135½ lbs. [61.2 kg.])

A: 8[10]; C: 1; D: 21–22 September.

1.	Harry Spanger	USA[11]
2.	Jack Eagan[12]	USA[13]
3.	Russell Van Horn	USA[14]
4.	Peter Sturholdt	USA
=5.	Kenneth Jewett	USA
	Arthur Seward	USA
	Joseph Lydon	USA[15]
DQ.	Carroll Burton/Bollinger	USA[16]

Tournament Draw

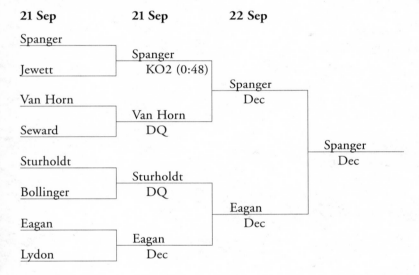

21 Sep	21 Sep	22 Sep
Spanger		
	Spanger	
Jewett	KO2 (0:48)	
		Spanger
		Dec
Van Horn		
	Van Horn	
Seward	DQ	
		Spanger
		Dec
Sturholdt		
	Sturholdt	
Bollinger	DQ	
		Eagan
		Dec
Eagan		
	Eagan	
Lydon	Dec	

Third-place match

22 Sep

Van Horn	
	Van Horn
Sturholdt	Dec

Welterweight Class (≦ 145 lbs. [65.8 kg.])

A: 4[17]; C: 1; D: 21–22 September.

1.	Albert Young	USA[18]
2.	Harry Spanger	USA[19]
=3.	Joseph Lydon[20]	USA[21]
	Jack Eagan[22]	USA[23]

Tournament Draw

21 Sep   **22 Sep**

Young

Young

Eagan

Young
Dec

Spanger

Spanger
Dec

Lydon

Middleweight Class (≦ 158 lbs. [71.7 kg.])

A: 2[24]; C: 1; D: 22 September.

1.	Charles Mayer	USA[25]
2.	Benjamin Spradley	USA[26]

Tournament Draw

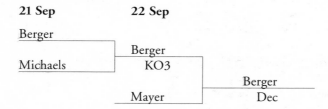

22 Sep

Mayer

Mayer
TKO3 (1:40)

Spradley

Heavyweight Class (> 158 lbs. [71.7 kg.])

A: 3[27]; C: 1; D: 21–22 September.

1.	Samuel Berger	USA[28]
2.	Charles Mayer	USA[29]
3.	William Michaels[30]	USA

Tournament Draw

21 Sep   **22 Sep**

Berger

Berger
KO3

Michaels

Berger
Dec

Mayer

NOTES

1. EK, FW, and VK have seven.
2. Burke weighed 107¾ pounds [48.9 kg.] for this bout, over the limit for the class. No explanation could be found for why he was allowed to compete. Finnegan weighed 104 lbs. [47.2 kg.].
3. EK, FW, and VK list six.
4. Kirk weighed 114 lbs. [51.7 kg.].
5. Finnegan weighed 104 lbs. [47.2 kg.].
6. EK, FW, and VK list five.
7. Kirk weighed 114 lbs. [51.7 kg.].
8. Haller weighed 125 lbs. [56.7 kg.].
9. FM and VK do not list a third-place finisher.
10. EK, FW, and VK list eight.
11. Spanger weighed 134¾ lbs. [61.1 kg.].
12. This athlete's name is seen variously in St. Louis newspapers of 1904 as either James/Jack and Eagan/Egan.
13. Eagan weighed 133 lbs. [60.3 kg.].
14. Van Horn weighed 135 lbs. [61.2 kg.].
15. Lydon weighed 132½ lbs. [60.1 kg.].
16. Carroll Burton was a well-known local boxer. An athlete named Bollinger entered using Burton's name and narrowly defeated Sturholdt by decision. When his identity was discovered, Bollinger/Burton was disqualified, and Sturholdt was advanced to the next round.
17. EK, FW, and VK list nine.
18. Young weighed 144¾ lbs. [65.7 kg.].
19. Spanger weighed 134¾ lbs. [61.1 kg.].
20. FM has Lydon as sole third.
21. Lydon weighed 132½ lbs. [60.1 kg.].
22. This athlete's name is spelled variously in 1904 St. Louis newspapers as James/Jack and Eagan/Egan.
23. Eagan weighed 133 lbs. [60.3 kg.].
24. EK, FW, and VK list six.
25. Mayer weighed 158 lbs. [71.7 kg.].
26. Spradley weighed 154¾ lbs. [70.2 kg.].
27. EK, FW, and VK list eight.
28. Berger weighed 180 lbs. [81.7 kg.].
29. Mayer weighed 158 lbs. [71.7 kg.].
30. FM did not list a third-place finisher.

Cycling

The cycling events[1]* of the 1904 Olympic Games were contested from 2–5 August on the Olympic stadium track at Francis Field. It was described as "a track of cinders, flat as a billiard table, very dry and dusty."[2] The cycling events were very poorly attended. *The Bicycling World* listed the crowd as 125 people on 2 August and noted that there were only "a few spectators" on 3–5 August.

Multiple events were contested at the 1904 Olympic Games. This included handicap events as well as events for professionals. In the past the cycling events of the 1904 Olympics have not always been included in the Olympic sports because of some suspicion that the amateurs and professionals competed together. That is not correct. They did not compete together in any event, although professional and amateur events were held on the same days on the same track. Certainly only the amateur events, which were not handicap events, should be considered as Olympic sports. Below I have listed all the results of all the events, including the amateur handicap, professional scratch, and professional handicap events. Of note, America's greatest track cyclist ever, Frank Kramer, competed in the 1904 professional events and won several of them.

Among the amateur cyclists, the events were dominated by Marcus Hurley who won four gold medals and six medals in all, from among the seven events contested. He was pressed by Burton Downing of San Jose, California and Teddy Billington of Vailsburg, New Jersey. Hurley, later that year, would win the world amateur sprint championship but never competed much in cycling after 1904. He entered Columbia University where he became an All-American basketball player and one of the greatest players of that era. Downing retired from cycling after the 1904 Olympics and eventually became a renowned architect. Almost nothing is known about Billington's life. However, it is known that his bicycle did not arrive in St. Louis on the train which brought him, and he competed at the St. Louis cycling competitions on a borrowed cycle.

No foreign cyclists competed at the 1904 cycling events. However, there were foreign entrants, specifically those from the Radfahrerbund from Berlin, Germany. Given that professionals and amateurs did not compete against each other, given that the competitions were open to all competitors, and since there were foreign entrants, there is every justification to regard the cycling events of the 1904 Olympics as Olympic events.

Site:	Francis Field
Dates/Times:	2–5 August

See Notes on pages 126–127.

Events: 7
Competitors: 18
Nations: 1

	Competitors	1st	2nd	3rd	Totals
United States	18	7	7	7	21
Totals	18	7	7	7	21
Nations	1	1	1	1	1

¼ Mile (402.34 meters)

A: 11; C: 1; D: 3 August; F: First two finishers in heats advance to the semi-finals. First two finishers in the semi-finals advance to the final.

Marcus Hurley won the quarter mile championship without being pressed. In the final there were four competitors: Hurley, Downing, Oscar Goerke, and Billington. Hurley took the lead at the start of the race and was never headed, winning by a length and a half over Downing, who had half a wheel on Billington, with Goerke trailing badly. The four heats were won by Billington, Hurley, Goerke, and Downing. The semi-finals went to Hurley and Goerke.

Final A: 4; C: 1; D: 3 August.

1.	Marcus Hurley	USA	31.8
2.	Burton Downing	USA	at 1½ lengths
3.	Teddy Billington	USA	at ½ wheel
4.	Oscar Goerke	USA	

Semi-Finals A: 8; C: 1; D: 3 August.

Heat 1 A: 4; C: 1

1.	Marcus Hurley	USA	34.8
2.	Teddy Billington	USA	
AC.	Frank Bizzoni	USA	
	Frank Montaldi	USA	

Heat 2 A: 4; C: 1

1.	Oscar Goerke	USA	33.4
2.	Burton Downing	USA	
AC.	A. F. Andrews	USA	
	Henry Wittman	USA	

Round One A: 11; C: 1; D: 3 August.

Heat 1 A: 2; C: 1

1.	Teddy Billington	USA	36.0
2.	Frank Bizzoni	USA	

Heat 2 A: 3; C: 1

1.	Marcus Hurley	USA	35.6
2.	Frank Montaldi	USA	
3.	Oscar Schwab	USA	

Heat 3 A: 3; C: 1

1.	Oscar Goerke	USA	34.8
2.	A. F. Andrews	USA	
3.	Fred Grinham	USA	

Heat 4 A: 3; C: 1

1.	Burton Downing	USA	35.2
2.	Henry Wittman	USA	
3.	Anthony Williamson	USA	

⅓ *Mile (536.45 meters)*

A: 10; C: 1; D: 4–5 August; F: First two finishers in heats advance to the semi-finals. First two finishers in the semi-finals advance to the final.

The one-third mile event was contested with two semi-finals followed by a final. The semi-final winners were Teddy Billington and Marcus Hurley. In the final Burton Downing took the lead and led Hurley until the last few yards of the stretch when Hurley jumped past him and won the race by a length. Teddy Billington was third with Charles Schlee fourth.

Final A: 4; C: 1; D: 5 August.

1.	Marcus Hurley	USA	43.8
2.	Burton Downing	USA	at 1 length
3.	Teddy Billington	USA	
4.	Charles Schlee	USA	

Semi-Finals A: 8; C: 1; D: 5 August.

Heat 1 A: 4; C: 1

1.	Teddy Billington	USA	50.2
2.	Charles Schlee	USA	
AC.	Oscar Goerke	USA	
	Fred Grinham	USA	

Heat 2 A: 4; C: 1

1.	Marcus Hurley	USA	44.2
2.	Burton Downing	USA	

Round One A: 10; C: 1; D: 4–5 August.

Heat 1 A: 2; C: 1

1.	Charles Schlee	USA
2.	Teddy Billington	USA

Heat 2 A: 2; C: 1

1.	Oscar Goerke	USA
2.	Fred Grinham	USA

Heat 3 A: [3]; C: 1

Heat 4 A: ; C: 1

½ Mile (804.67 meters)

A: 16; C: 1; D: 2 August; F: First two finishers in heats advance to the semi-finals. First two finishers in the semi-finals advance to the final.

The half-mile competition was the first Olympic event held in 1904. Marcus Hurley won it in convincing style with the big surprise being Teddy Billington defeating Burton Downing for second. Four heats were contested, won by Hurley, A. L. G. Fritz, Billington, and Downing. The semi-finals went to Hurley and Billington. In the final, Billington was on the pole with Hurley next to him, Downing in third position, and George Wiley on the outer lane. Wiley set the pace for the first quarter of a mile at which time all three cyclists passed him easily. Hurley stayed on the pole in the stretch and won by a length and a half over Billington who defeated Downing by almost two lengths.

Final A: 4; C: 1; D: 2 August.

1.	Marcus Hurley	USA	1:09.0
2.	Teddy Billington	USA	at 1½ lengths
3.	Burton Downing	USA	at 2 lengths
4.	George Wiley	USA	

Semi-Finals A: 8; C: 1; D: 2 August.

Heat 1 A: 4; C: 1

1.	Marcus Hurley	USA	1:12.8
2.	George Wiley	USA	
AC.	A. L. G. Fritz[4]	USA	
	Charles Schlee	USA	

Heat 2 A: 4; C: 1

1.	Teddy Billington	USA	1:09.0
2.	Burton Downing	USA	at ½ lengths
AC.	Fred Grinham	USA	
	Henry Wittman	USA	

Round One A: 16; C: 1; D: 2 August.

Heat 1 A: 4; C: 1

1.	Marcus Hurley	USA	1:08.6
2.	George Wiley	USA	
3.	A. F. Andrews	USA	

Heat 2 A: 4; C: 1

1.	A. L. G. Fritz	USA	1:07.0
2.	Charles Schlee	USA	
3.	Oscar Goerke	USA	

Heat 3 A: 4; C: 1

1.	Teddy Billington	USA	1:18.6[5]
2.	Henry Wittmann	USA	at 3 lengths
3.	Anthony Williamson	USA	

Heat 4 A: 4; C: 1

1.	Burton Downing	USA	1:13.6
2.	Fred Grinham	USA	
3.	Leo Larson	USA	

6

One Mile (1,609.34 meters)

A: 8; C: 1; D: 5 August; F: First two finishers in the semi-finals advance to the finals.

Although heats were planned for the one mile championship, they were not contested because there were not enough entries. The two semi-finals were won by Marcus Hurley and Burton Downing. The finals were contested by Marcus Hurley, Burton Downing, Teddy Billington, and Oscar Goerke. The quartet took turns pacing in the final with Goerke leading at the bell at which time Teddy Billington pulled alongside him. On the first turn of the last lap, Downing's back wheel slipped and he barely stayed upright, losing at least five lengths. Hurley took the lead on the backstretch of the last lap and won the race by four lengths from Downing, who had come back to defeat Billington in the stretch by inches.

Final A: 4; C: 1; D: 5 August.

1.	Marcus Hurley	USA	2:41.6[7]
2.	Burton Downing	USA	at 5 lengths
3.	Teddy Billington	USA	at 4 inches
4.	Oscar Goerke	USA	

Semi-Finals A: 8; C: 1; D: 5 August.

Heat 1 A: 4; C: 1

1.	Marcus Hurley	USA	2:34.2
2.	Oscar Goerke	USA	at 1 length
3.	Charles Schlee	USA	
	J. Nash McCrea	USA	DNF

Heat 2 A: 4; C: 1

1.	Burton Downing	USA	2:33.0
2.	Teddy Billington	USA	at 1 foot
3.	George Wiley	USA	
4.	Anthony Williamson	USA	

Two Miles (3,218.69 meters)

A: 13; C: 1; D: 3 August; F: Final only, no heats.

The two mile race was contested in one round with 13 starters. Unfortunately, many of them are not known to us. Marcus Hurley led at the start of the race with Downing, Billington, and Oscar Goerke following closely behind him. Charles Schlee, a well-known rider from the National Turnverein in Newark, New Jersey rode in last place through most of the race as was his custom, relying on his excellent finish. However, because of the crowded field he could not get through the field to make a chase for the championship. On the home stretch, Hurley's cycle slipped on the dusty cinder track and he was passed by both Downing and Goerke. Downing won by approximately one wheel over Goerke with Hurley in third place, defeating Billington by a length.

1.	Burton Downing	USA	4:57.8[8]
2.	Oscar Goerke	USA	at 4 feet
3.	Marcus Hurley	USA	
4.	Teddy Billington	USA	at 1 length
AC.	Charles Schlee	USA	

Five Miles (8,046.72 meters)

A: [9]; C: 1; D: 5 August; F: Final only, no heats.

The five mile race was spoiled by a large crash, precipitated by the rough riding of J. Nash McCrea of Springfield, Illinois. For his rough riding, he earned the nickname, "Crash McCrea." *The Bicycling World* noted that "he does not seem to be a vicious rider, but simply 'rides all over the track' and is dangerous for that reason." The crash took out the best riders in St. Louis in 1904, notably Marcus Hurley, Burton Downing, Teddy Billington, and Oscar Goerke. It was observed, however, that they deserved this somewhat because they rode near the end of the pack for much of the race, and thus were susceptible to a crash. The crash occurred on the penultimate lap when McCrea swerved into the rider alongside him and they struck two other riders. Hurley, Downing, Billington, and Goerke were behind them and fell over the fallen riders. Charles Schlee, of Newark, New Jersey, had been in last place, as was his customary strategy, but escaped the fall, and he and George Wiley of Syracuse, New York, fought out the championship on the last lap. Wiley led going around the last turn but Schlee overhauled him in the straight and won by five open lengths.

1.	Charles Schlee	USA	13:08.2
2.	George Wiley	USA	at 5 lengths
3.	A. F. Andrews	USA	
4.	Julius Schaefer	USA	
AC.	Marcus Hurley	USA	DNF
	Burton Downing	USA	DNF
	Oscar Goerke	USA	DNF
	Teddy Billington	USA	DNF
	J. Nash McCrea	USA	DNF[10]

25 Miles (40,233.61 meters)

A: 10; C: 1; D: 5 August; F: Final only, no heats.

In the 25-mile championship there were ten starters but only four finished due to punctures and falls. Marcus Hurley did not compete, for unknown reasons. Charles Schlee retired after two miles due to a puncture, and Teddy Billington quit after three miles for the same reason. Oscar Goerke briefly went out in the tenth mile when one of his tires exploded. He remounted on another bike, and kept riding until the 17th mile when he punctured again and withdrew. Four riders remained together going into the last two laps: Burton Downing, George Wiley, Samuel Lavoice, and A. F. Andrews. Andrews led beginning the next-to-last lap but Downing jumped him on the backstretch of the last lap and won by a length and a half, with Wiley third, four lengths behind Downing. Wiley did win a special lap prize for having led 35 laps of the race.

1.	Burton Downing	USA	1-10:55.4
2.	A. F. Andrews	USA	at 1½ lengths
3.	George Wiley	USA	at 4 lengths[11]
4.	Samuel LaVoice	USA	
AC.	Charles Schlee	USA	DNF
	Teddy Billington	USA	DNF
	Julius Schaefer	USA	DNF
	Oscar Goerke	USA	DNF[12]
	Anthony Williamson	USA	DNF[13]
	Marcus Hurley	USA	DNF

NON-OLYMPIC EVENTS

½ Mile (804.67 meters) Handicap, Amateur

A: 10; C: 1; D: 2 August.

1.	W. L. Snider	USA	1:02.8	(70 yds.)
2.	Henry C. Wittman	USA		(70 yds.)
3.	Teddy Billington	USA		(scratch)
4.	A. F. Andrews	USA		(40 yds.)
AC.	Oscar Goerke	USA		(15 yds.)
	Charles Schlee	USA		(15 yds.)

One Mile (1,609.34 meters) Handicap, Amateur

A: ?; C: ?; D: 3 August.

1.	Oscar Goerke	USA	2:13.0	(20 yds.)
2.	Henry C. Wittman	USA		(90 yds.)
3.	Fred Grinham	USA		(100 yds.)
4.	Samuel LaVoice	USA		(80 yds.)

One Mile (1,609.34 meters) Novice, Amateur

A: ?; C: ?; D: 2 August.

1.	A. L. G. Fritz/W. L. Snider[14]	USA	2:45.8
2.	Frank Bizzoni	USA	
3.	Henry C. Wittman	USA	

Five Mile (8,046.72 meters) Handicap, Amateur

A: ?; C: ?; D: 5 August.

1.	Oscar Goerke	USA	12:15.0	(100 yds.)
2.	Charles Schlee	USA		(50 yds.)
3.	George Wiley	USA		(150 yds.)
4.	Samuel LaVoice	USA		(250 yds.)

⅓ Mile (536.45 meters)
Grand Circuit Championship, Professional

A: 16; C: 2; D: 2 August.

Final A: 4; C: 1; D: 2 August.

1.	W. S. Fenn	USA	43.4
2.	Frank Kramer	USA	at 5 lengths
3.	Menus Bedell	USA	at 8 lengths
4.	Floyd Krebs	USA	bad fourth

Semi-finals A: 8; C: 2; D: 2 August.

Heat 1 A: 4; C: 1.

1.	Frank L. Kramer	USA	
2.	Floyd Krebs	USA	at 1 length
AC.	George H. Collett	USA	
	James B. Bowler	USA	

Heat 2 A: 4; C: 2.

1.	W. S. Fenn	USA	
2.	Menus Bedell	USA	at 5 lengths
3.	Floyd A. McFarland	USA	
4.	Fred H. Schepps	AUS	

Round One A: 16; C: 2; D; 2 August.

Heat 1 A: 5; C: 1.

1.	Frank Kramer	USA
2.	Floyd Krebs	USA
3.	E. F. Root	USA
AC.	Floyd Krebs	USA
	W. S. Sanderson	USA

Heat 2 A: 4; C: 1.

1.	James B. Bowler	USA
2.	George H. Collett	USA
3.	James Moran	USA
4.	John Bedell	USA

Heat 3 A: 4; C: 2.

1.	W. S. Fenn	USA	
2.	Fred H. Schepps	AUS	at 3 lengths
3.	Frank J. Cadwell	USA	
4.	Joseph Fogler	USA	

Heat 4 A: 3; C: 1.

1.	Menus Bedell	USA
2.	Floyd A. McFarland	USA
3.	J. P. Jacobson	USA

½ Mile (804.67 meters)
Grand Circuit Championship, Professional

A: ?; C: ?; D: 4–5 August.

Final A: 4; C: 1; D: 5 August.

1.	Frank L. Kramer	USA	1:09.0
2.	W. S. Fenn	USA	
3.	John Bedell	USA	
4.	Frank J. Cadwell	USA	

Semi-finals A: 8; C: 1; D: 5 August.

Heat 1 A: 4; C: 1.

1.	W. S. Fenn	USA	1:18.6
2.	John Bedell	USA	
AC.	Floyd A. McFarland	USA	
	Floyd Krebs	USA	

Heat 2 A: 4; C: 1.

1.	Frank L. Kramer	USA	1:07.0
2.	Frank J. Cadwell	USA	
3.	E. F. Root	USA	
4.	W. S. Sanderson	USA	

Round One A: ?; C: ?; D; 4 August.

Heat 1 A: ?; C: ?.

1.	W. S. Fenn	USA
2.	Floyd A. McFarland	USA

Heat 2 A: ?; C: ?.

1.	John Bedell	USA
2.	Floyd Krebs	USA

Heat 3 A: ?; C: ?.

1.	Frank L. Kramer	USA
2.	E. F. Root	USA

Heat 4 A: ?; C: ?.

1.	Frank J. Cadwell	USA
2.	W. S. Sanderson	USA
3.	Menus Bedell	USA

⅔ Mile (1,072.90 meters)
Grand Circuit Championship, Professional

A: 8; C: 1; D: 5 August.

Final A: 4; C: 1; D: 5 August.

1.	Frank L. Kramer	USA	1:46.6
2.	W. S. Fenn	USA	at inches
3.	Floyd Krebs	USA	
4.	Menus Bedell	USA	

Semi-finals A: 8; C: 1; D: 5 August.

Heat 1 A: 4; C: 1.

1.	Frank L. Kramer	USA	
2.	Floyd Krebs	USA	at 5 feet
3.	John Bedell	USA	
4.	James B. Bowler	USA	

Heat 2 A: 4; C: 1.

1.	W. S. Fenn	USA
2.	Menus Bedell	USA
3.	Frank J. Cadwell	USA
4.	Floyd A. McFarland	USA

One Mile (1,609.34 meters)
Grand Circuit Championship, Professional

A: ?; C: ?; D: 3 August.

Final A: 4; C: 1; D: 3 August.

1.	W. S. Fenn	USA	2:32.4
2.	James B. Bowler	USA	
3.	E. F. Root	USA	
4.	Frank L. Kramer	USA	

⅓ Mile (536.45 meters) Consolation, Professional

A: 8; C: 2; D: 5 August.

1.	Oliver Dorlon	USA	42.6
2.	George H. Collett	USA	
3.	Fred H. Schepps	AUS	
4.	Joseph Fogler	USA	
AC.	J. P. Jacobson	USA	
	Frank J. Cadwell	USA	
	Floyd A. McFarland	USA	DNF
	James B. Bowler	USA	DNF

One Mile (1,609.34 meters) Professional, Consolation #1

A: ?; C: 2; D: 2 August.

1.	James B. Bowler	USA	2:13.6
2.	George Collett	USA	
3.	Joseph Fogler	USA	
4.	Fred H. Schepps	AUS	
AC.	Oliver Dorlon	USA	

One Mile (1,609.34 meters) Professional, Consolation #2

A: ?; C: ?; D: 3 August.

1.	Frank J. Cadwell	USA	2:19.0
2.	Menus Bedell	USA	at one tire
3.	George Collett	USA	close 3rd
4.	J. P. Jacobson	USA	
AC.	Floyd A. McFarland	USA	DNF

½ Mile (804.67 meters) Handicap, Professional

A: ?; C: ?; D: 5 August.

Final A: 6; C: 1; D: 5 August.

1.	Oliver Dorlon	USA	58.8	(35 yds.)
2.	John Bedell	USA	at 2 lengths	(15 yds.)
3.	E. F. Root	USA	at 2 lengths	(25 yds.)
4.	Frank L. Kramer	USA	close to 3rd	(scratch)
5.	Menus Bedell	USA		(10 yds.)
6.	Floyd A. McFarland	USA		(20 yds.)

Semi-finals A: ?; C: ?; D: 5 August.

Heat 1 A: ?; C: ?.

1.	John Bedell	USA	59.4	(15 yds.)
2.	Frank L. Kramer	USA		(scratch)
3.	Oliver Dorlon	USA		(35 yds.)

Heat 2 A: ?; C: ?.

1.	Floyd A. McFarland	USA	59.4	(20 yds.)
2.	E. F. Root	USA		(25 yds.)
3.	Menus Bedell	USA		(10 yds.)

One Mile (1,609.34 meters) Professional, Handicap #1

A: ?; C: ?; D: 2 August.

1.	Floyd Krebs	USA	2:17.8	(50 yds.)
2.	Frank J. Cadwell	USA	at ½ length	(40 yds.)
3.	John Bedell	USA		(20 yds.)
4.	E. F. Root	USA	close to 4th	
AC.	W. S. Fenn	USA		

One Mile (1,609.34 meters) Professional, Handicap #2

A: 8; C: 2; D: 3 August.

1.	John Bedell	USA	2:07.6	(20 yds.)
2.	E. F. Root	USA	at 2 inches	(40 yds.)
3.	Oliver Dorlon	USA	at 4 inches	(60 yds.)
4.	Floyd Krebs	USA		(30 yds.)
AC.	Joseph Fogler	USA		
	Fred H. Schepps	AUS		
	J. P. Jacobson	USA		
	W. S. Sanderson	USA		

Two Miles (3,218.69 meters) Handicap, Professional

A: 11; C: 2; D: 5 August.

1.	E. F. Root	USA	4:17.4	(50 yds.)
2.	John Bedell	USA		(50 yds.)
3.	Menus Bedell	USA		(75 yds.)
4.	Frank J. Cadwell	USA		(75 yds.)
AC.	Floyd A. McFarland	USA		
	Joseph Fogler	USA		

Oliver Dorlon	USA		
James Moran	USA		
W. S. Sanderson	USA		
Fred H. Schepps	AUS		
James B. Bowler	USA	DNF	(25 yds.)
Floyd Krebs	USA	DNF	(25 yds.)

Australian Team Pursuit Race, Professional

A: 8; C: 2; D: 5 August; F: 6 miles and 1 lap, or 6⅓ miles (*circa* 10 km.).

1. East   USA   15:37.4
     (Oliver Dorlon, James Moran, J. P. Jacobson, Floyd Krebs)
2. West   USA/AUS   caught
     (James B. Bowler, Floyd A. McFarland, George H. Collett, Fred H. Schepps (AUS))

One Mile (1,609.34 meters) Motorcycle Exhibition #1

A: ?; C: ?; D: ?.

1. A. N. Jordan   USA   2:10.0

One Mile (1,609.34 meters) Motorcycle Exhibition #2

A: ?; C: ?; D: ?.

1. Eugene Holloway   USA   1:54.4

NOTES

1. The cycling results are almost exclusively derived from the magazine *The Bicycling World*.
2. *The Bicycling World*, 2 August 1904.
3. Heats three and four in the ⅓ mile were postponed from 4 August because of rain. Marcus Hurley and Burton Downing must have advanced from these heats but no results of these heats could be found.
4. This cyclist was listed originally as Fritz Snider. He entered a handicap event on 2 August under both names — Fritz and Snider. He then competed as Snider because he was given a better handicap. When this ruse was discovered, he was disqualified from subsequent events.
5. Billington won this heat despite using a borrowed bicycle as the trunk carrying his bicycle to the track did not arrive until just before the semi-finals of this event.
6. J. Nash McCrea and Oscar Schwab also competed in the heats, but it is not known in which heats they competed.
7. VK has the time as 2:41.4.
8. Downing's split times in this race were 2:37.8 for the first mile and 2:20.0 for the second mile.
9. The number of entrants is not given in any source.

10. All of the riders who are listed as "Did Not Finish" crashed in one large accident precipitated by the wild riding of J. Nash McCrea, who was given the nickname "Crash" for his wild style of riding.

11. Wiley led the lap prize, having led for 35 of the 75 laps.

12. Goerke went out at 17 miles with a flat tire. He had also flatted at 10 miles but re-mounted and continued.

13. Williamson was called off the track after finishing 24 miles because he was so far behind.

14. The race was won by this rider, who entered as "Snider." His name was revealed to be "Fritz" the day after his victory.

Diving

A diving competition was held at the life-saving exhibition lake in the middle of the World's Fairgrounds on 7 September 1904, concurrent with the swimming events. Only one event was held, a fancy diving competition. A St. Louis doctor, Dr. George Sheldon, won the competition, defeating Germany's Georg Hoffmann fairly easily. The controversy in this event occurred in the battle for the bronze medal. The American, Frank Kehoe, and a German, Alfred Braunschweiger, tied for third with 11.33 points. The Germans protested this result, thinking that Braunschweiger had easily outperformed Kehoe. A "dive-off" for third place was scheduled, but Braunschweiger refused to compete and Kehoe was awarded the bronze medal. The German commissioner to the World's Fair, Dr. Theodore Lewald, had donated a trophy for the winning diver, but he was so incensed at the outcome that he refused to award it to Sheldon. The controversy occurred because the Germans thought that they did fancier dives than the Americans, although the Americans protested that the Germans had poorer entries into the water. The Germans, noting that the event was called a fancy diving contest, thought that was immaterial. On 29 September, James Sullivan announced the ruling that the protest had not been allowed, although the decision had been made two weeks earlier.

Site:	Life Saving Exhibition Lake	
Dates/Times:	7 September	
Events:	1	
Competitors:	5	
Nations:	2	

	Competitors	1st	2nd	3rd	Totals
Germany	3	-	1	-	1
United States	2	1	-	1	2
Totals	5	1	1	1	3
Nations	2	1	1	1	2

Fancy Diving

A: 5[1]; C: 2; D: 7 September; F: Unknown.

1.	George Sheldon[2]	USA	12.66
2.	Georg Hoffmann	GER	11.66
3.	Frank Kehoe[3]	USA	11.33
4.	Alfred Braunschweiger[4]	GER	11.33
5.	Otto Hooff[5]	GER	

NOTES

1. FW has four.

2. Sheldon's victory was protested by the German team and his trophy withheld while the protest was considered. On 15 September 1904 the protest was rejected by James E. Sullivan.

3. FM has Kehoe and Braunschweiger tied for third.

4. Most sources list Kehoe and Braunschweiger as having tied for third, probably based on OR. The *St. Louis Republic* states that they were to have a dive-off of the tie and that Braunschweiger refused to dive, and that third was then awarded to Kehoe. The *St. Louis Republic* was the only paper that mentioned much about the diving event.

5. Hooff is not usually listed by other sources but his name was given in the *St. Louis Republic.*

Fencing

The 1904 Olympic fencing events were contested in the Physical Culture Gymnasium adjacent to Francis Field on 7–8 September 1904. There were five events: foil, saber, dueling swords (épée), single sticks, and team foil.

There were foreign competitors in the fencing events, both from Cuba and Germany. Germany sent one competitor, Gustav Casmir. The two Cuban fencers were Ramón Fonst and Manuel Diaz. Fonst had competed at the 1900 Olympics in Paris, where he had won the épée, and in St. Louis he repeated in that event and also won a gold medal in the foil competition. He also led a mixed Cuban/U.S. team to the championship in the team foil.

The 1904 fencing competitions were not simply United States championships, as the AAU Fencing Championships were held earlier in the year. Thus, with foreign competitors, amateur competition only, and events open to all competitors, the fencing events definitely should be considered part of the Olympic games.

Strangely, although the events were held in the United States and in most sports the best American athletes competed, the best American fencer of that era, Charles Bothner, who had been a multiple national champion in foil, épée, and saber, did not show up in St. Louis to compete.

Site:	Physical Culture Gymnasium			
Dates/Times:	7–8 September			
Events:	5			
Competitors:	11			
Nations:	3			

	Competitors	1st	2nd	3rd	Totals
Cuba	2	3	-	-	3
Cuba/United States	-	1	-	-	1
Germany	1	-	-	-	-
United States	8	1	5	4	10
Totals	11	5	5	4	14
Nations	3	2	1	1	2

130

Foil, Individual

A: 9[1]*; C: 3; D: 7 September[2]; F: The top two finishers in each semi-final advanced to the final. The final and semi-finals were round-robin affairs. All bouts were four minutes in duration with the contestants changing positions after two minutes.

Final A: 4; C: 3; D: 7 September.

1.	Ramón Fonst Segundo	CUB	3-0
2.	Albertson Van Zo Post	USA[3]	2-1
3.	Charles Tatham	USA[4]	1-2
4.	Gustav Casmir	GER	0-3

Finals Matches

Fonst Segundo d. Casmir
Fonst Segundo d. Tatham
Fonst Segundo d. Van Zo Post
Van Zo Post d. Tatham
Van Zo Post d. Casmir
Tatham d. Casmir

Semi-Finals

Pool 1 A: 5; D: 7 September.

1.	Ramón Fonst Segundo	CUB	4-0
2.	Albertson Van Zo Post	USA	3-1
3.	Fitzhugh Townsend[5]	USA	2-2
4.	Theodore Carstens	USA	1-3
5.	William Grebe	USA	0-4

Pool 1 Matches

Fonst Segundo d. Van Zo Post
Fonst Segundo d. Townsend
Fonst Segundo d. Carstens
Fonst Segundo d. Grebe
Van Zo Post d. Townsend
Van Zo Post d. Carstens
Vam Zo Post d. Grebe
Townsend d. Carstens
Townsend d. Grebe
Carstens d. Grebe

Pool 2 A: 4; D: 7 September.

1.	Gustav Casmir	GER	3-0
2.	Charles Tatham	USA	2-1
3.	Wilfred Holroyd	USA	1-2
4.	Arthur Fox	USA	0-3

*See Notes on pages 133–134.

Pool 2 Matches

    Casmir d. Tatham
    Casmir d. Holroyd
    Casmir d. Fox
    Tatham d. Holroyd
    Tatham d. Fox
    Holroyd d. Fox

Dueling Swords,[6] Individual

A: 5[7]; C: 3; D: 7 September; F: Each contestant fenced one bout with every other competitor. The winner of the bout was the first person to score a touch.

1.	Ramón Fonst Segundo	CUB
2.	Charles Tatham	USA
3.	Albertson Van Zo Post	USA
4.	Gustav Casmir	GER
5.	Fitzhugh Townsend	USA

Saber, Individual

A: 5[8]; C: 2; D: 8 September; T: 1000; F: The event was a round-robin affair.[9] The winner of each bout was the first person to score seven touches.

1.	Manuel Diaz Martinez	CUB	3-0	21 touches
2.	William Grebe	USA	2-1	20 touches[10]
3.	Albertson Van Zo Post	USA	2-1	18 touches
4.	Theodore Carstens	USA	1-2	
5.	Arthur Fox	USA	0-4	

Finals Matches[11]

    Diaz Martinez d. Grebe, 7-6
    Diaz Martinez d. Carstens
    Diaz Martinez d. Fox
    Grebe d. Van Zo Post, 7-4
    Grebe d. Fox
    Van Zo Post d. Carstens
    Van Zo Post d. Fox
    Carstens d. Fox

Single Sticks, Individual

A: 3[12]; C: 1; D: 8 September; T: 1000; F: Unknown

1.	Albertson Van Zo Post	USA	11 touches
2.[13]	William Scott O'Connor	USA	8 touches
3.	William Grebe	USA	2 touches

Foil, Team

A: 6; C: 2; D: 8 September; F: It appears that this was a round-robin affair with every fencer on each team facing every fencer on the opposing team.

1. Cuba/United States[14]   7–2
   (Ramón Fonst Segundo [CUB], Albertson Van Zo Post [USA], Manuel Diaz Martinez [CUB])
2. United States[15]   2–7
   (Charles Tatham, Fitzhugh Townsend, Arthur Fox)

NON-OLYMPIC EVENTS

Junior Foil[16]

A: ?; C: ?; D: 9 September.

1.	Arthur G. Fox	USA
2.	Theodore Carstens	USA
3.	Wilfred G. Holroyd	USA

NOTES

1. EK, FW, and VK list 12 competitors but both the *Globe-Democrat* and the *Post-Dispatch* list all competitors and all matches fenced.

2. The fencing events were scheduled to start on 6 September but were postponed because many of the competitors had not shown up.

3. Van Zo Post is listed in most sources as Cuban. However, his obituary in *The New York Times* states that he was born in New York City, was descended from an old New York family, and had a father who fought for the Union in the Civil War. In addition, Van Zo Post was several times U.S. champion and fenced for the United States in the 1912 Olympics.

4. Tatham is listed in all sources as Cuban. However, his obituary in *The New York Times* states that he was born in New York City and was descended from an old Philadelphia family.

5. EK has this athlete listed incorrectly as Charles Townsend.

6. This event is now known as the épée.

7. EK, FW, and VK list eleven starters but St. Louis papers have only five listed. A Chicago newspaper also listed several fencers who did not compete which corroborates that five competed but that eleven were entered.

8. EK, FW, and VK list six starters but the St. Louis papers listed all the fencers who competed and the results of all matches.

9. Although the event was purportedly a round-robin affair, for some reason, no match between Van Zo Post and Diaz Martinez can be found in any source. In addition, Diaz Martinez's record is given as 3–0 in several sources. There is also no match between Grebe and Carstens recorded.

10. In a deciding match for second place, Grebe defeated Van Zo Post.

11. It is likely that two other matches were fenced — Diaz Martinez vs. Van Zo Post and Grebe vs. Carstens. This assumes a round robin format, which it appears to have been. However, no record of these other two matches could be found.

12. EK, FW, and VK list six starters and four nations competing. There were only three competitors according to the *St. Louis Globe-Democrat*. Van Zo Post's affiliation with the United States makes it the only country to have been represented.

13. EK, FM, FW, and OR have Grebe second and O'Connor third but all the St. Louis papers show the order to be reversed.

14. Usually listed as a Cuban team but that assumes, incorrectly, that Van Zo Post was a Cuban citizen.

15. Usually listed as an international team (USA/CUB) but that assumes, incorrectly, that Tatham was a Cuban citizen.

16. Listed in FM and VK as an Olympic event.

Football (Soccer)

The 1904 football (soccer) tournament was contested by three teams, two from the United States and one from Canada. The Canadian team was from Galt, Ontario. The American teams were both from St. Louis and represented Christian Brothers College and St. Rose Parish. The events were held in November 1904 at the Olympic Stadium of the Washington University campus.

The two St. Louis teams became involved in the Olympics because of one of the athletes competing in soccer, Joseph P. Lydon. He was one of the outstanding amateur athletes in the St. Louis area and had competed in the Olympic boxing matches earlier in the summer. Local AAU officials encouraged Lydon to form a soccer league for amateur soccer players only, as most of the local clubs in St. Louis were actually semi-professional soccer teams. Lydon helped form a Parish League composed of three teams: Christian Brothers College, St. Rose Parish, and St. Anne's Parish. Shortly thereafter, a meeting was held at Christian Brothers College, chaired by Lydon, at which the Amateur Association Football League of St. Louis was established, which was really just an extension of the Parish League, although a fourth team, St. Alphonsus Parish, was added.

On 16 November, the Christian Brothers College played the Galt Football Club of Canada and lost decisively, 7–0. Lydon played half back for the CBC team. The Galt (Ontario) team was the Canadian national champion while at that time the CBC team had been in existence for approximately two weeks. Christian Brothers College was then both a college and a high school providing college preparatory courses, although eight of the CBC soccer players were college students.

The next day the Galt team defeated St. Rose 4–0 to win the Olympic soccer championship. On 18 November, CBC and St. Rose played off for second and third place in the Olympic tournament, but neither team could score, despite three overtimes, and after 90 minutes the game was postponed because of darkness. The playoff match was rescheduled for 23 November, and on that day CBC defeated St. Rose 2–0. Three days prior, however, CBC and St. Rose had actually played to a scoreless tie as part of the regular Parish League schedule. This scoreless tie was often listed as the first playoff for the Olympic championship, but the local newspapers in that era make it clear that it definitely was not part of the Olympic tournament.

Football (soccer) at the 1904 Olympics has a solid claim to having been an Olympic sport. Although it had an American and fairly local flavor, it did have international teams and even an international champion.

	Site:	Francis Field
	Dates/Times:	16–18, 23 November
	Events:	1
	Competitors:	34
	Nations:	2

	Competitors	1st	2nd	3rd	Totals
Canada	11	1	-	-	1
United States	23	-	1	1	2
Totals	34	1	1	1	1
Nations	2	1	1	1	1

Final Standings

A: 34[1]*; D: 16–18, 23 November; L: Francis Field; F: Games consisted of two thirty-minute halves with 10 minute overtimes if necessary.

1. Canada   (Galt Football Club)
    (Ernest Linton [G], George Ducker [FB], John Gourley [FB], John Fraser [FB], Albert Johnson [HB], Robert Lane [HB], Tom Taylor [F/RW], Frederick Steep [F/RW], Alexander Hall [F/C], Gordon McDonald [F/LW], William Twaits [F/LW])

2. United States   (Christian Brothers College)[2]
    (Louis Menges [G], Oscar Brockmeyer [FB/F][3], Thomas January [FB], John January [HB], Charles January [HB], Peter Ratican [HB], Warren Brittingham [F], Alexander Cudmore [F], Charles Bartliff [F], Joseph Lydon [F/FB], Raymond Lawlor [F])

3. United States   (St. Rose Parish)[4]
    (Frank Frost [G], George Cooke [FB], Henry Jameson [FB], Joseph Brady [HB], Dierkes [HB], Martin Dooling [HB], Cormic Cosgrove [F/RW], O'Connell [F/RW], Claude Jameson [F/C], Harry Tate [F/LW], Thomas Cooke [F/LW], Johnson [F/LW][5])

    Results of Matches

16 November	Galt FC	4	-	3	7					
	Christian Brothers	0	-	0	0					
	Goals: Hall [3], McDonald [2], Steep, Taylor									
17 November	Galt FC	4	-	0	4					
	St. Rose	0	-	0	0					
	Goals: Taylor [2], Twaits, one own goal									
18 November	Christian Brothers	0	-	0	0	0	-	0	-	0	0
	St. Rose	0	-	0	0	0	-	0	-	0	0
23 November[6]	Christian Brothers	1	-	1	2					
	St. Rose	0	-	0	0					

*See Notes on page 137.

NON-OLYMPIC FOOTBALL EVENT

Olympic Irish Sports Gaelic Football Championship

D: 20 July 1904

1. Chicago Fenians
2. St. Louis Innisfalls

> *Match Score*

Chicago Fenians defeated St. Louis Innisfalls, 10–0.

NOTES

1. VK lists 37.
2. Many of the Christian Brothers' players' full names were discovered by St. Louis researchers June Wuest Becht and Wayne McFarland.
3. In the games against Galt, Lydon played forward and Brockmeyer fullback. Against St. Rose, Lydon played fullback, and Brockmeyer forward.
4. Many of the names of the St. Rose players were found with assistance from the St. Louis Old-Tymers Soccer Club.
5. Johnson replaced Thomas Cooke in the second game against Christian Brothers after Cooke sustained a broken leg.
6. Most sources also list Christian Brothers and St. Rose as having also played on 20 November. They did play on that date but it was not part of the Olympic tournaments but rather a match in the parish league schedule of which they were both members. The play-off of the tie match from 18 November was specifically scheduled for 23 November.

Golf

Olympic golf was contested at the 1900 Olympic Games in Paris, with the golf tournaments held at the Compiègne Club in Compiègne, about 30 miles north of Paris. There were two Olympic golf events in 1900, one for gentlemen and one for ladies. A third competition was held on the final day. However, this was a handicap event for the men, and cannot be considered of Olympic caliber. It was, however, won by an American, Albert Lambert, whose participation was critical to a 1904 Olympic golf tournament taking place.

Lambert was a wealthy man, who founded Lambert Pharmacal Co., later Warner-Lambert, best-known as the makers of Listerine. His avocation in later years became flying, and he was the primary benefactor for Charles Lindbergh's transatlantic flight. For his contributions to aviation, the St. Louis airport was named Lambert International Field.

In 1900 Lambert played the Olympic golf event while on a business trip to his Paris office. On his return he mentioned the Olympic golf event to his father-in-law, Colonel George McGrew. McGrew was the founder and president of Glen Echo Golf Club in St. Louis, and with the Olympics coming to St. Louis in 1904, Lambert and McGrew made plans to conduct an Olympic golf tournament at Glen Echo.

Seventy-four Americans and three Canadians came to Glen Echo to contest the Olympic individual championship.[1]* They were greeted by a plethora of golf events — driving contests, putting contests at night under the lights, handicap events, flights for non-qualifiers and match-play losers, and team Nassau competitions. Just two of the many events can be considered Olympic championships: a team event of 36 holes stroke play on Saturday, 17 September, and an individual match-play event which ran the week of 19–24 September.

Of the six ten-man teams which had entered, only two showed up on 17 September, the Western Golf Association and the Trans-Mississippi Golf Association. A third team was organized at the last minute from among the golfers present, and it represented, very loosely, the USGA. The Western GA, led by current U.S. and Western Amateur champion H. Chandler Egan, won fairly easily. (The previous week, Egan had defeated Walter Travis to win the U.S. Amateur. Travis, considered America's top amateur, entered the Olympic tournament but declined to compete, citing illness.)

On Monday, 19 September, 75 golfers teed off for the match play qualifying. First player off the tee was Raymond Havemeyer, later donor of the Havemeyer Trophy given to the U.S.

*See Notes on pages 147–148.

138

Amateur champion. Qualifying medalists were Stuart Stickney and Ralph McKittrick of the St. Louis Country Club, with a 36-hole total of 163, though McKittrick later defeated Stickney, 84–86, in a play-off for the medal. A score of 183 was sufficient to move on to match play. Only one of the three Canadians survived the qualifying, George Lyon of the Lambton Golf & Country Club in Toronto. Match play began Tuesday and consisted of daily 36-hole matches. Advancing to the semi-finals were Egan, Lyon, Frank Newton of the Seattle CC, and Burt McKinnie of the Normandie Park Golf Club in St. Louis. McKinnie, a music teacher, was the current St. Louis city champion, while Newton was Pacific Northwest champion in 1902 and would win, in 1926, the first New England Amateur at the age of 52. Egan easily defeated McKinnie while Lyon bested Newton to move to the finals.

Egan, based on his summer record, was the favorite in the final, but Lyon was a fine player. Before Lyon's career was done he would win the Canadian Amateur eight times and finish second in both the U.S. Amateur and Canadian Open. Lyon was known as one of Canada's great all-around athletes, having been in the 1890s their top cricket batsman. After five straight days of 36 holes, one factor against him in the final, it was thought, was his age, 46.

The day of the final dawned cold and gloomy and both contestants would fight the rain for the entire day. When the battle was over, George Lyon was Olympic champion by 3 and 2. His body, hardened by years of athletic endeavor, had pulled him through. While Egan was a classic stylist, Lyon had an ungainly, flat swing, relying on his natural coordination and great strength, which made him easily the longest driver in the tournament. After the match, Egan went to bed exhausted. Lyon went to the awards dinner and further showed his stamina by walking the length of the dining room — on his hands!

Site:	Glen Echo Country Club, St. Louis, Missouri
Dates/Times:	17, 19–24 September
Events:	2
Competitors:	77
Nations:	2

	Competitors	1st	2nd	3rd	Totals
Canada	3	1	-	-	1
United States	74	1	2	2	5
Totals	77	2	2	2	6
Nations	2	2	1	1	2

Men's Individual Event

A: 75[2]; C: 2; D: 19–24 September; F: All players played 36 holes stroke play on 19 September to qualify for 32 positions in match play. Play continued at match play with all matches being 36 holes.

1.	George Lyon	CAN		=9.	Robert Hunter	USA
2.	H. Chandler Egan[3]	USA			Simpson Foulis	USA
=3.	Burt McKinnie	USA			W. Arthur Stickney	USA
	Francis Newton[4]	USA			Nathaniel Moore	USA
=5.	Daniel "Ned" Sawyer	USA			Stuart Stickney	USA
	Harry Allen	USA			Ralph McKittrick	USA
	Albert Lambert	USA			Arthur Havemeyer	USA
	Mason Phelps	USA			Allen Lard	USA

Match Play Summary

Qualifying Score	Round One 20 September	Round Two 21 September	Round Three 22 September	Semi-finals 23 September	Final 24 September	
86-84 170 [=11]	Burt McKinnie (USA)	McKinnie 37 holes	McKinnie 7 & 6	McKinnie 4 & 3	HC Egan 4 & 3	Lyon 3 & 2
88-86 174 [=16]	Harold Weber (USA)					
87-84 171 [14]	Robert Hunter (USA)	Hunter 8 & 7				
94-89 183 [=29]	Raymond Havemeyer (USA)					
89-85 174 [=16]	Simpson Foulis (USA)	Foulis 5 & 3	Sawyer 2 & 1			
87-86 173 [15]	Henry Potter[5] (USA)					
90-79 169 [=9]	Daniel "Ned" Sawyer (USA)	Sawyer 8 & 7				
92-82 174 [=16]	Jesse Carleton (USA)					
84-81 165 [=4]	W. Arthur Stickney (USA)	WA Stickney 2 & 1	Allen 4 & 3	HC Egan 4 & 3		
91-87 178 [=22]	Clement Smoot (USA)					
93-85 178 [=22]	Harry Allen (USA)	Allen 6 & 4				
84-86 170 [=11]	Warren Wood (USA)					
87-90 177 [=19]	Nathaniel Moore (USA)	Moore 12 & 10	HC Egan 7 & 6			
83-94 177 [=19]	Orus Jones (USA)					
88-78 166 [=6]	H. Chandler Egan (USA)	HC Egan 8 & 6				
90-93 183 [=29]	Harold Fraser (USA)					
81-82 163 [2][6]	Stuart Stickney (USA)[7]	SA Stickney 7 & 6	Lyon 11 & 9	Lyon 5 & 4	Lyon 1 up	
93-90 183 [=29]	William Smith (USA)					
84-85 169 [=9]	George Lyon (CAN)	Lyon 5 & 4				
93-89 182 [=27]	John Cady (USA)					
86-82 168 [8]	Albert Lambert (USA)	Lambert 7 & 6	Lambert 1 up			
80-85 165 [=4]	Walter Egan (USA)					
81-82 163 [1]	Ralph McKittrick (USA)	McKittrick 2 & 1				
88-82 170 [=11]	Douglas Cadwalader (USA)					
86-80 166 [=6]	Mason Phelps (USA)	Phelps 6 & 4	Phelps 12 & 10	Newton 2 & 1		
89-91 180 [26]	Frederick Semple (USA)					
88-90 178 [=22]	Arthur Havemeyer (USA)	Havemeyer 8 & 7				
85-92 177 [=19]	Simeon Price (USA)					
93-90 183 [=29]	Allen Lard (USA)	Lard 10 & 9	Newton 2 & 1			
92-90 182 [=27]	Abner Vickery (USA)					
80-84 164 [3]	Francis Newton (USA)	Newton 8 & 7				
88-91 179 [25]	Edward "Ned" Cummins (USA)					

Non-Qualifiers for Match Play

=33.	Bart Adams	USA	91	–	93	–	184
	William Burton	USA	94	–	90	–	184
=35.	Charles Scudder	USA	90	–	95	–	185
	Louis Boyd	USA	88	–	97	–	185
=37.	Edwin Hunter	USA	90	–	90	–	187
	Harold Simkins	USA	93	–	94	–	187
39.	John Rahm	USA	93	–	95	–	188
=40.	Arthur Hussey	USA	93	–	98	–	191
	Herbert Sumney	USA	92	–	99	–	191
=42.	E. M. Davis	USA	94	–	98	–	192
	E. Campbell Brown	USA	100	–	92	–	192
	Henry Case	USA	94	–	98	–	192
=45.	George Powell	USA	96	–	99	–	195
	R. H. Flack	USA	98	–	97	–	195
	C. E. Williard	USA	97	–	98	–	195
=48.	George Thomas	USA	96	–	100	–	196
	Charles Potter	USA	92	–	104	–	196
50.	George Oliver	USA	95	–	102	–	197
51.	W. A. Hersey	USA	101	–	97	–	198
=52.	E. C. Edmunds	USA	100	–	99	–	199
	J. S. Brandt	USA	97	–	102	–	199
54.	F. C. Newberry	USA	99	–	102	–	201
=55.	L. J. Hazleton	USA	99	–	103	–	202
	A. H. Annan	USA	102	–	100	–	202
57.	Murray Carleton	USA	104	–	99	–	203
58.	Louis Allis	USA	101	–	104	–	205
59.	John Watson	USA	99	–	107	–	206
=60.	Alexander Mackintosh	USA	102	–	105	–	207
	Jarvis Hunt	USA	103	–	104	–	207
=62.	William Withers	USA	108	–	101	–	209
	Wallace Shaw	USA	107	–	102	–	209
64.	J. J. Howard	USA	100	–	110	–	210
65.	Adam Austin	CAN	105	–	106	–	211
=66.	Mead Yates	USA	104	–	109	–	213
	J. L. Stack	USA	112	–	101	–	213
=68.	William Groseclose	USA	98	–	116	–	214
	Simon Harbaugh	USA	111	–	103	–	214
70.	E. W. Lansing	USA	114	–	105	–	219
71.	Edward Gould	USA	114	–	108	–	222
72.	Clarence Angier	USA	114	–	112	–	226
73.	Albert Austin	CAN	117	–	113	–	230
74.	E. Lee Jones	USA	125	–	115	–	240
	Charles Cory	USA	94	–	WD		

Men's Team Event

A: 30; C: 1; D: 17 September; F: 10 players per team with 36 holes stroke play per player.

1.	Western Golf Association	USA	882	–	867	–	1,749	
	H. Chandler Egan	81	–	84	–	165		
	Daniel "Ned" Sawyer	83	–	85	–	168		
	Robert Hunter	86	–	83	–	169		
	Kenneth Edwards	86	–	84	–	170		
	Clement Smoot	86	–	86	–	172		
	Warren Wood	90	–	83	–	173		
	Mason Phelps	89	–	88	–	177		
	Walter Egan	91	–	89	–	180		
	Edward "Ned" Cummins	94	–	93	–	187		
	Nathaniel Moore	96	–	92	–	188		
2.	Trans-Mississippi Golf Association	USA	892	–	878	–	1,770	
	Francis Newton	84	–	88	–	172		
	Henry Potter	83	–	89	–	172		
	Ralph McKittrick	87	–	87	–	174		
	Albert Lambert	89	–	86	–	175		
	Frederick Semple	89	–	87	–	176		
	Stuart Stickney	92	–	85	–	177		
	William Stickney	96	–	82	–	178		
	Burt McKinnie	89	–	89	–	178		
	John Maxwell	90	–	92	–	182		
	John Cady	93	–	93	–	186		
3.	United States Golf Association[8]	USA	926	–	913	–	1,839	
	Douglas Cadwalader	84	–	84	–	168		
	Allen Lard	85	–	87	–	172		
	Jesse Carleton	90	–	85	–	175		
	Simeon Price	93	–	88	–	181		
	Harold Weber	89	–	94	–	183		
	John Rahm	94	–	92	–	186		
	Arthur Hussey	89	–	98	–	187		
	Orus Jones	98	–	89	–	187		
	Harold Fraser	99	–	95	–	194		
	George Oliver	105	–	101	–	206		

NON-OLYMPIC EVENTS

International President's Match

A: 2; C: 2; D: 23 September

This match was between the club presidents of Glen Echo Country Club (McGrew), where the Olympic events were held, and Lambton Golf & Country Club in Toronto, Ontario, Canada (Austin). It was international as they represented the only two countries which competed at the 1904 Olympic golf events.

1.	Col. George S. McGrew	USA	87
2.	Adam W. Austin	CAN	92

Driving Contest

A: 25; C: ?; D: 16 September; F: Each contestant had three drives. To count, a drive had to be at least 175 yards and in the landing zone. The championship was decided by an unknown scoring system, although it was noted that the drives landed in a "checkerboard-like" grid.

1.	H. Chandler Egan	USA	6 pts.	(234 yds, 202 yds)
2.	Arthur Havemeyer	USA	4 pts.	

Putting Contest

A: ?; C: ?; D: 17 September; F: 9 holes stroke play

1.	Burt P. McKinnie	USA	21	22
2.	Clement Smoot	USA	21	26

Team Nassau Match

A: 24; C: 1; D: 16 September; F: The match was over 36 holes. One point was awarded the winner of the morning 18, one point was awarded the winner of the afternoon 18, and one point to the winner of the 36-hole match. Teams were composed of 12 men and the teams were not identical to those which took part in the Olympic Team championship on Saturday, 17 September.

1. Trans-Mississippi Golf Association   USA   20½

	AM	PM	36	Total[9]
Frank C. Newton	0	1	1	2
Burt P. McKinnie	0	1	1	2
John R. Maxwell	0	1	0	1
Ardo W. Mitchell	1	0	0	1
John D. Cady	0	0	0	0
Leon W. Mitchell	1	0	0	1
Ralph McKittrick	1	1	1	3
Frederick Semple	1	1	1	3
Stuart Stickney	1	0	0	1
Arthur Stickney	1	1	1	3
Henry Potter	½	1	1	2½
Albert B. Lambert	0	1	0	1

2. Western Golf Association   USA   15½

	AM	PM	36	Total
Clement Smoot	1	0	0	1
Ned Sawyer	1	0	0	1
Warren K. Wood	1	0	1	2
Benjamin Cummins	0	1	1	2
Mason Phelps	1	1	1	3
Kenneth P. Edwards	0	1	1	2

Robert Hunter	0	0	0	0
Simpson Foulis	0	0	0	0
H. Chandler Egan	0	1	1	2
Louis T. Boyd	0	0	0	0
Louis Allis	½	0	0	½
Walter Egan	1	0	1	2

Qualifying for Consolation Flights

A: 50; C: 2; D: 21 September; F: 18 holes stroke play.

1.	Douglas Cadwalader	USA	85
2.	Charles Scudder	USA	86
3.	Harold D. Fraser	USA	88
4.	Orus W. Jones	USA	89
=5.	L. J. Hazleton	USA	91
	H. L. Case	USA	91
	Walter E. Egan	USA	91
	Abner C. Vickery	USA	91
9.	J. S. Brandt	USA	92
=10.	Dr. Herbert Sumney	USA	93
	Sim T. Price, Jr.	USA	93
=12.	Adam E. Austin	CAN	94
	John T. Watson	USA	94
=14.	Mead W. Yates	USA	95
	Jesse L. Carleton	USA	95
	Louis T. Allis	USA	95
	Henry H. Potter	USA	95
	L. T. Boyd	USA	95
=19.	J. J. Howard	USA	97
	Warren K. Wood	USA	97
	E. C. Edmunds	USA	97
	Edwin Hunter	USA	97
=23.	Arthur D. Hussey	USA	98
	George C. Oliver	USA	98
	A. C. McIntosh	USA	98
=26.	Harold W. Sinkins	USA	99
	R. H. Flack	USA	99
28.	C. E. Williard	USA	99
=29.	Frederick H. Semple	USA	100
	Dr. Wallace Shaw	USA	100
	G. A. Thomas	USA	100
	Raymond Havemeyer	USA	100
	F. C. Newberry	USA	100
	Bart Adams	USA	100
35.	E. W. Lansing	USA	101
=36.	Murray Carleton	USA	103
	W. W. Burton	USA	103
	A. H. Annan	USA	103

=39.	William T. Withers	USA	104
	W. A. Hersey	USA	104
	—— Carleton	USA	104
	—— McArdle	USA	104
43.	George F. Powell	USA	105
=44.	Col. George S. McGrew	USA	106
	—— Miller	USA	106
	William Groseclose	USA	106
47.	—— Ballard	USA	107
48.	—— Lincoln	USA	112
49.	Simon Harbaugh	USA	119
50.	Albert Austin	CAN	123

First Flight Consolation Championship

A: 15; C: 2; D: 22-25 September; F: 18 holes match play, except the final was at 36 holes.

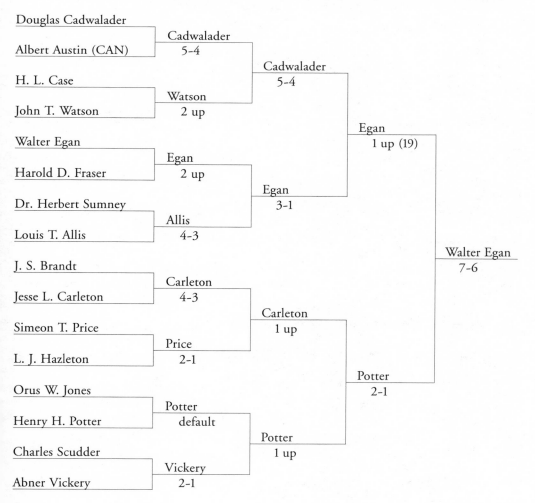

Second Flight Consolation Championship

A: 16; C: 1; D: 22–25 September; F: 18 holes match play, except the final was at 36 holes.

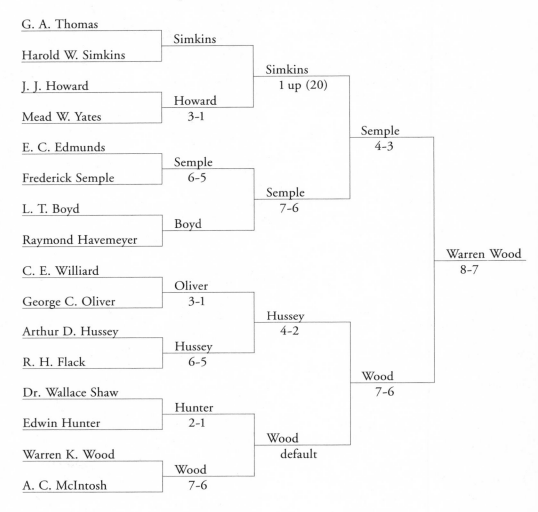

G. A. Thomas
Harold W. Simkins
— Simkins

J. J. Howard
Mead W. Yates
— Howard 3–1

Simkins 1 up (20)

E. C. Edmunds
Frederick Semple
— Semple 6–5

L. T. Boyd
Raymond Havemeyer
— Boyd

Semple 7–6

Semple 4–3

C. E. Williard
George C. Oliver
— Oliver 3–1

Arthur D. Hussey
R. H. Flack
— Hussey 6–5

Hussey 4–2

Dr. Wallace Shaw
Edwin Hunter
— Hunter 2–1

Warren K. Wood
A. C. McIntosh
— Wood 7–6

Wood default

Wood 7–6

Warren Wood 8–7

Third Flight Consolation Championship

A: 15; C: 1; D: 22–25 September; F: 18 holes match play, except the final was at 36 holes.

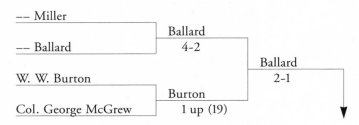

–– Miller
–– Ballard
— Ballard 4–2

W. W. Burton
Col. George McGrew
— Burton 1 up (19)

Ballard 2–1

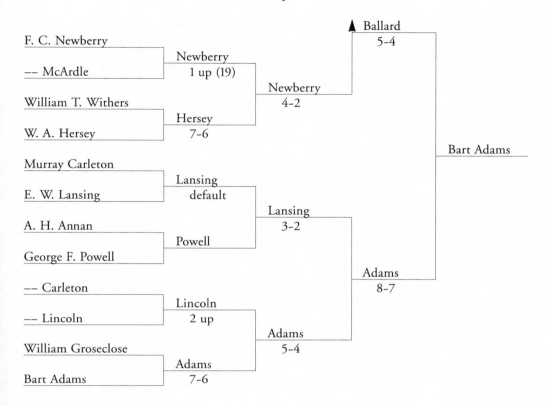

F. C. Newberry

Newberry
1 up (19)

-- McArdle

Newberry
4-2

William T. Withers

Hersey
7-6

W. A. Hersey

Ballard
5-4

Newberry

Murray Carleton

Lansing
default

E. W. Lansing

Lansing
3-2

A. H. Annan

Powell

George F. Powell

Bart Adams

Adams
8-7

-- Carleton

Lincoln
2 up

-- Lincoln

Adams
5-4

William Groseclose

Adams
7-6

Bart Adams

Fourth Flight Consolation Championship

A: 2; C: 2; D: 23 September; F: 36 holes match play final only.

Albert W. Austin

A. W. Austin
5-4

Simon Harbaugh

NOTES

1. There were also entrants from Chile (Hector Beeche), Cuba (M. Albertini), and France (Pierre Deschamps), though they did not compete.

2. EK and VK did not know of the early round matches and listed only 21 players.

3. EK lists incorrectly as Charles Chandler Egan. His name was Henry Chandler Egan.

4. EK lists this golfer incorrectly as Fred Newton. His correct name was Francis Clement Newton.

5. EK lists as Harry Potter. His son, T. Randolph Potter, confirmed that his real name was Henry.

6. Stuart Stickney and Ralph McKittrick tied at 163 for the qualifying medal. They played off the tie on Thursday, 22 September at 18 holes stroke play, with McKittrick winning 84–86.

7. Stickney's name is variously spelled as Stuart and Stewart. His daughter, Mrs. Peter Lindsay, confirmed the correct spelling.

8. The United States Golf Association (USGA) team was not a true representative of the USGA. When only two of the six entered teams showed up to play on the morning of 17 September, several

of the players who were on hand and not entered decided to form a team and enter the event. Since they were all members of USGA member clubs, they loosely represented the USGA. VK and EK did not know of a third team entered and listed only two finishers.

9. The players are arranged in the order of their matches, i.e., Newton vs. Smoot, McKinnie vs. Sawyer, etc.

Gymnastics

There were really two gymnastics competitions held at the 1904 Olympics. On 1–2 July 1904 Turnverein gymnastics was contested on the field of the Olympic Stadium. Turnverein gymnastics originated in Germany and Eastern Europe, sparked by the Bohemian Sokol movement. It often consisted of a combination of both gymnastics exercises and track & field exercises. At this time Turnverein gymnastics competed with Swedish gymnastics and their proponents for control of the sport. Swedish gymnastics consisted basically of only gymnastics exercises without the track & field events associated with them. Swedish gymnastics-type events were held at the 1904 Olympics as well, this time on 28 October 1904, or almost four months after the Turnverein gymnastics.

The Turnverein gymnastics consisted essentially of six events: horizontal bar, parallel bars, side and long horses, 100 yard run, shot put, and long jump. On the horizontal bar, parallel bars and horses, each contestant executed three different exercises, two compulsory and one optional. In a sense, then, the Turnverein gymnastics consisted of 12 events, as it is often listed. The official rules noted that the events would be conducted under the rules of the North American Gymnastic Union (Turnerbund).

Medals were given out for the top individual and team performances in the 12 events or basically an all-around competition in Turnverein gymnastics. However, medals were also given out for the best performance in the nine events consisting of only gymnastics work. Finally, a "triathlon" consisting of scores obtained only in the three track & field events was also scored, and medals were given out for that competition. This was definitely held as part of the Turnverein gymnastics competition, and not part of the track & field events. However, in many Olympic reference books it is listed with the track & field program, which can hardly be faulted since they were all track & field events. In fact, two days after the Turnverein gymnastics finished, on 4 July 1904, the all-around competition was held on the same field by several of the same competitors who competed in the triathlon. This was two months prior to the track & field events of the 1904 Olympics but that event is almost always considered as part of the track & field competition.

Turnverein gymnastics in this country was contested almost entirely by athletes of German and Scandinavian descent who had emigrated to this country. The 1904 Turnverein gymnastic events are certainly of Olympic caliber. A team of multiple gymnasts from Berlin competed, representing Germany. In addition, we know that many of the athletes representing other American Turnvereins were still almost certainly of foreign nationality, not yet having obtained their American nationality. In many cases their precise nationality cannot be determined.

149

The Swedish gymnastics competitions which were held in October 1904 are of marginal Olympic caliber. These were the AAU Gymnastics Championships for that year and there were no foreign entrants or foreign competitors. In all Olympic reference books they have been listed as an Olympic event, which I consider acceptable as the rules in no way excluded foreign athletes.

Perhaps the best story from the AAU Gymnastics concerns the exploits of George Eyser. George Eyser competed in the Turnverein gymnastics and the Swedish gymnastics of the 1904 Olympics. In the Turnverein gymnastics he did superbly on the gymnastics apparatus events but finished dead last in the track & field competition, hampered especially by very poor scores in the 100 yard dash and long jump. At the Swedish gymnastics competition, he won six Olympic medals including three gold. He did this entirely with his upper body strength, and it becomes more clear why he scored so poorly in the running events at the Turnverein gymnastics when one realizes that he had lost one of his legs as a youth when it was run over by a train. He competed at the Olympics as a gymnast with a wooden leg.

Strangely, the complete results of the AAU Gymnastic Championships have never been found. However, the Turnverein gymnastics results do exist, courtesy of the original score sheets that were in possession of the son of Julius Lenhart, who won the individual all-around competition. These score sheets were later given to Erich Kamper, the great historian of the Olympic movement, who kindly provided them to me. They are difficult to read, being written in German black letter, and some of the scores cannot be determined with absolute certainty from the printout that is available.

Site:	Francis Field	
Dates/Times:	1–2 July, 28 October	
Events:	12	
Competitors:	121	
Nations:	4	

	Competitors	1st	2nd	3rd	Totals
Austria	1	1	1	-	2
Austria/United States	-	1	-	-	1
Germany	7	-	1	1	2
Switzerland	1	1	-	1	2
United States	112	11	8	10	29
Totals	121	14	10	12	36
Nations	4	3	3	3	4

Combined Exercises, Apparatus Work, and Field Sports, Individual

A: 119; C: 4; D: 1–2 July; F: Each competitor executed three routines on the horizontal bar and parallel bars — two compulsory and one optional. All competitors performed a compulsory routine on the long horse, a compulsory routine on the side horse, and an optional routine on the side horse. Scoring was from 0–5, with 5 being the maximum score for any of the 9 routines, permitting a maximum of 45 overall. Each athlete also competed in the long jump, shot put, and 100 yard dash as part of the overall combined exercises. Scoring was from 0 to a maximum of 10 for each of the three events. In the long jump, 18 feet (5.48 m.) earned 10 points, and ⅒ point was subtracted for each ⅒ foot short of 18 feet. In the shot put, 30 feet (9.14 m.) earned 10 points, and ⅒ point was subtracted for each ⅕ foot short of 30 feet. In the 100 yard dash, 11.0 seconds earned 10 points, and ½ point was subtracted for each ⅕ second slower than 11.0 seconds. In this portion of the competition, 10 points was the maximum for each of the three track & field events, or 30 points total maximum for the track & field events, and an over-all maximum of 75 points.

		Total	PB	HB	SH	LJ Dist	SP Dist	100 Time	LJ Scor	SP Scor	100 Scor	GYM Total	TAF Total
1. Julius Lenhart	AUT[1]*	69.80	14.40	14.60	14.00	18.0	28.5	12.0	10.0	9.3	7.5	43.00	26.8
2. Wilhelm Weber	GER	69.10	14.17	13.93	13.50	18.1	30.1	12.0	10.0	10.0	7.5	41.60	27.5
3. Adolf Spinnler	SUI	67.99	14.53	14.53	14.43	16.2	29.6	12.4	8.2	9.8	6.5	43.49	24.5
4. Ernst Mohr	GER	67.90	12.90	13.00	13.00	18.7	30.0	11.4	10.0	10.0	9.0	38.90	29.0
5. Otto Wiegand	GER[2]	67.82	13.12	14.20	13.50	17.5	30.4	12.0	9.5	10.0	7.5	40.82	27.0
6. Otto Steffen	USA	67.03	12.80	14.10	12.63	18.1	30.8	12.0	10.0	10.0	7.5	39.53	27.5
7. Hugo Peitsch	GER	66.66	14.03	14.30	13.23	16.9	27.4	12.0	8.9	8.7	7.5	41.56	25.1
8. John Bissinger	USA	66.57	13.10	12.37	12.10	18.4	32.8	11.4	10.0	10.0	9.0	37.57	29.0
9. Christian Busch	GER	66.12	13.80	11.25	12.57	18.9	31.3	11.6	10.0	10.0	8.5	37.62	28.5
10. William Merz	USA	65.26	11.56	12.40	11.30	19.9	31.1	10.8	10.0	10.0	10.0	35.26	30.0
11. Phillip Kassell	USA	64.56	11.26	12.40	12.00	19.2	28.8	11.2	10.0	9.4	9.5	35.66	28.9
12. Theodore Gross	USA	64.39	12.19	13.60	11.40	18.1	28.3	11.8	10.0	9.2	8.0	37.19	27.2
13. Wilhelm Lemke	GER	64.15	12.02	13.43	12.30	18.2	24.7	11.4	10.0	7.4	9.0	37.75	26.4
14. Otto Boehnke	USA	64.10	12.69	11.97	11.84	19.1	28.2	11.6	10.0	9.1	8.5	36.50	27.6
15. William Andelfinger	USA	63.53	12.77	13.93	12.33	16.8	28.4	12.4	8.8	9.2	6.5	39.03	24.5
16. George Stapf	USA	63.47	10.73	11.70	12.84	18.5	26.4	11.0	10.0	8.2	10.0	35.27	28.2
17. Charles Umbs	USA	63.19	13.23	12.93	11.33	17.6	29.1	12.4	9.6	9.6	6.5	37.49	25.7
18. Anton Heida	USA	62.72	12.10	13.86	11.76	17.7	24.6	11.8	9.7	7.3	8.0	37.72	25.0
19. Adolph Weber	GER	62.62	11.53	13.83	11.36	18.0	26.8	12.0	10.0	8.4	7.5	36.72	25.9
20. Andreas Kempf	USA	62.57	13.63	13.97	11.37	16.7	27.7	12.6	8.7	8.9	6.0	38.97	23.6
21. George Mayer	USA	61.66	10.83	11.37	10.46	18.1	36.6	11.4	10.0	10.0	9.0	32.66	29.0
22. Fred Schmind	USA	61.40	11.03	10.67	11.20	19.4	30.2	11.6	10.0	10.0	8.5	32.90	28.5
23. Andrew Neu	USA	61.21	10.74	12.83	9.04	16.9	29.4	11.0	8.9	9.7	10.0	32.61	28.6
24. John Duha	USA	61.02	12.56	13.20	9.56	18.8	27.4	12.2	10.0	8.7	7.0	35.32	25.7
25. Reinhard Wagner	USA	60.73	11.23	10.77	11.73	18.4	30.0	12.2	10.0	10.0	7.0	33.73	27.0
26. Lorenz Spann	USA	60.32	10.03	12.93	9.96	17.9	30.0	12.0	9.9	10.0	7.5	32.92	27.4
27. Emil Rothe	USA	60.27	13.04	11.70	10.13	16.7	27.4	11.8	8.7	8.7	8.0	34.87	25.4
28. Ragnar Berg	USA	60.24	11.74	11.07	10.03	17.8	28.2	11.6	9.8	9.1	8.5	32.84	27.4
29. Robert Herrmann	USA	59.99	11.67	10.46	10.86	17.0	30.6	11.8	9.0	10.0	8.0	32.99	27.0
30. Emil Beyer	USA	59.70	11.20	12.60	9.40	17.2	28.5	11.8	9.2	9.3	8.0	33.20	26.5
31. Max Hess	USA	59.29	10.06	10.93	9.80	18.8	30.7	11.6	10.0	10.0	8.5	30.79	28.5
32. Edward Siegler	USA	59.03	11.77	10.23	8.63	18.8	28.8	11.4	10.0	9.4	9.0	30.63	28.4
33. Harry Hansen	USA	59.00	11.80	12.60	9.80	17.3	25.9	12.0	9.3	8.0	7.5	34.20	24.8
34. Max Wolf	USA	57.85	11.73	11.20	10.32	16.9	28.3	12.4	8.9	9.2	6.5	33.25	24.6
35. Frank Schicke	USA	57.47	9.37	11.30	8.40	18.1	27.8	11.2	10.0	8.9	9.5	29.07	28.4
36. John Dellert	USA	57.41	12.51	12.00	9.20	15.9	27.6	12.2	7.9	8.8	7.0	33.71	23.7
37. Charles Sorum	USA	57.40	11.50	12.90	9.00	16.6	24.8	11.8	8.6	7.4	8.0	33.40	24.0
38. William Horschke	USA	57.33	12.26	12.90	10.47	15.8	25.8	12.6	7.8	7.9	6.0	35.63	21.7
39. Oliver Olsen	USA	57.27	9.97	10.30	10.60	17.6	28.5	12.0	9.6	9.3	7.5	30.87	26.4
40. Rudolf Krupitzer	USA	57.18	11.32	11.63	8.73	17.3	27.4	12.0	9.3	8.7	7.5	31.68	25.5
41. Gustav Mueller	USA	57.12	12.34	12.45	10.33	15.8	25.4	12.4	7.8	7.7	6.5	35.12	22.0
42. Emil Schwegler	USA	56.87	11.90	11.80	11.87	16.1	24.4	12.6	8.1	7.2	6.0	35.57	21.3
43. Henry Koeder	USA	56.58	8.45	11.93	9.60	17.1	30.3	12.0	9.1	10.0	7.5	29.98	26.6
44. Louis Kniep	USA	56.57	9.67	10.23	10.77	17.7	26.4	11.8	9.7	8.2	8.0	30.67	25.9
45. William Traband	USA	56.26	11.37	11.20	9.39	17.7	23.2	11.8	9.7	6.6	8.0	31.96	24.3

See Notes on page 164.

		Total	PB	HB	SH	LJ Dist	SP Dist	100 Time	LJ Scor	SP Scor	100 Scor	GYM Total	TAF Total
46. Leander Keim	USA	56.16	8.13	12.23	9.40	15.9	31.8	11.6	7.9	10.0	8.5	29.76	26.4
47. Ernst Reckeweg	USA	56.15	9.06	11.03	8.26	18.4	29.5	11.8	10.0	9.8	8.0	28.35	27.8
48. Charles Krause	USA	56.11	11.37	9.64	10.60	16.6	26.7	12.0	8.6	8.4	7.5	31.61	24.5
49. Jacob Hertenbahn	USA	55.77	10.81	12.96	7.00	16.9	26.2	11.8	8.9	8.1	8.0	30.77	25.0
50. Edward Hennig	USA	55.63	7.22	12.97	9.74	16.7	31.6	12.2	8.7	10.0	7.0	29.93	25.7
51. Philip Schuster	USA	55.44	10.60	10.87	8.87	16.5	29.2	12.2	8.5	9.6	7.0	30.34	25.1
52. John Grieb	USA	55.21	8.11	8.43	8.67	20.2	33.6	11.0	10.0	10.0	10.0	25.21	30.0
53. P. Gussmann	USA	54.92	9.36	12.63	9.83	16.3	28.5	12.8	8.3	9.3	5.5	31.82	23.1
54. G. Hermerrling	USA	54.87	11.80	13.54	8.63	16.0	24.8	12.8	8.0	7.4	5.5	33.97	20.9
55. William Tritschler	USA	54.73	9.70	11.00	9.03	17.1	28.8	12.4	9.1	9.4	6.5	29.73	25.0
56. Christian Deubler	USA	54.63	9.20	11.50	10.43	16.6	23.9	11.8	8.6	6.9	8.0	31.13	23.5
57. Julian Schmitz	USA	54.58	12.31	11.67	9.40	14.9	26.5	12.6	6.9	8.3	6.0	33.38	21.2
58. Otto Neimand	USA	54.54	7.24	8.73	10.17	19.2	29.7	11.6	10.0	9.9	8.5	26.14	28.4
59. Robert Maysack	USA	54.53	10.76	10.90	8.67	16.8	25.8	12.0	8.8	7.9	7.5	30.33	24.2
60. Emil Voigt	USA	54.33	11.11	13.10	7.72	16.2	25.4	12.4	8.2	7.7	6.5	31.93	22.4
61. Anthony Jahnke	USA	53.94	10.24	8.57	8.73	17.4	26.9	11.6	9.4	8.5	8.5	27.54	26.4
62. Phillip Sontag	USA	53.83	8.37	11.10	8.16	17.7	27.9	12.0	9.7	9.0	7.5	27.63	26.2
63. Oluf Landnes	USA	53.64	9.07	8.00	9.37	17.0	28.3	11.4	9.0	8.7	8.0	27.97	25.5
64. George Aschenbrener	USA	53.47	9.54	9.47	8.96	16.8	27.3	11.8	9.5	8.7	7.5	27.73	25.7
65. John Wolf	USA	53.43	9.10	9.70	8.93	17.5	27.3	12.0	8.4	7.6	7.5	29.66	23.5
66. Edward Tritschler	USA	53.16				16.4	25.2	12.0	8.4	7.6	7.5	29.66	23.5
67. Max Emmerich	USA	52.85				21.6	32.2	10.6	10.0	10.0	10.0	22.85	30.0
68. Henry Prinzler	USA	52.81	8.56	10.05	7.80	17.0	26.8	11.4	9.0	8.4	9.0	26.41	26.4
69. Frank Raad	USA	52.39	10.45	12.20	8.24	16.0	25.9	12.8	8.0	8.0	5.5	30.89	21.5
70. L. Hunger	USA	52.22	7.56	11.73	7.03	17.7	25.3	11.6	9.7	7.7	8.5	26.32	25.9
71. George Eyser	USA	52.20	12.10	14.30	12.30	13.4	26.1	15.4	5.4	8.1	0.0	38.70	13.5
72. William Berewald	USA	51.87	9.53	10.37	5.37	17.1	30.9	12.0	9.1	10.0	7.5	25.27	26.6
=73. Martin Ludwig	USA	51.83	10.07	11.96	9.40	15.1	25.6	12.8	7.1	7.8	5.5	31.43	20.4
George Mastrovich	USA	51.83	9.90	10.53	7.30	16.0	27.1	12.0	8.0	8.6	7.5	27.73	24.1
75. M. Bascher	USA	51.53	9.80	10.53	9.80	15.7	26.4	12.8	7.7	8.2	5.5	30.13	21.4
76. Henry Kraft	USA	51.40	9.10	11.10	8.50	15.2	31.5	12.8	7.2	10.0	5.5	28.70	22.7
77. Willard Schrader	USA	51.22	7.53	9.63	7.56	18.5	28.1	12.0	10.0	9.0	7.5	24.72	26.5
78. James Dwyer	USA	51.00	10.37	9.00	7.33	17.6	27.4	12.6	9.6	8.7	6.0	26.70	24.3
79. George Schroeder	USA	50.90	9.17	9.37	6.96	16.8	28.3	12.0	8.8	9.1	7.5	25.50	25.4
80. Robert Reynolds	USA	50.74	7.13	8.37	6.94	18.2	29.6	11.6	10.0	9.8	8.5	22.44	28.3
81. Harry Warnken	USA	50.53	8.09	10.24	7.10	17.2	26.8	12.0	9.2	8.4	7.5	25.43	25.1
82. Bergin Nilsen	USA	50.45	7.91	9.54	8.60	16.8	27.2	12.2	8.8	8.6	7.0	26.05	24.4
83. John Leichinger	USA	50.00	5.64	7.90	8.76	17.7	32.9	11.8	9.7	10.0	8.0	22.30	27.7
84. Rudolf Schrader	USA	49.64	9.87	11.20	7.27	15.1	24.4	12.2	7.1	7.2	7.0	28.34	21.3
85. Michael Lang	USA	49.44	8.70	9.20	8.54	16.8	25.4	12.4	8.8	7.7	6.5	26.44	23.0
86. Charles Dellert	USA	49.35	8.64	10.10	10.31	14.3	24.0	12.2	6.3	7.0	7.0	29.05	20.3
87. Alvin Kritschmann	USA	48.97	10.77	13.50	5.80	15.0	24.8	13.2	7.0	7.4	4.5	30.07	18.9
88. Richard Tritschler	USA	48.80	7.30	10.67	8.43	15.5	23.8	11.8	7.5	6.9	8.0	26.40	22.4
89. Arthur Rosenkampff	USA	48.34	9.81	9.77	7.66	15.5	23.2	12.2	7.5	6.6	7.0	27.24	21.1
90. Clarence Kiddington	USA	48.30	5.27	9.03	7.50	18.0	26.0	11.6	10.0	8.0	8.5	21.80	26.5
91. Hy. Meyland	USA	47.94	7.31	10.10	8.13	15.7	26.4	12.4	7.7	8.2	6.5	25.54	22.4
92. Barney Chimberoff	USA	47.93	8.23	8.93	7.37	16.9	25.0	12.2	8.9	7.5	7.0	24.53	23.4
93. K. Woerner	USA	47.67	8.80	9.27	9.90	14.6	23.1	12.4	6.6	6.6	6.5	27.97	19.7
94. K. Roedek	USA	47.63	8.63	10.10	9.90	15.0	22.9	12.8	7.0	6.5	5.5	28.63	19.0
95. M. Barry	USA	47.43	8.57	10.73	8.03	15.4	24.3	12.8	7.4	7.2	5.5	27.33	20.1
96. P. Ritter	USA	47.09	7.46	10.80	6.03	17.1	25.4	12.6	9.1	7.7	6.0	24.29	22.8
97. Otto Feyder	USA	47.05	5.75	9.80	6.30	17.6	25.2	11.8	9.6	7.6	8.0	21.85	25.2
98. Bernard Berg	USA	46.73	7.10	8.57	7.66	15.4	31.1	12.6	7.4	10.0	6.0	23.33	23.4
99. Max Thomas	USA	45.85	6.11	7.67	5.67	16.9	30.5	12.0	8.9	10.0	7.5	19.45	26.4
100. M. Fischer	USA	45.35	9.14	8.74	6.27	14.9	25.5	12.4	6.9	7.8	6.5	24.15	21.2
101. Charles Schwartz	USA	45.34	8.51	10.23	7.50	14.7	24.8	13.0	6.7	7.4	5.0	26.24	19.1

			Total	PB	HB	SH	LJ Dist	SP Dist	100 Time	LJ Scor	SP Scor	100 Scor	GYM Total	TAF Total
102.	Wilhelm Zabel	USA	45.13	8.30	8.63	6.70	15.8	23.3	12.2	7.8	6.7	7.0	23.63	21.5
103.	L. Rathke	USA	44.93	6.00	7.36	6.47	16.3	28.6	12.0	8.3	9.3	7.5	19.83	25.1
104.	L. Guerner	USA	44.90	8.04	7.80	5.86	15.8	27.7	12.4	7.8	8.9	6.5	21.70	23.2
105.	William Herzog	USA	44.60	7.80	8.54	7.16	16.7	23.8	12.8	8.7	6.9	5.5	23.50	21.1
106.	August Placke	USA	44.41	7.03	8.84	7.24	14.9	28.7	13.0	6.9	9.4	5.0	23.11	21.3
107.	Otto Roissner	USA	43.90	5.63	9.40	6.87	16.6	24.8	12.6	8.6	7.4	6.0	21.90	22.0
108.	Paul Studel	USA	43.38	7.11	9.07	6.30	17.0	21.8	12.6	9.0	5.9	6.0	22.48	20.9
109.	Arthur Sundbye	USA	43.21	7.11	7.37	8.53	15.8	20.3	12.6	7.8	6.4	6.0	23.01	20.2
110.	Christian Sperl	USA	42.66	8.03	8.03	5.30	16.3	26.1	13.0	8.3	8.0	5.0	21.36	21.3
111.	William Kruppinger	USA	42.50	5.30	7.60	8.30	16.1	24.4	12.6	8.1	7.2	6.0	21.20	21.3
112.	J. Wassow	USA	42.46	5.30	5.53	6.13	17.4	28.2	12.2	9.4	9.1	7.0	16.96	25.5
113.	Walter Real	USA	42.44	8.14	6.80	7.30	15.7	23.9	12.8	7.7	7.0	5.5	22.24	20.2
114.	John Messel	USA	41.97	5.54	7.93	8.30	15.8	22.8	12.6	7.8	6.4	6.0	21.77	20.2
115.	Otto Thomsen	USA	41.67	6.23	6.30	5.54	15.1	28.1	12.0	7.1	9.0	7.5	18.07	23.6
116.	Edward Pueschell	USA	40.36	5.93	7.27	7.86	14.4	23.7	12.6	6.4	6.9	6.0	21.06	19.3
117.	Otto Knerr	USA	39.87	5.30	6.54	7.63	13.9	33.8	13.2	5.9	10.0	4.5	19.47	20.4
118.	William Friedrich	USA	39.57	8.20	8.87	4.80	15.1	21.2	13.0	7.1	5.6	5.0	21.87	17.7
119.	Theodore Studler	USA	13.14	3.67	2.77	6.70				0.0	0.0	0.0	13.14	0.0

Combined Exercises, Apparatus Work, Individual

A: 119; C: 4; D: 1–2 July; F: Each competitor executed three routines on the horizontal bar and parallel bars — two compulsory and one optional. All competitors performed a compulsory routine on the long horse and a compulsory routine on the side horse, and an optional routine on the side horse. Scoring was from 0–5, with 5 being the maximum score for any of the 9 routines, permitting a maximum of 45 overall.

			Total	PB	HB	Horses
1.	Adolf Spinnler	SUI	43.49	14.53	14.53	14.43
2.	Julius Lenhart	AUT	43.00	14.40	14.60	14.00
3.	Wilhelm Weber	GER	41.60	14.17	13.93	13.50
4.	Hugo Peitsch	GER	41.56	14.03	14.30	13.23
5.	Otto Wiegand	GER	40.82	13.12	14.20	13.50
6.	Otto Steffen	USA	39.53	12.80	14.10	12.63
7.	William Andelfinger	USA	39.03	12.77	13.93	12.33
8.	Andreas Kempf	USA	38.97	13.63	13.97	11.37
9.	Ernst Mohr	GER	38.90	12.90	13.00	13.00
10.	George Eyser	USA	38.70	12.10	14.30	12.30
11.	Wilhelm Lemke	GER	37.75	12.02	13.43	12.30
12.	Anton Heida	USA	37.72	12.10	13.86	11.76
13.	Christian Busch	GER	37.62	13.80	11.25	12.57
14.	John Bissinger	USA	37.57	13.10	12.37	12.10
15.	Charles Umbs	USA	37.49	13.23	12.93	11.33
16.	Theodore Gross	USA	37.19	12.19	13.60	11.40
17.	Adolph Weber	GER	36.72	11.53	13.83	11.36
18.	Otto Boehnke	USA	36.50	12.69	11.97	11.84
19.	Phillip Kassell	USA	35.66	11.26	12.40	12.00
20.	William Horschke	USA	35.63	12.26	12.90	10.47
21.	Emil Schwegler	USA	35.57	11.90	11.80	11.87

			Total	PB	HB	Horses
22.	John Duha	USA	35.32	12.56	13.20	9.56
23.	George Stapf	USA	35.27	10.73	11.70	12.84
24.	William Merz	USA	35.26	11.56	12.40	11.30
25.	Gustav Mueller	USA	35.12	12.34	12.45	10.33
26.	Emil Rothe	USA	34.87	13.04	11.70	10.13
27.	Harry Hansen	USA	34.20	11.80	12.60	9.80
28.	G. Hermerrling	USA	33.97	11.80	13.54	8.63
29.	Reinhard Wagner	USA	33.73	11.23	10.77	11.73
30.	John Dellert	USA	33.71	12.51	12.00	9.20
31.	Charles Sorum	USA	33.40	11.50	12.90	9.00
32.	Julian Schmitz	USA	33.38	12.31	11.67	9.40
33.	Max Wolf	USA	33.25	11.73	11.20	10.32
34.	Emil Beyer	USA	33.20	11.20	12.60	9.40
35.	Robert Herrmann	USA	32.99	11.67	10.46	10.86
36.	Lorenz Spann	USA	32.92	10.03	12.93	9.96
37.	Fred Schmind	USA	32.90	11.03	10.67	11.20
38.	Ragnar Berg	USA	32.84	11.74	11.07	10.03
39.	George Mayer	USA	32.66	10.83	11.37	10.46
40.	Andrew Neu	USA	32.61	10.74	12.83	9.04
41.	William Traband	USA	31.96	11.37	11.20	9.39
42.	Emil Voigt	USA	31.93	11.11	13.10	7.72
43.	P. Gussmann	USA	31.82	9.36	12.63	9.83
44.	Rudolf Krupitzer	USA	31.68	11.32	11.63	8.73
45.	Charles Krause	USA	31.61	11.37	9.64	10.60
46.	Martin Ludwig	USA	31.43	10.07	11.96	9.40
47.	Christian Deubler	USA	31.13	9.20	11.50	10.43
48.	Frank Raad	USA	30.89	10.45	12.20	8.24
49.	Oliver Olsen	USA	30.87	9.97	10.30	10.60
50.	Max Hess	USA	30.79	10.06	10.93	9.80
51.	Jacob Hertenbahn	USA	30.77	10.81	12.96	7.00
52.	Louis Kniep	USA	30.67	9.67	10.23	10.77
53.	Edward Siegler	USA	30.63	11.77	10.23	8.63
54.	Philip Schuster	USA	30.34	10.60	10.87	8.87
55.	Robert Maysack	USA	30.33	10.76	10.90	8.67
56.	M. Bascher	USA	30.13	9.80	10.53	9.80
57.	Alvin Kritschmann	USA	30.07	10.77	13.50	5.80
58.	Henry Koeder	USA	29.98	8.45	11.93	9.60
59.	Edward Hennig	USA	29.93	7.22	12.97	9.74
60.	Leander Keim	USA	29.76	8.13	12.23	9.40
61.	William Tritschler	USA	29.73	9.70	11.00	9.03
62.	Edward Tritschler	USA	29.66			
63.	Frank Schicke	USA	29.07	9.37	11.30	8.40
64.	Charles Dellert	USA	29.05	8.64	10.10	10.31
65.	Henry Kraft	USA	28.70	9.10	11.10	8.50
66.	K. Roedek	USA	28.63	8.63	10.10	9.90
67.	Ernst Reckeweg	USA	28.35	9.06	11.03	8.26
68.	Rudolf Schrader	USA	28.34	9.87	11.20	7.27

		Total	PB	HB	Horses
=69.	K. Woerner	USA	27.97	8.80	9.27	9.90
	George Aschenbrener	USA	27.97	9.54	9.47	8.96
=71.	John Wolf	USA	27.73	9.10	9.70	8.93
	George Mastrovich	USA	27.73	9.90	10.53	7.30
73.	Phillip Sontag	USA	27.63	8.37	11.10	8.16
74.	Anthony Jahnke	USA	27.54	10.24	8.57	8.73
75.	M. Barry	USA	27.33	8.57	10.73	8.03
76.	Arthur Rosenkampff	USA	27.24	9.81	9.77	7.66
77.	James Dwyer	USA	26.70	10.37	9.00	7.33
=78.	Oluf Landnes	USA	26.44	9.07	8.00	9.37
	Michael Lang	USA	26.44	8.70	9.20	8.54
80.	Henry Prinzler	USA	26.41	8.56	10.05	7.80
81.	Richard Tritschler	USA	26.40	7.30	10.67	8.43
82.	L. Hunger	USA	26.32	7.56	11.73	7.03
83.	Charles Schwartz	USA	26.24	8.51	10.23	7.50
84.	Otto Neimand	USA	26.14	7.24	8.73	10.17
85.	Bergin Nilsen	USA	26.05	7.91	9.54	8.60
86.	Hy. Meyland	USA	25.54	7.31	10.10	8.13
87.	George Schroeder	USA	25.50	9.17	9.37	6.96
88.	Harry Warnken	USA	25.43	8.09	10.24	7.10
89.	William Berewald	USA	25.27	9.53	10.37	5.37
90.	John Grieb	USA	25.21	8.11	8.43	8.67
91.	Willard Schrader	USA	24.72	7.53	9.63	7.56
92.	Barney Chimberoff	USA	24.53	8.23	8.93	7.37
93.	P. Ritter	USA	24.29	7.46	10.80	6.03
94.	M. Fischer	USA	24.15	9.14	8.74	6.27
95.	Wilhelm Zabel	USA	23.63	8.30	8.63	6.70
96.	William Herzog	USA	23.50	7.80	8.54	7.16
97.	Bernard Berg	USA	23.33	7.10	8.57	7.66
98.	August Placke	USA	23.11	7.03	8.84	7.24
99.	Arthur Sundbye	USA	23.01	7.11	7.37	8.53
100.	Max Emmerich	USA	22.85			
101.	Paul Studel	USA	22.48	7.11	9.07	6.30
102.	Robert Reynolds	USA	22.44	7.13	8.37	6.94
103.	John Leichinger	USA	22.30	5.64	7.90	8.76
104.	Walter Real	USA	22.24	8.14	6.80	7.30
105.	Otto Roissner	USA	21.90	5.63	9.40	6.87
106.	William Friedrich	USA	21.87	8.20	8.87	4.80
107.	Otto Feyder	USA	21.85	5.75	9.80	6.30
108.	Clarence Kiddington	USA	21.80	5.27	9.03	7.50
109.	John Messel	USA	21.77	5.54	7.93	8.30
110.	L. Guerner	USA	21.70	8.04	7.80	5.86
111.	Christian Sperl	USA	21.36	8.03	8.03	5.30
112.	William Kruppinger	USA	21.20	5.30	7.60	8.30
113.	Edward Pueschell	USA	21.06	5.93	7.27	7.86
114.	L. Rathke	USA	19.83	6.00	7.36	6.47
115.	Otto Knerr	USA	19.47	5.30	6.54	7.63

			Total	PB	HB	Horses
116.	Max Thomas	USA	19.45	6.11	7.67	5.67
117.	Otto Thomsen	USA	18.07	6.23	6.30	5.54
118.	J. Wassow	USA	16.96	5.30	5.53	6.13
119.	Theodore Studler	USA	13.14	3.67	2.77	6.70

Combined Exercises, Field Sports, Individual (Triathlon)

A: 118³; C: 4; D: 1–2 July; F: Each athlete competed in the long jump, shot put, and 100 yard dash as part of the overall combined exercises. Scoring was basically from 0–10 for each of the three events. In the long jump, 18 feet (5.48 m.) earned 10 points, and ¹⁄₁₀ point was added or subtracted for each ¹⁄₁₀ foot short of or beyond 18 feet. In the shot put, 30 feet (9.14 m.) earned 10 points, and ¹⁄₁₀ point was added or subtracted for each ⅓ foot short of or beyond 30 feet. In the 100 yard dash, 11.0 seconds earned 10 points, and ½ point was added or subtracted for each ⅓ second faster or slower than 11.0 seconds.

			Total	LJ Distance	SP Distance	100 Time	LJ Score	SP Score	100 Score
1.	Max Emmerich	USA	35.7	21.6	32.2	10.6	13.6	11.1	11.0
2.	John Grieb	USA	34.0	20.2	33.6	11.0	12.2	11.8	10.0
3.	William Merz	USA	32.9	19.9	31.1	10.8	11.9	10.5	10.5
4.	George Mayer	USA	32.4	18.1	36.6	11.4	10.1	13.3	9.0
5.	John Bissinger	USA	30.8	18.4	32.8	11.4	10.4	11.4	9.0
6.	Phillip Kassell	USA	30.1	19.2	28.8	11.2	11.2	9.4	9.5
=7.	Fred Schmind	USA	30.0	19.4	30.2	11.6	11.4	10.1	8.5
	Christian Busch	GER	30.0	18.9	31.3	11.6	10.9	10.6	8.5
9.	Ernst Mohr	GER	29.7	18.7	30.0	11.4	10.7	10.0	9.0
=10.	Otto Neimand	USA	29.6	19.2	29.7	11.6	11.2	9.9	8.5
	Max Hess	USA	29.6	18.8	30.7	11.6	10.8	10.3	8.5
12.	Edward Siegler	USA	29.2	18.8	28.8	11.4	10.8	9.4	9.0
13.	John Leichinger	USA	29.1	17.7	32.9	11.8	9.7	11.4	8.0
=14.	Otto Boehnke	USA	28.7	19.1	28.2	11.6	11.1	9.1	8.5
	George Stapf	USA	28.7	18.5	26.4	11.0	10.5	8.2	10.0
16.	Andrew Neu	USA	28.6	16.9	29.4	11.0	8.9	9.7	10.0
=17.	Robert Reynolds	USA	28.5	18.2	29.6	11.6	10.2	9.8	8.5
	Frank Schicke	USA	28.5	18.1	27.8	11.2	10.1	8.9	9.5
19.	Ernst Reckeweg	USA	28.2	18.4	29.5	11.8	10.4	9.8	8.0
20.	Otto Steffen	USA	28.0	18.1	30.8	12.0	10.1	10.4	7.5
21.	Wilhelm Weber	GER	27.6	18.1	30.1	12.0	10.1	10.0	7.5
=22.	Reinhard Wagner	USA	27.4	18.4	30.0	12.2	10.4	10.0	7.0
	Ragnar Berg	USA	27.4	17.8	28.2	11.6	9.8	9.1	8.5
	Lorenz Spann	USA	27.4	17.9	30.0	12.0	9.9	10.0	7.5
=25.	Theodore Gross	USA	27.3	18.1	28.3	11.8	10.1	9.2	8.0
	Robert Herrmann	USA	27.3	17.0	30.6	11.8	9.0	10.3	8.0
	Leander Keim	USA	27.3	15.9	31.8	11.6	7.9	10.9	8.5
=28.	Otto Wiegand	GER	27.2	17.5	30.4	12.0	9.5	10.2	7.5
	Oluf Landnes	USA	27.2	17.0	28.3	11.4	9.0	9.2	9.0

		Total	LJ Distance	SP Distance	100 Time	LJ Score	SP Score	100 Score
=30.	William Berewald	USA	27.0	17.1	30.9	12.0	9.1	10.4	7.5
	Willard Schrader	USA	27.0	18.5	28.1	12.0	10.5	9.0	7.5
32.	Julius Lenhart	AUT	26.8	18.0	28.5	12.0	10.0	9.3	7.5
33.	Henry Koeder	USA	26.7	17.1	30.3	12.0	9.1	10.1	7.5
=34.	Wilhelm Lemke	GER	26.6	18.2	24.7	11.4	10.2	7.4	9.0
	Max Thomas	USA	26.6	16.9	30.5	12.0	8.9	10.2	7.5
=36.	John Duha	USA	26.5	18.8	27.4	12.2	10.8	8.7	7.0
	Emil Beyer	USA	26.5	17.2	28.5	11.8	9.2	9.3	8.0
	Edward Hennig	USA	26.5	16.7	31.6	12.2	8.7	10.8	7.0
	Clarence Kiddington	USA	26.5	18.0	26.0	11.6	10.0	8.0	8.5
=40.	Oliver Olsen	USA	26.4	17.6	28.5	12.0	9.6	9.3	7.5
	Henry Prinzler	USA	26.4	17.0	26.8	11.4	9.0	8.4	9.0
	Anthony Jahnke	USA	26.4	17.4	26.9	11.6	9.4	8.5	8.5
43.	Phillip Sontag	USA	26.2	17.7	27.9	12.0	9.7	9.0	7.5
=44.	Louis Kniep	USA	25.9	17.7	26.4	11.8	9.7	8.2	8.0
	L. Hunger	USA	25.9	17.7	25.3	11.6	9.7	7.7	8.5
	Adolph Weber	GER	25.9	18.0	26.8	12.0	10.0	8.4	7.5
=47.	John Wolf	USA	25.7	17.5	27.3	12.0	9.5	8.7	7.5
	Charles Umbs	USA	25.7	17.6	29.1	12.4	9.6	9.6	6.5
=49.	Rudolf Krupitzer	USA	25.5	17.3	27.4	12.0	9.3	8.7	7.5
	J. Wassow	USA	25.5	17.4	28.2	12.2	9.4	9.1	7.0
	George Aschenbrener	USA	25.5	16.8	27.3	11.8	8.8	8.7	8.0
=52.	George Schroeder	USA	25.4	16.8	28.3	12.0	8.8	9.1	7.5
	Emil Rothe	USA	25.4	16.7	27.4	11.8	8.7	8.7	8.0
54.	Otto Feyder	USA	25.2	17.6	25.2	11.8	9.6	7.6	8.0
=55.	Philip Schuster	USA	25.1	16.5	29.2	12.2	8.5	9.6	7.0
	L. Rathke	USA	25.1	16.3	28.6	12.0	8.3	9.3	7.5
	Hugo Peitsch	GER	25.1	16.9	27.4	12.0	8.9	8.7	7.5
	Harry Warnken	USA	25.1	17.2	26.8	12.0	9.2	8.4	7.5
=59.	William Tritschler	USA	25.0	17.1	28.8	12.4	9.1	9.4	6.5
	Jacob Hertenbahn	USA	25.0	16.9	26.2	11.8	8.9	8.1	8.0
	Anton Heida	USA	25.0	17.7	24.6	11.8	9.7	7.3	8.0
62.	Harry Hansen	USA	24.8	17.3	25.9	12.0	9.3	8.0	7.5
63.	Max Wolf	USA	24.6	16.9	28.3	12.4	8.9	9.2	6.5
=64.	William Andelfinger	USA	24.5	16.8	28.4	12.4	8.8	9.2	6.5
	Charles Krause	USA	24.5	16.6	26.7	12.0	8.6	8.4	7.5
	Adolf Spinnler	SUI	24.5	16.2	29.6	12.4	8.2	9.8	6.5
67.	Bergin Nilsen	USA	24.4	16.8	27.2	12.2	8.8	8.6	7.0
=68.	William Traband	USA	24.3	17.7	23.2	11.8	9.7	6.6	8.0
	James Dwyer	USA	24.3	17.6	27.4	12.6	9.6	8.7	6.0
70.	Robert Maysack	USA	24.2	16.8	25.8	12.0	8.8	7.9	7.5
71.	George Mastrovich	USA	24.1	16.0	27.1	12.0	8.0	8.6	7.5
72.	Charles Sorum	USA	24.0	16.6	24.8	11.8	8.6	7.4	8.0
73.	Bernard Berg	USA	23.9	15.4	31.1	12.6	7.4	10.5	6.0
74.	John Dellert	USA	23.7	15.9	27.6	12.2	7.9	8.8	7.0
=75.	Otto Thomsen	USA	23.6	15.1	28.1	12.0	7.1	9.0	7.5
	Andreas Kempf	USA	23.6	16.7	27.7	12.6	8.7	8.9	6.0

			Total	LJ Distance	SP Distance	100 Time	LJ Score	SP Score	100 Score
=77.	Edward Tritschler	USA	23.5	16.4	25.2	12.0	8.4	7.6	7.5
	Christian Deubler	USA	23.5	16.6	23.9	11.8	8.6	6.9	8.0
=79.	Henry Kraft	USA	23.4	15.2	31.5	12.8	7.2	10.7	5.5
	Barney Chimberoff	USA	23.4	16.9	25.0	12.2	8.9	7.5	7.0
81.	L. Guerner	USA	23.2	15.8	27.7	12.4	7.8	8.9	6.5
82.	P. Gussmann	USA	23.1	16.3	28.5	12.8	8.3	9.3	5.5
83.	Michael Lang	USA	23.0	16.8	25.4	12.4	8.8	7.7	6.5
84.	P. Ritter	USA	22.8	17.1	25.4	12.6	9.1	7.7	6.0
=85.	Richard Tritschler	USA	22.4	15.5	23.8	11.8	7.5	6.9	8.0
	Hy. Meyland	USA	22.4	15.7	26.4	12.4	7.7	8.2	6.5
	Emil Voigt	USA	22.4	16.2	25.4	12.4	8.2	7.7	6.5
88.	Otto Knerr	USA	22.3	13.9	33.8	13.2	5.9	11.9	4.5
=89.	Otto Roissner	USA	22.0	16.6	24.8	12.6	8.6	7.4	6.0
	Gustav Mueller	USA	22.0	15.8	25.4	12.4	7.8	7.7	6.5
91.	William Horschke	USA	21.7	15.8	25.8	12.6	7.8	7.9	6.0
=92.	Wilhelm Zabel	USA	21.5	15.8	23.3	12.2	7.8	6.7	7.0
	Frank Raad	USA	21.5	16.0	25.9	12.8	8.0	8.0	5.5
94.	M. Bascher	USA	21.4	15.7	26.4	12.8	7.7	8.2	5.5
=95.	William Kruppinger	USA	21.3	16.1	24.4	12.6	8.1	7.2	6.0
	Rudolf Schrader	USA	21.3	15.1	24.4	12.2	7.1	7.2	7.0
	Emil Schwegler	USA	21.3	16.1	24.4	12.6	8.1	7.2	6.0
	Christian Sperl	USA	21.3	16.3	26.1	13.0	8.3	8.0	5.0
	August Placke	USA	21.3	14.9	28.7	13.0	6.9	9.4	5.0
=100.	M. Fischer	USA	21.2	14.9	25.5	12.4	6.9	7.8	6.5
	Julian Schmitz	USA	21.2	14.9	26.5	12.6	6.9	8.3	6.0
=102.	William Herzog	USA	21.1	16.7	23.8	12.8	8.7	6.9	5.5
	Arthur Rosenkampff	USA	21.1	15.5	23.2	12.2	7.5	6.6	7.0
=104.	Paul Studel	USA	20.9	17.0	21.8	12.6	9.0	5.9	6.0
	G. Hermerrling	USA	20.9	16.0	24.8	12.8	8.0	7.4	5.5
106.	Martin Ludwig	USA	20.4	15.1	25.6	12.8	7.1	7.8	5.5
107.	Charles Dellert	USA	20.3	14.3	24.0	12.2	6.3	7.0	7.0
=108.	Walter Real	USA	20.2	15.7	23.9	12.8	7.7	7.0	5.5
	John Messel	USA	20.2	15.8	22.8	12.6	7.8	6.4	6.0
	Arthur Sundbye	USA	20.2	15.8	20.3	12.6	7.8	6.4	6.0
111.	M. Barry	USA	20.1	15.4	24.3	12.8	7.4	7.2	5.5
112.	K. Woerner	USA	19.7	14.6	23.1	12.4	6.6	6.6	6.5
113.	Edward Pueschell	USA	19.3	14.4	23.7	12.6	6.4	6.9	6.0
114.	Charles Schwartz	USA	19.1	14.7	24.8	13.0	6.7	7.4	5.0
115.	K. Roedek	USA	19.0	15.0	22.9	12.8	7.0	6.5	5.5
116.	Alvin Kritschmann	USA	18.9	15.0	24.8	13.2	7.0	7.4	4.5
117.	William Friedrich	USA	17.7	15.1	21.2	13.0	7.1	5.6	5.0
118.	George Eyser	USA	13.5	13.4	26.1	15.4	5.4	8.1	0.0

Combined Exercises, Apparatus Work, and Field Sports, Team

A: 78; C: 2; D: 1–2 July; F: Each team consisted of six competitors. The team score was derived by adding up the total of the individual scores. In the track & field events, scores past 10 were allowed for the team event. However, in each track & field event, the maximum a team could score was 60 points, or 10 points per competitor. Thus, the maxima were 180 points for the three track & field events, 270 points for the apparatus work, and 450 points overall.

1.[4] Philadelphia Turngemeinde, Philadelphia, PA   USA/AUT[5]   370.13[6]
    Raw Scores   64.3   57.9   51.5   200.73   374.43
    Adjusted Totals   60.0   57.9   51.5   200.73   370.13
    (Julius Lenhart, Phillip Kassell, Anton Heida, Max Hess, Ernst Reckeweg, John Grieb)

2. New York Turnverein, New York, NY   USA   356.37
    Raw Scores   53.0   55.2   44.0   204.17   356.37
    Adjusted Totals   53.0   55.2   44.0   204.17   356.37
    (Otto Steffen, John Bissinger, Emil Beyer, Max Wolf, Julian Schmitz, Arthur Rosenkampff)

3. Central Turnverein, Chicago, IL   USA   352.79[7]
    Raw Scores   57.6   57.3   47.0   190.89   352.79
    Adjusted Totals   57.6   57.3   47.0   190.89   352.79
    (George Mayer, John Duha, Edward Siegler, Charles Krause, Philip Schuster, Robert Maysack)

4. Concordia Turnverein, St. Louis, MO   USA   344.01
    Raw Scores   51.6   51.5   40.5   200.41   344.01
    Adjusted Totals   51.6   51.5   40.5   200.41   344.01
    (William Merz, George Stapf, John Dellert, Emil Voigt, George Eyser, Hy. Meyland)

5. South St. Louis Turnverein, St. Louis, MO   USA   338.32[8]
    Raw Scores   54.3   54.6   46.5   182.92   338.32
    Adjusted Totals   54.3   54.6   46.5   182.92   338.32
    (Charles Umbs, Andrew Neu, William Tritschler, Christian Deubler, Edward Tritschler, John Leichinger)

6. Norwegier Turnverein, Brooklyn, NY   USA   338.00[9]
    Raw Scores   55.1   51.6   47.5   183.80   338.00
    Adjusted Totals   55.1   51.6   47.5   183.80   338.00
    (Ragner Berg, Harry Hansen, Charles Sorum, Oliver Olsen, Oluf Landnes, Bergin Nilsen)

7. Turnverein Vorwärts, Chicago, IL   USA   329.68
    Raw Scores   52.0   54.0   42.0   181.68   329.68
    Adjusted Totals   52.0   54.0   42.0   181.68   329.68
    (Theodore Gross, Henry Koeder, Jacob Hertenbahn, Henry Kraft, James Dwyer, Rudolf Schrader)

8. Davenport Turngemeinde, Davenport, IA   USA   325.52
    Raw Scores   55.8   58.7   45.0   166.02   325.52
    Adjusted Totals   55.8   58.7   45.0   166.02   325.52
    (Reinhard Wagner, Leander Keim, Otto Neimand, Phillip Sontag, Harry Warnken, Bernard Berg)

9. La Salle Turnverein, Chicago, IL   USA   318.13
   Raw Scores   52.7   48.8   45.0   171.63   318.13
   Adjusted Totals 52.7   48.8   45.0   171.63   318.13
   (Emil Rothe, Frank Schicke, William Horschke, George Aschenbrener, Otto Feyder, Walter Real)

10. Passaic Turnverein, Passaic, NJ   USA   301.39
    Raw Scores   47.0   46.9   34.5   172.99   301.39
    Adjusted Totals 47.0   46.9   34.5   172.99   301.39
    (P. Gussmann, G. Hermerrling, M. Bascher, K. Roedek, P. Ritter, M. Fischer)

11. Milwaukee Turnverein, Milwaukee, WI   USA   286.97
    Raw Scores   51.6   53.8   41.0   140.57   286.97
    Adjusted Totals 51.6   53.8   41.0   140.57   286.97
    (Robert Herrmann, L. Hunger, L. Rathke, August Placke, Christian Sperl, J. Wassow)

12. Socialer Turnverein, Detroit, MI   USA   273.65
    Raw Scores   50.7   44.6   38.5   139.85   273.65
    Adjusted Totals 50.7   44.6   38.5   139.85   273.65
    (Robert Reynolds, Alvin Kritschmann, Clarence Kiddington, Otto Roissner, John Messel, William Friedrich)

13. Turnverein Vorwärts, Cleveland, OH   USA   271.84
    Raw Scores   44.9   43.5   34.5   148.94   271.84
    Adjusted Totals 44.9   43.5   34.5   148.94   271.84
    (Rudolf Krupitzer, Edward Hennig, William Berewald, Michael Lang, Paul Studel, Theodore Studler)

Combined Exercises, Individual

A: ?[10]; C: 1; D: 28 October; F: The total score was based on the competitors' scores on the parallel bars, horizontal bar, side horse, and long horse. Overall maximum was 180 points.[11]

1.	Anton Heida	USA	161 pts.	[43-36-42-40]
2.	George Eyser[12]	USA	152 pts.	[44-36-33-39]
3.	William Merz	USA	135 pts.	[-31-29-]
4.	John Duha[13]	USA		[40- - -]
5.	Edward Hennig	USA		[- - -40]

Parallel Bars

A: ?; C: 1; D: 28 October; F: Each competitor performed three exercises, all optional. Each exercise was judged by three judges on a 0–5 scale, giving a maximum of 15 points for each exercise. Overall maximum was 45 points.

1.	George Eyser	USA	44 pts.
2.	Anton Heida	USA	43 pts.
3.	John Duha	USA	40 pts.

Long Horse

A: ?; C: 1; D: 28 October; F: Each competitor performed three exercises, all optional. Each exercise was judged by three judges on a 0–5 scale, giving a maximum of 15 points for each exercise. Overall maximum was 45 points.

=1.	Anton Heida	USA	36 pts.
	George Eyser	USA	36 pts.
3.	William Merz	USA	31 pts.

Side Horse

A: ?; C: 1; D: 28 October; F: Each competitor performed three exercises, all optional. Each exercise was judged by three judges on a 0–5 scale, giving a maximum of 15 points for each exercise. Overall maximum was 45 points.

1.	Anton Heida	USA	42 pts.
2.	George Eyser	USA	33 pts.
3.	William Merz	USA	29 pts.

Horizontal Bar

A: ?; C: 1; D: 28 October; F: Each competitor performed three exercises, all optional. Each exercise was judged by three judges on a 0–5 scale, giving a maximum of 15 points for each exercise. Overall maximum was 45 points.

=1.	Anton Heida	USA	40 pts.
	Edward Hennig	USA	40 pts.
3.	George Eyser	USA	39 pts.

Rings

A: ?; C: 1; D: 28 October; F: Maximum 45 points.

1.	Herman Glass	USA	45 pts.
2.	William Merz	USA	35 pts.
3.	Emil Voigt	USA	32 pts.

Rope Climbing

A: ?; C: 1; D: 28 October; F: The rope was 25 feet [7.62 meters] high. Each contestant was allowed three trials, the fastest time to count.

1.	George Eyser	USA	7.0 seconds
2.	Charles Krause	USA	7.2 seconds
3.	Emil Voigt	USA	9.8 seconds

Club Swinging

A: ?; C: 1; D: 28 October; F: Each contestant was allowed five minutes for the performance with three-pound clubs. Three judges were to score each competitor a maximum of five points each, thus an overall maximum of 15 points.

1.	Edward Hennig	USA	13 pts.
2.	Emil Voigt	USA	9 pts.
3.	Ralph Wilson	USA	5 pts.

NON-OLYMPIC EVENTS

YMCA Individual Gymnastic Championships

D: 17 August 1904; F: Side horse, long horse, with springboard (leaping), horizontal bar, parallel bars.

Side Horse

1.	Fred Prosch	27.16
2.	George Ketcham	25.00
3.	E. F. Kettner	23.00
4.	Robert E. Maysack	22.50
5.	N. C. Tuska	21.83
6.	E. E. Utz	20.66
7.	D. K. McDonald	18.50
8.	H. A. Barth	18.16
9.	E. McClain	17.66

Long Horse

1.	H. A. Barth	22.83
2.	Fred Prosch	22.00
3.	E. E. Utz	21.33
4.	Robert E. Maysack	20.66
5.	George Ketcham	18.66
6.	N. C. Tuska	14.66

Parallel Bars

1.	E. F. Kettner	28.83
2.	George Ketcham	28.66
3.	Fred Prosch	27.16
4.	E. E. Utz	26.83
5.	G. L. Cameron	25.16
=6.	James Hall	23.83
	Robert E. Maysack	23.83

8.	E. McClain	23.00
9.	N. C. Tuska	21.83
10.	H. A. Barth	21.33
11.	D. K. McDonald	21.00
12.	J. T. Rapp	18.16
13.	C. L. Johnson	16.00

Horizontal Bars

1.	E. F. Kettner	25.83
2.	E. McClain	25.75
3.	E. E. Utz	22.41
4.	G. L. Cameron	25.16
5.	S. T. Davis	21.66
6.	James Hall	20.66
7.	George Ketcham	19.83
8.	C. L. Johnson	16.33

All-Around

Name	Club	SH	LH	PB	HB	Total
George Ketcham	Newark, N.J.	25.00	18.66	28.66	19.83	92.15
E. E. Utz	Chicago Central	20.66	21.33	26.83	22.41	91.23
E. F. Kettner	Newark, N.J.	23.00		28.83	25.83	77.66
Fred Prosch	Newark, N.J.	27.16	22.00	27.16		76.32
Robert E. Maysack	Chicago Central	22.50	20.66	23.83		66.99
E. McClain	Seattle	17.66		23.00	25.75	66.41
H. A. Barth	Seattle	18.16	22.83	21.33		62.32
N. C. Tuska	St. Louis Central	21.83	14.66	21.83		58.32
G. L. Cameron	Newark, N.J.			25.16	25.16	50.32
James Hall	St. Louis Central			23.83	20.66	44.49
D. K. McDonald	Seattle	18.50		21.00		39.50
C. L. Johnson	St. Louis Central			16.00	16.33	32.33
S. T. Davis	St. Louis Central				21.66	21.66
J. T. Rapp	St. Louis Central		18.16			18.16

Athletic-Gymnastic Team Championship

D: 19 August 1904; F: Events — Marching calisthenic drill, side horse, horizontal bars, parallel bars, running high jump, basketball, 1-mile relay. Teams composed of eight men.

Team Championships

High jump

| 1. Chicago | 497 |
| 2. St. Louis | 296 |

Marching calisthenics apparatus

1. Chicago   669
2. St. Louis   527

Basketball

1. Chicago   100

Relay race

1. St. Louis   100

Totals

1. Chicago   1,266
2. St. Louis   923

NOTES

1. FM, FW, and OR give Lenhart's score as 70.5.

2. Wiegand's score is incorrectly given as 67.52 in several sources, notably EK, FW (67.5), and VK.

3. EK lists 119, but Theodore Studler, who started in the turners' contests, withdrew during the apparatus work, and did not compete in any of the field sports.

4. FW lists a German team composed of W. Weber, Spinnler [SUI], Mohr, Wiegand, Peitsch, Busch, Lemke, and A. Weber as first, with the Philadelphia team second. No scores are given. The Germans tried to enter a team but were again rebuffed, as not all the German turners were members of the same club. It could be considered that this should disqualify the event from consideration as Olympic calibre.

5. This is always listed as a U.S. team. However, Kamper was able to show that Lenhart was of Austrian citizenship in 1904. Lenhart had been living and working in Philadelphia for only a short time at the time of the Olympics.

6. The score is often seen as 374.43, the unadjusted raw score.

7. VK has the score as 349.69.

8. VK has the score as 338.65.

9. VK has the score as 334.00.

10. The number of competitors is not known with certainty. However, the *Chicago Tribune* of 29 October 1904 commented that of the original 38 entries only 10 showed up. Nine different names are listed below so only one of the ten competitors remains unknown. However, the *Richmond Times-Dispatch* of 1 November 1904 stated that Herman Glass, winner of the rings event, was a specialist and competed only in that event.

11. EK stated that this event was held on seven apparatuses, but the daily programs and the rules and regulations both said that the event was contested only on the above four apparatuses. This also seems quite reasonable in light of the scores made by Heida and Eyser.

12. Several newspapers describe Eyser as having, incredibly enough, a wooden leg.

13. No previous source has listed any finisher beyond third place. This result is derived from a comment in the 30 October 1904 edition of the *Cleveland Plain-Dealer* which stated that Edward Hennig, a native of Cleveland, barely lost fourth place to John Duha.

Lacrosse

Lacrosse[1]* was contested in the 1904 Olympics, and it deserves that classification as an Olympic sport. Although only three teams competed, two of them were from a foreign country, Canada, and one of the Canadian teams won the championship.

The events were contested on the infield of the Olympic stadium on July 5–7, 1904. There were four teams entered: the Winnipeg Shamrocks of Winnipeg, Manitoba, Canada; the St. Louis AAA (Amateur Athletic Association); the Mohawk Indians of Canada; and the Brooklyn Crescents. The Brooklyn Crescents did not appear.

Until my earlier work on the 1904 Olympic Games was compiled in 1981, the Mohawk Indian team was unknown, and the Brooklyn Crescents entry was not recorded either. Some sources list the Mohawk Indian team as actually an Iroquois Indian team. They apparently were from the area surrounding Brantford, Ontario. The discovery of their roster allows us to add the following wonderful Native American names to the list of Olympic medalists: Black Hawk, Black Eagle, Almighty Voice, Flat Iron, Spotted Tail, Half Moon, Lightfoot, Snake Eater, Red Jacket, Night Hawk, Man Afraid Soap, and Rain in Face.

The Winnipeg Shamrocks were the class of the three teams, easily defeating the St. Louis AAA in the final 8–2. Lacrosse was contested again at the 1908 Olympics as an official Olympic sport, but has not appeared on the Olympic program since. However, the 1904 lacrosse tournament is certainly of Olympic caliber, having been contested by amateur athletes of both America and foreign countries with no restrictions placed on them.

Site:	Francis Field
Dates/Times:	2, 7 July
Events:	1
Competitors:	36
Nations:	2

*See Notes on pages 166–167.

	Competitors	1st	2nd	3rd	Totals
Canada	24	1	-	1	2
United States	12	-	1	-	1
Totals	36	1	1	1	3
Nations	2	1	1	1	2

Final Standings

A: 36²; C: 2; D: 2, 7 July.

1. Canada   [Shamrock Lacrosse Team]
    (George Cloutier [G], George Cattanach [P], Benjamin Jamieson [CP], Jack Flett [D], George
    Bretz [D], Eli Blanchard [D], Hilliard Laidlaw [C], H. Lyle [H], W. Brennaugh [H], L.
    H. Pentland [H], Sandy Cowan [IH], William Burns [OH])

2. United States   [St. Louis Amateur Athletic Association]
    (Hunter [G], Patrick Grogan [P], William Passmore [CP], George Passmore [D], Partridge
    [D], J. W. Dowling [D], A. H. Venn [C], Murphy [H], Gibson [H], Sullivan [H], Ross
    [IH], Woods [OH])

3. Canada   [Mohawk Indians³]
    (Black Hawk [G], Black Eagle [P], Almighty Voice [CP], Flat Iron [D], Spotted Tail [D],
    Half Moon [D], Lightfoot [C], Snake Eater [H], Red Jacket [H], Night Hawk [H], Man
    Afraid Soap [IH], Rain in Face [OH])

Match Results

2 July	St. Louis AAA						2
	Mohawks						2
7 July⁴	Shamrock	0	1	2	5	-	8⁵
	St. Louis AAA	0	0	2	0	-	2

NON-OLYMPIC "LACROSSE-TYPE" EVENT

Olympic Irish Sports Hurling Championship

D: 20 July 1904.

1. Innisfall Hurling Club of St. Louis

NOTES

1. The St. Louis newspapers barely mentioned the lacrosse tournament. The best results were contained in the *Manitoba Free Press* which supplied most of the details.

2. EK and VK had only 26 players but they did not know about the third team. In addition, they listed one extra player for both the Shamrock and St. Louis teams. Milton Roberts, lacrosse his-

torian, has confirmed that these players were non-playing captains and should not be listed as competitors.

3. Called the Iroquois Indians by the *Globe-Democrat*. The *Manitoba Free Press* and the *Chicago Tribune* both called them the Mohawk Indians. The team roster came from the *Chicago Tribune*.

4. This match was scheduled for 5 July and then again for 6 July, but rain postponed it on both occasions.

5. EK lists the score of this match as 12–8. This is also given in several other sources. But the *Manitoba Free Press* gave the above score and the score by quarters and this seems the most reliable.

Rowing & Sculling

The 1904 rowing events were held at Creve Coeur Lake. They were contested on 29 and 30 July 1904 as part of the Olympic Games. The bulk of the entrants were from the United States, although the Toronto Argonaut Club did send an eight-oar crew which competed in the Olympic senior eight-oared shells. The events doubled as the United States Championships of the National Association of Amateur Oarsmen (NAAO).

Multiple ancillary events in addition to the Olympic events were contested, such as association single sculls, intermediate eight-oared shells, intermediate single sculls, and intermediate coxed pairs. The Americans dominated, with the only foreign competitor in the events that are usually considered of Olympic caliber having been the Toronto Argonauts' coxed eight. There were other entrants from Canada as well as from Germany in the ancillary events. These cannot be considered of Olympic caliber because they were essentially restricted events for rowers of lesser skill.

The single sculls event had the potential to be a great event for the time, as the world's top two amateur scullers, James Ten Eyck (USA) and Louis Scholes (CAN) both entered. Scholes had won the Diamond Sculls at Henley earlier in the year, but neither he nor the American champion Ten Eyck participated in the Olympic event.

Creve Coeur Lake still exists today. In 1995, during the filming of some television shows concerning Olympic history, I had the opportunity to spend part of an afternoon there. It is still the training ground of several of the St. Louis rowing clubs. When I told one of the local fishermen that the 1904 Olympic rowing events had been contested here, his comment was one of incredulity, "This place? It's just a mud hole." Perhaps. But for two days in 1904, it was a very famous mud hole.

All the races were over 1½ miles (2,414.02 meters). The fours and eights were held straight-away. The pair and both sculls rowed out ¾ mile (1,207.01 meters), turned, and then rowed back over the same course.

Site:	Creve Coeur Lake
Dates/Times:	29 July [1530–1800]; 30 July [1530–1740]
Events:	5
Competitors:	44
Nations:	2

Competitors		1st	2nd	3rd	Totals
Canada	9	–	1	–	1
United States	35	5	4	4	13
Totals	44	5	5	4	14
Nations	2	1	2	1	2

Single Sculls

A: 4[1]*; C: 1; D: 30 July; T: 1710.

1.	Frank Greer	USA	10:08.5
2.	James Juvenal	USA	at 2 lengths
3.	Constance Titus	USA	at ½ length
4.	Dave Duffield	USA	

Double Sculls

A: 6; C: 1; D: 30 July; T: 1650.

1. United States (Atalanta Boat Club)   10:03.2
   (John Mulcahy [bow], William Varley [stroke])
2. United States (Ravenswood Boat Club)   at 2 lengths
   (James McLoughlin [bow], John Hoben [stroke])
3. United States (Independent Rowing Club)
   (Joseph Ravanack [bow], John Wells [stroke])

Coxless Pairs[2]

A: 6; C: 1; D: 30 July; T: 1730.

1. United States (Seawanhaka Boat Club)   10:57.0
   (Robert Farnam [bow], Joseph Ryan [stroke])
2. United States (Atalanta Boat Club)   at 4 lengths
   (John Mulcahy [bow], William Varley [stroke])
3. United States (Western Rowing Club)
   (John Joachim [bow], Joseph Buerger [stroke])

Coxless Fours

A: 12[3]; C: 1; D: 30 July; T: 1710.

*See Notes on page 172.

1. United States (Century Boat Club)   9:05.8
   (Arthur Stockhoff [bow], August Erker [2], George Dietz [3], Albert Nasse [stroke])

2. United States (Mound City Rowing Club)   at 2 lengths
   (Frederick Suerig [bow], Martin Fromanack [2], Charles Aman [3], Michael Begley [stroke])

3. United States (Western Rowing Club)
   (Gustav Voerg [bow], John Freitag [2], Louis Helm [3], Frank Dummerth [stroke])

Coxed Eights

A: 18; C: 2; D: 30 July; T: 1730.

1. United States (Vesper Boat Club)   7:50.0
   (Louis Abell [coxswain], Frederick Cresser [bow], Michael Gleason [2], Frank Schell [3], James Flanagan [4], Charles Armstrong [5], Harry Lott [6], Joseph Dempsey [7], John Exley [stroke])

2. Canada (Toronto Argonauts)   at 3 lengths
   (Thomas Loudon [coxswain], A. B. Bailey [bow], William "Colonel" Rice [2], George "Pat" Reiffenstein [3], Phil Boyd [4], George Strange [5], William Wadsworth [6], Donald MacKenzie [7], Joseph Wright [stroke])

NON-OLYMPIC EVENTS

Single Sculls, Intermediate[4]

A: 7; C: 2; D: 29–30 July; F: 1½ mile with a turn.

Final A: 4; C: 1; D: 30 July; T: 1530.

1. Frederick Shepherd (Ravenswood BC)	USA	10:30.0
2. George H. Lloyd (Arlington [MA] BC)	USA	easy win
3. James A. Ten Eyck (Wachusett BC)	USA	
4. Ernest J. Hess (Century BC)	USA	

Round One A: 7; C: 2; D: 29 July.

Heat 1 A: 4; C: 1; T: 1550.

1. James A. Ten Eyck (Wachusetts BC)	USA	10:49.6
2. Ernest J. Hess (Century BC)	USA	10:53.2
AC. Edward C. Atherton (Hartford BC)	USA	
Herman Kirtman (Arlington [MA] BC)	USA	

Heat 2 A: 3; C: 2; T: 1610.

1. Frederick Shepherd (Ravenswood BC)	USA	11:21.4
2. George H. Lloyd (Arlington [MA] BC)	USA	at 20 lengths
3. W. Obernesse (Toronto RC)	CAN	

Single Sculls, Association[5]

A: 8; C: 2; D: 29–30 July; F: 1½ mile with a turn.

Final A: 5; C: 1; D: 30 July; T: 1550.

1. David B. Duffield (Detroit BC)	USA	10:08.8
2. Frank Vesely (First Bohemian BC)	USA	
3. Fred Fuessel (Harlem RC)	USA	
AC. Clarence E. Johnston (Arlington [MA] BC)	USA	
Edward C. Atherton (Hartford BC)	USA	

Round One A: 8; C: 2; D: 29 July.

Heat 1 A: 3; C: 1; T: 1630.[6]

1. Frank Vesely (First Bohemian BC)	USA	11:18.0
2. Clarence E. Johnston (Arlington [MA] BC)	USA	
Fred Fuessel (Harlem RC)	USA	DQ[7]

Heat 2 A: 5; C: 2; T: 1650.

1. David B. Duffield (Detroit BC)	USA	11:00.6
2. Edward C. Atherton (Hartford BC)	USA	at 8 feet
AC. Frank Smith (Toronto RC)	CAN	
Ernest J. Hess (Century BC)	USA	
Jesse Williamson (University Barge C)	USA	

Double Sculls, Intermediate[8]

A: 6; C: 1; D: 30 July; T: 1610; F: 1½ mile with a turn.

1. Ravenswood Boat Club, Long Island City	USA	10:05¼
(John Hoben [bow], Joseph McLaughlin [stroke])		
2. Pensacola Boat Club, Pensacola	USA	at 15 lengths
(William McGowan [bow], M. A. Garrett [stroke])		
3. St. Louis Rowing Club, St. Louis	USA	
(Louis Joachim [bow], Joseph E. Dilg [stroke])		

Coxless Pairs, Intermediate[9]

A: 8; C: 1; D: 29 July; T: 1530; F: 1½ mile with a turn.

1. Seawanhaka Boat Club, Brooklyn	USA	11:05.0
(Robert Farnam [bow], Joseph Ryan [stroke])		
2. Century Boat Club, St. Louis	USA	
(William H. Fisse [bow], Frank M. Lansing [stroke])		
3. Detroit Boat Club, Detroit	USA	
(W. B. Maurice [bow], C. S. Ritter [stroke])		

4. Western Rowing Club, St. Louis   USA
   (A. Boeher [bow], O. Wolff [stroke])

Coxless Fours, Intermediate[10]

A: 12; C: 1; D: 30 July; T: 1630; F: 1½ mile with a turn.

1. South Side Boat Club, Quincy, IL   USA   9:39½
   (George Zimmerman [bow], Charles Honer [2], George Duesdecker [3], Charles Bisser [stroke])
2. Mound City Rowing Club, St. Louis   USA
   (Fred Suerig [bow], Martin Fromanack [2], Charles Aman [3], Michael Begley [stroke])
3. Central Rowing Club, St. Louis   USA
   (Ernest Beal [bow], H. Petchoneck [2], William Rother [3], A. Tebeau [stroke])

Coxed Eights, Intermediate[11]

A: 18; C: 1; D: 29 July; T: 1750; F: 1½ mile with a turn.

1. Detroit Boat Club, Detroit   USA   8:25¼
   (R. H. Clark [coxswain], M. D. Richardson [bow], L. C. Hammer [2], R. Craig [3], H.
      H. Emmons [4], E. Q. Wasley [5], R. Inglis [6], J. Symington [7], I. W. Craig [stroke])
2. Western Rowing Club, St. Louis   USA
   (O. Becker [coxswain], A. Boeher [bow], W. Fischer [2], H. Bruehmer [3], O. Wolff [4],
      J. Schott [5], John Joachim [6], J. Maurer [7], H. Bensen [stroke])

NOTES

1. EK, FW, and VK list five.
2. Not listed in EK, FW, or VK.
3. EK, FM, FW, and VK list eight and did not list a third-place finisher.
4. Listed as an Olympic event in FM.
5. Listed as an Olympic event in FM.
6. Adolf Möller of the Berlin Rowing Club (Germany) was entered in this heat but did not start.
7. Fuessel won the race but was disqualified for failing to go around the marker at the turn. He was allowed to start in the final despite this.
8. Listed as an Olympic event in FM.
9. Listed as an Olympic event in FM.
10. Listed as an Olympic event in FM.
11. Listed as an Olympic event in FM, although he did not have any results listed.

Swimming

The 1904 swimming events were held on 5–7 September 1904. After track & field athletics, swimming was perhaps the most international sport of any contested at the 1904 Olympics as there were competitors from Hungary, Germany, and Austria in addition to the United States. Unlike track & field, however, the swimming competition was not totally dominated by the American athletes, and the international competition was the best of the 1904 Olympics. The 1904 Olympic events doubled as the United States National Championships, or the AAU Championships. Still, there was no prohibition against foreign entrants or competitors.

There were 10 events held at the 1904 swimming competitions. The events were held in a man-made lake that was used each day by the Coast Guard for life-saving exhibitions at the World's Fair. The races were held on the opposite side of the lake between a pier and rafts floating on the lake. The lake was fed from a river, creating a slight current, although the swimmers agreed that the current had not been a major consideration.

Site:	Life Saving Exhibition Lake
Dates/Times:	5–7 September[1]
Events:	9
Competitors:	23
Nations:	4

	Competitors	1st	2nd	3rd	Totals
Austria	1	-	-	1	1
Germany	4	4	2	2	8
Hungary	2	2	1	1	4
United States	16	3	6	5	14
Totals	23	9	9	9	27
Nations	4	3	3	4	4

*See Notes on pages 179–180.

50 Yard [45.72 meters] Freestyle

A: 9[2]; C: 2; D: 6 September; F: Three fastest in heats advance to the final. The event was swum on a straight course.

The 50-yard freestyle was won by Zoltán von Halmay of Hungary after a swim-off with America's J. Scott Leary. It was a very controversial race. There were two heats contested, one by von Halmay and Leary. Six athletes, five Americans and von Halmay, competed in the final on 6 September. The *St. Louis Globe Democrat* reported the results of that final as follows, "Scarcely had the men finished than Leary threw up his arms in the air and yelled to the officials on the float and in the stands 'Foul.' As soon as he could swim to the float, he did so and claimed that Halmay interfered with him near the finish and tried to pull him back. While it was acknowledged that Halmay's course was the strongest in the world, all thoughts of his attempting to deliberately foul Leary were cast to the winds and the foul was disallowed.

"Up in the stands, however, the judges weren't able to decide who won the event. One of the judges, a Hungarian, began to call Halmay the winner before he was within three yards of the finish and finally selected his countryman as the winner. On the other hand, the judges trying to pick the second man selected Halmay for that place and finally when the judges could not pick a winner the heat was ordered to be run over."

In the swim-off, both men were charged with one false start, but on the third start Halmay got far better at the beginning, Leary could not catch him, and von Halmay won easily. The photo of the finish of the first race at the Missouri Historical Society indicates that the dead heat was very generous to Leary.

Final A: 6; C: 1; D: 6 September.

1.	Zoltán von Halmay	HUN	28.2[3]
2.	J. Scott Leary	USA	28.2
3.	Charles Daniels	USA	
4.	David Gaul[4]	USA	
5.	Leo "Budd" Goodwin	USA	
6.	Raymond Thorne	USA	

Semi-Finals A: 9; C: 2; D: 6 September.

Heat 1 A: 5; C: 2

1.	Zoltán von Halmay	HUN	29.6
2.	Leo "Budd" Goodwin	USA	
3.	Raymond Thorne	USA	

Heat 2 A: 4; C: 1

1.	J. Scott Leary	USA	28.2
2.	Charles Daniels	USA	
3.	David Gaul	USA	

100 Yard [91.44 meters] Freestyle

A: ?[5]; C: 2; D: 5 September; F: Three fastest in heats advance to the final. The event was swum on a straight course.

There were two heats in the 100-yard freestyle, which were won by Zoltán von Halmay and Charles Daniels. Six competitors reported for the finals, von Halmay and five Americans, led by Daniels and J. Scott Leary. Although Leary had recently become the first man to swim a 100 yards under one minute, he was no match for von Halmay or Daniels and finished third. Von Halmay easily defeated Daniels.

Final A: 6; C: 1; D: 5 September.

1.	Zoltán von Halmay	HUN	1:02.8
2.	Charles Daniels	USA	
3.	J. Scott Leary	USA	
4.	David Gaul[6]	USA	
5.	David Hammond[7]	USA	
6.	Leo "Budd" Goodwin	USA	

[8]

Semi-Finals A: ?; C: 2; D: 5 September.

Heat 1 A: 5; C: 2.

1.	Zoltán von Halmay	HUN	1:06.2
2.	J. Scott Leary	USA	
3.	David Hammond	USA	

Heat 2 A: 4; C: ?.

1.	Charles Daniels	USA	1:07.4
2.	David Gaul	USA	
3.	Leo "Budd" Goodwin	USA	

220 Yard [201.17 meters] Freestyle

A: 4[9]; C: 2; D: 6 September; F: Final only, no heats. The event was two laps of a 110 yard [100.58 meters] course.

Charles Daniels recovered from his loss of the day before in the 100-yard freestyle and easily won the 220-yard freestyle. He defeated three other competitors, led by America's Francis Gailey and Germany's Emil Rausch. Daniels and Gailey had a fairly close race with Daniels winning by less than two seconds.

1.	Charles Daniels	USA	2:44.2
2.	Francis Gailey	USA	2:46.0
3.	Emil Rausch	GER	2:56.0
4.	Edgar Adams	USA	

440 Yard [402.34 meters] Freestyle

A: 4[10]; C: 2; D: 7 September; F: Final only, no heats. The event was four laps of a 110 yard [100.58 meters] course.

Charles Daniels won his second gold medal of the 1904 Olympics in the 440-yard freestyle. There were only four competitors and he won comfortably over Francis Gailey.

1.	Charles Daniels	USA	6:16.2
2.	Francis Gailey	USA	6:22.0
3.	Otto Wahle	AUT	6:39.0
4.	Leo "Budd" Goodwin	USA[11]	

880 Yard [804.67 meters] Freestyle

A: 6[12]; C: 4; D: 7 September; F: Final only, no heats. The event was eight laps of a 110 yard [100.58 meters] course.

Emil Rausch added the 880-yard championship to the mile freestyle that he had won the day before, winning by 12 seconds over Francis Gailey, who earned his third silver medal of the Olympics. With Hungary's Géza Kiss finishing in third, this was one of the very few events at the 1904 Olympics in which the three medalists came from three different countries.

1.	Emil Rausch	GER	13:11.4
2.	Francis Gailey	USA	13:23.4
3.	Géza Kiss	HUN	
4.	Edgar Adams[13]	USA	
5.	Otto Wahle	AUT	
6.	Jamison Handy	USA	

One Mile [1,609.34 meters] Freestyle

A: 7[14]; C: 4; D: 6 September; F: Final only, no heats. The event was sixteen laps of a 110 yard [100.58 meters] course.

There were seven swimmers in the mile race, with four countries represented, which was almost unheard of for any event at the 1904 Olympics. For the first half of the race the swimmers contented themselves with a steady even pace and nobody took a significant lead. Near the end, Géza Kiss (HUN) and Emil Rausch (GER) pulled away from the other competitors. Rausch then easily distanced himself from Kiss and won the race with a margin described in the papers as 65 feet and listed in some results as one minute and ten seconds.

1.	Emil Rausch	GER	27:18.2[15]
2.	Géza Kiss	HUN	28:28.2
3.	Francis Gailey	USA	28:54.0
4.	Otto Wahle	AUT	
AC.	John Meyers	USA	DNF
	Louis Handley	USA	DNF
	Edgar Adams	USA	DNF

100 Yard [91.44 meters] Backstroke

A: 6[16]; C: 2; D: 6 September; F: Final only, no heats. The event was swum on a straight course.

The 100-yard backstroke was contested by six swimmers, three Americans and three Germans. The Americans were no contest at all for the Germans who dominated the backstroke and breaststroke events in this era. The Germans swept the medals, led by Walter Brack who finished in 1:16.8, followed by Georg Hoffmann, and Georg Zacharias.

1.	Walter Brack	GER	1:16.8
2.	Georg Hoffmann	GER	
3.	Georg Zacharias	GER	
4.	William Orthwein[17]	USA	
AC.	Edwin Swatek	USA	
	David Hammond	USA	

440 Yard [402.34 meters] Breaststroke

A: 4; C: 2; D: 7 September; F: Final only, no heats. The event was four laps of a 110 yard [100.58 meters] course.

Originally only three Germans were going to compete in the 440-yard breaststroke, as it was an event rarely contested in the United States at that time. Jamison "Jam" Handy entered at the last second because he saw a chance to win a medal for himself at the Olympics. He narrowly defeated Georg Hoffmann and won a bronze medal. Germany's George Zacharias easily defeated his countryman, Walter Brack, by about five meters to win the gold medal.

"Jam" Handy's medal would later earn him some notoriety as, born in 1886, he lived until 1983, and was the last surviving medalist of the 1904 Olympic Games.

1.	Georg Zacharias	GER	7:23.6
2.	Walter Brack	GER	at 5 meters[18]
3.	Jamison Handy	USA	
4.	Georg Hoffmann[19]	GER	

Plunge for Distance

A: 5[20]; C: 1; D: 5 September; F: The distance was measured when the athlete's face appeared above the surface of the water or at the end of the time limit, 60 seconds. Each athlete had three trials.

The plunge for distance is an unusual event now, but was a common one in that era. It was based on the distance the athlete achieved with no attempt to propel himself after entering the water. There were five competitors, all American. William Dickey won the event easily with a distance of 62 feet 6 inches. The American record holder, Charles Pyrah, was far off form and finished fifth and last.

1.	William Dickey	USA	62-6	[19.05 m.]
2.	Edgar Adams	USA	57-6	[17.52 m.]
3.	Leo "Budd" Goodwin	USA	57-0	[17.37 m.]
4.	Newman Samuels	USA	55-0	[16.76 m.]
5.	Charles Pyrah	USA	46-0	[14.02 m.]

NON-OLYMPIC EVENTS

4 × 50 Yard [45.72 meters] Freestyle Relay

A: 16[21]; C: 1; D: 7 September

Similar to the controversy that occurred in the 1904 water polo events, a German team attempted to enter the freestyle relay competition. The American teams protested this, stating that the German team was not all from the same club but in fact constituted an all-star team. The judges upheld the American protest and disqualified the Germans. After the meet was over some Americans offered to pick their own all-star team to compete against the Germans but the Germans refused this offer. This event has always been listed as an Olympic event in the record books but because of this it probably should be disqualified from Olympic consideration.

Four teams eventually competed: two from the New York Athletic Club, one from the Chicago Athletic Association, and one from the Missouri Athletic Club. The #1 team from the New York AC won easily, trailed by the Chicago Athletic Association.

1. United States   [New York Athletic Club #1]   2:04.6
   (Joseph Ruddy, Leo "Budd" Goodwin, Louis Handley, Charles Daniels)
2.[22] United States   [Chicago Athletic Association]
   (David Hammond, William Tuttle, Hugo Goetz[23], Raymond Thorne)
3. United States   [Missouri Athletic Club]
   (Amedee Reyburn, Gwynne Evans, Marquard Schwarz[24], William Orthwein)
4. United States   [New York Athletic Club #2[25]]
   (Edgar Adams, David Bratton, George Van Cleaf, David Hesser)

100 Yard [91.44 meters] Handicap

A: ?; C: ?; D: 6 September[26].

1.	H. B. Warren	USA	1:14.2
2.	Edwin Swatek	USA	
3.	James A. Ruddy	USA	

220 Yards [201.17 meters] Handicap

A: ?; C: ?; D: 7 September.

1.	Marquard Schwarz	USA	3:06.2	(off 0:25)
2.	Rex E. Beach	USA		(off 0:25)
3.	David Hammond	USA		(off 0:30)

440 Yards [402.34 meters] Handicap

A: ?; C: ?; D: 6 September.

1.	Edgar H. Adams	USA	6:44.4	(off 0:35)
2.	Géza Kiss	HUN		(off 0:10)
3.	Marquard Schwarz	USA		(off 0:35)
AC.	Jamison Handy	USA		
	Max Pape	GER		

880 Yards [804.67 meters] Handicap

A: ?; C: ?; D: 7 September.

1.	Leo "Budd" Goodwin	USA	14:18.0
2.	Jamison Handy	USA	
3.	Max Pape	GER	
4.	Frank Kehoe	USA	

One Mile [1,609.34 meters] Handicap

A: ?; C: ?; D: 6 September.

1.	Rex E. Beach	USA	32:03.6	(off 6:45)
2.	H. B. Warren	USA		(off 7:45)
3.	Jamison Handy	USA		(off 1:00)

NOTES

1. Swimming was originally scheduled for July but the Life Saving Exhibition Lake was not available at that time.

2. EK and VK list 11 but the number was confirmed by photos of the heats.

3. In the original race von Halmay and Leary dead-heated. In the swim-off of the tie, Halmay won easily by 28.0 to 28.6. A photo of the first race finish at the Missouri Historical Society indicates that the dead-heat was quite generous to Leary.

4. EK lists Francis Gailey in fourth, but all St. Louis newspapers have Gaul in fourth place.

5. It is not certain how many swimmers competed in the first heat but it is almost certainly either four or five, making the total competitors in this event either eight or nine. EK, FW, and VK have 17 competitors, which is almost certainly wrong, and based on the number of entries. There were 17 entrants

6. EK lists Francis Gailey in fourth, but all St. Louis newspapers have Gaul in fourth place.

7. VK has Goodwin fifth and Hammond sixth but St. Louis papers gave this description.

8. EK states that only four competed in the final but the St. Louis newspaper descriptions indicate that there were six who finished as listed above.

9. EK and VK have nine starters, but a photo of the start of the race confirms that there were only four finalists. No evidence of any heats could be found.

10. EK, FW, and VK have eleven starters but a photo of the start of the race confirms that there were only four finalists. No evidence of any heats could be found.

11. EK stated that there were only three swimmers in the final, but that is wrong.

12. EK and VK have ten starters, but a photo of the start of the race confirms that there were six finalists. In addition, conversation in 1981 with Jamison Handy, who swam in this event in the 1904 Olympics, confirmed that there were six starters and no heats.

13. EK lists Otto Wahle in fourth but all St. Louis newspapers listed Edgar Adams as fourth.

14. EK and FW have nine starters, and VK has eleven, but a photo of the start of the race confirms that only seven started. In addition, the *Chicago Daily News* commented that seven started but only four finished. The St. Louis papers listed the first four finishers and mentioned Meyers and Handley as having competed. Adams was identified from the start photo. EK also noted that there were only four swimmers in the final. That was incorrect, and the implication that there were heats in this event was also wrong.

15. The splits in this race were as follows: Gailey at 550 yards in 8:12.2; Rausch led the remainder of the race in the following splits: 660 yards — 9:55.4; 770 yards —11:39.6; 990 yards —15:08.4; 1,100 yards —16:52.4; 1,210 yards —18:40.2; 1,320 yards — 20:25.0; 1,430 yards — 22:10.2; 1,540 yards — 23:57.2; and 1,650 yards — 25:44.0.

16. EK, FW, and VK list four starters but a photo of the start confirms that there were six. The complete starting list was found in the *New York Athletic Club Journal*.

17. EK lists Charles Daniels in fourth but he did not compete. Orthwein is listed as fourth in all St. Louis papers.

18. EK lists Brack as finishing 20 meters behind but the St. Louis papers describe him as losing by only 5 yards (4.57 m.).

19. EK lists Edgar Adams as fourth but all St. Louis papers have Georg Hoffmann in that position. There were only three entries in the daily program. Handy entered at the last minute because, in his words, "I thought I could win a medal."

20. FW and VK list six.

21. FW has 20 swimmers from 5 teams. No fifth team competed, although the Germans tried to enter a fifth team but were rebuffed.

22. FW incorrectly has Germany second and Hungary third.

23. This swimmer's name is usually seen as Thorne Goetz. However, the *Chicago Tribune* calls him Hugo, and most other sources list him as H. L. In addition, no person with the name Thorne Goetz is listed in the Chicago City Directory for 1904. Likely the name is bastardized by combining it with his teammate's, Raymond Thorne.

24. Usually spelled Schwartz. The above spelling was confirmed by a brother and a nephew.

25. EK calls this a team from San Francisco which is unlikely, as only two swimmers from San Francisco were in St. Louis — J. Scott Leary and Francis Gailey. The above team is mentioned in the St. Louis papers and the roster came from the daily programs and the *New York Athletic Club Journal*.

26. This was scheduled for 5 September but was not held until the next day.

Tennis (Lawn)

There were several tennis events held at the 1904 Louisiana Purchase Exposition. From the newspaper reports, it is actually fairly difficult to sort out exactly which matches were part of the Olympics and which were not. The events that were contested were as follows: Olympic Men's Singles, Olympic Men's Doubles, World's Fair Men's Singles, World's Fair Men's Doubles, Louisiana Purchase Men's Singles, and an Interscholastic Championship. Only the Olympic Singles and Doubles should probably be considered part of the Olympic Games. Strangely, however, there were no restrictions on the entrants in the other sports and there were even foreign competitors in several of them.

Also of note, although no women competed in the Olympic events, one woman did enter for the Interscholastic Championships. This was Miss Carrie M. Dwan and a story concerning her entry ran in the St. Louis newspapers of 28 August. She was the girls' champion of the St. Louis high school district in 1903 and had also won the double championships, partnered by Carrie Briback. Although Miss Dwan was entered for the interscholastic championships, and was scheduled to play F. E. Sheldon, neither player appeared and she did not compete.

The only foreign entrant in the Olympic events was Dr. Hugo Hardy of Berlin, Germany. He competed in both the Olympic Singles and Doubles and also competed in the World's Fair Singles and Doubles. The Japanese champion, Shunzo Tokaki, attended the World's Fair and enterd the Missouri State Championships in early July, but he is not mentioned as having entered the "Olympic" tennis events.

All these events were contested during the same time period with multiple events being held on multiple courts. It is not always clear from the newspaper reports which of the events they are discussing, as the events were simply numbered in some of the newspaper articles rather than giving their names.

The director of the Olympic tennis competitions was Dwight Davis, who was a well-known St. Louis politician and later was U.S. Secretary of War. He managed to win the singles championship in the Louisiana Purchase event. He also achieved long-term tennis immortality when he donated a cup as an international team trophy (in 1900), now called the Davis Cup. Davis played on the U.S. teams that won the first two Davis Cup competitions (1900, 1902).

Site:	Dirt Courts adjacent to the stadium at Francis Field
Dates/Times:	29 August–3 September

181

	Competitors	1st	2nd	3rd	Totals
Events: 2					
Competitors: 36					
Nations: 2					
Germany	1	-	-	-	-
United States	35	2	2	4	8
Totals	36	2	2	4	8
Nations	2	1	1	1	1

Olympic Men's Singles

A: 27[1]*; C: 2[2]; D: 29 August–3 September; F: Single elimination. All matches were best of three sets.[3]

The Olympic Men's Singles championship was won by Beals Wright of Boston who was the defending U.S. doubles champion, having been partnered by Holcolmbe Ward to win that championship in 1903. Wright won the title by defeating Robert LeRoy of Columbia University, who was the 1903 European champion. The final match score was 6–4, 6–4. The *St. Louis Globe Democrat* reported the results of the final as follows, "Wright showed himself to be worthy of the reputation with which he is accredited. His play was steadily brilliant and he invoked the applause of the highly interested spectators, of whom there were a goodly number, not withstanding the counter attraction offered by the final events of the Olympic games. LeRoy's playing bordered on the sensational throughout the game, and the execution of difficult strokes was frequent. He made such a showing as to make him a logical candidate for championship honors when he has gained the strength which comes with maturity."

LeRoy had advanced to the finals by defeating Edgar Leonard of Boston, 6–3, 6–3. Wright had advanced to the finals by defeating Los Angeles' Alphonzo Bell, 6–3, 6–4. Wright was the son of George Wright, one of the early pioneers of baseball in the United States.

1.	Beals Wright	USA
2.	Robert LeRoy	USA
=3.	Edgar Leonard	USA
	Alphonzo Bell	USA
=5.	Charles Cresson	USA
	W. E. Blatherwick	USA
	John Neely	USA
	Semp Russ	USA
=9.	Fred Sanderson	USA
	Ralph McKittrick	USA
	J. Cunningham	USA
	Hugo Hardy	GER
	F. R. Feltshans	USA
	Dwight F. Davis	USA
	McKittrick Jones	USA
=16.	Frank Wheaton	USA

*See Notes on page 190.

=16.	Chris Forney	USA
	William Easton	USA
	Nathaniel Semple	USA
	Forest Montgomery	USA
	Malcolm Macdonald	USA
	Joseph Charles	USA
	Orien Vernon	USA
	J. Stewart Tritle	USA
	Douglas Turner	USA
	Andrew Drew	USA
27.	George Stadel	USA

Olympic Men's Doubles

A: 30[4]; C: 2; D: 31 August–3 September; F: The final was played at best three of five sets.

The Olympic Men's Doubles championship was won by Beals Wright and Edgar Leonard, who defeated Robert LeRoy and Alphonzo Bell in the final, 6–4, 6–4, 6–2. The newspaper report was as follows, "The teamwork of the winners was superb, while LeRoy and Bell were not far behind the champions in skill. Wright and Leonard have played together before and know each other's style well enough to be able to anticipate just where the ball would next be sent. Their victory was a well-earned one."

1.	Beals Wright/Edgar Leonard	USA
2.	Robert LeRoy/Alphonzo Bell	USA
=3.	Joseph Wear/Allen West	USA
	Clarence Gamble/Arthur Wear	USA
=5.	Frank Wheaton/–– Hunter	USA
	Charles Cresson/Semp Russ	USA
	Ralph McKittrick/Dwight Davis	USA
	Hugh McKittrick Jones/Harold Kauffman	USA
=9.	N. M. Smith/Joseph Charles	USA
	W. E. Blatherwick/Orien Vernon	USA
	Forest Montgomery/J. Stewart Tritle	USA
	Nathaniel Semple/Malcolm Macdonald	USA
	Paul Gleason/Hugo Hardy	USA/GER
	George Stadel/Frederick Semple	USA
	Andrew Drew/Douglas Turner	USA

Men's Singles Tournament Summary

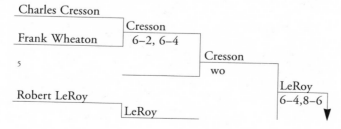

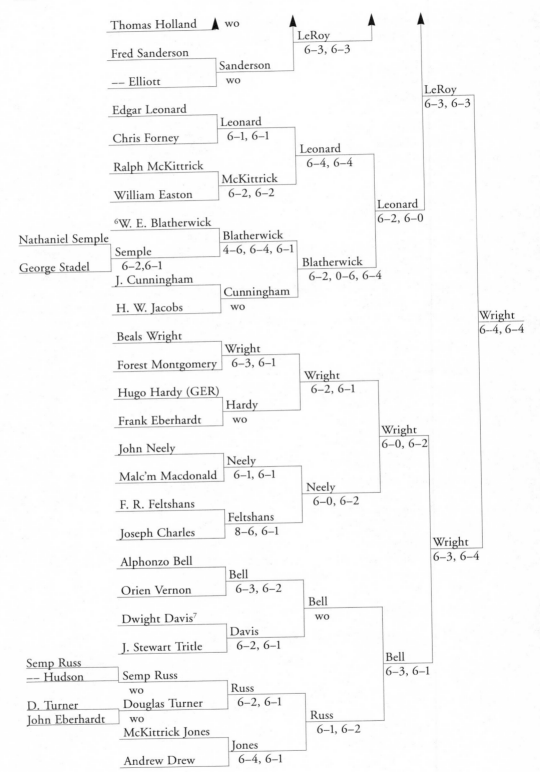

Thomas Holland — wo

LeRoy
6–3, 6–3

Fred Sanderson

Sanderson
wo

—— Elliott

LeRoy
6–3, 6–3

Edgar Leonard

Leonard
6–1, 6–1

Chris Forney

Leonard
6–4, 6–4

Ralph McKittrick

McKittrick
6–2, 6–2

William Easton

Leonard
6–2, 6–0

[6]W. E. Blatherwick

Blatherwick
4–6, 6–4, 6–1

Nathaniel Semple
Semple
6–2, 6–1

George Stadel

J. Cunningham

Cunningham
wo

H. W. Jacobs

Blatherwick
6–2, 0–6, 6–4

Wright
6–4, 6–4

Beals Wright

Wright
6–3, 6–1

Forest Montgomery

Wright
6–2, 6–1

Hugo Hardy (GER)

Hardy
wo

Frank Eberhardt

Wright
6–0, 6–2

John Neely

Neely
6–1, 6–1

Malc'm Macdonald

Neely
6–0, 6–2

F. R. Feltshans

Feltshans
8–6, 6–1

Joseph Charles

Wright
6–3, 6–4

Alphonzo Bell

Bell
6–3, 6–2

Orien Vernon

Bell
wo

Dwight Davis[7]

Davis
6–2, 6–1

J. Stewart Tritle

Bell
6–3, 6–1

Semp Russ
—— Hudson
Semp Russ
wo

Russ
6–2, 6–1

D. Turner
John Eberhardt
Douglas Turner
wo

Russ
6–1, 6–2

McKittrick Jones

Jones
6–4, 6–1

Andrew Drew

Men's Doubles Tournament Summary

Wheaton/Hunter
— Wheaton/Hunter
bye

Gamble/Wear
6–1, 6–4

Gamble/Wear
Smith/Charles — Gamble/Wear
6–3, 7–5

Wright/Leonard
6–1, 6–2

Wright/Leonard
Blatherwick/Vernon — Wright/Leonard
6–4, 7–5

Wright/Leonard
6–2, 5–7, 6–3

Cresson/Russ
Montgomery/Tritle — Cresson/Russ
7–5, 6–2

Wright/Leonard
6–4, 6–4, 6–2

McKittrick/Davis
Semple/Macdonald — McKittrick/Davis
6–1, 6–1

LeRoy/Bell
9–7, 6–4

LeRoy/Bell
Hardy/Gleason — LeRoy/Bell
6–3, 6–1

LeRoy/Bell
2–6, 6–1, 6–2

Jones/Kauffman
Stadel/Semple — Jones/Kauffman
6–1, 8–6

Wear/West
6–3, 4–6, 6–4

Wear/West
Drew/Turner — Wear/West
6–3, 6–4

NON-OLYMPIC EVENTS

World's Fair Men's Singles

A: 26; C: 2; D: 29 August–3 September; F: Single elimination. Matches were best of three sets, except the final which was best of five sets.[8]

1.	Edgar Leonard	USA
2.	Alphonzo Bell	USA
=3.	–– Neely	USA
	Dwight Davis	USA
=5.	Frank Wheaton	USA
	Paul Gleason	USA

| =5. | H. C. Auld | USA |
| | Robert LeRoy | USA |

World's Fair Men's Doubles

A: 18; C: 2; D: 1–3 September; F: Single elimination. Matches were best of three sets, except the final which was best of five sets.[9]

1.	Ralph McKittrick/Dwight Davis	USA
2.	Charles Cresson/Semp Russ	USA
=3.	Clarence Gamble/Arthur Wear	USA
	W. E. Blatherwick/Orien Vernon	USA
=5.	Joseph Wear/Allen West	USA
	Hugo Hardy/Paul Gleason	GER/USA
	N. M. Smith/Joseph Charles	USA
=8.	Nathaniel Semple/Malcolm Macdonald	USA
	Forest Montgomery/J. Stewart Tritle	USA

Louisiana Purchase Open[10] Singles

A: 14; C: 1; D: 31 August–2 September; F: Single elimination. Matches were best of three sets, except the final which was best of five sets.[11]

1.	Dwight Davis	USA
2.	Orien Vernon	USA
=3.	Ralph McKittrick	USA
	H. C. Auld	USA
=5.	H. McKittrick Jones	USA
	William Easton	USA
	Joseph Charles	USA
	Douglas Turner	USA
=9.	W. E. Blatherwick	USA
	F. R. Feltshans	USA
	Nathaniel M. Semple	USA
	L. E. Moore	USA
=13.	J. Stewart Tritle	USA
	Malcolm Macdonald	USA

Interscholastic Men's Singles

A: 3; C: 1; D: 1–2 September; F: Single elimination. Matches were best of three sets, except the final which was best of five sets.

1.	L. Stern	USA
2.	F. J. Tobin	USA
3.	J. C. Tobin	USA

World's Fair Men's Singles Tournament Summary

R. McKittrick
　　　　McKittrick
　　　　bye
E. W. Leonard
　　　　Leonard
N. M. Semple　62, 60
　　　　　　　Leonard
　　　　　　　26, 60, 63

C. Forney
　　　　Forney
M. N. Smith　wo
F. A. Wheaton
　　　　Wheaton
J. S. Tritle　46, 75, 63
　　　　　　　Wheaton
　　　　　　　wo
　　　　　　　　　　　Leonard
　　　　　　　　　　　60, 62

A. Drew
　　　　Drew
G. Stadel　68, 63, 62
　　　　　　　Neely
Neely　　　　61, 61
　　　　Neely
Ths. Holland　wo
　　　　　　　　　　　Neely
　　　　　　　　　　　86, 63

F. H. Montgomery
　　　　Montgomery
H. Gautier　36, 63, 60
　　　　　　　Gleason
P. Gleason　　63, 63
　　　　Gleason
C. C. Cresson　57, 75, 64

　　　　　　　　　　　　　　　　Leonard
　　　　　　　　　　　　　　　　64, 60

D. Davis
　　　　Davis
R. Pierson　wo
　　　　　　　Davis
H. McK Jones　64, 75
　　　　Jones
J. W. Charles　64, 61
　　　　　　　　　　　Davis
　　　　　　　　　　　61, 61

H. Hardy
　　　　Hardy
W. S. Easton　68, 61, 62
　　　　　　　Auld
H. C. Auld　　61, 46, 75
　　　　Auld

　　　　　　　　　　　　　　　　Leonard
　　　　　　　　　　　　　　　　64, 46, 62

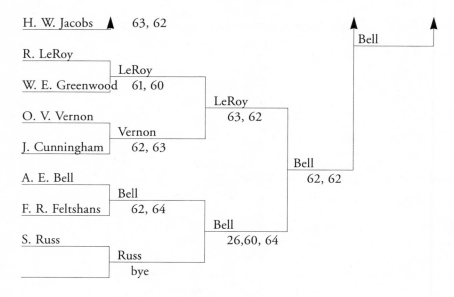

Louisiana Purchase Men's Singles Tournament Summary

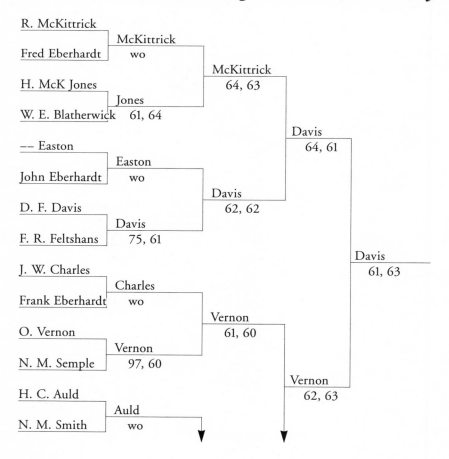

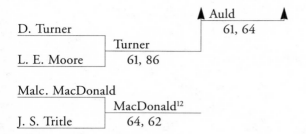

Interscholastic Men's Singles Tournament Summary

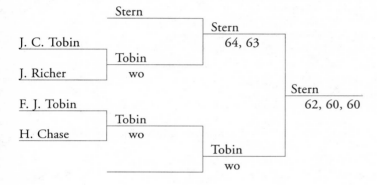

World's Fair Men's Doubles Tournament Summary

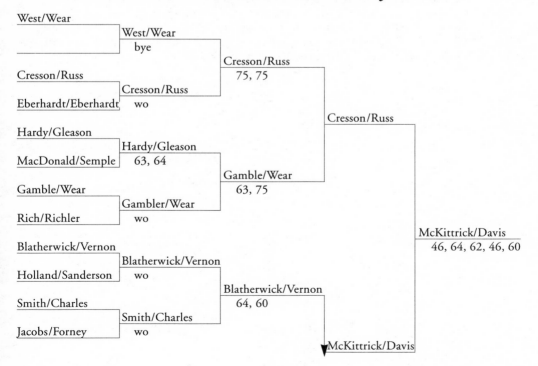

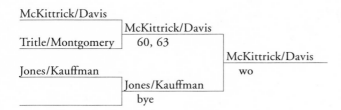

McKittrick/Davis

Tritle/Montgomery

Jones/Kauffman

NOTES

1. There were 36 entries but 9 players failed to show up or defaulted in round one. EK and VK did not know of the early round matches and listed only six players.

2. All players were from the United States with the exception of Dr. Hugo Hardy of Germany, who was the only foreigner in both singles and doubles.

3. This was listed as "Event No. 1" in the St. Louis daily newspapers.

4. EK and VK did not know of the early round matches and listed only eight players.

5. A match was scheduled for this slot between H. M. Holland and Rahn? (Rehm?) but neither player showed up.

6. Blatherwick was to have played a preliminary match against Melville Bergfeld but Bergfeld defaulted.

7. Dwight Davis later became quite famous and is the man who donated the Davis Cup of tennis.

8. This was listed as "Event No. 2" in the St. Louis daily newspapers.

9. This was listed as "Event No. 3" in the St. Louis daily newspapers.

10. Miss Carrie Dwan of 6370 Vermont Avenue in St. Louis was entered in the Louisiana Purchase Singles, the only woman entered in the tennis events during the 1904 World's Fair. She did not compete, and no explanation for that was given in the newspapers.

11. This was listed as "Event No. 7" in the St. Louis daily newspapers.

12. This match definitely took place. It is listed in the St. Louis newspapers and the Spalding Lawn Tennis Annual. However, neither player competed again in the Louisiana Purchase Singles. In addition, it is not even possible to tell where they should fit in the draw.

Tug-of-War

This event was won by the Milwaukee Athletic Club team, which was actually composed of athletes from Chicago, who were members of other athletic clubs in that town. Apparently, Milwaukee, looking for team points, had in some way induced the Chicago tuggers to pull for them. They won two easy matches.

The New York Athletic Club withdrew after losing to Milwaukee and did not pull as scheduled against the first St. Louis team. As a result, although New York had finished fourth, Chicago tried to protest their finish, which was worth one point in the team race, but to no avail.

Each match had a five-minute time limit. The winner was the first team to pull the other team over a line six feet from their starting point. If no team pulled the other over the line by the time limit, then the losing team was the team closest to that line.

Site:	Francis Field	
Dates/Times:	31 August–1 September	
Events:	1	
Competitors:	30	
Nations:	3	

	Competitors	1st	2nd	3rd	Totals
Greece	5	-	-	-	-
South Africa	5	-	-	-	-
United States	20	1	1	1	3
Totals	30	1	1	1	3
Nations	3	1	1	1	1

Tug-of-War Tournament

A: 30; C: 3[1]*; D: 31 August–1 September; F: To win a team had to pull the other team six feet (1.83 m.) within a five-minute time limit.

See Notes on page 193.

1. Milwaukee Athletic Club[2]   USA
    (Oscar Olson, Sidney Johnson, Henry Seiling, Conrad Magnusson, Patrick Flanagan)
2. St. Louis Southwest Turnverein #1[3] USA
    (Max Braun, William Seiling, Orrin Upshaw, Charles Rose, August Rodenberg)
3. St. Louis Southwest Turnverein #2[4] USA
    (Charles Haberkorn, Frank Kungler, Charles Thias, Harry Jacobs, Oscar Friede)
4. New York Athletic Club   USA
    (Charles Dieges, Samuel Jones, Lawrence Feuerbach[5], Charles Chadwick, James Mitchel[6])
=5. Boer Team   SAF
    (C. Walker, P. Hillense, J. Schutte, B. Lombard, P. Visser)
=5. Pan-Hellenic Athletic Club   GRE
    (Nikolaos Georgantas, Perikles Kakousis, Dimitrios Dimitrakopoulos, Anastasios Georgopoulos, Vasilios Metalos)

Results of Matches

31 August	Milwaukee defeated Boers	0:20
	St. Louis #1 defeated Pan-Hellenic	2 feet (0.61 m.) at 5:00
	Milwaukee defeated St. Louis #1	1:44
	New York defeated St. Louis #2	4 feet (1.22 m.) at 5:00
1 September	Milwaukee defeated New York	2–0
	St. Louis #1 defeated St. Louis #2	
	St. Louis #1 defeated New York	Default

Tournament Summary

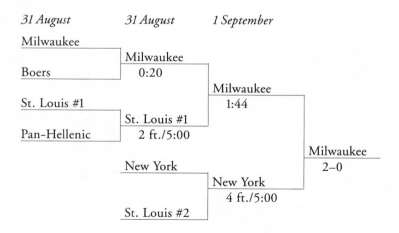

Second-Place Tournament Summary

1 September

St. Louis #1
⌐ St. Louis #1
St. Louis #2
       ⌐ St. Louis #1
         Default
     New York

NOTES

1. EK and VK list 30 competitors correctly, but have only 1 nation represented.

2. This team was composed solely of Chicago athletes. Depending on the paper read they were either members of the Columbian Knights Athletic Association or the Sleipner Athletic Club, both of Chicago. Because of this fact, the victory was later protested by the St. Louis Southwest Turnverein but it was apparently overruled.

3. The *Weltliche Post* of 4 September 1904 has a photo of the team which was discovered by June Becht. The photo lists George Dietzler instead of Orrin Upshaw. However, a photo at the Missouri Historical Society shows #91 pulling in an action shot for the St. Louis Southwest Turnverein #1. In the daily program #91 is Orrin Upshaw. Most sources list Upshaw.

4. Full names not listed in EK. These were found in entry lists in the *Globe-Democrat*.

5. Lawrence Edward Joseph Feuerbach's name is usually seen incorrectly as Leon E. J. Feuerbach.

6. EK has Stangland in place of Mitchel but the *Globe-Democrat* lists Mitchel. This seems more likely as Mitchel was a weight-thrower and Stangland was a long jumper. Mitchel is commonly misspelled as Mitchell.

Weightlifting

The weightlifting events[1]* were contested on 1–3 September on the infield of Francis Field at the Olympic Stadium. There were two events, a two-handed lift of unlimited style and an all-around dumbbell contest. The two-handed lift was won easily by the Greek Perikles Kakousis. The all-around dumbbell contest was contested by three Americans: Oscar Osthoff, Frederick Winters, and Frank Kungler. It was an unusual event which was essentially a weightlifting decathlon in which nine different dumbbell movements were contested. In addition, the tenth section was for optional feats, which saw the two remaining athletes, Osthoff and Winters, doing variations of push-ups to earn points.

The Olympic weightlifting contests of 1904 were held as part of the track & field competition as was common in that era. They were an open competition with foreign entrants and no handicaps and are correctly always considered Olympic caliber.

Site: Francis Field
Dates/Times: 1, 3 September
Events: 2
Competitors: 5
Nations: 2

	Competitors	1st	2nd	3rd	Totals
Greece	1	1	-	-	1
United States	4	1	2	2	5
Totals	5	2	2	2	6
Nations	2	2	1	1	2

Two-Hand Lift (Unlimited Class)

A: 4; C: 2; D: 3 September.

1.	Perikles Kakousis	GRE	246.25 lbs.	[111.70 kg.][2]
2.	Oscar Osthoff	USA	186.00 lbs.	[84.37 kg.]
3.	Frank Kungler	USA	175.50 lbs.	[79.61 kg.]
4.	Oscar Olson	USA	149.50 lbs.	[67.81 kg.][3]

All-Around Dumbbell Contest

A: 3; C: 1; D: 1, 3 September; F: The scoring for the first nine sections gave five points for first, three points for second, and one point for third. In section ten, the judges and referee had the power to award the points in any number thought proper but the total number of points awarded in section ten was not to exceed 25.

1.	Oscar Osthoff	USA	48 pts.[4]
2.	Frederick Winters	USA	45 pts.
3.	Frank Kungler	USA	10 pts.

Results of Each Section

1 September

Section One: Holding out one dumbbell in each hand at arm's length, the bells to be started with the arm perpendicular above the head and dropped down from there to straight out at arm's length from the shoulder, horizontally.

Winters	R	79.50 lbs	[36.06 kg]	L	57.50 lbs	[26.08 kg]	5 pts.	[5]
Osthoff	R	49.75 lbs	[22.57 kg]	L	49.75 lbs	[22.57 kg]	3 pts.	[3]
Kungler	R	40.00 lbs	[18.14 kg]	L	39.50 lbs	[17.92 kg]	1 pt.	[1]

Section Two: Curling one dumbbell in one hand.

Winters	100.25 lbs	[45.47 kg]	5 pts.	[10]
Osthoff	73.875 lbs	[33.51 kg]	3 pts.	[6]
Kungler	53.25 lbs	[24.15 kg]	1 pt.	[2]

Section Five: Tossing one dumbbell in one hand from the ground to arm's length above the shoulders in one motion without stopping at the shoulder.

Winters	130.00 lbs	[58.97 kg]	5 pts.	[15]
Osthoff	116.75 lbs	[52.96 kg]	3 pts.	[9]
Kungler	94.125 lbs	[42.69 kg]	1 pt.	[3]

Section Seven: Jerking up one dumbbell with one hand from the shoulder to arm's length above the shoulder.

Osthoff	150.00 lbs	[68.04 kg]	5 pts.	[14]
Winters	130.00 lbs	[58.97 kg]	2 pts.	[17]
Kungler	130.00 lbs	[58.97 kg]	2 pts.	[5]

Section Eight: Pushing up slowly one dumbbell in each hand from the shoulder to arm's length above the shoulder.

Winters	R	100.25 lbs	[45.47 kg]	L	79.50 lbs	[36.06 kg]	5 pts.	[22]
Osthoff	R	74.75 lbs	[33.91 kg]	L	73.875 lbs	[33.51 kg]	3 pts.	[17]
Kungler	R	57.50 lbs	[26.08 kg]	L	49.75 lbs	[22.57 kg]	1 pt.	[6]

3 September

Section Three: Curling one dumbbell in each hand at the same time.

Winters	R	78.00 lbs	[35.38 kg]	L	57.50 lbs	[26.08 kg]	5 pts.	[27]
Osthoff	R	74.00 lbs	[33.57 kg]	L	53.00 lbs	[24.04 kg]	3 pts.	[20]
Kungler	R	53.00 lbs	[24.04 kg]	L	49.875 lbs	[22.62 kg]	1 pt.	[7]

Section Four: Tossing up one dumbbell from the ground to the shoulder with one hand.

Osthoff	151.00 lbs	[68.49 kg]	5 pts.	[25]
Winters	140.50 lbs	[63.73 kg]	3 pts.	[30]
Kungler	94.25 lbs	[42.75 kg]	1 pt.	[8]

Section Six: Pushing up slowly one dumbbell with one hand from the shoulder to arm's length above the shoulder.

Winters	126.50 lbs	[57.38 kg]	5 pts.	[35]
Osthoff	116.75 lbs	[52.96 kg]	3 pts.	[28]
Kungler	78.00 lbs	[35.38 kg]	1 pt.	[9]

Section Nine: Jerking up one dumbbell in each hand from the shoulder to arm's length above the shoulder.

Osthoff	R	100.25 lbs	[45.47 kg]	L	94.25 lbs	[42.75 kg]	5 pts.	[33]
Winters	R	94.25 lbs	[42.75 kg]	L	74.875 lbs	[33.96 kg]	3 pts.	[38]
Kungler	R	74.00 lbs	[33.57 kg]	L	73.50 lbs	[33.34 kg]	1 pt.	[10]

Section Ten: Original feats at the option of the contestant.

Osthoff— putting up in a bridge with two hands, 177 lbs. [80.29 kg.], six times 15 pts.   [48]
Winters — one-arm push-up, 105.25 lbs. [47.74 kg.], six times   7 pts.   [45]

NOTES

1. In 1904, the weightlifting events were considered a part of the athletics (track & field) competition.

2. En route to the final lift, Kakousis also lifted 186 lbs. (84.37 kg.) and 200 lbs (90.72 kg.).

3. EK gives the weights lifted for the four finishers as follows: 111.58 kg., 84.36 kg., 79.83 kg., and 68.04 kg. The weights given here were taken in their original Imperial measure from the *Globe-Democrat* and converted to their metric equivalents.

4. FM has the "mark" as 86.75 kg. (191¼ lb.), but obviously he did not understand the format of the competition.

Wrestling

The Olympic wrestling championships for 1904 were held on 14–15 October in the infield of the Olympic Stadium at Francis field. The events doubled as the United States AAU Championships. There were no foreign entrants and no foreign competitors. The rules for the 1904 Olympic wrestling championships, however, did allow entrants from any country. There was no restriction on nationality at all. It was simply that no foreigners elected to compete. Some of this may have been due to the fact that the events were held very late in the year, and many of the foreign athletes had returned to Europe by then.

Of the seven weight classes none had more than ten entrants. Several Americans defended their national titles, among them Robert Curry who had been national champion at 105 pounds in 1903 and also won in 1904; George Mehnert, who won his third consecutive national championship at 115 pounds; and Isidor "Jack" Niflot who won his fourth consecutive national championship at 125 pounds.

Despite the fact that no foreign competitors competed, there was no real reason not to include the wrestling competitions as an Olympic sport in 1904. They meet all our criteria for consideration as an Olympic sport, and although they were far from memorable, they should be included.

The format was that all weight classes were held as single elimination tournaments. All those losing to the winner and runner-up had the right to compete for third-place in a a new tournament, though results of those matches are not known to any degree. Bouts were to be six minutes with three minute overtimes, should they be necessary. In the final the first overtime was to be six minutes.[1]*

Site:	Francis Field	
Dates/Times:	14–15 October	
Events:	7	
Competitors:	41	
Nations:	1	

	Competitors	1st	2nd	3rd	Totals
United States	41	7	7	7	21
Totals	41	7	7	7	21
Nations	1	1	1	1	1

*See Notes on pages 202–203.

197

≦*105 lb. [47.63 kg.] Class*

A: 4[2]; C: 1; D: 14–15 October.

1.	Robert Curry	USA
2.	John Hein	USA
3.	Gustav Thiefenthaler	USA
4.	Claude Holgate	USA

Tournament Summary

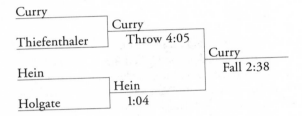

Curry
Thiefenthaler — Curry — Throw 4:05
Hein
Holgate — Hein — 1:04
Curry — Fall 2:38

≦*115 lb. [52.16 kg.] Class*

A: 3[3]; C: 1; D: 14–15 October.

1.	George Mehnert	USA
2.	Gustav Bauer	USA
3.	William Nelson	USA

Tournament Summary

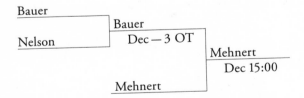

Bauer
Nelson — Bauer — Dec — 3 OT
Mehnert
Mehnert — Dec 15:00

≦*125 lb. [56.70 kg.] Class*

A: 7[4]; C: 1; D: 14–15 October.

1.	Isidor "Jack" Niflot	USA
2.	August Wester	USA
3.	Z. B. Strebler	USA
AC.	Milton Whitehurst	USA

AC.	Frederick Ferguson	USA
	Charles Stevens	USA
	J. M. Cardwell	USA

Tournament Summary

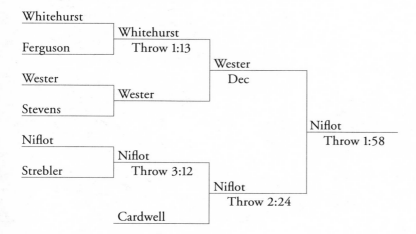

Whitehurst
Whitehurst
Ferguson — Throw 1:13
Wester — Dec
Wester
Wester
Stevens
Niflot — Throw 1:58
Niflot
Niflot — Throw 3:12
Strebler
Niflot — Throw 2:24
Cardwell

≦*135 lb. [61.23 kg.] Class*

A: 9[5]; C: 1; D: 14–15 October.

1.	Benjamin Bradshaw	USA
2.	Theodore McLear	USA
3.	Charles Clapper	USA
4.	Frederick Ferguson	USA
AC.	J. C. Babcock	USA
	Z. B. Strebler	USA
	Dietrich Wortmann	USA
	Max Miller	USA
	Hugo Toeppen	USA

Tournament Summary

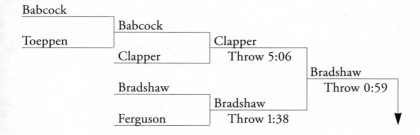

Babcock
Babcock
Toeppen
Clapper
Clapper — Throw 5:06
Bradshaw — Throw 0:59
Bradshaw
Bradshaw
Ferguson — Throw 1:38

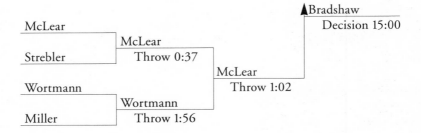

```
McLear
              McLear
Strebler      Throw 0:37
                                McLear
                                Throw 1:02
Wortmann
              Wortmann
Miller        Throw 1:56
```

Bradshaw
Decision 15:00

Third-place Match

```
Clapper
              Clapper
Ferguson      Throw 0:54
```

≦*145 lb. [65.77 kg.] Class*

A: 10[6]; C: 1; D: 14–15 October.

1.	Otto Roehm	USA
2.	Rudolph Tesing	USA
3.	Albert Zirkel	USA
AC.	Fred Koenig	USA
	Fred Hussman	USA
	Jerry Winholtz	USA
	Charles Haberkorn	USA
	Rudolph Wolken	USA
	William Hennessy	USA
	Charles Eng	USA

Tournament Summary

```
Roehm
              Roehm
Koenig
                          Roehm
                          Throw 11:51
Hussman
              Hussman
Winholtz      Dec
                                     Roehm

Zirkel
              Zirkel
              Throw 4:10
Haberkorn
                                          Roehm
```

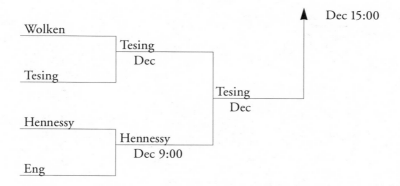

≦*158 lb. [71.67 kg.] Class*

A: 10[7]; C: 1; D: 14–15 October.

1.	Charles Ericksen	USA
2.	William Beckmann	USA
3.	Jerry Winholtz	USA
AC.	A. J. Betchestobill	USA
	William Schaefer	USA
	S. A. Filler	USA
	Otto Roehm	USA
	Hugo Toeppen	USA
	William Hennessy	USA
	A. Mellinger	USA

Tournament Summary

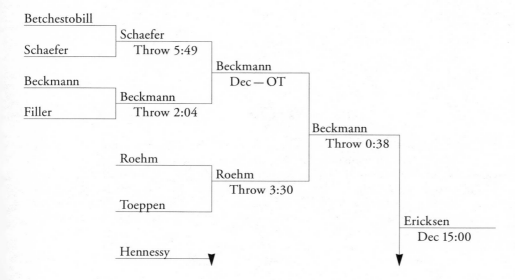

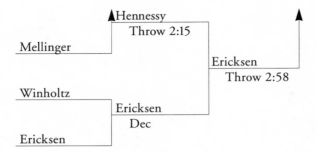

Unlimited Class (> 158 lbs. [71.67 kg.])

A: 5; C: 1; D: 14–15 October.

1.	Bernhuff Hansen	USA
2.	Frank Kungler	USA
3.	Fred Warmboldt	USA
AC.	William Hennessy	USA
	Joseph Dilg	USA

Tournament Summary

NOTES

1. The third-place finishers listed here are as listed in EK. Third-place was apparently awarded in conformation with Rule 10 stating that all who have been defeated by the winners of either first or second place shall have been entitled to compete for third place. Only one such match is known — that between Clapper and Ferguson in the 135 lb. class. It might seem more reasonable to list the losing semi-finalists as equal third in the other classes, but it is possible that deciding third-place matches took place in all classes but were not recorded or have not been found, despite extensive efforts. Consequently, I have left the results as usually recorded.

2. EK and VK list six.

3. EK and VK list seven.

4. EK and VK list six.
5. EK and VK list six.
6. EK and VK list five.
7. EK and VK list five.

Non-Olympic Sports

American Football (Colleges)

Quoting from the *Spalding Official Athletic Almanac*, "The Department knew perfectly well that it would be unable to have an Olympic Foot Ball Championship, though it felt incumbent to advertise it. Owing to the conditions in American colleges it would be utterly impossible to have an Olympic foot ball championship decided. The only college that seemed absolutely willing to give up its financial interest to play for the World's Fair Championship was the St. Louis University and there is more apparently in this honor than appears in this report. There were many exhibition contests held in the Stadium under the auspices of the Department wherein teams from the St. Louis University and Washington University took part and competed against other teams from universities east and west of the Mississippi River. The Missouri-Purdue game was played in the Stadium on October 28, as was the Carlisle-Haskell game on November 26, when the men from the Government Indian Schools competed against each other for the first time.

"The Olympic College Foot Ball Championship was won by St. Louis University, St. Louis, Mo. by default."

Although other sources have occasionally mentioned that American college football was contested as part of the 1904 Olympic Games, quite obviously all that occurred was that several college football games were contested at Francis Field on the campus of Washington University. Even more obviously, only one of these games, the match between Haskell and Carlisle, did not involve the Washington University team, which was thus simply playing all home games as part of its regular college football schedule. St. Louis University, which apparently agreed to compete for the Olympic championship, did not play any of its games at the Olympic Stadium.

There is no justification for giving these college football games any Olympic status. Remember, also, that no foreigners competed nor were invited, and to my knowledge, American football was not played in any other country, with the possible exception of Canada, in 1904.

Football Games Played in the Olympic Stadium

28 September	Washington University	10	Shurtleff College	0
5 October	Washington University	16	Rose Polytechnic	5
8 October	University of Illinois	31	Washington University	0

15 October	Sewanee College	17	Washington University	0
19 October	Washington University	36	Drury College	0
22 October	Indiana University	21	Washington University	6
29 October	University of Texas	23	Washington University	0
5 November	Washington University	11	University of Missouri	0
12 November	University of Kansas	12	Washington University	0
19 November	University of West Virginia	6	Washington University	5
24 November	Haskell Indian School	47	Washington University	0
26 November	Carlisle Indian School	38	Haskell Indian School	4

Anthropology Days at the Stadium

12–13 August 1904

As was noted in the introduction to this work, an unusual set of "athletic" events took place on 12–13 August 1904 during the 1904 Olympic Games, termed "Anthropology Days." These events were contests among minority, aboriginal or native peoples from several lands who were present at the Physical Culture exhibits of the Louisiana Purchase Exhibition. They certainly have no Olympic status, as the events were open only to these groups of people. In addition, though the events were purportedly a "scientific experiment" to demonstrate the supposed prowess of these participants, it was relatively obvious that the events were actually meant to demean them. One interesting note: one of the spectators on the field that day was the famous Chiricahua Apache Indian Chief Geronimo (1829–1909). The description of these events, as given in on pp. 249–259 of *Spalding's Official Athletic Almanac for 1905: Special Olympic Number, Containing the Official Report of the Olympic Games of 1904* is as follows:

In the early months of the Exposition, the Chief of the Department of Physical Culture had several conferences with Dr. W. J. McGee, Chief of the Department of Anthropology, in relation to the athletic ability of the several savage tribes, and owing to the startling rumors and statements that were made in relation to the speed, stamina and strength of each and every particular tribe that was represented at St. Louis, it was decided to inaugurate a two-days athletic meet for them, to be known as "Anthropology Days," the days being named after the Department of Anthropology, in honor of Dr. McGee, who used his influence toward making the days the brilliant success which they terminated in.

It would be unfair, however, to proceed with the narrative of the Anthropology Days without giving a great deal of credit to Dr. Simms, of the Field Museum, Chicago, for the part he took in arranging the details and successfully carrying them out, and to Dr. Luther Halsey Gulick, who did much preliminary work and acted as referee. The first day the various tribes competed amongst themselves in the different athletic events elected, and on the second day occurred the final contests between those finishing first and second in each one of the tribal events on the opening day.

The Department very wisely held this meeting during the month of August, so that the many physical directors and gentlemen interested in scientific work could be present and benefit by the demonstrations. That the ones interested were deeply disappointed in what this meeting demonstrated is well known. We have for years been led to believe from statements made by those who should know and from newspaper articles and books, that the average savage was fleet of foot, strong of limb, accurate with the bow and arrow and expert in throwing the stone, and that some, particularly the Patagonians, were noted for their great size and strength, and owing to the peculiar life that many have been called upon to lead they have been termed natural athletes. Of course none expected that the Patagonians would be John Flanagans or the Indians Arthur Duffeys or Alexander Grants, but they certainly expected a great deal more from the savages who competed in the Anthropology Days than events proved.

We have heard of the marvelous qualities of the Indian as a runner; of the stamina of the Kaffir, and the natural all around ability of the savage in athletic feats, but the events at St. Louis disprove the tales. The records that are published herewith will prove most interesting, as they are the results of the first athletic meeting held anywhere, in which savages were exclusive participants.

On the first day of the Anthropology sports the one hundred yards run was decided in heats, subdivided as follows: six heats, one for each of the followings classes, Africans, Moros (Philippines), Patagonians, and the Ainu (Japanese), Cocopa (Mexican), and Sioux Indian tribes. The fastest time was made by George Mentz, of the Sioux tribe, an Americanized Indian. His time was 11.8, time that almost any winner of a schoolboy event would eclipse at will. Lamba, an African Pygmy, ran one hundred yards in 14.6. Now the African Pygmy leads an outdoor life, hunts, runs, swims, jumps and uses the bow and arrow and spear, and if anything, his life might be termed a natural athletic one, but, nevertheless, we find it takes him 14.6 to run one hundred yards. Arthur Duffey, or any of our American champion sprinters could easily, in this particular race, have given the African Pygmy forty yards and a beating.

No particular speed, of course, was expected from the Patagonians. The winner's time, 13.6, might be considered very poor running for even an ordinary man in a healthy condition. A Cocopa Indian ran the one hundred yards in 13.0.

The shot putting contest had a great many entries, each tribe competing among themselves. The tribes entered consisted of the Patagonians, the Cocopas, the Indian tribe, the Ainu (Japanese), the Turks, and the Africans. It was in this particular competition that every one naturally supposed the Patagonians would excel, on account of their size, strength and remarkable performances credited to them in strength contests, but nevertheless, the best performance of the Patagonian was that of 30–5 (9.27). This, for putting the 16-lb. shot, is such a ridiculously poor performance that it astonished all who witnessed it. It is 18–2 (5.54) behind the American record, many feet behind the interscholastic record, and it is doubtful if there is a high school championship that is not won with a better performance. This was one of the disappointing features of the day's sport.

A glance at the other performances will prove interesting. The shot competition was won by an Americanized Indian, W. Dietz, who put it 33–10½ (10.32). The Japanese Ainus, a very small tribe — a gentlemanly tribe at that — performed very poorly, one of them putting the shot but 13–7½ (4.15). The best performance among the Pygmies was by Shambo, who put 17–6 (5.33), the poorest performance being 11–1½ (3.39).

A comparison of these records and the other records in the Almanac will prove particularly interesting. Of course the argument may be made that these savages have not been taught the art of shot putting. Quite true, but one would think that the life these men have led should enable them to easily have put this shot many feet further. With the Pygmies, however, it is only fair to state that they entered into the spirit of this competition for fun, and only became interested in the pole climbing and their mud fight.

The four hundred and forty yards run had four heats, the Americanized Indian, George Rye, making the fastest time — 63.0 — the slowest time being 1:10.6, which was made by Gondola, from one of the African tribes.

In the running broad jump the different tribes sent forward their best men, the Americanized Indian, Mentz, of the Sioux tribe, clearing 17 feet (5.18). The jumping of the Pygmies, the Ainus, and some of the Indians was really ridiculous. Ray Ewry jumped further in the standing jump than any of them could go in a running broad jump. The broad jumping, like other sports the savages took part in, proves conclusively that the savage is not the natural athlete we have been led to believe.

When the competition in throwing the baseball was called, it was particularly noticeable that all the savages, as well as the Americanized Indians, were anxious to throw. There seemed to be a weird fascination about the ball that appealed to them. No less than two dozen took part in throwing the baseball. The first, second and third places were won by Americanized Indians, the best throw of the savages being that of Coloho, the Patagonian, who threw 214 feet (65.22).

The savages did not take kindly at all to the 56-lb. weight. That is naturally a game for muscular athletes, but nevertheless it was thought advisable to obtain the records in a performance of this kind, to see how they compared with our own. Here is where the Patagonian was supposed to excel, because weight throwing is primarily a sport that large men excel at, particularly large, athletic, healthy men. Three Patagonians competed among themselves, but the best performance was 10–6. This is ludicrous when one considers Flanagan's great record, in fact, Flanagan in one throw sent the 56-lb. weight many feet further than the combined score of the three Patagonians. The best performance this day at this particular competition was by a young Sioux Indian named Mentz, who threw it 15–11 (4.85), and the performances of the Ainus would compel many to believe that they had a great deal to accomplish in the way of developing their bodies. Three Ainus took part, one 28 years of age, one 38 and one 57. The young man threw it 7–4 (2.23), the old man 5–0 (1.52) and the man 38 years old threw it 3–6 (1.06). It can probably be said, without fear of contradiction, that never before in the history of sport in the world were such poor performances recorded for weight throwing.

The second, and the final day of the Anthropology sports showed the savage off somewhat better, because they were given a chance to show what they could accomplish in some of their own particular sports. The most marvelous performances at pole climbing ever witnessed in this country was given by an Igorotte, who climbed a pole about 50 feet (15.24) in height in 20.4; the best American record for rope climbing being 15.8 for 35–8 (10.87), made by C. E. Raynor, South Bethlehem, Pa., in 1887. This performance showed conclusively the marvelous agility, strength of limb, and great endurance of this particular Igorotte, and it is doubtful if we have any trained athlete in America who could duplicate that performance with years of training. The nearest approach to this feat was that of an African who took 39.2 seconds to climb the pole. The times of all the savages in this particular event were praiseworthy and worthy of record.

Throwing the javelin was another disappointment. The javelin is 3–6 (1.06) in length, and is made of wood, except the head, which is spear-shaped and made of steel and measures 16 inches (40 centimeters). The instrument is thrown with one hand only, from a seven-foot circle, at an object post of soft wood, one foot square, placed some distance from the circle and four feet above the ground.

The javelin, it will be seen, is thrown in the same style as the savages throw their spears, and it is to a certain extent an enlarged spear. At this particular sport it was hoped the savages would excel, but far from it; they did not, and in three attempts each, only three out of a couple of dozen hit the post 25 feet (7.62) away.

In the running high jump, the Americanized Indian again outclassed the savage, the savages showing in very poor form.

The archery contest was another disappointment. We have been led to believe that the Igorottes, the Africans, the Pygmies, the Cocopas, and the Ainus, who have been living for years with the bow and arrow, and with whom shooting with the arrow is an everyday occurrence, would exhibit the most marvelous target shooting that had ever been witnessed. The target, actually four feet by six, was placed forty-two yards away, and astonishing to relate, only two of the entrants pierced the target, the others striking at the bottom of it. The winner turned up in a little Cocopa Indian boy named Shake, who pierced the target once. The other Indians, some of them old and gray-haired, found it impossible to hit it. The reason for this was explained perhaps to a certain extent by Dr. Simms, who claimed they did most of their shooting from horseback at moving objects. Be that as it may, the exhibition of archery shooting by the savage tribes was very disappointing, particularly to those, who, a few weeks later had the pleasure of seeing the American archers use their bows and arrows. The difference was just the same as in other sports.

The Patagonians, in the tug-of-war with the giants, showed remarkable ability. At bolo and perhaps at pulling, hauling and dragging, they must have developed muscles that are useful and strong, but the muscles for shot putting and throwing the weights had certainly been neglected.

In throwing the baseball for accuracy only two out of a couple of dozen were able to strike an ordinary telegraph pole at a distance of 25 feet (7.62), the best throw being by Chief Guechico, a Patagonian.

Many started in the one-mile run, and it was believed that the Kaffirs and Indians would show great speed. This event, like all the other runs went to the Americanized Indians in the slow time of 5:38.0; Lehouw, a Kaffir, finished third in this race, showing fine form but no speed.

The Pygmies and the Cocopa Indians at the conclusion of the day's sport gave an exhibition of their shinny game, which required team work and the uninteresting exhibition showed conclusively the lack of the necessary brain to make the team and its work a success, for they absolutely gave no assistance to each other, and so far as team work was concerned, it was a case of purely individual attempt on the part of the players. The same could be said of both games.

The Pygmies indulged in one of their favorite pastimes, a mud fight, two sides being selected, and it reminded one very much of a snowball fight of the average American boy. The exhibition was clever. They showed great dexterity in ducking, throwing and running, and they altogether redeemed themselves for their lack of interest in the other sports.

The records that follow should be kept and, no doubt, in years to come, there may perhaps be another meeting that the savages can take part in and better performances may be recorded.

Dr. McGee attributes this utter lack of athletic ability on the part of the savages to the fact they have not been shown, or educated. He thinks perhaps if they could have the use of a professional trainer for a short time that they would become as proficient as many Americans. The writer doubts it, as the exhibitions given on these particular days do not speak well for them. The whole meeting proves conclusively that the savage has been a very much overrated man from an athletic point of view.

It may be claimed that these particular days did not thoroughly establish the athletic ability of the savage tribes. It was a very hard meeting to handle and many of them did not perhaps know that they were expected to do their very best. The Pygmies from Africa were full of mischief. They took nothing whatever seriously, outside of their own shinny game and the tree climbing. For the other sports, they seemed to think that they were brought there to do certain things, and they did them, which may account for their poor performances. They tried to run, but did not persevere. The Ainus, a very small tribe from the north of Japan, were without doubt the most polite savages the writer has ever met, extremely so. They willingly, and with pleasant bows to the officials and everyone else, took part in every sport they were asked to, but it is doubtful if they extended themselves to any great effort. One of the Ainus was particularly interesting and decidedly anxious to jump, and he tried hard, but could not.

In the one hundred yards run the savages proved, of course, that they knew nothing whatever about sprint racing. With eight or ten men on the mark it was a pretty hard thing to explain to them to run when the pistol was fired. In running their heats, when coming to the finish tape, instead of breasting it or running through, many would stop and others run under it.

In all these field sports, Mr. Martin Delaney, of the St. Louis University, gave them examples in advance, so that they knew what was expected of them. It may have been a mistake in not having another day, when perhaps, the different interpreters could have explained to the savages more about what was expected of them, but nevertheless, the "Anthropology Days" were most successful and interesting, and ones that scientific men will refer to for many years to come. It taught a great lesson.

Lecturers and authors will in the future please omit all reference to the natural athletic ability of the savage, unless they can substantiate their alleged feats.

100 yard run

Africans—1) Lamba, Pygmy Tribe, 14.6; 2) Prince Lotuna, Bacuba Tribe; 3) Loumbungo, Bacuba Tribe.

Lanao Moros (Filipinos)—1) Sumdud, Samal Tribe, 12.4.

Patagonians—1) Bonifacio, 13.6; 2) Casimido; 3) Colofor.

Asians (Syrians from Beirut)—1) Yousouf Hana 12.6; 2) Maroof Zaytoun.

Cocopa Tribe—1) John Roy, 13.0; 2) Chempuko; 3) Jack.

Sioux Indian Tribe—1) George Mentz, Sioux Tribe, 11.8; 2) Frank Moore, Pawnee Tribe.

Putting 16-lb. shot

Patagonian Tribe—1) Casimido, 30–5 (9.27); 2) Bonifacio, 29–6 (8.99); 3) Coloho, 28–0 (8.53); 4) Cinchel, 27–4 (8.33); 5) Chief Guechico, 17–0 (5.18).

Cocopa Tribe—1) Chief Pueblo Colorado, 24–4½ (7.43); 2) Jerry, 22–3 (6.78); 3) John Roy, 20–3½ (6.18); 4) Chizi, 17–0 (5.18).

Indian Tribes—1) W. Deitz, Sioux Tribe, 33–10½ (10.32); 2) Poitre, Chippewa Tribe, 33–10½ (10.32); 3) Black White Bear, Crow Tribe, 32–10 (10.01); 4) George Mentz, Sioux Tribe, 26–0½ (7.94); 5) Simon Max, Sioux Tribe, 26–0 (7.92).

Japanese Ainu Tribe—1) Kuto Roz, 20–0½ (6.11), 2) Goro, 16–10 (5.13), 3) Oschawa, 15–7 (4.75); 4) Sangea, 13–7½ (4.15).

Pueblo Santa Clara Tribe—1) Aniseto Suas, 19–6 (5.94).

Asians—1) Yousouf Hana, 20–9½ (6.34); 2) Maroof Zaytoun 20–6½ (6.26).

Africans—1) John Gondola, Battatella Tribe, 26–4½ (8.04); 2) Shamba, Pygmy Tribe, 17–6 (5.33); 3) Malango, Pygmy Tribe, 17–4½ (5.29); 4) Prince Lotuna, Bacuba Tribe, 14–8 (4.47); 5) Lumu, Pygmy Tribe, 12–3½ (3.74); 6) Loumbungo, Bacuba Tribe, 12–3 (3.73); 7) Bushubba, Pygmy Tribe, 11–7½ (3.54); 8) Otabenga, Pygmy Tribe, 11–1½ (3.39).

440 yard run

Indians—1) George Rye, Cherokee Tribe, 1:00.3; 2) Simon Max, Sioux Tribe; 3) W. Deitz, Sioux Tribe.

Mexican Cocopas—1) John Roy, 1:06.8; 2) Nethab.

Asians—1) Yousouf Hana, 1:06.0s; 2) Maroof Zaytoun.

Africans—1) John Gondola, Battatella Tribe, 1:10.6; 2) Shamba, Pygmy Tribe; 3) Prince Lotuna, Bacuba Tribe.

Running broad jump

Indians—1) George Mentz, Sioux Tribe, 17–0 (5.18); 2) Frank Moore, Pawnee Tribe, 15–6½ (4.74); 3) Poitre, Chippewa Tribe, 15–0 (4.57); 4) Simon Max, Sioux Tribe 15–0 (4.57); 5) Black White Bear, Crow Tribe, 14–0½ (4.28).

Filipinos—1) Mande Cochero, Lanao Moro Samal Tribe, 15–2 (4.62); 2) Sumdud, Lanao Moro Samal Tribe, 15–2 (4.62).

Cocopa Tribe—1) Coldwater 11–6 (3.50); 2) Chizi, 11–4½ (3.47).

Japanese Ainu Tribe—1) Goro, 9–11 (3.02).

Pueblo Santa Clara Tribe—1) Vincenta Suaz, 9–6 (2.89).

Africans—1) Prince Lotuna, Bacuba Tribe (age 15), 10–4 (3.15); 2) John Gondola, Battatella Tribe (age 23), 11–1¹* (3.38).

Throwing bolos

Patagonians only—1) Coloho, [128–0 (39.02), 142–0 (43.28), 187–0 (57.00), 209–0 (63.70)]; 2) Bonifacio, [142–0 (43.28), 187–0 (57.00), 209–0 (63.70)]; 3) Casimido, [187–0 (57.00), 209–0 (63.70)].

Throwing baseball

Indians—1) Poitre, Chippewa Tribe, 266–0 (81.08); 2) W. Deitz, Sioux Tribe, 260–0 (79.26); 3) DePoe, Rock River Tribe, 251–0 (76.50); 4) George Mentz, Sioux Tribe, 239–0 (72.84); 5) Simon Max, Sioux Tribe, 234–0 (71.32); 6) Black White Bear, Crow Tribe, 198–0 (60.36); 7) Warrior, 160–0 (48.78).

Patagonians—1) Coloho, 214–0 (65.22); 2) Bonifacio, 211–0 (64.32); 3) Casimido, 172–0 (52.42).

Cocopa Tribe—1) Coldwater, 203–0 (61.88); 2) John Roy, 180–0 (54.86); 3) El Puk, 138–0 (42.06).

*See Notes on pages 220–221.

Japanese Ainu Tribe—1) Kuto Roz, 124–0 (37.80); 2) Goro, 115–6 (35.20); Oschawa, 73–6 (22.40).

Pueblo Santa Clara Tribe—1) Vincenta Suaz, 142–0 (43.28).

Africans—1) John Gondola, Battatella Tribe, 200–0 (60.96); 2) Prince Lotuna, Bacuba Tribe, 151–0 (46.02); 3) Malhen, left-hand throw, Batua Tribe, 139–0 (42.36); 4) Teobang, cannibal, Badihna Tribe, 111–0 (33.84).

Throwing 56-lb. weight

Patagonian Tribe—1) Casimido, 10–6 (3.20); 2) Coloho, 10–0½ (3.06); 3) Bonifacio, 7–11 (2.41).

Indians—1) George Mentz, Sioux Tribe, 15–11 (4.85); 2) Black White Bear, Crow Tribe, 15–9 (4.80); 3) DePoe, Rock River Tribe, 14–6 (4.42); 4) Frank Moore, Pawnee Tribe, 14–6 (4.42); 5) Poitre, Chippewa Tribe, 13–0½ (3.97).

Cocopa Tribe—1) Chief Pueblo Colorado, 12–2½ (3.72); 2) Coldwater, 9–3 (2.82); 3) Capt. Tom Moore, Pawnee Tribe, 7–4 (2.23).

Japanese Ainus Tribe—1) Goro (28 yrs.old), 7–4 (2.23); 2) Sangea (57 yrs.old), 5–0 (1.52); 3) Kuto Roz (age 38 yrs.old), 3–6 (1.06).

120 yard hurdle race

Indians only—1) George Mentz, Sioux Tribe, 19.0; 2) Capt. Tom Moore, Pawnee Tribe.

Throwing the ball for accuracy

1) Chief Guechico, Patagonian, 75–0 (22.86); 2) Capt. Tom Moore, Pawnee Tribe.

1-mile run

1) Black White Bear, Crow Tribe, 5:38.0; 2) Yousouf Hana, Asian; 3) Lehouw, Zulu.

100-meter run

1) George Mentz, Sioux Tribe, 11.6; 2) Sumdud, Lanao Moro Samal Tribe, Filipino; 3) Frank Moore, Pawnee Tribe.

Throwing Javelin, 25-foot distance

1) Teman, Lanao Moro, Filipino; 2) Shamba, Pygmy Tribe; 3) Koutourokee, Ainu, Japan.

120 yard hurdle race

1) Poitre, Chippewa Tribe, 18.8; 2) Sumdud, Lanao Moro Samal Tribe, Filipino; 3) George Mentz, Sioux Tribe.

Climbing pole

1) Basilio, Negrito, Filipino, 20.4; 2) Bushubba, Pygmy Tribe, 39.2; 3) Sayas, Negrito, Filipino, 42.4; 4) Teman, Lanao Moro, Filipino, 52.8; 5) Prince Lotuna, Bacuba Tribe, 56.8; 6) Loumbungo, Bacuba Tribe, 58.6.

Running high jump

1) George Mentz, Sioux Tribe, 4–7 (1.39); 2) Black White Bear, Crow Tribe, 4–0 (1.22); 3) Poitre, Chippewa Tribe, 4–0 (1.22).

Archery

1) Shake, Cocopa Indian, 126–0 (38.40); 2) Sangea, Ainu, Japanese; 3) Shamba, Pygmy Tribe.

440 yard run

1) George Mentz, Sioux Tribe; 2) Simon Max, Sioux Tribe; 3) J. Hana, Asia.

Tug-of-war

1) Patagonians; 2) Asians.

Baseball

Was baseball held in any way as a part of the sporting events at the Louisiana Purchase Exposition? Some records books (see Appendix I), occasionally mention that baseball was held as an "exhibition" sport during the 1904 Olympic Games. Probably some baseball games were conducted during the 1904 Louisiana Purchase Exposition on which Director James Sullivan hung the label "Olympic." However, the evidence for even this in the newspapers is scant at best.

In the *St. Louis Post-Dispatch* on 18 May, it was mentioned that Washington University and Indiana University were to play at 3:00 P.M. on Francis Field to commence the Olympic Intercollegiate Baseball championship. This is the only mention I can find of that tournament. It was likely, in analogy to American Football, that some of the regularly scheduled college baseball games for St. Louis universities were held at Francis Field. But there is no further mention of this tournament at all. And on 18 May, colleges had to be getting near the end of their spring semesters.

On 3 June, the *St. Louis Post-Dispatch* described another event, the Olympic Amateur Baseball tournament. It was mentioned that 12 teams had already entered, that entries closed the next day, and that the teams would play a series of six games each to decide the championship. Again, there is nothing further in the papers. This is especially troubling when one considers that the *Post-Dispatch* sports pages contained a small column entitled "Amateur Baseball," giving the results and summaries of the games involving amateur baseball clubs in the St. Louis area. The Olympic Amateur Baseball tournament never finds its way into that column.

Thus, there seems to be minimal evidence that any amateur baseball games were considered to be part of the "Olympics" even by the authorities in charge that year. Perhaps a few games were played as exhibitions at the fair, but nothing more.

Basketball

The Olympic basketball tournament of 1904 was listed in the *Spalding's Official Basketball Guide* as "The First Olympic World's Basket Ball Championship." The events were held on 11–12

July in the infield at the Olympic Stadium on a court measuring 50 feet by 70 feet. The event was absolutely dominated by the Buffalo German Y.M.C.A. who won games by such scores as 97–8, 77–6, and 105–50. The Buffalo Germans were the greatest basketball team of that era and were later enshrined in the Basketball Hall of Fame as a team. They had won the Pan-American Exposition in 1901 and had not been defeated since that time.

Donald Sayenga has written about the famous Buffalo German YMCA team, which was later inducted into the Basketball Hall of Fame as a team. Portions of his article are as follows:

> The Buffalo Germans were a very small group of German-speaking men who played together as one of several teams sponsored by the Buffalo (New York) Young Men's Christian Association (YMCA). The new Buffalo Central YMCA (which opened in 1903) was a huge organization with thousands of members, one of the world's largest YMCA associations.
>
> The famous Buffalo Germans basketball team had carried away all honors at the Pan-American Exposition [in 1901]. At that Exposition eight of the country's leading basketball teams were entered in competition and the Buffalo Germans won the championship by defeating all of the others. They scored a total of 81 points in the tournament to their opponents' 27. This is more remarkable because the average age of this team in the Pan-American year was only 18.
>
> Following their Olympic triumph, the team manager arranged a country-wide tour which included the playing of 87 games and of these they won 69 and lost 18. In 1907 the team started the greatest winning streak of their career, playing 111 games from then through the season of 1910-11 without a single loss. During all these years the team included only nine different men and they carried only six on their tours. This great team began its career in the gymnasium of the German department of the Buffalo YMCA and played games and practised there until 1905. An unfortunate misunderstanding with the administration of the German department forced them to leave the YMCA just as they were beginning the greatest years of their career. They reluctantly moved across the street to Orioles Hall and continued there for the rest of their career. In retrospect, it seems that the YMCA gave up a tremendous asset through this action.
>
> The Buffalo Germans represent a rare case of a whole team which has been inducted into the Basketball Hall of Fame. As single individuals, however, they remain obscure. Historian William G. Mokray credits the Buffalo Germans as perhaps being the first great professional basketball team.[2]

However, the basketball events in the 1904 Olympics are hardly of Olympic caliber. No foreign teams entered or competed. The championship doubled as the AAU Championship for 1904. In addition, restrictions on team events at the 1904 Olympics put severe restrictions on many foreign countries entering teams. It was required that the athletes not only represent a single country but that they all be members of the same club. This rarely happened with foreign teams. Finally, in 1904, there were essentially no foreign countries playing basketball. I do not consider the basketball events of the 1904 World's Fair as part of the Olympic games.

Site:	Francis Field and the Physical Culture Gymnasium
Dates/Times:	11–12 July
Events:	1
Competitors:	40
Nations:	1

	Competitors
United States	40
Totals	40
Nations	1

Final Standings

A: 40[3]; C: 1; D: 11–12 July; L: Francis Field (11 July), Physical Culture Gymnasium (11–12 July)[4]; F: Round-robin tournament.

			Won	Lost	Points For	Points Agst
1.	Buffalo German YMCA	USA	5	0	354	120
2.	Chicago Central YMCA	USA	4	1	90	54
3.	Missouri Athletic Club	USA	3	2	51	136
4.	St. Louis Central YMCA	USA	2	3	76	121
=5.	Xavier Athletic Club	USA	0	4	80	133
	Turner Tigers	USA	0	4	18	105

Game Results

11 July	–	Buffalo German YMCA	28	49	–	77				
		Turner Tigers	4	2	–	6				
		Buffalo German YMCA	11	25	–	36				
		Xavier Athletic Club	10	18	–	28				
		Buffalo German YMCA				105				
		St. Louis Central YMCA				50				
		Chicago Central YMCA	26	30	–	56				
		Xavier Athletic Club	5	10	–	15				
		Chicago Central YMCA[5]				2				
		Turner Tigers				0				
		Missouri Athletic Club				2				
		St. Louis Central YMCA				0				
		Chicago Central YMCA				2[6]				
		Missouri Athletic Club				0				
		Missouri Athletic Club[7]	16	21	–	37	–	2	–	39
		Xavier Athletic Club	15	22	–	37	–	0	–	37
		St. Louis Central YMCA[8]				24				
		Turner Tigers				12				
12 July	–	Buffalo German YMCA	17	22	–	39				
		Chicago Central YMCA	14	14	–	28				
		Buffalo German YMCA	56	41	–	97				
		Missouri Athletic Club	2	6	–	8				

Chicago Central YMCA	2	
St. Louis Central YMCA	0	
Missouri Athletic Club	2	
Turner Tigers	0	
St. Louis Central YMCA	2	
Xavier Athletic Club	0	
Xavier Athletic Club[9]		
Turner Tigers		

Box Scores

Buffalo — Turner [11 July] 77–6

Buffalo	FG	FT	Pts	Fouls
Rhode	13	3-3	29	3
Redlein	2	3-3	7	3
Heerdt	17	1-1	35	2
Miller	2	–	4	1
Manweiler	1	–	2	2
Totals	35	7-7	77	11

Turner	FG	FT	Pts	Fouls
Holden	0	0-5	0	2
Beebe	0	0-1	0	1
Cunningham	0	1-1	1	0
Hincke	1	–	2	1
Keating	1	1-1	3	0
Totals	2	2-8	6	4

Buffalo — Xavier [11 July] 36–28

Buffalo	FG	FT	Pts	Fouls
Rhode	4	5-6	13	1
Redlein	5	4-6	14	7[10]
Heerdt	3	1-1	7	3
Miller	0	–	0	3
Manweiler	1	–	2	2
Totals	13	10-13	36	16

Xavier	FG	FT	Pts	Fouls
Kenny	2	–	4	2
Leitz	2	–	4	2
Donovan	2	5-7	9	3
Roach	1	4-7	6	3
Craven	2	1-1	5	1
Totals	9	10-15	28	11

Chicago — Xavier [11 July] 56–15

Chicago	FG	FT	Pts	Fouls
Jardine	7	10-17	24	1
Berggren	6	–	12	2
Schommer	7	–	14	2
Armstrong	2	–	4	3
Williams	1	–	2	2
Totals	23	10-17	56	11

Xavier	FG	FT	Pts	Fouls
Kenny	0	1-6	1	4
Leitz	2	–	4	4
Cleveland	1	0-2	2	3
Craven	4	0-2	8	5
Roach	0	–	0	1
Smith	0	–	0	0
Totals	7	1-10	15	17

Buffalo — Chicago [12 July] 39–28

Buffalo	FG	FT	Pts	Fouls
Rhode	7	7-10	21	0
Redlein	3	–	6	4
Heerdt	4	–	8	3

Chicago	FG	FT	Pts	Fouls
Jardine	1	6-9	8	1
Berggren	4	–	8	2
Schommer	4	–	8	4

Manweiler	1	-	2	1	Williams	1	-	2	3
Miller	1	-	2	1	Armstrong	1	-	2	0
Totals	16	7-10	39	9	Totals	11	6-9	28	10

Buffalo — Missouri [12 July] 97–8

Buffalo	FG	FT	Pts	Fouls	Missouri	FG	FT	Pts	Fouls
Rhode	13	1-3	27	1	Newman	2	-	4	2
Redlein	12	-	24	0	Rauscher	1	0-2	2	2
Heerdt	13	0-5	26	0	Busch	0	0-2	0	1
Miller	8	-	16	2	Arhelger	1	0-1	2	2
Manweiler	2	-	4	1	[11]				
Totals	48	1-8	97	4	Totals	4	0-5	8	7

Team Rosters

Buffalo German YMCA, Buffalo, New York, USA
   (Alfred Heerdt [captain], Albert Manweiler, George Redlein, William Rhode, Edward Miller, Charles Monahan)

Chicago Central YMCA, Chicago, Illinois, USA
   (J. A. Jardine, Axel Berggren, John Schommer, Melvin Idarius, Carl Watson, W. K. Armstrong, W. A. Williams, Seth Collins)

Missouri Athletic Club, St. Louis, Missouri, USA
   (William Newman, Martin Arhelger, William Busch, Robert Rauscher, H. C. Waldman, Harvey Kiener)

St. Louis Central YMCA, St. Louis, Missouri, USA
   (LaRue Weber, John McKnight, L. N. Forbes, William Hardin, Tracy Farnham, Harold J. Barker)

Xavier Athletic Club, New York, New York, USA
   (E. J. Roach [captain], James Donovan, Charles R. Cleveland, James Kenny, J. S. Smith, Julius Leitz, Frank Craven, W. Herschel)

Turner Tigers, Los Angeles, California, USA
   (J. Holden [captain], Thomas Keating, Henry Hincke, Arba Cunningham, Frank Beebe, George Karstens)

Non-Olympic Events

Olympic Basketball Championships of the Public Schools Athletic League

   D: 4–6 July 1904; F: Open to High School and Elementary School Boys under 19 and 15 years of age, respectively.

High School

1. New York Team
2. Chicago Team

3. San Francisco Team
4. St. Louis Team

   Elementary Schools

1. New York Team
2. Chicago Team
3. San Francisco Team
4. St. Louis Team

YMCA Basketball Championships

D: 15–17 August 1904.

15 August

Cincinnati YMCA	43	Joplin YMCA	28
Chicago Central YMCA	31	Hamilton YMCA	22
Sioux City YMCA	43	Hamilton YMCA	31
Denver YMCA	39	Joplin YMCA	34
Chicago Central YMCA	79	Cincinnati YMCA	33
Sioux City YMCA	53	Denver YMCA	30

16 August

Sioux City YMCA	55	Joplin YMCA	8
Chicago Central YMCA	53	Denver YMCA	19
Hamilton YMCA	44	Cincinnati YMCA	19
Cincinnati YMCA	38	Sioux City YMCA	38
Hamilton YMCA	44	Denver YMCA	16
Hamilton YMCA	wo	Joplin YMCA	dns
Denver YMCA	wo	Cincinnati YMCA	dns

17 August

| Chicago Central YMCA | 35 | Sioux City YMCA | 29 |

		W	L	T
1.	Chicago Central YMCA	4	0	0
2.	Sioux City YMCA	3	1	1
3.	Hamilton YMCA	3	2	0
4.	Cincinnati YMCA	1	3	1
5.	Denver YMCA	2	3	0
6.	Joplin YMCA	0	4	0

Olympic College Basketball Championship

D: 11–12 July 1904.

Hiram College	25	Wheaton College	20
Hiram College	25	Latter Day Saints University	18
Wheaton College	40	Latter Day Saints University	35

Public Schools Athletic League Basketball

D: 11–12 July 1904.

High Schools		W	L
1.	New York	3	0
2.	Chicago	2	1
3.	St. Louis	1	2
4.	San Francisco	0	3

Elementary Schools		W	L
1.	New York	2	0
2.	Chicago	1	1
3.	San Francisco	0	2

Roque[12]

Roque is a variant of the sport croquet, and the name is derived by dropping the initial "c" and the trailing "t" from the name of the sport, croquet. It was contested at the 1904 Olympics as part of the program at the Louisiana Purchase Exposition. However, no foreign athlete competed or entered. In addition, the championship doubled as the United States National Championship. The events were organized by the leading exponent of roque in this country, Charles Jacobus of Springfield, Massachusetts. Jacobus was the author of the *Spaulding Official Roque Guide* and was the president of the national association in 1904. He had been national champion several times, the first time in 1883.

Four athletes competed in the 1904 "Olympic" roque. Jacobus won the competition which was contested as a double round robin with each athlete playing a match against the other athlete twice.

Croquet had been held in the 1900 Olympics with competitors from both France and Belgium. Croquet, or roque, or a variant would never again appear on an Olympic program. There is almost no justification for calling the 1904 roque event an Olympic sport, as it was the United States National Championship, there were no foreign entrants, and there were no foreign competitors. It has always been listed as such by previous Olympic reference books but I would recommend that it be deleted.

Site:	Francis Field
Dates/Times:	3–6, 8 August
Events:	1
Competitors:	4
Nations:	1

Competitors	
United States	4
Totals	4
Nations	1

Men's Singles

A: 4[13]; C: 1; D: 3–6, 8 August; F: Double round-robin.

			W	L
1.	Charles Jacobus	USA	5	1
2.	Smith Streeter	USA	4	2
3.	Charles Brown[14]	USA	2[15]	4
4.	William Chalfant	USA	1	5

Match Results

3 August	–	Streeter d. Chalfant	32	–	7
4 August	–	Jacobus d. Chalfant	32	–	23
5 August	–	Jacobus d. Chalfant	32	–	9
		Jacobus d. Streeter	32	–	18
		Streeter d. Brown	32	–	18
6 August	–	Jacobus d. Brown	32	–	14
		Streeter d. Jacobus	32	–	27
		Brown d. Chalfant	32	–	9
8 August	–	Jacobus d. Brown	32	–	13
		Streeter d. Chalfant	32	–	26
		Brown d. Streeter	32	–	10
		Chalfant d. Brown			

Water Polo

Water polo events were held during the 1904 St. Louis World's Fair on 5–6 September at the man-made Life Saving Exhibition lake in the center of the World's Fair. There is no justification whatsoever for calling this sport an Olympic one in 1904.

Three teams competed in the 1904 water polo events during the St. Louis World's Fair: the New York Athletic Club, the Chicago Athletic Association, and the Missouri Athletic Club. The New York Athletic Club beat Missouri 5–0 and Chicago 6–0. A fourth team tried to enter representing Germany. However, the Germans were not allowed to compete because their athletes did not represent a single club. Basically, therefore, foreign participation was attempted but was rebuffed and by itself this should disqualify the sport from Olympic consideration in 1904. There is nothing in the Olympic rules now nor was there anything mentioned by Coubertin or at any of the IOC sessions prior to 1904 mandating that foreign teams had to represent one club.

A sad footnote did occur after the water polo event. The artificial lake created in the middle of the World's Fair for the life-saving exhibition was also used for some of the agricultural exhibits, and many of the cattle of the agricultural exhibits grazed and wandered into the lake. Although the swimming and water polo events were held at the other end of the lake, before the middle of 1905, less than one year after the water polo events in that lake, four of the water poloists died from typhus.

Site:	Life Saving Exhibition Lake
Dates/Times:	5–6 September
Events:	1
Competitors:	21
Nations:	1

	Competitors
United States	21
Totals	21
Nations	1

Final Standings

A: 21; C: 1; D: 5–6 September; L: Life Saving Exhibition Lake; F: Each game consisted of two halves of eight minutes each with a five-minute rest in between the halves.

1. United States   (New York Athletic Club)
    (David Bratton, George Van Cleaf, Leo "Budd" Goodwin, Louis Handley, David Hesser, Joseph Ruddy, James Steen)
2. United States   (Chicago Athletic Association)[16]
    (Rex Beach, Jerome Steever, Edwin Paul Swatek, Charles Healy, Frank Kehoe[17], David Hammond, William Tuttle)
3. United States   (Missouri Athletic Club)
    (John Meyers, Manfred Toeppen, Gwynne Evans, Amedee Reyburn, Fred Schreiner, Augustus Goessling, William Orthwein)

Results of Matches

5 September	–	New York	5
		Missouri	0
		Goals: Goodwin [3], Hesser, Handley	
6 September	–	New York	6
		Chicago	0
		Goals: Goodwin [5], Hesser	

Tournament Summary

5 September

New York

New York
5–0

Missouri

New York
6–0

Chicago

NOTES

1. Gondola's mark is listed as longer than that of Prince Lotuna, but Prince Lotuna was listed as the winner by OR.

2. Sayenga D. "The 1904 Basketball Championship ... or ... Were the 'Buffalo Germans' the Original Dream Team?", *Citius, Altius, Fortius, 4(3)*: 7-8, 1996.

3. EK lists only 34 players and 5 teams. His results were taken from Spalding which did not mention the St. Louis Central YMCA team. This same mistake was made by *Spalding's Official Basketball Guide 1905*, despite the fact that they printed a picture of the St. Louis team as one of the teams competing in the Olympics. The results given herein are taken from the *St. Louis Globe-Democrat* newspaper with the box scores from *Spalding's Official Basketball Guide 1905*. These results differ a great deal from most earlier results published (notably EK and FM), because of their lack of knowledge of the sixth team.

4. The games were supposed to be played outdoors on a court set up on Francis Field, but rain on 11 July forced many of the games indoors to the Physical Culture Gymnasium.

5. Chicago Central YMCA won this match by forfeit.

6. With Chicago leading 6-0, this match was stopped by rain, after it had been started outdoors on Francis Field. After the deluge Missouri refused to play on the rain-soaked court, requesting that the game be moved indoors. When this request was denied, they forfeited the game. The committee, in an unusual decision, then decided to play the remainder of the games indoors because the courts were, indeed, too wet.

7. This game was held in the gymnasium due to the court conditions.

8. This game was held in the gymnasium due to the court conditions.

9. This game was scheduled but neither team showed up to play, so it was cancelled.

10. The rules concerning fouling out of a game must have been liberal in 1904.

11. Missouri had only four players show up for this game, but rather than forfeit they played with just four players.

12. Roque is similar to croquet but is not the exact same game.

13. EK and VK list six starters but gave only three names. However, the *St. Louis Globe-Democrat* stated clearly that there were four competitors.

14. Seen in EK and OR as D. Charles Brown, this is probably a mistranscription of Dr. Charles Brown since Brown was a veterinarian.

15. EK lists Brown as having won three matches, but the final results given above were listed clearly in the *Globe-Democrat*. The match results were pieced together from all St. Louis and Chicago newspapers and confirm the above final standings.

16. Confusion has existed over the exact composition of the Missouri and Chicago teams for some time. The Chicago team composition is derived from Chicago papers, descriptions of the matches in the *Globe-Democrat*, and correspondance with Jamison Handy, who was a Chicago resident at the time. The Missouri team composition is derived from the *Globe-Democrat* and personal conversations with relatives of William Orthwein and Marquard Schwarz.

17. EK lists this player as Keough with no known first name. The name is spelled many different ways but Frank Kehoe seems most likely. Pictures of the Chicago AA team show only one athlete with a spelling similar to this — Frank Kehoe, who finished third in diving. Kehoe definitely competed in water polo for Chicago the night after the Olympics in an exhibition match, and in addition, Jamison Handy was of the opinion that Kehoe also played in the Olympic match for Chicago.

Appendix I
1904 Olympic Sports and Events in the Literature

In the Introduction the convoluted organization of the 1904 Olympic Games was described. A section was also inserted to discuss which events and sports were Olympic and which were not in 1904. No consensus has previously been reached but I did attempt to reach certain conclusions in this book.

What follows are the events listed at various times by other authors. Notably, I have used all the standard well-known Olympic reference books and listed which of the myriad sporting events of the 1904 Louisiana Purchase Exposition they included as part of the 1904 Olympic Games.

[253 events]: x = indicates listed as a 1904 Olympic event in that book

BH	=	Henry, Bill. *An Approved History of the Olympic Games.*
DW	=	Wallechinsky, David. *The Complete Book of the Olympics.*
EK	=	Kamper, Erich. *Enzyklopädie der olympischen Spiele.*
FM	=	Mező, Ferenc. *The Modern Olympic Games.*
FW	=	Wasner, Fritz. *Olympia-Lexikon.*
OR	=	*Spalding's Official Athletic Almanac for 1905: Special Olympic Number.*
SG	=	Greenberg, Stan. *The Guinness Book of Olympics Facts and Feats.*
VK	=	Kluge, Volker. *Die olympischen spiele von 1896 bis 1980.*

	BH	DW	EK	FM	FW	OR	SG	VK
Anthropology Days						x		
Archery	x	x	x	x		x	x	x
Double York Round, Men	x	x	x	x		x	x	x
Double American Round, Men	x	x	x	x		x	x	x
Team Round, Men	x	x	x	x		x	x	x

223

	BH	DW	EK	FM	FW	OR	SG	VK
Double Columbia Round, Women	x	x	x	x		x	x	x
Double National Round, Women	x	x	x	x		x	x	x
Team Round, Women	x		x	x		x	x	x
Flight Shooting, Men								
Flight Shooting, Women								
Athletics (Track & Field)	x	x	x	x	x	x	x	x
Olympic Track & Field Athletics	x	x	x	x	x	x	x	x
60 meters	x	x	x	x	x	x	x	x
100 meters	x	x	x	x	x	x	x	x
200 meters	x	x	x	x	x	x	x	x
400 meters	x	x	x	x	x	x	x	x
800 meters	x	x	x	x	x	x	x	x
1,500 meters	x	x	x	x	x	x	x	x
Marathon	x	x	x	x	x	x	x	x
110 meter hurdles	x	x	x	x	x	x	x	x
200 meter hurdles	x	x	x	x	x	x	x	x
400 meter hurdles	x	x	x	x	x	x	x	x
2,590 meter steeplechase	x	x	x	x	x	x	x	x
4-mile team race	x	x	x	x	x	x	x	x
High jump	x	x	x	x	x	x	x	x
Pole vault	x	x	x	x	x	x	x	x
Broad jump	x	x	x	x	x	x	x	x
Hop, step, and jump	x	x	x	x	x	x	x	x
Standing high jump	x	x	x	x	x	x	x	x
Standing broad jump	x	x	x	x	x	x	x	x
Standing hop, step, and jump	x	x	x	x	x	x	x	x
Shot put	x	x	x	x	x	x	x	x
Discus throw	x	x	x	x	x	x	x	x
Hammer throw	x	x	x	x	x	x	x	x
56-lb. weight throw	x	x	x	x	x	x	x	x
All-Around	x	x	x	x		x	x	x
Olympic Handicap Meet						x		
Missouri Interscholastic Meet						x		
Open Handicap Meeting						x		
School Meet for LPE Territory						x		
St. Louis Elementary School Meet						x		
AAU Handicap Meet						x		
AAU Junior Championships						x		
AAU Championships								
Olympic Collegiate Championships						x		
Interscholastic Handicap Meet						x		
Interscholastic Championships						x		
Special Athletic Events						x		
Public Schools Athletic League Meet						x		
Irish Sports						x		
Western AAU Handicap Meet						x		
Western AAU Championship Meet						x		

	BH	DW	EK	FM	FW	OR	SG	VK
YMCA Team Pentathlon Championships						x		
YMCA Handicap Track and Field Meet						x		
YMCA Track and Field Championship						x		
Military Athletic Carnival								
Baseball					x			
Basketball		x	x	x	x	x		x
Olympic Basketball Championship		x	x	x	x	x		x
Olympic College Basketball Championship						x		
Public School Ath. League Basketball						x		
YMCA Basketball Championships						x		
Boxing	x	x	x	x	x	x	x	x
Flyweight	x	x	x	x	x	x	x	x
Bantamweight	x	x	x	x	x	x	x	x
Featherweight	x	x	x	x	x	x	x	x
Lightweight	x	x	x	x	x	x	x	x
Welterweight	x	x	x	x	x	x	x	x
Middleweight	x	x	x	x	x	x	x	x
Heavyweight	x	x	x	x	x	x	x	x
Cycling	x			x		x		x
Olympic Amateur Events	x			x		x		x
¼ mile	x			x		x		x
⅓ mile	x			x		x		x
½ mile	x			x		x		x
1 mile	x			x		x		x
2 miles	x			x		x		x
5 miles	x			x		x		x
25 miles	x			x		x		x
Olympic Amateur Events, Handicap						x		
Olympic Professional Events						x		
Olympic Professional Events, Handicap						x		
Diving	x	x	x	x	x	x	x	x
Fancy Diving	x	x	x	x	x	x	x	x
Fencing	x	x	x	x	x	x	x	x
Foil	x	x	x	x	x	x	x	x
Dueling Swords (Épée)	x	x	x	x	x	x	x	x
Saber	x	x	x	x	x	x	x	x
Single Sticks	x	x	x	x	x	x	x	x
Team foil	x	x	x	x	x	x	x	x
Junior foil	x			x		x		x
Football		x	x	x		x	x	
Olympic Association Football		x	x	x		x	x	
Olympic College Football						x		
Gaelic Football Championships						x		

	BH	DW	EK	FM	FW	OR	SG	VK
Golf		x	x	x		x	x	x
Men's Individual		x	x	x		x	x	x
Men's Team Championship		x	x			x	x	x
President's Match								
Consolation Flights								
Team Nassau Match								
Driving Contest								
Putting Contest								
Gymnastics	x	x	x	x	x	x	x	x
AAU Events	x	x	x	x		x	x	x
Combined exercises, individual	x	x	x	x		x	x	x
Parallel bars	x	x	x	x		x	x	x
Horizontal bar	x	x	x	x		x	x	x
Long Horse	x	x	x	x		x	x	x
Side Horse		x	x	x		x	x	x
Rings	x	x	x	x		x	x	x
Rope climbing	x	x	x	x		x	x	x
Club swinging	x	x	x	x		x	x	x
Turnverein Gymnastics		x	x	x	x	x	x	x
Combined exercises, team		x	x	x	x	x	x	x
Combined exercises, apparatus/field, ind.		x	x	x	x	x	x	x
Combined exercises, apparatus, ind.			x	x	x	x	x	x
Triathlon (combined ex., field)		x	x	x	x	x	x	x
YMCA Individual Gymnastics						x		
YMCA Team Athletic-Gymnastics						x		
Lacrosse	x	x	x	x	x	x	x	x
Olympic Lacrosse Championships	x	x	x	x	x	x	x	x
Irish Hurling Championships						x		
Roque	x	x	x	x		x	x	x
Rowing & Sculling	x	x	x	x	x	x	x	x
Single Sculls	x	x	x	x	x	x	x	x
Double Sculls	x	x	x	x	x	x	x	x
Coxless Pairs	x	x		x		x		
Coxless Fours	x	x	x	x	x	x	x	x
Coxed Eights	x	x	x	x	x	x	x	x
Intermediate Single Sculls	x			x		x		
Association Single Sculls	x			x		x		
Intermediate Double Sculls	x			x		x		
Intermediate Coxless Pairs	x			x		x		
Intermediate Coxless Fours	x			x		x		
Senior International Coxless Fours[1]	x			x		x		
Intermediate Coxed Eights				x		x		

See Note on page 227.

	BH	DW	EK	FM	FW	OR	SG	VK
Swimming	x	x	x	x	x	x	x	x
Olympic Swimming Championships	x	x	x	x	x	x	x	x
50 yard freestyle	x	x	x	x	x	x	x	x
100 yard freestyle	x	x	x	x	x	x	x	x
220 yard freestyle	x	x	x	x	x	x	x	x
440 yard freestyle	x	x	x	x	x	x	x	x
880 yard freestyle	x	x	x	x	x	x	x	x
One mile freestyle	x	x	x	x	x	x	x	x
100 yard backstroke	x	x	x	x	x	x	x	x
440 yard breaststroke	x	x	x	x	x	x	x	x
Plunge for distance	x	x	x	x	x	x	x	x
4 × 50 yard relay	x	x	x	x	x	x	x	x
Olympic Handicap Meet						x		
Tennis (Lawn)	x	x	x	x	x	x	x	x
Olympic Men's Singles	x	x	x	x	x	x	x	x
Olympic Men's Doubles	x	x	x	x	x	x	x	x
World's Fair Men's Singles						x		
World's Fair Men's Doubles						x		
Louisiana Purchase Open Singles						x		
Interscholastic Men's Singles						x		
Tug-of-War	x	x	x	x	x	x		x
Water Polo	x	x	x	x	x	x	x	x
Weightlifting	x	x	x	x	x	x	x	x
Two-Hand Lift	x	x	x	x	x	x	x	x
All-Around Dumbbell Contest	x	x	x	x	x	x	x	x
Wrestling	x	x	x	x	x	x	x	x
105 lb. class	x	x	x	x	x	x	x	x
115 lb. class	x	x	x	x	x	x	x	x
125 lb. class	x	x	x	x	x	x	x	x
135 lb. class	x	x	x	x	x	x	x	x
145 lb. class	x	x	x	x	x	x	x	x
158 lb. class	x	x	x	x	x	x	x	x
Heavyweight class	x	x	x	x	x	x	x	x

NOTES

1. This event is listed in the sources noted. It is not described in any 1904 St. Louis newspaper account of the rowing events as a separate event but was apparently the Olympic coxless fours.

Appendix II
Non-Competing
Foreign Entrants

Australia

Athletics (Track & Field)
　　Gardner, Cornelius H., "Corrie." Broad jump.
　　McPherson, Leslie M. 400 meter hurdles.

Canada

Athletics (Track & Field)
　　Deer, Peter. 1,500 meters.
　　Hapenny, William. Pole vault.
　　Lukeman, Frank L. 200 meters; 400 meters.
　　Molson, Percival. 200 meters; Broad jump.
　　Sherring, William John. Marathon.
　　Vernon, Lee. 100 meters.

Football (Association Football/Soccer)
　　Berlin Rangers (team composition unknown).

Rowing & Sculling
　　Obernesse, W. Single sculls.
　　Smith, Frank. Single sculls.

Chile

Golf
　　Beeche, Hector.

Cuba

Golf
  Albertini, M.

France

Golf
  Deschamps, Pierre.

Germany

Athletics (Track & Field)
  Runge, Johannes. 1,500 meters.
  Weinstein, Paul. Hop, step, and jump; Standing hop, step, and jump.

Cycling
  Deutsche Radfahrerbund (team members unknown).

Diving
  Stotz, Gustav. Fancy diving.
  Wundrum, Will. Fancy diving.

Gymnastics
  Hofmann, Fritz.
  Neumann, Oscar.
  Rehbock, Franz.
  Selchow, Wilhelm.
  Trippel, Carl.
  Wolf, Frederick.

Rowing & Sculling
  Müller, Adolph. Double sculls.
  Sand, Waldemar. Single sculls, Double sculls.

Swimming
  Brack, Walter. 50 yard freestyle.
  Hoffmann, Georg. 50 yard freestyle, 100 yard freestyle, 440 yard freestyle.
  Pape, Max. 220 yard freestyle, 440 yard freestyle, 880 yard freestyle.
  Rausch, Emil. 100 yard freestyle, 440 yard freestyle.

Greece

Athletics (Track & Field)
  Lontos, Constantinos. Marathon.
  Tsohas, Dimitrios. Marathon.

Tug-of-War
  Tofalos, Dimitrios.

Weightlifting
  Dimitrakopoulos, Dimitrios. All-Around dumbbell contest.
  Kakousis, Perikles. All-Around dumbbell contest.
  Tofalos, Dimitrios. Two-handed Lift; All-Around dumbbell contest.

Hungary

Athletics (Track & Field)
  Mező, Béla de. 200 meters; Hop, step, and jump.

Fencing
  Békessy, Béla.
  Mésváros, Ervin.

Swimming
  Kiss, Géza. 50 yard freestyle, 440 yard freestyle.
  Halmay, Zoltán van. 220 yard freestyle, 440 yard freestyle, 880 yard freestyle.

Ireland

Athletics (Track & Field)
  Daly, John J. Marathon.

New Zealand

Athletics (Track & Field)
  Gunn, Will. 800 meters; 1,500 meters; 400 meter hurdles.

The Philippines

Archery
  Lanao Moro Tribe entered several archers — names not given.

South Africa

Weightlifting
  Lombard, B. All-Around dumbbell contest.

Appendix III
Competitors (by Country)

Australia (Total: 2; Men: 2; Women: 0)

Athletics (Track & Field) (Total: 2; Men: 2; Women: 0)
 Gardner, Cornelius H. "Corrie." (b.1880) 110 meter hurdles [4h1r1/2]; Broad Jump [ac] (Melbournian Hare & Hounds Athletic Club).
 McPherson, Leslie M. 110 meter hurdles [ach2r1/2]; Broad Jump [ac] (Melbournian Hare & Hounds Athletic Club).

Austria (Total: 2; Men: 2; Women: 0)

Gymnastics (Total: 1; Men: 1; Women: 0)
 Lenhart, Julius. (b.27 November 1875–d.10 November 1962) All-around, apparatus work [2]; All-around, individual [1]; Combined exercises, team [1]; Triathlon [32]. (Philadelphia Turnegmeinde).

Swimming (Total: 1; Men: 1; Women: 0)
 Wahle, Otto. (b.5 November 1879–d.11 August 1963) 880 yard freestyle [5]; One mile freestyle [4]; 440 yard freestyle [3]. (New York Athletic Club).

Canada (Total: 52; Men: 52; Women: 0)

Athletics (Track & Field) (Total: 5; Men: 5; Women: 0)
 Deer, Peter. 800 meters [ac]; 1,500 meters [6]. (Montreal Athletic Club).
 Desmarteau, Étienne. (b.4 February 1873–d.29 October 1905) 56-lb. Weight Throw [1]. (Montreal Athletic Club).

Kerr, Robert. (b.9 June 1882–d.12 May 1963) 60 meters [acr 2/3]; 100 meters [3h2r1/2]; 200 meters [3h2r1/2]. (West End Pleasure Club, Hamilton, Ontario).

Molson, Percival. (b.14 August 1880–d.5 July 1917) 400 meters [ac]. (Montreal Athletic Club).

Peck, John B. 800 meters [ac]. (Montreal Athletic Club).

Football (Association Football/Soccer) (Total: 11; Men: 11; Women: 0)

Ducker, George. [1] (Galt Football Club).

Fraser, John Alexander. (b.19 December 1881) [1] (Galt Football Club).

Gourley, John. [1] (Galt Football Club).

Hall, Alexander. [1] (Galt Football Club).

Johnson, Albert. [1] (Galt Football Club).

Lane, Robert. [1] (Galt Football Club).

Linton, Ernest. (b.17 February 1880) [1] (Galt Football Club).

McDonald, Gordon. [1] (Galt Football Club).

Steep, Frederick. [1] (Galt Football Club).

Taylor, Thomas "Tom." [1] (Galt Football Club).

Twaits, William. [1] (Galt Football Club).

Golf (Total: 3; Men: 3; Women: 0)

Austin, Adam E. (b.1888) Individual [65qr]. (Lambton Golf & Country Club).

Austin, Albert William. (b.27 March 1857) Individual [73qr]. (Lambton Golf & Country Club).

Lyon, George Seymour. (b.27 August 1858–d.11 May 1938) Individual [1]. (Lambton Golf & Country Club).

Lacrosse (Total: 24; Men: 24; Women: 0)

Almighty Voice. [3] (Mohawk Indians).

Black Eagle. [3] (Mohawk Indians).

Black Hawk. [3] (Mohawk Indians).

Blanchard, Eli. [1] (Shamrock Lacrosse Team, Winnipeg, Manitoba).

Brennaugh, W. [1] (Shamrock Lacrosse Team, Winnipeg, Manitoba).

Bretz, George. [1] (Shamrock Lacrosse Team, Winnipeg, Manitoba).

Burns, William Laurie. (b.24 March 1875) [1] (Shamrock Lacrosse Team, Winnipeg, Manitoba).

Cattanach, George. [1] (Shamrock Lacrosse Team, Winnipeg, Manitoba).

Cloutier, George. [1] (Shamrock Lacrosse Team, Winnipeg, Manitoba).

Cowan, Sandy. [1] (Shamrock Lacrosse Team, Winnipeg, Manitoba).

Flat Iron. [3] (Mohawk Indians).

Flett, Jack. [1] (Shamrock Lacrosse Team, Winnipeg, Manitoba).

Half Moon. [3] (Mohawk Indians).

Jamieson, Benjamin. [1] (Shamrock Lacrosse Team, Winnipeg, Manitoba).

Laidlaw, Hilliard. [1] (Shamrock Lacrosse Team, Winnipeg, Manitoba).

Lightfoot. [3] (Mohawk Indians).

Lyle, H. [1] (Shamrock Lacrosse Team, Winnipeg, Manitoba).

Man Afraid Soap. [3] (Mohawk Indians).

Night Hawk. [3] (Mohawk Indians).

Pentland, L. H. [1] (Shamrock Lacrosse Team, Winnipeg, Manitoba).

Rain in Face. [3] (Mohawk Indians).

Red Jacket. [3] (Mohawk Indians).

Snake Eater. [3] (Mohawk Indians).

Spotted Tail. [3] (Mohawk Indians).

Rowing & Sculling (Total: 9; Men: 9; Women: 0)
 Bailey, A. B. Coxed eights [2] (Toronto Argonauts).
 Boyd, Phillip Ewing. (b.1876) Coxed eights [2] (Toronto Argonauts).
 Loudon, Thomas Richardson. (b.1 September 1883–d.6 January 1968) Coxed eights [2]
  (Toronto Argonauts).
 MacKenzie, Donald. Coxed eights [2] (Toronto Argonauts).
 Reiffenstein, George Patrick "Pat." Coxed eights [2] (Toronto Argonauts).
 Rice, William C. "Colonel." Coxed eights [2] (Toronto Argonauts).
 Strange, George M. Coxed eights [2] (Toronto Argonauts).
 Wadsworth, William Ridout. (b.17 December 1875) Coxed eights [2] (Toronto Argonauts).
 Wright, Joseph W. H. (b.14 January 1864–d.18 October 1950) Coxed eights [2] (Toronto Arg-
  onauts).

Cuba (Total: 3; Men: 3; Women: 0)

Athletics (Track & Field) (Total: 1; Men: 1; Women: 0)
 Carbajal de Soto, Felix de la Caridad. (b.18 March 1875) Marathon [4].

Fencing (Total: 2; Men: 2; Women: 0)
 Diaz Martinez, Manuel Dionysios. (b.8 April 1874–d.20 February 1929) Saber [1]; Team foil
  [1]. (Harvard University).
 Fonst Segundo, Ramón. (b.31 August 1883–d.10 September 1959) Épée [1]; Foil [1]; Team
  foil [1].

France (Total: 1; Men: 1; Women: 0)

Athletics (Track & Field) (Total: 1; Men: 1; Women: 0)
 Coray, Albert J. (b.1881) 4-mile team race [2]; Marathon [2]. (Chicago Athletic Association).

Germany (Total: 17; Men: 17; Women: 0)

Athletics (Track & Field) (Total: 2; Men: 2; Women: 0)
 Runge, Johannes. (b.24 January 1878–d.1949) 400 meters [ac]; 800 meters [5]; 1,500 meters [5].
 Weinstein, Paul. (b.5 April 1878–d.1965) High Jump [3]; Pole Vault [7].

Diving (Total: 3; Men: 3; Women: 0)
 Braunschweiger, Alfred. (b.1883) Fancy diving [4].
 Hoffmann, Georg. (b.1880–d.1947) Fancy diving [2]. [See also Swimming].
 Hooff, Otto. (b.1881–d.1960) Fancy diving [5].

Fencing (Total: 1; Men: 1; Women: 0)
 Casmir, Gustav. (b.5 November 1872–d.2 October 1910) Foil [4]; Épée [4].

Gymnastics (Total: 7; Men: 7; Women: 0)
 Busch, Christian. (b.8 January 1880) Combined exercises, apparatus work [13]; All-around,
  individual [9]; Triathlon [=7]. (Turngemeinde Elberfeld).

Lemke, Wilhelm. (b.1885) Combined exercises, apparatus work [11]; All-around, individual [13]; Triathlon [=34]. (Berlin Turngemeinde).

Mohr, Ernst. (b.1878) Combined exercises, apparatus work [9]; Combined exercises, individual [4]; Triathlon [9]. (Berlin Turngemeinde).

Peitsch, Hugo. (b.1874) Combined exercises, apparatus work [4]; Combined exercises, individual [7]; Triathlon [=55]. (Berlin Turnrath).

Weber, Adolph. (b.1879) Combined exercises, apparatus work [17]; Combined exercises, individual [19]; Triathlon [=44]. (Berlin Turnerschaft).

Weber, Wilhelm. (b.1880–d.28 April 1963) Combined exercises, apparatus work [3]; Combined exercises, individual [2]; Triathlon [21]. (Berlin Turnerschaft).

Wiegand, Otto. (b.1875) Combined exercises, apparatus work [5]; Combined exercises, individual [5]; Triathlon [=28]. (Berlin Turnrath).

Swimming (Total: 4; Men: 4; Women: 0)

Brack, Walter. (b.20 November 1880–d.19 July 1919) 100 yard backstroke [1]; 440 yard breaststroke [2].

Hoffmann, Georg. (b.1880–d.1947) 100 yard backstroke [2]; 440 yard breaststroke [4]. [See also Diving].

Rausch, Emil A. (b.11 September 1882–d.14 December 1954) 220 yard freestyle [3]; 880 yard freestyle [1]; One mile freestyle [1].

Zacharias, Georg. (b.14 June 1884–d.31 July 1953) 100 yard backstroke [3]; 440 yard breaststroke [1].

Tennis (Lawn Tennis) (Total: 1; Men: 1; Women: 0)

Hardy, Dr. Hugo, Jr. Singles [=9]; Doubles [=9].

Greece (Total: 14; Men: 14; Women: 0)

Athletics (Track & Field) (Total: 10; Men: 10; Women: 0)

Drosos, Georgios. Marathon [ac/dnf].

Georgantas, Nikolaos. (b.12 March 1880–d.23 January 1958) Discus Throw [3]; Shot Put [ac/dq]. [See also Tug-of-War].

Giannakas, Charilaos. Marathon [ac/dnf].

Loungitsas, Ioannis. Marathon [ac/dnf].

Louridas, Georgios L. Marathon [ac/dnf].

Oikonomou, Andrew Ioannis. Marathon [14].

Pipiles, Petros. Marathon [ac/dnf].

Vamkaitis, Georgios D. Marathon [ac/dnf].

Veloulis, Dimitrios. Marathon [5].

Zekhouritis, Christos D. Marathon [10].

Tug-of-War (Total: 5; Men: 5; Women: 0)

Dimitrakopoulos, Dimitrios. [=5] (Pan-Hellenic Athletic Club).

Georgantas, Nikolaos. (b.12 March 1880–d.23 January 1958) [=5] (Pan-Hellenic Athletic Club). [See also Track & Field Athletics].

Georgopoulos, Anastasios. [=5] (Pan-Hellenic Athletic Club).

Kakousis, Perikles. (b.1879) [=5] (Pan-Hellenic Athletic Club). [See also Weightlifting].

Metalos, Vasilios. [=5] (Pan-Hellenic Athletic Club).

Weightlifting (Total: 1; Men: 1; Women: 0)
    Kakousis, Perikles. (b.1879) Two-hand lift [1]. [See also Tug-of-War].

Hungary (Total: 4; Men: 4; Women: 0)

Athletics (Track & Field) (Total: 2; Men: 2; Women: 0)
    Gönczy, Lajos. (b.24 February 1881–d.1914) High Jump [4]; Standing High Jump [5].
    Mező, Béla de. (b.1 July 1883) 60 meters [4h3r1/3]; 100 meters [3h1r1/2]; Broad Jump [ac].

Swimming (Total: 2; Men: 2; Women: 0)
    Halmay, Zoltán von. (b.18 June 1881-d.20 May 1956) 50 yard freestyle [1]; 100 yard freestyle [1].
    Kiss, Géza. (b.22 October 1882–d.23 August 1952) 880 yard freestyle [3]; One mile freestyle [2].

Ireland/Great Britain (Total: 3; Men: 3; Women: 0)

Athletics (Track & Field) (Total: 3; Men: 3; Women: 0)
    Daly, John James. (b.22 February 1880) 2,590 meter steeplechase [2].
    Holloway, John J. All-Around [4]. (Greater New York Irish Athletic Association).
    Kiely, Thomas Francis. (b.25 August 1869–d.6 November 1951) All-Around [1].

South Africa (Total: 8; Men: 8; Women: 0)

Athletics (Track & Field) (Total: 3; Men: 3; Women: 0)
    Harris, Robert W., "Bertie" (b.1884) Marathon [ac/dnf].
    Mashiani, Jan. Marathon [12]. (Tswana Tribe).[1]*
    Tau, Len. Marathon [9]. (Tswana Tribe).[2]

Tug-of-War (Total: 5; Men: 5; Women: 0)
    Hillense, P. [=5] (Boer Team).
    Lombard, B. [=5] (Boer Team).
    Schutte, J. [=5] (Boer Team).
    Visser, P. [=5] (Boer Team).
    Walker, C. [=5] (Boer Team).

Switzerland (Total: 1; Men: 1; Women: 0)

Gymnastics (Total: 1; Men: 1; Women: 0)
    Spinnler, Adolf. (b.18 July 1879–d.20 November 1951) Combined exercises, apparatus work [1]; Combined exercises, individual [3]; Triathlon [=64]. (Turnverein Esslingen, Esslingen, GER).

*See Notes on pages 255–256.

United States (Total: 523; Men: 517; Women: 6)

Archery (Total: 29; Men: 23; Women: 6].

Women

Cooke, Emma C. (b.14 March 1884–d.May 1975) Double Columbia Round [2]; Double National Round [2]. (Potomac Archers).

Howell, Lida Scott. (b.28 August 1859–d.20 December 1939) Double Columbia Round [1]; Double National Round [1]. (Cincinnati Archers).

Pollock, Jessie. Double Columbia Round [3]; Double National Round [3]. (Cincinnati Archers).

Taylor, Louise. Double Columbia Round [6]; Double National Round [6]. (Cincinnati Archers).

Taylor, Mabel. Double Columbia Round [5]; Double National Round [5]. (Cincinnati Archers).

Woodruff, Laura. Double Columbia Round [4]; Double National Round [4]. (Cincinnati Archers).

Men

Bruce, Edward. Double American Round [19]; Double York Round [16]; Team Round [4]. (Chicago Archers).

Bryant, George Phillip. (b.22 February 1878–d.18 April 1938) Double American Round [1]; Double York Round [1]; Team Round [3]. (Boston Archers).

Bryant, Wallace. (b.22 February 1878–d.18 April 1938) Double American Round [5]; Double York Round [4]; Team Round [3]. (Boston Archers).

Casselman, Amos. Double American Round [16]. (Potomac Archers).

Clark, William A. (d.20 October 1913) Double American Round [6]; Team Round [2]. (Cincinnati Archers).

Dallin, Cyrus Edwin. (b.22 November 1861–d.14 November 1944) Double American Round [8]; Double York Round [10]; Team Round [3]. (Boston Archers).

Duvall, Samuel Harding. (b.11 March 1836–d.26 September 1908) Double American Round [14]; Team Round [2]. (Cincinnati Archers).

Frentz, Edward. Double American Round [15]; Double York Round [6]. (Boston Archers).

Hubbard, Charles R. Double American Round [11]; Team Round [2]. (Cincinnati Archers).

Keys, Benjamin. Double American Round [7]; Double York Round [5]; Team Round [4]. (Chicago Archers).

Maxson, Lewis W. (b.1850–d.20 July 1918) Double American Round [12]; Double York Round [12]; Team Round [1]. (Potomac Archers).

McGowan, D. F. Double York Round [11]. (Potomac Archers).

Richardson, Henry Barber. (b.19 May 1889–d.19 November 1963) Double American Round [9]; Double York Round [9]; Team Round [3]. (Boston Archers).

Scott, Thomas F. Double American Round [17]; Double York Round [13]. (Cincinnati Archers).

Spencer, Galen Carter. (b.19 September 1840–d.19 October 1904) Double American Round [13]; Team Round [1]. (Potomac Archers).

Taylor, Homer S. Double American Round [10]; Double York Round [7]; Team Round [4]. (Chicago Archers).

Taylor, Ralph B. Double American Round [18]; Double York Round [14]. (Cincinnati Archers).

Thompson, William Henry. (b.10 March 1848–d.1918) Double American Round [3]; Double York Round [3]; Team Round [1]. (Potomac Archers).

Valentine, W. G. Double American Round [22]. (Chicago Archers).

Weston, E. H. Double American Round [20]. (Chicago Archers).

Weston, Edward Bruce. Double American Round [21]; Double York Round [15]; Team Round [4]. (Chicago Archers).

Williams, Robert W., Jr. (b.24 January 1841–d.10 December 1914) Double American Round [2]; Double York Round [2]; Team Round [1]. (Potomac Archers).

Woodruff, C. S. Double American Round [4]; Double York Round [8]; Team Round [2]. (Cincinnati Archers).

Athletics (Track & Field) (Total: 88; Men: 88; Women: 0)

Allen, Claude Arthur. (b.29 April 1885) Pole Vault [5]. (Greater New York Irish Athletic Association).

Ashburner, Lesley. (b.2 October 1883–d.12 November 1950) 110 meter hurdles [3]. (Cornell University).

Bacon, Charles Joseph, Jr. (b.9 January 1885) 1,500 meters [9]. (Greater New York Irish Athletic Association).

Barker, Ervin Jerold. (b.1883) High Jump [6]. (University of Iowa).

Biller, John A. (b.14 November 1879–d.February 1960) Discus Throw [5]; Standing Broad Jump [3]; Standing High Jump [4]. (National Turnverein, Newark, NJ).

Blair, Clyde Amel. (d.1953) 60 meters [4]; 100 meters [3h3r1/2]; 400 meters [ac]. (University of Chicago; Chicago Athletic Association).

Bonhag, George V. (b.31 January 1882–d.30 October 1960) 800 meters [ac]. (Greater New York Irish Athletic Association).

Brawley, Henry A. (b.29 December 1880–d.March 1963) Marathon [7]. (St. Alphonsus Athletic Association, Roxbury, MA).

Breitkreutz, Emil William. (b.16 November 1883–d.3 May 1972) 800 meters [3]. (Milwaukee Athletic Club).

Carr, Edward P. Marathon [ac/dnf]. (Xavier Athletic Club, New York).

Cartmell, Nathaniel John "Nate." (b.13 January 1883–d.23 August 1967) 60 meters [acr2/3]; 100 meters [2]; 200 meters [2]. (University of Pennsylvania; Louisville YMCA).

Castleman, Frank Riley. (b.17 March 1887–d.9 October 1946) 60 meters [6]; 100 meters [4h3r1/2]; 110 meter hurdles [4]; 200 meter hurdles [2]. (Colgate University; Greater New York Irish Athletic Association).

Chadwick, Charles. (b.19 November 1874) 56-lb. Weight Throw [5]; Hammer Throw [4]; Shot Put [5]. [See also Tug-of-War]. (Yale University; New York Athletic Club).

Clark, Ellery Harding. (b.13 March 1874–d.27 July 1949) All-Around [5]. (Boston Athletic Association).

Coe, William Wesley, Jr. (b.8 May 1879–d.24 December 1926) Shot Put [2]. (Yale University).

Cohn, Harvey Wright. (b.4 December 1884–d.July 1965) 800 meters [ac]; 1,500 meters [8]; 2,590 meter steeplechase [ac]. (Greater New York Irish Athletic Association).

Devlin, F. P. Marathon [11]. (Mott Haven Athletic Club, New York).

DeWitt, John Riegel. (b.29 October 1881–d.28 July 1930) Hammer Throw [2]. (Princeton University).

Dray, Walter. (b.21 March 1886–d.April 1973) Pole Vault [6]. (Oxford School, Chicago; Yale University).

Dvorak, Charles Edward. (b.27 November 1878–d.18 December 1969) Pole Vault [1]. (University of Michigan; Chicago Athletic Association).

Emmerich, Max. All-Around [ac/dnf]. [See also Gymnastics]. (Socialer Turnverein, Indianapolis).

Englehardt, Fred. Broad Jump [4]; Hop, Step, and Jump [2]. (Mohawk Athletic Club, New York).

Ewry, Raymond Clarence. (b.14 October 1873–d.29 September 1937) Standing Broad Jump [1]; Standing High Jump [1]; Standing Hop, Step, and Jump [1]. (Purdue University; New York Athletic Club).

Feuerbach, Lawrence Edward Joseph. (b.1884–d.16 November 1911) Shot Put [3]. [See also Tug-of-War]. (New York University; New York Athletic Club).

Field, Henry W. Standing Broad Jump [4].

Flanagan, John Jesus. (b.9 January 1873–d.4 June 1938) 56-lb. Weight Throw [2]; Discus Throw [4]; Hammer Throw [1]. (Greater New York Irish Athletic Association).

Fleming, Joseph S. 400 meters [4]. (Washington University; Missouri Athletic Club).

Fowler, Robert J. Marathon [ac/dnf]. (Cambridgeport Gymnasium, Cambridge, MA).

Foy, John J. Marathon [ac/dnf]. (Star Athletic Club, New York).

Frank, Daniel. (d.20 March 1965) Broad Jump [2]. (New Westside Athletic Club, New York).

Freymark, Emil. High Jump [5]. (Missouri Athletic Club).

Fuhler, John W. Hop, Step, and Jump [4]. (Milwaukee Athletic Club).

Furla, John. Marathon [13].

Garcia, William R. Marathon [ac/dnf]. (Pacific Athletic Association, San Francisco).

Grieb, John. All-Around [6]. (Philadelphia Turngemeinde).

Groman, Herman Charles. (b.18 August 1882–d.21 July 1954) 400 meters [3]. (Yale University; Chicago Athletic Association).

Guiney, John J. Shot Put [7]. (Missouri Athletic Club).

Gunn, Adam B. All-Around [2]. (Buffalo Central YMCA).

Hagerman, John Percival. (b.25 October 1881) Broad Jump [6]; Hop, Step, and Jump [6]. (Pacific Athletic Association, San Francisco).

Hahn, Charles Archibald "Archie." (b.14 September 1880–d.21 January 1955) 60 meters [1]; 100 meters [1]; 200 meters [1]. (University of Michigan; Milwaukee Athletic Club).

Hare, Thomas Truxtun.[3] (b.12 October 1878–d.2 February 1956) All-Around [3]. (University of Pennsylvania).

Hatch, Sidney H. (b.18 August 1883–d.January 1974) Marathon [8]; 4-mile team race [2]. (Chicago Athletic Association).

Hearn, Lacey Earnest. (b.23 March 1881–d.19 October 1969) 800 meters [ac]; 1,500 meters [3]; 4-mile team race [2]. (Chicago Athletic Association).

Heckwolf, Frederick. 100 meters [5]. (Missouri Athletic Club).

Hennemann, Charles Henry. (b.15 February 1866–d.23 June 1938) 56-lb. Weight Throw [4].

Hicks, Thomas J. (b.7 January 1875–d.2 December 1963) Marathon [1]. (Cambridgeport YMCA, Cambridge, MA).

Hillman, Harry Livingston, Jr. (b.8 September 1881–d.9 August 1945) 200 meter hurdles [1]; 400 meter hurdles [1]; 400 meters [1]. (New York Athletic Club).

Hogensen, William P. (b.26 October 1884–d.14 October 1965) 60 meters [2]; 100 meters [3]; 200 meters [3]. (Lewis Institute; University of Chicago; Chicago Athletic Association).

Hunter, William B. 60 meters [ach1r1/3].

Johnson, Albert A. Hammer Throw [6]; Shot Put [6]. (St.Louis YMCA).

Jones, Samuel Symington. (b.1879–d.13 April 1954) High Jump [1]; Hop, Step, and Jump [7]. [See also Tug-of-War]. (New York University; New York Athletic Club).

Joyce, John J. 800 meters [ac].

Kennedy, Thomas J. Marathon [ac/dnf]. (National Athletic Club, New York).

King, Charles M. Standing Broad Jump [2]; Standing Hop, Step, and Jump [2].

Kneeland, David J. Marathon [6]. (St. Philipps Athletic Association, Boston).

Lightbody, James Davies. (b.17 March 1882–d.2 March 1953) 800 meters [1]; 1,500 meters [1]; 2,590 meter steeplechase [1]; 4-mile team race [2] (Chicago Athletic Association). (University of Chicago; Chicago Athletic Association).

Lordon, John C. (b.1875) Marathon [ac/dnf]. (Cambridgeport Gymnasium, Cambridge, MA).

Lorz, Fred. (b.1880) Marathon [ac/dnf]. (Mohawk Athletic Club, New York).

McLanahan, Ward. (b.15 January 1883–d.December 1974) 110 meter hurdles [3h1r1/2]; Pole Vault [4]. (Yale University; New York Athletic Club).

Mellor, Samuel Alexander. (b.15 February 1878–d.July 1970) Marathon [ac/dnf]. (Mohawk Athletic Club, New York).

Mitchel, James Sarsfield. (b.30 January 1864–d.3 July 1921) 56-lb. Weight Throw [3]; Discus Throw [6]; Hammer Throw [5]. [See also Tug-of-War]. (New York Athletic Club).

Moulton, Fay R. (b.7 April 1876–d.19 February 1945) 60 meters [3]; 100 meters [4]; 200 meters [4]. (Yale University; Kansas City Athletic Club).

Munson, David Curtiss. (b.19 May 1884–d.17 September 1953) 1,500 meters [4]; 2,590 meter steeplechase [ac]; 4-mile team race [1] (New York Athletic Club). (Cornell University; New York Athletic Club).

Newton, Arthur Lewis. (b.31 January 1883 –d.19 July 1950) 2,590 meter steeplechase [3]; Marathon [3]; 4-mile team race [1]. (New York Athletic Club).

Oxley, John Taylor. (b.13 October 1881–d.10 November 1925) Broad Jump [ac]. (Yale University; Chicago Athletic Association).

Pierce, Frank C. Marathon [ac/dnf]. (Pastime Athletic Club, New York).

Pilgrim, Paul Harry. (b.26 October 1883–d.8 January 1958) 400 meters [ac]; 800 meters [ac]; 4-mile team race [1] (New York Athletic Club). (New York Athletic Club).

Poage, George Coleman. (b.6 November 1880–d.11 April 1962) 60 meters [ach1r1/3]; 200 meter hurdles [3]; 400 meter hurdles [3]; 400 meters [6]. (University of Wisconsin; Milwaukee Athletic Club).

Porter, Guy J. (b.26 May 1875–d.July 1966) Marathon [ac/dnf]. (Cambridgeport YMCA, Cambridge, MA).

Prinstein, Meyer. (b.1880–d.10 March 1925) 60 meters [5]; 100 meters [4h2r1/2]; 400 meters [5]; Broad Jump [1]; Hop, Step, and Jump [1]. (Syracuse University; Greater New York Irish Athletic Association).

Robertson, Lawson N. (b.24 September 1883–d.22 January 1951) 60 meters [3h3r1/3]; 100 meters [6]; Standing High Jump [3]. (Greater New York Irish Athletic Association).

Rose, Ralph Waldo. (b.17 March 1885–d.16 October 1913) 56-lb. Weight Throw [6]; Discus Throw [2]; Hammer Throw [3]; Shot Put [1]. (University of Michigan; Chicago Athletic Association).

Samse, LeRoy Perry. (b.1885–d.1 May 1956) Pole Vault [2]. (Indiana University).

Sandford, Richard L. 2,590 meter steeplechase [ac]. (Brooklyn YMCA).

Schule, Frederick William. (b.27 September 1879) 110 meter hurdles [1]; 200 meter hurdles [5]. (University of Michigan; Milwaukee Athletic Club).

Serviss, Garrett Putnam. (b.23 December 1878–d.23 December 1908) High Jump [2]; Standing Hop, Step, and Jump [4]. (Cornell University).

Sheridan, Martin Joseph. (b.28 March 1881–d.27 March 1918) Discus Throw [1]; Shot Put [4]. (Greater New York Irish Athletic Association).

Shideler, Thaddeus Rutter. (b.1884–d.22 June 1966) 110 meter hurdles [2]. (Indiana University; Chicago Athletic Association).

Spring, Michael. (b.14 December 1879–d.17 March 1970) Marathon [ac/dnf]. (Pastime Athletic Club, New York).

Stadler, Joseph F. Standing High Jump [2]; Standing Hop, Step, and Jump [3]. (Franklin Athletic Club, Cleveland).

Stangland, Robert Sedgwick. (b.1881–d.15 December 1953) Broad Jump [3]; Hop, Step, and Jump [3]. (Columbia University; New York Athletic Club).

Underwood, George B. (b.1884–d.28 August 1943) 400 meters [ac]; 800 meters [4]; 4-mile team race [1] (New York Athletic Club). (New York Athletic Club).

Valentine, Howard V. (b.1881–d.25 June 1932) 400 meters [ac]; 800 meters [2]; 1,500 meters [7]; 4-mile team race [1] (New York Athletic Club). (New York Athletic Club).

Van Cleaf, George A. (b.1880–d.6 January 1905) Broad Jump [5]; Hop, Step, and Jump [5]. (New York Athletic Club).

Varnell, George. (b.10 August 1882–d.4 February 1967) 200 meter hurdles [4]; 400 meter hurdles [4]. (University of Chicago; Chicago Athletic Association).

Verner, William Frank. (b.24 June 1883–d.1969) 800 meters [6]; 1,500 meters [2]; 2,590 meter steeplechase [4]; 4-mile team race [2]. (Chicago Athletic Association).

Waller, Frank Laird. (b.1886–d.29 November 1941) 400 meter hurdles [2]; 400 meters [2]. (University of Wisconsin; Chicago Athletic Association).

Wilkins, Louis Gary. (b.10 December 1882) Pole Vault [3]. (University of Chicago; Chicago Athletic Association).

Boxing (Total: 18; Men: 18; Women: 0)

Berger, Samuel. (b.25 December 1884–d.23 February 1925) Heavyweight [1]. (Olympic Club, San Francisco).

Burke, Miles J. Flyweight [2].

Burton/Bollinger, Carroll. Lightweight [dq].

Eagan, Jack. Lightweight [2]; Welterweight [=3].

Finnegan, George V. Bantamweight [2]; Flyweight [1]. (Olympic Club, San Francisco).

Gilmore, Fred. Featherweight [3].

Haller, Frank. Featherweight [2]. (Cincinnati Athletic Club and Gymnasium).

Jewett, Kenneth. Lightweight [=5].

Kirk, Oliver L. (b.20 April 1884) Bantamweight [1]; Featherweight [1]. (Business Men's Gymnasium, St. Louis).

Lydon, Joseph Patrick. (b.2 February 1878–d.19 August 1937) Lightweight [=5]; Welterweight [=3]. [See also Football (Soccer)]. (Christian Brothers College, St. Louis).

Mayer, Charles. Heavyweight [2]; Middleweight [1]. (St. George's Athletic Club, New York).

Michaels, William M. Heavyweight [3].

Seward, Arthur. Lightweight [=5].

Spanger, Harry J. Lightweight [1]; Welterweight [2]. (National Turnverein, Newark, NJ).

Spradley, Benjamin. Middleweight [2]. (Business Men's Gymnasium, St. Louis).

Sturholdt, Peter J. Lightweight [4].

Van Horn, Russell. Lightweight [3]. (South Broadway Athletic Club, St. Louis).

Young, Albert. Welterweight [1]. (Olympic Club, San Francisco).

Cycling (Total: 18; Men: 18; Women: 0)

Andrews, A. F. ¼ mile [ach2r2/3]; ½ mile [3h1r1/3]; 5 miles [3]; 25 miles [2].

Billington, Edwin "Teddy." (b.14 July 1882–d. August 1966) ¼ mile [3]; ⅓ mile [3]; ½ mile [2]; 1 mile [3]; 2 miles [4]; 5 miles [ac]; 25 miles [ac].

Bizzoni, Frank. ¼ mile [ach1r2/3].

Downing, Burton Cecil. (b.5 February 1885–d.1 January 1929) ¼ mile [2]; ⅓ mile [2]; ½ mile [3]; 1 mile [2]; 2 miles [1]; 5 miles [ac]; 25 miles [1].

Fritz, A. L. G. ½ mile [ach1r2/3].

Goerke, Oscar. ¼ mile [4]; ⅓ mile [ach1r2/3]; ½ mile [3h2r1/3]; 1 mile [4]; 2 miles [2]; 5 miles [ac]; 25 miles [ac].

Grinham, Fred. (b.22 November 1881–d.March 1972) ¼ mile [3h3r1/3]; ⅓ mile [ach1r2/3]; ½ mile [ach2r2/3].

Hurley, Marcus Latimer. (b.22 December 1883–d.28 March 1941) ¼ mile [1]; ⅓ mile [1]; ½ mile [1]; 1 mile [1]; 2 miles [3]; 5 miles [ac]; 25 miles [ac]. (Columbia University; New York Athletic Club).

Larson, Leo. ½ mile [3h4r1/3].

LaVoice, Samuel. 25 miles [4].

McCrea, J. Nash. 1 mile [dnf h1r1/2]; 5 miles [ac].

Montaldi, Frank. ¼ mile [ach1r2/3].

Schaefer, Julius. 5 miles [4]; 25 miles [ac].

Schlee, Charles. ⅓ mile [4]; ½ mile [ach1r2/3]; 1 mile [3h1r1/2]; 2 miles [ac]; 5 miles [1]; 25 miles [ac].

Schwab, Oscar. ¼ mile [3h2r1/3].

Wiley, George E. (b.1882–d.3 March 1954) ½ mile [4]; 1 mile [3h2r1/2]; 5 miles [2]; 25 miles [3].

Williamson, Anthony. ¼ mile [3h4r1/3]; ½ mile [3h3r1/3]; 1 mile [4h2r1/2]; 25 miles [ac].

Wittman, Henry. ¼ mile [ach2r2/3]; ½ mile [ach2r2/3].

Diving (Total: 2; Men: 2; Women: 0)

Kehoe, Frank. Fancy diving [3]. (Chicago Athletic Association).

Sheldon, George Herbert. (b.17 May 1874–d.25 November 1907) Fancy diving [1]. (Muegge Institute, St. Louis).

Fencing (Total: 8; Men: 8; Women: 0)

Carstens, Theodore. Foil [4p1r1/2]; Saber [4].

Fox, Arthur G. Foil [4p2r1/2]; Saber [5]; Team foil [2].

Grebe, William. Foil [5p1r1/2]; Saber [2]; Single sticks [2].

Holroyd, Wilfred. Foil [3p2r1/2].

O'Connor, William Scott. (d.16 January 1939) Single sticks [2]. (New York Fencer's Club).

Tatham, Charles T. (b.1853–d.24 September 1939) Épée [2]; Foil [3]; Team foil [2]. (New York Fencer's Club).

Townsend, Charles Fitzhugh. (d.11 December 1906) Épée [5]; Foil [3p1r1/2]; Team foil [2]. (New York Fencer's Club).

Van Zo Post, Albertson. (b.1866–d.23 January 1938) Épée [3]; Foil [2]; Saber [3]; Single sticks [1]; Team foil [1]. (New York Fencer's Club).

Football (Association Football/Soccer) (Total: 23; Men: 23; Women: 0)

Bartliff, Charles Albert. [2]. (Christian Brothers College).

Brady, Joseph J. [3]. (St. Rose Parish).

Brittingham, Warren G. (b.2 September 1886–d.December 1962) [2]. (Christian Brothers College).

Brockmeyer, Oscar B. (b.14 November 1883–d.10 January 1954) [2]. (Christian Brothers College).

Cooke, George Edwin. (b.17 February 1883–d.3 June 1969) [3]. (St. Rose Parish).

Cooke, Thomas J. (b.1885) [3]. (St. Rose Parish).

Cosgrove, Cormic F. [3]. (St. Rose Parish).

Cudmore, Alexander. (b.1888) [2]. (Christian Brothers College).

Dierkes, –– [3]. (St. Rose Parish).

Dooling, Martin T. [3]. (St. Rose Parish).

Frost, Frank. [3]. (St. Rose Parish).

Jameson, Claude Stanley. (b.1883) [3]. (St. Rose Parish).

Jameson, Henry Wood. (b.1885) [3]. (St. Rose Parish).

January, Charles James, Jr. (b.1 February 1888–d.1975) [2]. (Christian Brothers College).

January, John Hartnett. (b.6 March 1882–d.1 December 1917) [2]. (Christian Brothers College).

January, Thomas Thurston. (b.8 January 1886–d.25 January 1957) [2] (Christian Brothers College).

Johnson, –– [3]. (St. Rose Parish).

Lawlor, Raymond E. [2]. (Christian Brothers College).

Lydon, Joseph Patrick. (b.2 February 1878–d.19 August 1937) [2]. (Christian Brothers College). [See also Boxing].

Menges, Louis John. (b.30 October 1888–d.10 March 1961) [2]. (Christian Brothers College).

O'Connell, –– [3]. (St. Rose Parish).

Ratican, Peter Joseph. (b.1887–d.20 November 1922) [2]. (Christian Brothers College).

Tate, Harry. [3]. (St. Rose Parish).

Golf (Total: 74; Men: 74; Women: 0)

Adams, Bart. Individual [=33qr]. (Algonquin Country Club, St. Louis).

Allen, Harry. Individual [=5]. (St. Louis Field Club [Bellerive Country Club]).

Allis, Louis. Individual [58qr]. (Milwaukee Country Club).

Angier, Clarence. Individual [72qr]. (Birmingham Country Club, AL).

Annan, A. H. Individual [=55qr]. (Algonquin Country Club, St. Louis).

Boyd, Louis T. Individual [=35qr]. (Milwaukee Country Club).

Brandt, J. S. Individual [=52qr]. (Glen Echo Country Club).

Brown, E. Campbell. Individual [=42qr]. (Springfield Country Club, MA).

Burton, William W. Individual [=33qr]. (Lakewood Country Club, St. Louis).

Cadwalader, Douglas P. Individual [=16]; Team [3]. (United States Golf Association; Springfield Country Club, IL).

Cady, John Deere. (b.26 January 1886–d.12 November 1933) Individual [=16]; Team [2] (Trans-Mississippi Golf Association; Rock Island Arsenal Club, Rock Island, IL).

Carleton, Jesse L. (b.20 August 1862–d.6 December 1921) Individual [=16]; Team [3] (United States Golf Association; Glen Echo Country Club).

Carleton, Murray. Individual [57qr]. (Glen Echo Country Club).

Case, Henry L. Individual [=42qr]. (Oil City Country Club, Oil City, PA).

Cory, Charles B. Individual [dnfqr]. (Wollaston Country Club, Quincy, MA).

Cummins, Edward "Ned." Individual [=16]; Team [1] (Western Golf Association; Exmoor Country Club, Chicago).

Davis, E. M. Individual [=42qr]. (Tekoa Golf Club, Westfield, MA).

Edmunds, E. C. Individual [=52qr]. (Glen Echo Country Club).

Edwards, Kenneth Paine. (b.9 March 1886) Team [1] (Western Golf Association; Exmoor Country Club, Chicago).

Egan, H. Chandler. (b.21 August 1884–d.5 April 1936) Individual [2]; Team [1] (Harvard University; Western Golf Association; Exmoor Country Club, Chicago).

Egan, Walter Eugene. (b.2 June 1881–d.12 September 1971) Individual [=16]; Team [1] (Harvard University; Western Golf Association; Exmoor Country Club, Chicago).

Flack, R. H. Individual [=45qr]. (Birmingham Country Club, AL).

Foulis, Simpson. Individual [=9]. (Chicago Golf Club).

Fraser, Harold D. Individual [=16]; Team [3] (United States Golf Association; Inverness Club, Toledo, OH).

Gould, Edward M. Individual [71qr]. (Glen Echo Country Club).

Groseclose, William B. Individual [=68qr]. (Glen Echo Country Club).

Harbaugh, Simon J. Individual [=68qr]. (Glen Echo Country Club).

Havemeyer, Arthur. Individual [=9]. (Seabright Country Club, Deal, NJ).

Havemeyer, Raymond. Individual [=16]. (Seabright Country Club, Deal, NJ).

Hazleton, L. J. Individual [=55qr]. (Tekoa Golf Club, Westfield, MA).

Hersey, W. A. Individual [51qr]. (Normandie Park Golf Club, St. Louis).

Howard, J. J. Individual [64qr]. (Glen Echo Country Club).

Hunt, Jarvis. Individual [=60qr]. (Chicago Golf Club).

Hunter, Edwin L. Individual [=37qr]. (Midlothian Country Club, Chicago).

Hunter, Robert Edward. (b.20 November 1886–d.28 March 1971) Individual [=9]; Team [1] (Yale University; Western Golf Association; Midlothian Country Club, Chicago).

Hussey, Arthur D. Individual [=40qr]; Team [3] (United States Golf Association; Inverness Club, Toledo, OH).

Jones, E. Lee. Individual [74qr]. (Lake Geneva Country Club, Lake Geneva, WI).

Jones, Orus W. Individual [=16]; Team [3] (United States Golf Association; Inverness Club, Toledo, OH).

Lambert, Albert Bond. (b.6 December 1875–d.12 November 1946) Individual [=5]; Team [2] (Trans-Mississippi Golf Association; Glen Echo Country Club).

Lansing, E. W. Individual [70qr]. (Glen Echo Country Club).

Lard, Allen E. Individual [=9]; Team [3] (United States Golf Association; Columbia Country Club, Chevy Chase, MD).

Mackintosh, Alexander C. Individual [=60qr]. (Pueblo Golf & Country Club, Pueblo, CO).

Maxwell, John R. (b.16 July 1871–d.3 June 1906) Team [2] (Keokuk College of Physicians and Surgeons; Trans-Mississippi Golf Association; Keokuk Country Club, Keokuk, IA).

McKinnie, Burt P. Individual [=3]; Team [2] (Trans-Mississippi Golf Association; Normandie Park Golf Club, St. Louis).

McKittrick, Ralph. (b.17 August 1877–d.4 May 1923) Individual [=9]; Team [2] (Harvard University; Trans-Mississippi Golf Association; St. Louis Country Club). [See also Tennis (Lawn)].

Moore, Nathaniel Fish, II. (b.25 January 1876–d. October 1967) Individual [=9]; Team [1] (Western Golf Association; Lake Geneva Country Club, Lake Geneva, WI).

Newberry, F. C. Individual [54qr]. (Glen Echo Country Club).

Newton, Francis Clement. (b.3 January 1874–d.3 August 1946) Individual [=3]; Team [2] (The Johns Hopkins University; Trans-Mississippi Golf Association; Seattle Country Club).

Oliver, George C. Individual [50qr]; Team [3] (United States Golf Association; Birmingham Country Club, AL).

Phelps, Mason Elliott. (b.7 December 1885–d.2 September 1945) Individual [=5]; Team [1] (Yale University; Western Golf Association; Midlothian Country Club, Chicago).

Potter, Charles. Individual [=48qr]. (St. Louis Country Club).

Potter, Henry. (b.4 October 1881–d.24 January 1955) Individual [=16]; Team [2] (Yale University; Trans-Mississippi Golf Association; St. Louis Country Club).

Powell, George F. Individual [=45qr]. (St. Louis Field Club [Bellerive Country Club]).

Price, Simeon Taylor, Jr. Individual [=16]; Team [3] (United States Golf Association; Glen Echo Country Club).

Rahm, John B. Individual [39qr]; Team [3] (United States Golf Association; Omaha Country Club).

Sawyer, Daniel "Ned." (d.6 July 1937) Individual [=5]; Team [1] (Western Golf Association; Chicago Golf Club).

Scudder, Charles S. Individual [=35qr]. (Glen Echo Country Club).

Semple, Frederick Humphrey. (b.24 December 1872–d.21 December 1927) Individual [=16]; Team [2] (Trans-Mississippi Golf Association; St. Louis Field Club [Bellerive Country Club]). [See also Tennis (Lawn)].

Shaw, Wallace F. Individual [=62qr]. (Tekoa Country Club, Westfield, MA).

Simkins, Harold W. Individual [=37qr]. (Yarmouth Country Club, Yarmouth, MA).

Smith, William P. Individual [=16]. (Philadelphia Country Club).

Smoot, Clement E. (b.7 April 1884–d.January 1963) Individual [=16]; Team [1] (Western Golf Association). (Exmoor Country Club, Chicago).

Stack, J. L. Individual [=66qr]. (Midlothian Country Club, Chicago).

Stickney, Stuart Grosvenor. (b.9 March 1877–d.24 September 1932) Individual [=9]; Team [2] (Trans-Mississippi Golf Association; St. Louis Country Club).

Stickney, William Arthur. (b.25 May 1879–d.12 September 1944) Individual [=9]; Team [2] (Trans-Mississippi Golf Association; St. Louis Country Club).

Sumney, Herbert Clayton. Individual [=40qr]. (Omaha Country Club).

Thomas, George A. Individual [=48qr]. (Exmoor Country Club, Chicago).

Vickery, Abner C. Individual [=16]. (Glen Echo Country Club).

Watson, John T. Individual [59qr]. (Glen Echo Country Club).

Weber, Harold. Individual [=16]; Team [3] (United States Golf Association; Inverness Club, Toledo, OH).

Williard, C. E. Individual [=45qr]. (Homewood Country Club [Flossmoor Country Club], Flossmoor, IL).

Withers, William T. Individual [=62qr].

Wood, Warren K. Individual [=16]; Team [1] (Western Golf Association; Homewood Country Club [Flossmoor Country Club], Flossmoor, IL)).

Yates, Mead W. Individual [=66qr]. (Springfield Country Club, IL).

Gymnastics (Total: 112; Men: 112; Women: 0)

Andelfinger, William. (b.15 December 1880–d.December 1968) Combined exercises, apparatus work [7]; Combined exercises, individual [15]; Triathlon [=64]. (St. Louis Turnverein).

Aschenbrener, George. Combined exercises, apparatus work [=69]; Combined exercises, individual [64]; Combined exercises, team [9]; Triathlon [=49]. (Chicago La Salle Turnverein).

Barry, M. Combined exercises, apparatus work [75]; Combined exercises, individual [95]; Triathlon [111]. (Indianapolis Socialer Turnverein).

Bascher, M. Combined exercises, apparatus work [56]; Combined exercises, individual [75]; Combined exercises, team [10]; Triathlon [94]. (Passaic Turnverein, Passaic, NJ).

Berewald, William. Combined exercises, apparatus work [89]; Combined exercises, individual [72]; Combined exercises, team [13]; Triathlon [=30]. (Cleveland Turnverein Vorwärts).

Berg, Bernard. Combined exercises, apparatus work [97]; Combined exercises, individual [98]; Combined exercises, team [8]; Triathlon [73]. (Davenport Turngemeinde, Davenport, IA).

Berg, Ragnar. Combined exercises, apparatus work [38]; Combined exercises, individual [28]; Combined exercises, team [6]; Triathlon [=22]. (Brooklyn Norwegier Turnverein).

Beyer, Emil. (b.1876.–d.15 October 1934) Combined exercises, apparatus work [34]; Combined exercises, individual [30]; Combined exercises, team [2]; Triathlon [=36]. (New York Turnverein).

Bissinger, John. (b.29 October 1883–d.December 1968) Combined exercises, apparatus work [14]; Combined exercises, individual [8]; Combined exercises, team [2]; Triathlon [5]. (New York Turnverein).

Boehnke, Otto. Combined exercises, apparatus work [18]; Combined exercises, individual [14]; Triathlon [=14]. (Brooklyn Turnverein Vorwärts).

Chimberoff, Barney. Combined exercises, apparatus work [92]; Combined exercises, individual [92]; Triathlon [=79]. (Chicago Turnverein Vorwärts).

Dellert, Charles. (b.26 March 1882–d.October 1988) Combined exercises, apparatus work [64]; Combined exercises, individual [86]; Triathlon [107]. (St. Louis Concordia Turnverein).

Dellert, John. (b.18 November 1884–d.February 1985) Combined exercises, apparatus work [30]; Combined exercises, individual [36]; Combined exercises, team [4]; Triathlon [74]. (St. Louis Concordia Turnverein).

Deubler, Christian. Combined exercises, apparatus work [47]; Combined exercises, individual [56]; Combined exercises, team [5]; Triathlon [=77]. (South St. Louis Turnverein).

Duha, John. (b.25 June 1888–d.December 1970) Combined exercises, apparatus work [22]; Combined exercises, individual [24]; Combined exercises, team [3]; Triathlon [=36]; Combined exercises, individual, 4 events [4]; Parallel Bars [3]. (Chicago Central Turnverein).

Dwyer, James. Combined exercises, apparatus work [77]; Combined exercises, individual [78]; Combined exercises, team [7]; Triathlon [=68]. (Chicago Turnverein Vorwärts).

Emmerich, Max. Combined exercises, apparatus work [100]; Combined exercises, individual [67]; Triathlon [1]. (Socialer Turnverein, Indianapolis). [See also Athletics (Track & Field)].

Eyser, George. (b.1871) Combined exercises, apparatus work [10]; Combined exercises, individual [71]; Combined exercises, team [4]; Triathlon [118]; Combined exercises, individual, 4 events [2]; Horizontal Bar [3]; Long Horse [=1]; Parallel Bars [1]; Rope Climbing [1]; Side Horse [2]. (St. Louis Concordia Turnverein).

Feyder, Otto. Combined exercises, apparatus work [107]; Combined exercises, individual [97]; Combined exercises, team [9]; Triathlon [54]. (Chicago La Salle Turnverein).

Fischer, M. Combined exercises, apparatus work [94]; Combined exercises, individual [100]; Combined exercises, team [10]; Triathlon [=100]. (Passaic Turnverein, Passaic, NJ).

Friedrich, William. Combined exercises, apparatus work [106]; Combined exercises, individual [118]; Combined exercises, team [12]; Triathlon [117]. (Detroit Socialer Turnverein).

Glass, Herman T. (b.1879–d.31 January 1961) Rings [1]. (Richmond YMCA, Richmond, VA).

Grieb, John. Combined exercises, apparatus work [90]; Combined exercises, individual [52]; Combined exercises, team [1]; Triathlon [2]. (Philadelphia Turngemeinde).

Gross, Theodore. Combined exercises, apparatus work [16]; Combined exercises, individual [12]; Combined exercises, team [7]; Triathlon [=25]. (Chicago Turnverein Vorwärts).

Guerner, L. Combined exercises, apparatus work [110]; Combined exercises, individual [104]; Triathlon [81]. (Milwaukee Turnverein).

Gussmann, P. Combined exercises, apparatus work [43]; Combined exercises, individual [53]; Combined exercises, team [10]; Triathlon [82]. (Passaic Turnverein, Passaic, NJ).

Hansen, Harry. Combined exercises, apparatus work [27]; Combined exercises, individual [33]; Combined exercises, team [6]; Triathlon [62]. (Brooklyn Norwegier Turnverein).

Heida, Anton. (b.1878) Combined exercises, apparatus work [12]; Combined exercises, individual [18]; Combined exercises, team [1]; Triathlon [=59]; Combined exercises, individual, 4 events [1]; Horizontal Bar [=1]; Long Horse [=1]; Parallel Bars [2]; Side Horse [1]. (Philadelphia Turngemeinde).

Hennig, Edward A. (b.1880–d.28 August 1960) Combined exercises, apparatus work [59]; Combined exercises, individual [50]; Combined exercises, team [13]; Triathlon [=36]; Club Swinging [1]; Combined exercises, individual, 4 events [5]; Horizontal Bar [=1]. (Cleveland Turnverein Vorwärts).

Hermerrling, G. Combined exercises, apparatus work [28]; Combined exercises, individual [54]; Combined exercises, team [10]; Triathlon [=104]. (Passaic Turnverein, Passaic, NJ).

Herrmann, Robert. Combined exercises, apparatus work [35]; Combined exercises, individual [29]; Combined exercises, team [11]; Triathlon [=25]. (Milwaukee Turnverein).

Hertenbahn, Jacob. Combined exercises, apparatus work [51]; Combined exercises, individual [49]; Combined exercises, team [7]; Triathlon [=59]. (Chicago Turnverein Vorwärts).

Herzog, William. Combined exercises, apparatus work [96]; Combined exercises, individual [105]; Triathlon [=102]. (Chicago Turnverein Vorwärts).

Hess, Max. Combined exercises, apparatus work [50]; Combined exercises, individual [31]; Combined exercises, team [1]; Triathlon [=10]. (Philadelphia Turngemeinde).

Horschke, William. Combined exercises, apparatus work [20]; Combined exercises, individual [38]; Combined exercises, team [9]; Triathlon [91]. (Chicago La Salle Turnverein).

Hunger, L. Combined exercises, apparatus work [82]; Combined exercises, individual [70]; Combined exercises, team [11]; Triathlon [=44]. (Milwaukee Turnverein).

Jahnke, Anthony. Combined exercises, apparatus work [74]; Combined exercises, individual [61]; Triathlon [=40]. (Chicago Central Turnverein).

Kassell, Phillip. (b.1876) Combined exercises, apparatus work [19]; Combined exercises, individual [11]; Combined exercises, team [1]; Triathlon [6]. (Philadelphia Turngemeinde).

Keim, Leander. Combined exercises, apparatus work [60]; Combined exercises, individual [46]; Combined exercises, team [8]; Triathlon [=25]. (Davenport Turngemeinde, Davenport, IA).

Kempf, Andreas. Combined exercises, apparatus work [8]; Combined exercises, individual [20]; Triathlon [=75]. (Kansas City Turnverein).

Kiddington, Clarence. Combined exercises, apparatus work [108]; Combined exercises, individual [90]; Combined exercises, team [12]; Triathlon [=36]. (Detroit Socialer Turnverein).

Knerr, Otto. Combined exercises, apparatus work [115]; Combined exercises, individual [117]; Triathlon [88]. (Kansas City Turnverein).

Kniep, Louis. Combined exercises, apparatus work [52]; Combined exercises, individual [44]; Triathlon [=44]. (Newark Turnverein, Newark, NJ).

Koeder, Henry. Combined exercises, apparatus work [58]; Combined exercises, individual [43]; Combined exercises, team [7]; Triathlon [33]. (Chicago Turnverein Vorwärts).

Kraft, Henry. Combined exercises, apparatus work [65]; Combined exercises, individual [76]; Combined exercises, team [7]; Triathlon [=79]. (Chicago Turnverein Vorwärts).

Krause, Charles. Combined exercises, apparatus work [45]; Combined exercises, individual [48]; Combined exercises, team [3]; Triathlon [=64]; Rope Climbing [2]. (Chicago Central Turnverein).

Kritschmann, Alvin. Combined exercises, apparatus work [57]; Combined exercises, individual [87]; Combined exercises, team [12]; Triathlon [116]. (Detroit Socialer Turnverein).

Krupitzer, Rudolf. Combined exercises, apparatus work [44]; Combined exercises, individual [40]; Combined exercises, team [13]; Triathlon [=49]. (Cleveland Turnverein Vorwärts).

Kruppinger, William. Combined exercises, apparatus work [112]; Combined exercises, individual [111]; Triathlon [=95]. (South St. Louis Turnverein).

Landnes, Oluf. Combined exercises, apparatus work [=78]; Combined exercises, individual [63]; Combined exercises, team [6]; Triathlon [=28]. (Brooklyn Norwegier Turnverein).

Lang, Michael. Combined exercises, apparatus work [=78]; Combined exercises, individual [85]; Combined exercises, team [13]; Triathlon [83]. (Cleveland Turnverein Vorwärts).

Leichinger, John. Combined exercises, apparatus work [103]; Combined exercises, individual [83]; Combined exercises, team [5]; Triathlon [13]. (South St. Louis Turnverein).

Ludwig, Martin. Combined exercises, apparatus work [46]; Combined exercises, individual [=73]; Triathlon [106]. (Labor Lyceum, Baltimore).

Mastrovich, George. Triathlon [71]; Combined exercises, apparatus work [=71]; Combined exercises, individual [=73]. (Turnverein Germania, Los Angeles).

Mayer, George. Combined exercises, apparatus work [39]; Combined exercises, individual [21]; Combined exercises, team [3]; Triathlon [4]. (Chicago Central Turnverein).

Maysack, Robert. Combined exercises, apparatus work [55]; Combined exercises, individual [59]; Combined exercises, team [3]; Triathlon [70]. (Chicago Central Turnverein).

Merz, William A. (b.1878–d.20 March 1946) Combined exercises, apparatus work [24]; Combined exercises, individual [10]; Combined exercises, team [4]; Triathlon [3]; Combined exercises, individual, 4 events [3]; Long Horse [3]; Rings [2]; Side Horse [3]. (St. Louis Concordia Turnverein).

Messel, John. Combined exercises, apparatus work [109]; Combined exercises, individual [114]; Combined exercises, team [12]; Triathlon [=108]. (Detroit Socialer Turnverein).

Meyland, Hy. Combined exercises, apparatus work [86]; Combined exercises, individual [91]; Combined exercises, team [4]; Triathlon [=85]. (St. Louis Concordia Turnverein).

Mueller, Gustav. Combined exercises, apparatus work [25]; Combined exercises, individual [41]; Triathlon [=89]. (Chicago Central Turnverein).

Neimand, Otto. Combined exercises, apparatus work [84]; Combined exercises, individual [58]; Combined exercises, team [8]; Triathlon [=10]. (Davenport Turngemeinde, Davenport, IA).

Neu, Andrew. Combined exercises, apparatus work [40]; Combined exercises, individual [23]; Combined exercises, team [5]; Triathlon [16]. (South St. Louis Turnverein).

Nilsen, Bergin. Combined exercises, apparatus work [85]; Combined exercises, individual [82]; Combined exercises, team [6]; Triathlon [67]. (Brooklyn Norwegier Turnverein).

Olsen, Oliver. Combined exercises, apparatus work [49]; Combined exercises, individual [39]; Combined exercises, team [6]; Triathlon [=40]. (Brooklyn Norwegier Turnverein).

Placke, August. Combined exercises, apparatus work [98]; Combined exercises, individual [106]; Combined exercises, team [11]; Triathlon [=95]. (Milwaukee Turnverein).

Prinzler, Henry. Combined exercises, apparatus work [80]; Combined exercises, individual [68]; Triathlon [=40]. (Indianapolis Socialer Turnverein).

Pueschell, Edward. Combined exercises, apparatus work [113]; Combined exercises, individual [116]; Triathlon [113]. (Kansas City Turnverein).

Raad, Frank. Combined exercises, apparatus work [48]; Combined exercises, individual [69]; Triathlon [=92]. (Johnstown Turnverein, Johnstown, PA).

Rathke, L. Combined exercises, apparatus work [114]; Combined exercises, individual [103]; Combined exercises, team [11]; Triathlon [=55]. (Milwaukee Turnverein).

Real, Walter. Combined exercises, apparatus work [104]; Combined exercises, individual [113]; Combined exercises, team [9]; Triathlon [=108]. (Chicago La Salle Turnverein).

Reckeweg, Ernst. Combined exercises, apparatus work [67]; Combined exercises, individual [47]; Combined exercises, team [1]; Triathlon [19]. (Philadelphia Turngemeinde).

Reynolds, Robert. Combined exercises, apparatus work [102]; Combined exercises, individual [80]; Combined exercises, team [12]; Triathlon [=17]. (Detroit Socialer Turnverein).

Ritter, P. Combined exercises, apparatus work [93]; Combined exercises, individual [96]; Combined exercises, team [10]; Triathlon [84]. (Passaic Turnverein, Passaic, NJ).

Roedek, K. Combined exercises, apparatus work [66]; Combined exercises, individual [94]; Combined exercises, team [10]; Triathlon [115]. (Passaic Turnverein, Passaic, NJ).

Roissner, Otto. Combined exercises, apparatus work [105]; Combined exercises, individual [107]; Combined exercises, team [12]; Triathlon [=89]. (Detroit Socialer Turnverein).

Rosenkampff, Arthur H. (b.3 November 1884–d.6 November 1952) Combined exercises, apparatus work [76]; Combined exercises, individual [89]; Combined exercises, team [2]; Triathlon [=102]. (New York Turnverein).

Rothe, Emil. Combined exercises, apparatus work [26]; Combined exercises, individual [27]; Combined exercises, team [9]; Triathlon [=52]. (Chicago La Salle Turnverein).

Schicke, Frank. Combined exercises, apparatus work [63]; Combined exercises, individual [35]; Combined exercises, team [9]; Triathlon [=17]. (Chicago La Salle Turnverein).

Schmind, Fred. Combined exercises, apparatus work [37]; Combined exercises, individual [22]; Triathlon [=7]. (Chicago Central Turnverein).

Schmitz, Julian. Combined exercises, apparatus work [32]; Combined exercises, individual [57]; Combined exercises, team [2]; Triathlon [=100]. (New York Turnverein).

Schrader, Rudolf. (b.17 March 1875–d.January 1981) Combined exercises, apparatus work [68]; Combined exercises, individual [84]; Combined exercises, team [7]; Triathlon [=95]. (Chicago Turnverein Vorwärts).

Schrader, Willard. (b.17 February 1883–d.January 1967) Combined exercises, apparatus work [91]; Combined exercises, individual [77]; Triathlon [=30]. (Chicago Turnverein Vorwärts).

Schroeder, George. Combined exercises, apparatus work [87]; Combined exercises, individual [79]; Triathlon [=52]. (Kansas City Turnverein).

Schuster, Philip. Combined exercises, apparatus work [54]; Combined exercises, individual [51]; Combined exercises, team [3]; Triathlon [=55]. (Chicago Central Turnverein).

Schwartz, Charles. Combined exercises, apparatus work [83]; Combined exercises, individual [101]; Triathlon [114]. (Newark Turnverein, Newark, NJ).

Schwegler, Emil. Combined exercises, apparatus work [21]; Combined exercises, individual [42]; Triathlon [=95]. (St.Louis Schweitzer Turnverein).

Siegler, Edward. Combined exercises, apparatus work [53]; Combined exercises, individual [32]; Combined exercises, team [3]; Triathlon [12]. (Chicago Central Turnverein).

Sontag, Phillip. Combined exercises, apparatus work [73]; Combined exercises, individual [62]; Combined exercises, team [8]; Triathlon [43]. (Davenport Turngemeinde, Davenport, IA).

Sorum, Charles. Combined exercises, apparatus work [31]; Combined exercises, individual [37]; Combined exercises, team [6]; Triathlon [72]. (Brooklyn Norwegier Turnverein).

Spann, Lorenz. Combined exercises, apparatus work [36]; Combined exercises, individual [26]; Triathlon [=22]. (Newark Turnverein, Newark, NJ).

Sperl, Christian. Combined exercises, apparatus work [111]; Combined exercises, individual [110]; Combined exercises, team [11]; Triathlon [=95]. (Milwaukee Turnverein).

Stapf, George. Combined exercises, apparatus work [23]; Combined exercises, individual [16]; Combined exercises, team [4]; Triathlon [=14]. (St. Louis Concordia Turnverein).

Steffen, Otto I. (b.9 August 1874) Combined exercises, apparatus work [6]; Combined exercises, individual [6]; Combined exercises, team [2]; Triathlon [20]. (New York Turnverein).

Studel, Paul. Combined exercises, apparatus work [101]; Combined exercises, individual [108]; Combined exercises, team [13]; Triathlon [=104]. (Cleveland Turnverein Vorwärts).

Studler, Theodore. Combined exercises, apparatus work [119]; Combined exercises, individual [119]; Combined exercises, team [13]. (Cleveland Turnverein Vorwärts).

Sundbye, Arthur. Combined exercises, apparatus work [99]; Combined exercises, individual [109]; Triathlon [=108]. (Brooklyn Norwegier Turnverein).

Thomas, Max. Combined exercises, apparatus work [116]; Combined exercises, individual [99]; Triathlon [=34]. (South St. Louis Turnverein).

Thomsen, Otto. Combined exercises, apparatus work [117]; Combined exercises, individual [115]; Triathlon [=75]. (Davenport Turngemeinde, Davenport, IA).

Traband, William. Combined exercises, apparatus work [41]; Combined exercises, individual [45]; Triathlon [=68]. (Philadelphia Turngemeinde).

Tritschler, Edward. (b.5 June 1885–d.May 1963) Combined exercises, apparatus work [62]; Combined exercises, individual [66]; Combined exercises, team [5]; Triathlon [=77]. (South St. Louis Turnverein).

Tritschler, Richard. Combined exercises, apparatus work [81]; Combined exercises, individual [88]; Triathlon [=85]. (South St. Louis Turnverein).

Tritschler, William. Combined exercises, apparatus work [61]; Combined exercises, individual [55]; Combined exercises, team [5]; Triathlon [=59]. (South St. Louis Turnverein).

Umbs, Charles. Combined exercises, apparatus work [15]; Combined exercises, individual [17]; Combined exercises, team [5]; Triathlon [=47]. (South St. Louis Turnverein).

Voigt, Emil. Combined exercises, apparatus work [42]; Combined exercises, individual [60]; Combined exercises, team [4]; Triathlon [=85]; Club Swinging [2]; Rings [3]; Rope Climbing [3]. (St. Louis Concordia Turnverein).

Wagner, Reinhard. (b.16 November 1876–d.April 1964) Combined exercises, apparatus work [29]; Combined exercises, individual [25]; Combined exercises, team [8]; Triathlon [=22]. (Davenport Turngemeinde, Davenport, IA).

Warnken, Harry. (b.19 November 1883–d.October 1963) Combined exercises, apparatus work [88]; Combined exercises, individual [81]; Combined exercises, team [8]; Triathlon [=55]. (Davenport Turngemeinde, Davenport, IA).

Wassow, J. Combined exercises, apparatus work [118]; Combined exercises, individual [112]; Combined exercises, team [11]; Triathlon [=49]. (Milwaukee Turnverein).

Wilson, Ralph. Club Swinging [3]. (National Turnverein, Newark, NJ).

Woerner, K. Combined exercises, apparatus work [=69]; Combined exercises, individual [93]; Triathlon [112]. (Passaic Turnverein, Passaic, NJ).

Wolf, John. Combined exercises, apparatus work [=71]; Combined exercises, individual [65]; Triathlon [=47]. (Philadelphia Turngemeinde).

Wolf, Max. Combined exercises, apparatus work [33]; Combined exercises, individual [34]; Combined exercises, team [2]; Triathlon [63]. (New York Turnverein).

Zabel, Wilhelm. Combined exercises, apparatus work [95]; Combined exercises, individual [102]; Triathlon [=92]. (St. Louis Turnverein).

Lacrosse (Total: 12; Men: 12; Women: 0)

Dowling, J. W. [2]. (St. Louis Amateur Athletic Association).

Gibson, –– [2]. (St. Louis Amateur Athletic Association).

Grogan, Patrick. [2]. (St. Louis Amateur Athletic Association).

Hunter, –– [2]. (St. Louis Amateur Athletic Association).

Murphy, –– [2]. (St. Louis Amateur Athletic Association).

Partridge, –– [2]. (St. Louis Amateur Athletic Association).

Passmore, George. (b.22 January 1886–d.July 1970) [2]. (St. Louis Amateur Athletic Association).

Passmore, William. [2]. (St. Louis Amateur Athletic Association).

Ross, –– [2]. (St. Louis Amateur Athletic Association).

Sullivan, –– [2]. (St. Louis Amateur Athletic Association).

Venn, A. H. [2]. (St. Louis Amateur Athletic Association).

Woods, –– [2]. (St. Louis Amateur Athletic Association).

Rowing & Sculling (Total: 35; Men: 35; Women: 0)

Abell, Louis G. (b.21 July 1884–d.25 October 1962) Coxed eights [1]. (Vesper Boat Club).

Aman, Charles. Coxless fours [2]. (Mound City Rowing Club).

Armstrong, Charles E. Coxed eights [1]. (Vesper Boat Club).

Begley, Michael. Coxless fours [2]. (Mound City Rowing Club).

Buerger, John Joseph. (b.19 September 1870–d.1951) Coxless pairs [3]. (Western Rowing Club).

Cresser, Frederick. Coxed eights [1]. (Vesper Boat Club).

Dempsey, Joseph F. (b.27 September 1872–d.9 October 1930) Coxed eights [1]. (Vesper Boat Club).

Dietz, George. (b.1880–d.19 April 1965) Coxless fours [1]. (Century Boat Club).

Duffield, David B. Single sculls [4]. (Detroit Boat Club).

Dummerth, Frank. Coxless fours [3]. (Western Rowing Club).

Erker, August Casimir. (b.1879–d.29 November 1951) Coxless fours [1]. (Century Boat Club).

Exley, John Onins, Jr. (b.23 May 1867–d.27 July 1938) Coxed eights [1]. (Vesper Boat Club).

Farnam, Robert. Coxless pairs [1]. (Seawanhaka Boat Club).

Flanagan, James Showers. (b.1884–d.28 March 1937) Coxed eights [1]. (Vesper Boat Club).

Freitag, John. Coxless fours [3]. (Western Rowing Club).

Fromanack, Martin. Coxless fours [2]. (Mound City Rowing Club).

Gleason, Michael D. (d.11 January 1923) Coxed eights [1]. (Vesper Boat Club).

Greer, Frank B. (b.1879–d.7 May 1943) Single sculls [1]. (East Boston Amateur Athletic Boat Club).

Helm, Louis G. Coxless fours [3]. (Western Rowing Club).

Hoben, John Grey. (b.1884–d.6 July 1915) Double sculls [2]. (Ravenswood Boat Club).

Joachim, John L. Coxless pairs [3]. (Western Rowing Club).

Juvenal, James B. (b.12 January 1874–d.2 September 1942) Single sculls [2]. (Pennsylvania Barge Club, Philadelphia).

Lott, Harry Hunter. (b.1880–d.5 February 1949) Coxed eights [1]. (Vesper Boat Club).

McLoughlin, James. (b.1885–d.1 April 1946) Double sculls [2]. (Ravenswood Boat Club).

Mulcahy, John J. F. (b.1875–d.19 November 1942) Coxless pairs [2]; Double sculls [1]. (Atalanta Boat Club, New York).

Nasse, Albert F. (b.2 July 1878–d.21 November 1910) Coxless fours [1]. (Century Boat Club).

Ravanack, Joseph. Double sculls [3]. (Independent Rowing Club).

Ryan, Joseph. Coxless pairs [1]. (Seawanhaka Boat Club).

Schell, Frank Reamer. (b.1884–d.5 December 1959) Coxed eights [1]. (Vesper Boat Club).

Stockhoff, Arthur M. (b.19 November 1879–d.20 October 1934) Coxless fours [1]. (Century Boat Club).

Suerig, Frederick. Coxless fours [2]. (Mound City Rowing Club).

Titus, Constance Sutton. (b.14 August 1873–d.24 August 1967) Single sculls [3]. (Atalanta Boat Club, New York).

Varley, William P. Coxless pairs [2]; Double sculls [1]. (Atalanta Boat Club, New York).

Voerg, Gustav. (b.7 June 1870–d.21 April 1944) Coxless fours [3]. (Western Rowing Club).

Wells, John. Double sculls [3]. (Independent Rowing Club).

Swimming (Total: 16; Men: 16; Women: 0)

Adams, Edgar H. 220 yard freestyle [4]; 880 yard freestyle [4]; One mile freestyle [dnf]; Plunge for distance [2]. (New York Athletic Club).

Daniels, Charles Meldrum. (b.24 March 1885–d.9 August 1973) 50 yard freestyle [3]; 100 yard freestyle [2]; 220 yard freestyle [1]; 440 yard freestyle [1]. (New York Athletic Club).

Dickey, William Paul. (b.13 October 1883–d.17 February 1950) Plunge for distance [1]. (New York Athletic Club).

Gailey, Francis. 220 yard freestyle [2]; 440 yard freestyle [2]; 880 yard freestyle [2]; One mile freestyle [3]. (Olympic Club, San Francisco).

Gaul, David. (b.7 July 1886–d.August 1962) 50 yard freestyle [4]; 100 yard freestyle [4]. (Philadelphia Swimming Club).

Goodwin, Leo G. "Budd." (b.13 November 1883–d.25 May 1957) 50 yard freestyle [5]; 100 yard freestyle [6]; 440 yard freestyle [4]; Plunge for distance [3]. (New York Athletic Club).

Hammond, David. 100 yard backstroke [ac]; 100 yard freestyle [5]. (Chicago Athletic Association).

Handley, Louis de Breda. (b.14 February 1874–d.28 December 1956) One mile freestyle [dnf]. (New York Athletic Club).

Handy, Henry Jamison. (b.6 March 1886–d.13 November 1983) 440 yard breaststroke [3]; 880 yard freestyle [6]. (University of Michigan; Chicago Central YMCA).

Leary, J. Scott. 50 yard freestyle [2]; 100 yard freestyle [3]. (Olympic Club, San Francisco).

Meyers, John. One mile freestyle [dnf]. (Missouri Athletic Club).

Orthwein, William Robert. (b.16 October 1881–d.2 October 1955) 100 yard backstroke [4]. (Yale University; Missouri Athletic Club).

Pyrah, Charles H. Plunge for distance [5]. (New York Athletic Club).

Samuels, Newman. Plunge for distance [4]. (Missouri Athletic Club).

Swatek, Edwin Paul. (b.7 January 1885–d.December 1965) 100 yard backstroke [ac]. (Chicago Athletic Association).

Thorne, Raymond. 50 yard freestyle [6]. (Chicago Athletic Association).

Tennis (Lawn Tennis) (Total: 35; Men: 35; Women: 0)

Bell, Alphonzo Edward. (b.29 September 1875–d.27 December 1947) Doubles [2]; Singles [=3].

Blatherwick, W. E. Doubles [=9]; Singles [=5].

Charles, Joseph W. Doubles [=9]; Singles [=16].

Cresson, Charles C., Jr. Doubles [=5]; Singles [=5].

Cunningham, J. Singles [=9].

Davis, Dwight Filley. (b.5 July 1879–d.28 November 1945) Doubles [=5]; Singles [=9].

Drew, Andrew. Doubles [=9]; Singles [=16].

Easton, William. Singles [=16].

Feltshans, F. R. Singles [=9].

Forney, Chris. Singles [=16].

Gamble, Clarence Oliver. (b.16 August 1881–d.13 June 1952) Doubles [=3].

Gleason, Paul. Doubles [=9].

Hunter, –– Doubles [=5].

Jones, Hugh McKittrick. Doubles [=5]; Singles [=9].

Kauffman, Harold M. Doubles [=5].

Leonard, Edgar Welch. (b.19 June 1881–d.7 October 1948) Doubles [1]; Singles [=3].

LeRoy, Robert. (b.7 February 1885–d.7 September 1946) Doubles [2]; Singles [2].

Macdonald, Malcolm D. Doubles [=9]; Singles [=16].

McKittrick, Ralph. Doubles [=5]; Singles [=9]. [See also Golf].

Montgomery, Forest H. Doubles [=9]; Singles [=16].

Neely, John C. Singles [=5].

Russ, Semp. [*16 April 1878–d.March 1978] Doubles [=5]; Singles [=5].

Sanderson, Fred R. Singles [=9].

Semple, Frederick Humphrey. (b.24 December 1872–d.21 December 1927) Doubles [=9]. [See also Golf].

Semple, Nathaniel M. Doubles [=9]; Singles [=16].

Smith, N. M. Doubles [=9].

Stadel, George H. Doubles [=9]; Singles [27].

Tritle, J. Stewart. Doubles [=9]; Singles [=16].

Turner, Douglas. Doubles [=9]; Singles [=16].

Vernon, Orien V. Doubles [=9]; Singles [=16].

Wear, Arthur Yancey. (b.1 March 1880–d.6 November 1918) Doubles [=3].

Wear, Joseph Walker. (b.27 November 1876–d.4 June 1941) Doubles [=3].

West, Allen Tarwater. (b.1880–d.1924) Doubles [=3].

Wheaton, Frank. Doubles [=5]; Singles [=16].

Wright, Beals Coleman. (b.19 December 1879–d.23 August 1961) Doubles [1]; Singles [1].

Tug-of-War (Total: 20; Men: 20; Women: 0)

Braun, Max. (b.12 March 1883–d.May 1967) [2]. (St. Louis Southwest Turnverein #1).

Chadwick, Charles. (b.19 November 1874) [4]. (New York Athletic Club). [See also Track & Field Athletics].

Dieges, Charles J. (b.26 October 1865–d.14 September 1953) [4]. (New York Athletic Club).

Feuerbach, Lawrence Edward Joseph. (b.1884–d.16 November 1911) [4]. (New York Athletic Club). [See also Track & Field Athletics].

Flanagan, Patrick. [1]. (Milwaukee Athletic Club).

Friede, Oscar C. [3]. (St. Louis Southwest Turnverein #2).

Haberkorn, Charles. (b.31 March 1874–d.May 1968) [3]. (St. Louis Southwest Turnverein #2). [See also Wrestling].

Jacobs, Harry. [3]. (St. Louis Southwest Turnverein #2).

Johnson, Sidney B. [1]. (Milwaukee Athletic Club).

Jones, Samuel Symington. (b.1879–d.13 April 1954) [4]. (New York Athletic Club). [See also Track & Field Athletics].

Kungler, Frank. [3]. (St. Louis Southwest Turnverein #2). [See also Weightlifting and Wrestling].

Magnusson, Conrad. (b.1874–d.14 September 1924) [1]. (Milwaukee Athletic Club).

Mitchel, James Sarsfield. (b.30 January 1864–d.3 July 1921) [4]. (New York Athletic Club). [See also Track & Field Athletics].

Olson, Oscar G. (b.7 October 1878–d.February 1963) [1]. (Milwaukee Athletic Club). [See also Weightlifting].

Rodenberg, August. [2]. (St. Louis Southwest Turnverein #1).

Rose, Charles. [2]. (St. Louis Southwest Turnverein #1).

Seiling, Henry. [1]. (Milwaukee Athletic Club).

Seiling, William Bernard. (b.28 May 1863–d.5 January 1951) [2]. (St. Louis Southwest Turnverein #1).

Thias, Charles. (3 April 1886–d.February 1970) [3]. (St. Louis Southwest Turnverein #2).

Upshaw, Orrin Thomas. (b.1874–d.1937) [2]. (St. Louis Southwest Turnverein #1).

Weightlifting (Total: 4; Men: 4; Women: 0)

Kungler, Frank. All-Around Dumbbell Contest [3]; Two-hand lift [3]. (St. Louis Southwest Turnverein). [See also Tug-of-War and Wrestling].

Olson, Oscar G. (b.7 October 1878–d.February 1963) Two-hand lift [4]. [See also Tug-of-War].

Osthoff, Oscar Paul. (b.23 March 1883–d.9 December 1950) All-Around Dumbbell Contest [1]; Two-hand lift [2].

Winters, Frederick. All-Around Dumbbell Contest [2].

Wrestling (Catch-as-Catch-Can) (Total: 41; Men: 41; Women: 0)

Babcock, J. C. 135 lb. class [ac]. (Chicago Central YMCA).

Bauer, Gustav. (b.4 April 1884) 115 lb. class [2]. (National Turnverein, Newark, NJ).

Beckmann, William. 158 lb. class [2]. (New Westside Athletic Club, New York).

Betchestobill, A. J. 158 lb. class [ac]. (St. Louis Amateur Athletic Association).

Bradshaw, Benjamin Joseph. (b.15 August 1879–d.19 April 1960) 135 lb. class [1]. (Boys' Club, New York).

Cardwell, J. M. 125 lb. class [ac]. (Chicago Central YMCA).

Clapper, Charles E. (b.26 October 1883–d.October 1962) 135 lb. class [3]. (Chicago Central YMCA).

Curry, Robert. 105 lb. class [1]. (St. George's Athletic Club, New York).

Dilg, Joseph. Unlimited class [ac]. (St. Louis Rowing Club).

Eng, Charles. 145 lb. class [ac]. (Brooklyn Norwegier Turnverein).

Ericksen, Charles F. (b.1875–d.23 February 1916) 158 lb. class [1]. (Brooklyn Norwegier Turn-verein).

Ferguson, Frederick C. (b.7 August 1884–d.November 1971) 125 lb. class [ac]; 135 lb. class [4]. (Chicago Central YMCA).

Filler, S. A. 158 lb. class [ac]. (Chicago Central YMCA).

Haberkorn, Charles. (b.31 March 1874–d.May 1968) 145 lb. class [ac]. (St. Louis Southwest Turnverein). [See also Tug-of-War].

Hansen, Bernhuff. Unlimited class [1]. (Brooklyn Norwegier Turnverein).

Hein, John C. (b.27 January 1886–d.29 August 1963) 105 lb. class [2]. (Boys' Club, New York).

Hennessy, William Joseph. 145 lb. class [ac]; 158 lb. class [ac]; Unlimited class [ac].

Holgate, Claude. 105 lb. class [4]. (National Turnverein, Newark, NJ).

Hussman, Fred. 145 lb. class [ac]. (St. Louis Socialer Turnverein).

Koenig, Fred. 145 lb. class [ac]. (St. Louis Socialer Turnverein).

Kungler, Frank. Unlimited class [2]. (St. Louis Southwest Turnverein). [See also Tug-of-War and Weightlifting].

McLear, Theodore J. (b.29 June 1879) 135 lb. class [2]. (National Turnverein, Newark, NJ).

Mehnert, George Nicholas. (b.3 November 1881–d.8 July 1948) 115 lb. class [1]. (National Turnverein, Newark, NJ).

Mellinger, A. 158 lb. class [ac]. (St. Bartholomew's Athletic Club, New York).

Miller, Max. 135 lb. class [ac]. (St. Louis Central YMCA).

Nelson, William L. 115 lb. class [3]. (St. George's Athletic Club, New York).

Niflot, Isidor "Jack." (b.1882–d.29 May 1950) 125 lb. class [1]. (Pastime Athletic Club, New York).

Roehm, Otto F. (b.1882–d.1 May 1958) 145 lb. class [1]; 158 lb. class [ac]. (Buffalo Central YMCA).

Schaefer, William. 158 lb. class [ac].

Stevens, Charles. 125 lb. class [ac]. (St. Louis Socialer Turnverein).

Strebler, Z. B. 125 lb. class [3]; 135 lb. class [ac]. (South Broadway Athletic Club, St. Louis).

Tesing, Rudolph. 145 lb. class [2]. (St. George's Athletic Club, New York).

Thiefenthaler, Gustav. 105 lb. class [3]. (South Broadway Athletic Club, St. Louis).

Toeppen, Hugo. 135 lb. class [ac]; 158 lb. class [ac]. (St. Louis South Side Turnverein).

Warmboldt, Fred Charles. Unlimited class [3]. (North St. Louis Turnverein).

Wester, August, Jr. (b.12 February 1882) 125 lb. class [2]. (National Turnverein, Newark, NJ).

Whitehurst, Milton Morris. (b.1 December 1882–d.December 1966) 125 lb. class [ac]. (University of Maryland).

Winholtz, Jerry E. 145 lb. class [ac]; 158 lb. class [3]. (Chicago Central YMCA).

Wolken, Rudolph. 145 lb. class [ac]. (Boys' Club, New York).

Wortmann, Dietrich. (b.11 January 1884–d.21 September 1952) 135 lb. class [ac]. (Columbia University; University of Leipzig [GER]; German-American Athletic Club, Brooklyn).

Zirkel, Albert. (b.23 October 1885) 145 lb. class [3]. (National Turnverein, Newark, NJ).

NOTES

1. Yamasini and Lentauw, the usually seen spellings for Jan Mashiani and Len Tau, were in earlier days often termed Kaffirs (a racial slur), or members of the Kaffir Tribe (now considered offensive); they were and are also termed Xhosa or occasionally Zulus. Nowadays these individuals might most

commonly be referred to as black South Africans. FJGVDM, referring to the two black South African marathoners, states, "It can be stated that they were not Zulus and their names not 'Lentauw' and 'Yamasini'" (p. 15). Merwe describes Lau's affiliation with the Tswana Tribe, but is not as specific about Mashiani, only implying the same tribal origin.

2. See the previous footnote concerning tribal affiliation.

3. This athlete's name is spelled correctly as listed here, notably, the middle name, which he used, is spelled "Truxt*u*n." A number of other books attempt to correct the "obvious" spelling error and use the more common suffix ending "-ton," but that is incorrect according to the Alumni Records at both his prep school (St. Mark's Academy, Southborough, Massachusetts), and the University of Pennsylvania.

Index